Habits of Change

Habits of Change

An Oral History of American Nuns

CAROLE GARIBALDI ROGERS

OXFORD
UNIVERSITY PRESS

The original edition of this publication was made possible by a grant from the New Jersey Council for the Humanities, a state partner of the National Endowment for the Humanities. Any views, findings, conclusions, or recommendations in this publication do not necessarily represent those of the National Endowment for the Humanities or the New Jersey Council for the Humanities.

OXFORD
UNIVERSITY PRESS

Oxford University Press, Inc., publishes works that further
Oxford University's objective of excellence
in research, scholarship, and education.

Oxford   New York
Auckland   Cape Town   Dar es Salaam   Hong Kong   Karachi
Kuala Lumpur   Madrid   Melbourne   Mexico City   Nairobi
New Delhi   Shanghai   Taipei   Toronto

With offices in
Argentina   Austria   Brazil   Chile   Czech Republic   France   Greece
Guatemala   Hungary   Italy   Japan   Poland   Portugal   Singapore
South Korea   Switzerland   Thailand   Turkey   Ukraine   Vietnam

Copyright © 1996, 2011 by Carole Garibaldi Rogers

Published by Oxford University Press, Inc.
198 Madison Avenue, New York, New York 10016

www.oup.com

The first edition of this book was originally published in hardcover as *Poverty, Chastity, and Change: Lives of Contemporary American Nuns* (Twayne, 1996).

Oxford is a registered trademark of Oxford University Press

Library of Congress Cataloging-in-Publication Data
Rogers, Carole G.
  Habits of change : an oral history of American nuns / Carole Garibaldi Rogers.
  p.   cm.
  Rev. ed. of: Poverty, chastity, and change.
  Includes bibliographical references (p.   ). and index.
  ISBN 978-0-19-975706-0 (pbk. : alk. paper)   1. Nuns—United States—Biography.   2. Oral biography.
3. Monasticism and religious orders for women—United States—History—20th century. I. Rogers, Carole
G. Poverty, chastity, and change. II. Title.
  BX4225.R64 2011
  271'.9002273—dc22   2010038533
  [B]

1 3 5 7 9 8 6 4 2
Printed in the United States of America
on acid-free paper

Contents

Acknowledgments

An oral history collection simply does not exist without its narrators, and so I acknowledge first my great debt to all the women I interviewed, both those who appear here and those who unfortunately could not be included. I am particularly grateful to the first women who trusted me, a stranger carrying a tape recorder, with their life stories.

In the long interlude between editions I kept in touch with many of the women. A few I visited. Many more I followed via Christmas cards as their addresses changed. They offered consolation and prayers when my parents died. Over the years, my husband and I were able to contribute to some wonderful nonprofit organizations around the country because I had met these women religious and we had become familiar with their work. I also believe that some of their wisdom and courage and hope seeped into my life. For all of that I am profoundly grateful.

Because I wanted to include a broad cross section of women religious in the collection, I depended heavily on recommendations from friends, acquaintances, and the interviewees themselves—in addition to random calls to chancery offices and motherhouses in the areas I planned to visit. I am grateful to all who provided suggestions.

It would seem logical that Catholic friends would offer helpful leads—and they did. I would like to thank, in particular, the Benedictine monks of St. Mary's Abbey in Morristown, New Jersey, for their many excellent recommendations. Other wonderful suggestions, however, came from Jewish, Protestant, and agnostic friends who had met a nun, admired her work, and wanted to share her name. Their keen and continuing interest in the oral histories has meant a great deal to me.

As interview followed interview and the original collection took shape, I came to depend on critiques from some stalwart women in my writers' group, Marjorie Keyishian, Anne Homer Doerflinger, and Joan Morrison, a fine oral historian from whom I learned a great deal. I will never forget their friendship or their high professional standards. Over the years, I have also gained valuable insights from members of the Conference on History of Women Religious, a cohort of excellent scholars from many disciplines devoted to preserving and sharing the histories of women religious. I am particularly grateful to Sister Mary

Ellen Gleason, archivist for the College of Saint Elizabeth in Convent Station, New Jersey, for her many acts of kindness, both professional and personal.

The vital but unseen contributors to any oral history collection are the transcribers. I have been fortunate to have three excellent ones: Val Davia and Elizabeth Hauser for the first edition and Kate Hennessy for the second.

Transcribing costs for oral history work can be burdensome. I am very grateful to the New Jersey Council for the Humanities for a grant that assisted with those costs for the original collection. Fairleigh Dickinson University administered the grant, and I am indebted to Francis J. Mertz, President, for agreeing to do so. I would also like to thank the Lilly Endowment for a grant that assisted with some of my travel expenses for the first edition. The College of New Rochelle administered that grant, thanks to Sister Dorothy Ann Kelly, President.

Unless otherwise credited, photographs have been provided by the subjects of the interviews.

Over the years, this collection has benefited from three excellent editors. Mark Zadrozny, at Twayne Publishers, an imprint of Simon & Schuster Macmillan, for the first edition; and Nancy Toff, at Oxford University Press, for the second, displayed not only professional expertise but also sensitivity to the discipline of oral history and to the stories of women religious. Donald A. Ritchie, series editor for the first edition, who became the bridge to the second, is also an excellent oral historian whose work I much admire.

Finally, a word about my family. In the interlude between editions, my sons, Douglas and Matthew, grew from boys to fine men with careers and family responsibilities of their own. But I have never felt anything less than their whole-hearted enthusiasm for this project. It is my hope that they, too, absorbed some wisdom and courage from these women religious. I cannot adequately describe the role my husband, Leo, has played in my life and in the development of this book. He is the one with whom I first shared my idea, on a wintry weekend walk in 1991. Since then, despite some difficult times in our lives, he never faltered in his confidence that this book should happen and that I could make it happen. He read every word of the original manuscript, often more than once, and made invaluable suggestions. Then he willingly signed on to do the same chores all over again for this edition. The book belongs to the women whose stories are here, but I think they would not mind my saying that there is a sense in which it is also his.

Prologue: Where They've Been

Early in 2009, American Catholic women religious learned that the Vatican would be conducting two investigations, one into their lives and another into their doctrinal beliefs. The first, officially called an Apostolic Visitation, was designed to collect data, conduct on-site interviews, and issue a report to the Vatican on the "quality of life" of nearly 400 communities of active, not cloistered, nuns in the United States.

The second, initiated by the Vatican's Congregation for the Doctrine of the Faith, was announced to assess the doctrinal correctness of the Leadership Conference of Women Religious (LCWR), whose membership of 1,500 leaders of congregations of women religious represents 95 percent of American nuns. The Vatican specified three areas where it believed the Conference had not promoted official Church teaching: a male-only priesthood, homosexuality, and the unique role of Christ in salvation. Both investigations drew strong public reactions from American Catholics, including the nuns themselves, and the news spilled out of church circles into the secular media.

In the same early months of 2009, a traveling exhibit, "Women and Spirit: Catholic Sisters in America," organized under the auspices of LCWR, focused attention on the almost 300 years of service that women religious have provided since they first arrived in the United States in 1727. The exhibit, opening in Cincinnati and destined to tour museums around the country, highlighted the important historic roles nuns had played in cities like Baltimore, New Orleans, Galveston, San Francisco, and New York; on battlefields during the Civil War; in frontier outposts and mill towns and farming communities across the country and through the centuries. Information that had been known primarily to historians and archivists finally reached a wider audience.

And, in early 2010, Americans learned more about the role women religious play in the current fiber of American life. As the health care bill stalled and seemed unlikely to pass Congress, the Catholic Health Association, whose member hospitals and nursing homes are mostly operated by communities of women religious, spoke up in favor of the bill. Women religious, with centuries of caring for the sick, comforting the dying, building hospitals, and staffing clinics for the poor, brought their tradition of service into the political arena. Against the backdrop of the two Vatican investigations and the staunch opposition of the United States bishops to the health care bill, their action came at great risk to themselves and put them once again in public view. Sister Carol Keehan, CHA president, provided extraordinary leadership and was both vilified and praised for her work.

These early twenty-first century occurrences went a long way to erase the stereotypes of nuns that had lingered decades after the heyday of popular comedies like *Nunsense* and *Sister Act* in the 1980s and '90s. And, as the decades have gone by, the number of Catholics who remember, fondly or not so fondly, the ever-present Sisters from their grammar school days has decreased dramatically. For better or worse, ubiquitous nuns in habits, who spent their days teaching young children, were no longer a major part of American culture. Stereotypes and memories met reality. Many Americans, including Catholics, were caught by surprise. But, in fact, the events of 2009–2010 revealed both the change and continuity in the lives of American women religious during the previous half-century.

Prior to the 1960s, when young Catholic women entered the convent, they left behind family and friends, and the world itself, to live and pray together. Parents knew their daughters were leaving them forever; nuns were rarely allowed to return home, even for the death of a parent. When they entered their new and separate world, they were first postulants and then novices, studying the disciplines of their community. As "brides of Christ," they were then "professed," taking vows of poverty, chastity, and obedience. Those vows, solemn promises intended to last a lifetime, meant that they would never own property or manage their own money, that they would remain unmarried and celibate, and that they would follow the rules of their community as interpreted for them by their superior. Sisters of that era never questioned the centuries-old theology that formed the foundation of their commitment. They believed their way of life was immutable, as indeed it had been for centuries.

But, gradually, inexorably, as a result of events in both American society and the Catholic Church, their lives became improbable journeys. Every facet of their personal lives was altered, and these women had to respond to an amazing variety of challenges. Well into middle-age, they learned to drive cars and balance checkbooks, making the painful transition from a sheltered environment, where a mother superior handed out dimes for carfare, to independent living, where they assumed responsibility for their own lives. After years in which their time had been spent in either the classroom or the convent, they embarked on new ministries, spoke out publicly on issues they believed in, and stood up for people who needed champions.

My choice of oral history to capture the stories of women religious who lived through these changes was deliberate. Sociologists make sense of trends and statistics; historians discern cause and effect, which contribute much to our knowledge of events. There are solid sociological studies and numerous histories of women religious. But oral histories give us the opportunity to hear history in the language of the narrators. As Sherna Gluck, an early feminist oral historian, observed in *Rosie the Riveter Revisited*, "It is only when individual women talk about their lives that we are able to put the whole story together: the public and the private; the dramatic and the subtle; the gains and the losses."

I made another choice in collecting these oral histories. I could have used short excerpts from the transcripts and surrounded them with explications, as many good oral history collections do. I chose instead the long, almost free-standing model as most appropriate for narrators who were by and large articulate, who had already done the hard work of self-examination and could speak out of that self-knowledge, and whose histories dealt not just with participation in historical events but with subtle life changes. I also believed that model dealt most honestly with the outsider/insider issue; I am not and never was a woman religious.

For the last 50 years, nuns have lived at the epicenter of change—change in their personal lives, in their work, their church, and their country. This collection gives readers an opportunity to examine the way a group of women adapted to such uncommon change. Because many of the narrators played an active role in contemporary events, we also hear different perspectives on the dramatic changes that occurred in the wider world during those decades.

The oral histories frequently begin with what the women call "vocation stories," the complicated, sometimes sad, sometimes inspiring reasons they originally joined the convent. As their lives changed, the women revisited those reasons many times. Some found those reasons inadequate and left religious life; others found new and deeper reasons to stay.

In the earlier model of religious life, the days of a young nun were rigorous and filled with self-sacrifice, no matter which community she joined. The young nun was given a new name, which was not always one she would have chosen for herself. She wore the habit of her community, usually a floor-length black dress with a headdress that tightly framed her face, and a veil. The nun's habit was an important symbol. It was sometimes a replica of the clothing worn by the foundress. She might have been, for example, a well-to-do eighteenth-century widow who devoted her later life to serving the poor, but retained the dress of her former life. Or the habit may have been designed by the nineteenth-century bishop or priest who founded the congregation. In any case, the habit came to signify to the nuns themselves, to priests, and to the general public that the woman wearing it lived a dedicated, holy, chaste life.

With the exception of the relatively few women who entered the nursing profession and those who joined cloistered or missionary orders, Sisters in those days were teachers. But they rarely had a choice of what they taught or where they lived. Those decisions were made—sometimes wisely, sometimes mysteriously, occasionally capriciously—by superiors. A Sister of any age could be uprooted at any time and assigned to a new convent, a new school, a new city. Such decisions, wrenching though they were, were to be accepted because of the vow of obedience. The women in charge were usually called *mother, mother general,* or *mother superior*. Theirs was an authoritarian, rarely collegial, style of leadership.

Before the 1960s the spiritual life of a nun, like her ministry, also followed a predictable pattern. Sisters prayed together as a group, even meditated as a group. Few nuns had any familiarity with scripture. They attended daily Mass, which was perhaps said for them in a convent chapel; if it was not, they walked, hands hidden, heads down, to the parish church. There was an assigned amount of daily devotional reading; a priest preached an annual summer retreat.

What may now seem silly or dictatorial or even repressive was not necessarily so in its time. Many women lived productive, happy, even joyful lives in this model of religious life. They believed they had chosen a better way. And perhaps they had. In an era when a young woman, particularly one from a poor or lower-middle-class family, looked at her choices and saw a life of dedication, education, and professional accomplishment—versus a life, possibly like her mother's, of raising children and struggling to make ends meet—entering a convent became an appealing option. Outside of the convent there were few opportunities for a woman to become an executive; a nun with leadership abilities could become a school principal, the president of a college, or the administrator of a hospital.

Many of the women, speaking of their early choices, mentioned their teachers in grammar school and high school as the role models they followed. What they saw—and what they wanted to join—was a cadre of happy women who were fulfilled in their work, enjoying each other's company, and working together toward a higher goal. These are the women and that was the life they were living when history caught up with them and they reclaimed their baptismal names and changed their clothes, their jobs, and their basic assumptions about who they were.

For American Catholic nuns, the monumental changes that would envelop their lives actually began during the 1950s. In the fall of 1950 Pope Pius XII first urged religious communities to adapt their strict customs to the needs of modern life, and throughout that seemingly complacent decade the Pope issued several further calls for renewal. One of his chief concerns was an improvement in the training and education given young Sisters. The messages coming from Rome dovetailed with a similar concern already gathering support in the United States. In 1954 religious communities here, responding to evidence that Sisters in the classroom did not have adequate professional credentials, established the Sister Formation Conference to hasten and improve the education of young Sisters.

It is now clear that, for two reasons, the Sister Formation Conference, and the changes it wrought, became the cornerstone for the changes that followed during later decades. First, the Conference created a large group of highly educated Sisters. Prior to the late 1950s, it typically took a young Sister 20 years, attending classes on Saturdays and during the summers, to complete her college degree. The impetus of the Sister Formation Conference created new college curricula and, in some cases, new colleges, specifically to educate Sisters. Many of the women had an opportunity, for the first time, to study the works of prominent theologians like Henri de Lubac, Yves Congar, and Karl Rahner and were thus prepared to read and understand the pronouncements of Vatican II.

Second, the Conference provided communication links among religious communities so that members from different congregations and different parts of the country could exchange information and gather support and inspiration from each other. This, too, was something radically new for Sisters who had, by and large, remained sequestered within the convents of their own communities.

Recognition of the importance of these developments has come only in retrospect. In most essential aspects and to all outward appearances, the life of an American nun in 1960 had not changed much from previous decades. Except for the opportunity to attend college full time, few of the nuns I interviewed recalled any significant change in their routine during the 1950s.

Change began with a jolt during the 1960s. On October 11, 1962, Pope John XXIII convened the Second Vatican Council, the first such meeting of all the hierarchy in the Roman Catholic Church since the First Vatican Council almost a century earlier. John XXIII died the following year, but the Council continued, its work endured, and the changes it set in place reached into every area of Catholic life. Two documents promulgated by the Council, *Gaudium et Spes (Joy and Hope)* and *Lumen Gentium (Light of All Nations)*, had a major impact on the future of American nuns. Ironically, neither was devoted to the renewal of religious life.

Gaudium et Spes, also known, appropriately, as the *Pastoral Constitution on the Church in the Modern World*, decreed that the Church would no longer maintain an adversarial position toward the rest of the world as it had since nineteenth-century popes inveighed against the evils of modern society. Vatican II said the Church was to be "truly and intimately linked with humankind and its history." The mission of the Church was to be in solidarity with the world, actively working for and with the people. If that were so, then nuns had to reassess their own stance toward the world. They had to acknowledge that they, too, were part of human history and they had to find new ways to minister to—and in—the wider world.

In *Lumen Gentium*, also called the *Dogmatic Constitution on the Church*, the Council asserted that all Christians, by their baptism, are called "to the fullness of the Christian life and the perfection of charity." This doctrine, so simply stated, had a profound effect on women religious. In pre–Vatican II days, Catholics had thought that nuns lived on higher ground—closer to God than the laity—and many women had entered the convent believing they would always be special. The sacrifices they had made were somehow worthwhile; in return, they had received a certain status. Suddenly, according to the Council, everyone had the potential and the obligation to be holy. Members of religious orders no longer had an exclusive claim to spiritual perfection. Nuns would have to search for a new identity as well as new ways to minister.

These two revolutionary concepts, combined with renewed interest in the spirit and charism of the foundress, formed the basis of the agonizing self-assessments and reevaluations that occurred in convent after convent.

Many Sisters spoke to me of the excitement they felt when they first grasped the import of the Council documents. It was for them indeed the *aggiornamento*, the throwing open of the windows, that John XXIII had promised. Other women did not respond so positively to the Council's pronouncements. And there were many women who did not pay any attention at all. They were too immersed in day-to-day responsibilities. But change was in the air they breathed. It appeared in everyday conversations, on the agenda at community meetings, at workshops and retreats, on summer reading lists. Several Sisters mentioned *The Nun in the World*, by Leon Joseph Cardinal Suenens, a small book, they said, that had a large impact on their lives. When I read the book in 1993, it was not hard to see why 30 years later women could still recall reading it. In an early chapter, before making concrete suggestions for ways nuns could renew their lives, Cardinal Suenens wrote, "It has been said of certain congregations of nuns that they are the last stronghold of the very studied manners of the middle-class women of the nineteenth century. People would like to see more spontaneity, less inhibition, more natural and straightforward reactions. . . . To put it briefly, the dusty old wax flowers should be replaced by living blooms drawing nourishment direct from the earth."

Events in the United States during the 1960s and early 1970s also reverberated in convents around the country. Sisters, absorbing social justice doctrines from theologians as well as Vatican II documents, responded to contemporary demands for civil rights. Like many other Americans they were learning to look beyond individual acts of charity toward systemic change. Often to their own surprise, they were drawn into unfamiliar activist roles as participants in marches and protests. The civil rights movement affected nuns' ministries as well. Some of the Sisters who remained in the classroom began to teach social justice, on occasion angering pastors and local communities. More and more women chose to leave teaching, frequently to live and work with the poor. This growing political activism, which is a part of many of the oral histories that follow and which surfaces in many different guises, reinforced changes within religious communities and made it impossible to shut the windows that had been opened by Vatican II.

Sisters also responded to the stimulus of the women's movement. Facing their own struggles with a male hierarchy and bolstered by their already strong sense of community with other women, they found in feminism an answer to many of their own questions. They read the early work of feminist theologians; they also read Betty Friedan and other feminist writers whose turf was more political. They evaluated their own experiences as the educated, middle-class American Catholic women they had become, and they gradually found solidarity with other women who were not necessarily Catholic or educated or middle class. In some of my interviews I met outspoken radical feminists; more frequently the theme was somewhat muted. Rarely, however, was there a woman, even among the cloistered orders, who in some way or other did not allude to a heightened awareness of feminism.

To focus on the ways the lives of American nuns have changed over the last five decades is not to say that other groups have not also seen the absolutes in their world mutate, slide away, and become obsolete during the second half of the twentieth century. The events that altered the basic tenets of religious life affected other people as well.

American women of that generation, women who were raised to be wives and mothers, found that life did not unfold in quite the way they had been led to expect. Assuming an adulthood centered around the home, they faced instead divorce, economic insecurity, and the call of feminism, all of which thrust them into the workplace. Catholic laypeople, both women and men, old enough to remember pre-Vatican II Catholicism, endured many significant and unexpected alterations in what they believed were absolutes. Gone were penalties for eating meat on Friday; gone was the familiar Latin Mass. The mere fact that change could happen at all in the Roman Catholic Church was an unsettling reality for many people.

Such acute change in the lives of so many nuns did not happen without some bitterness and real pain. The pain radiated through individuals, local convents, and entire congregations. Some of these problems have proved intractable, lasting through the years into the present.

The struggles between women religious and the Catholic hierarchy, in Rome and in the United States, began shortly after the Second Vatican Council and have not abated, as the two investigations begun in 2009 attest. The men who had participated in Vatican II and supported its decrees came home to their own dioceses and within a few years were faced with the results of their decisions. Women religious, who had taken seriously the call for renewal, were moving out of habits into contemporary dress. They were also moving out of schools into other ministries. Some bishops saw renewal and read rebellion; they ordered the women to follow the guidance of the hierarchy in any attempts at renewal.

The controversy thus begun emerged over and over again, in a variety of places and on a variety of issues, pitting nuns against their local bishops and the authorities in Rome. It led to the punishment of individual women and to the dissolution of some religious congregations.

In 1965, for example, the Glenmary Sisters of Cincinnati came into serious conflict with the archbishop of Cincinnati, Karl Alter, and later disbanded. Two years later, when the Immaculate Heart of Mary Sisters (IHMs) of Los Angeles attempted renewal, James F. Cardinal McIntyre erupted in anger. Authorities in Rome sided with the cardinal and, at the end of 1969, more than 300 IHM Sisters voted to leave and form a noncanonical community.

The IHM conflict also had a major impact on the national organization that represented all American Sisters. At the 1969 annual gathering of the Conference of Major Superiors of Women, which had been established in 1956 and was approved by the Vatican, a resolution to support the IHM Sisters failed by one vote. The discussion caused anger and resentment on both sides of the issue—pro-hierarchy and pro-IHM—and Sisters at the meeting saw clearly the struggle that lay ahead.

In 1971 the Conference changed its name to the Leadership Conference of Women Religious (LCWR) and, more significantly, moved away from a posture that called for allegiance to the hierarchy and toward a sense of identification with the people of God. Some members, still reacting to the IHM issue of 1969 and preferring a conservative stance that preserved the alliance of the community with the hierarchy of the Church, left LCWR and formed their own group, Consortium Perfectae Caritatis (Association of Perfect Charity).

In 1992 the Vatican established a new organization to represent American Sisters, called the Council of Major Superiors of Women Religious (CMSWR). Consortium members joined CMSWR—in fact, were its core—and the Consortium disbanded. Many nuns interpreted the move as the hierarchy's way of trying to discredit or disband LCWR. Both groups continue to exist. Although the membership of LCWR still represents 95 percent of women religious in the United States, the divergence between the two views of religious life remains to the present and has perhaps even intensified. Allegiance to the hierarchy continues to be a divisive issue.

Throughout the oral histories there are many references to painful confrontations between Sisters and the clergy. Some had national significance; others were more personal and local. But in almost every case the women remember these moments as times when their lives changed irrevocably.

Another area where the changes caused intense pain and dislocation lies in the large number of women who left religious life during the 1970s and 1980s. The Official Catholic Directory reported that there were 173,351 nuns in the United States in 1962; the numbers continued to climb until 1966, when there were 181,421—the highest number ever reached. By 1992, there were 99,337 women in American religious communities, a decline of approximately 43 percent during a 30-year span. By 2008 there were 61,000, but these more recent statistics reflect the deaths of aging Sisters, not continuing departures.

During the same period, for a variety of reasons, very few women entered convents. As a result, the average age of nuns rose sharply, resulting in another significant figure: In 1968 the average age of women religious was 45; in 1995 it was 65. This upward trend has continued. A 2009 study, conducted by the Center for Applied Research in the Apostolate (CARA) and the National Religious Vocation Conference (NRVC), reported that 91 percent of women religious are 60 or older; most of the rest are at least 50.

The problems caused by aging Sisters and the dwindling number of younger women in ministry exacerbated a third area of stress caused by the changes in religious life—the financial health of communities of women religious. In the early years of the renewal, as more and more women moved out of teaching, religious communities began to lose the financial support from parishes and dioceses that had provided a stable financial base. Some congregations, like the School Sisters of St. Francis, found themselves in the position of temporarily discouraging young women from entering—or staying—because they were not sure they could find ways to support them. Other orders found themselves encouraging some members to work full time with the poor, where salaries were minimal or even nonexistent, while encouraging other members to remain in higher-paying positions to support the communal commitment to the poor.

For many years women religious had not been eligible for Social Security, and the majority had not received retirement benefits. Communities were confronted with an increased need for infirmaries and retirement facilities to care for their elderly Sisters, but most had woefully inadequate financial resources—and few young entrants to share the burden. In 1988 a nationwide fund-raising drive for retired Sisters was established, but despite public attention and heroic efforts, serious financial problems persisted.

In recent years the problems have only grown more severe. Many communities have combined their small geographic provinces into larger ones, sometimes stretching across half the country; others have sold land treasured by their founding Sisters and pulled back from schools and hospitals they can no longer staff. Almost all have seriously depleted their resources, both emotional and financial, to care for their elderly Sisters.

There is real and growing evidence that many religious communities are dying. Their work in the Church is finished. It is no longer necessary to take life-long vows of poverty, chastity, and obedience in order to serve the poor or care for the sick, as Sisters in the United States had done for almost 300 years.

Throughout the original interviews there are poignant comments by women who feel the ambiguity, who recognize that they may be living the end. "Last one here turns out the lights," was a rueful comment I heard several times. The passage of 15 more years has only brought that reality closer. In one of the 2010 interviews, Sister Virginia Johnson talks about the hard decisions her very small community is now making.

At a basic level, there is a consensus that religious life will endure. It survived massive change in earlier periods of history; it will do so again. But the future will be very different from the present. And therein lies perhaps the most significant reason for these oral histories. The women here have lived a unique moment in history. It is important to hear their voices before the stories are lost.

This collection is based on 94 oral history interviews I conducted between 1991 and 1995, 54 of which appeared in *Poverty, Chastity and Change: Lives of Contemporary American Nuns*, published in 1996. This second edition preserves the integrity of the original interviews. They have not been changed, but I have appended updates for all. To them I have added new oral histories of two women who add recent perspectives to the existing collection.

The women represent a wide cross section of religious life. This has been qualitative, not quantitative, research, but some facts and figures are pertinent:

- The women ranged in age from their forties to their nineties, with the majority in their sixties. Ages given in the text are their ages at the time of the interview.

- They come most commonly from Irish, German, and Italian families—immigrant groups that made up the bulk of American Catholics during the early decades of the twentieth century. Five African-American women and four Mexican-American women were interviewed.

- They are members of more than 40 different religious communities. I made every effort to include women from groups that could be described as conservative as well as those that could be called liberal, but I discovered that a project about change precludes, by its very nature, some participants. Some individual women, some convents, and one entire congregation—speaking through its superior—declined to be interviewed.

- The interviews took place in 15 states, representing most regions of the country, in a variety of settings—monasteries, motherhouses, apartments, convents, and offices located in inner-city neighborhoods, rural sanctuaries, and suburban towns.

- A large majority of the narrators in this collection are highly educated and many have been highly successful. Including so many of their voices does not detract from the representational factor of the collection; I would argue that it is essential for a fair portrayal. Sisters of this generation were belatedly, but effectively, educated and trained to be successful—not in worldly or financial ways, but in their ministries. They made great contributions to the Catholic Church and to American society because of that. Some of the women were initially educated because their superiors decided to send them to college (Sister Bonaventure Burke), while others had to persistently request further study (Sister Janet Ruffing). Once educated, Sisters, regardless of their background, continued to seek further credentialing as they moved into new ministries.

- Of the 96 women interviewed, seven had left religious life. Three of their narratives are included here. Only women who had been in the convent for at least 10 years, whether they left or stayed, were included in the research.

- Among the women who are still Sisters, 13 wore some form of recognizable habit; an additional three chose to retain only the veil. The rest wore a variety of contemporary outfits—slacks, suits, dresses.

Each interview lasted approximately two hours. Prior to the conversation, I sent each woman a letter describing the purpose of the research and explaining how the interview would be conducted. "I ask three basic questions," I wrote, "but each story takes the conversation in different directions and there is great latitude in the way we use our time. . . . The three basic questions are: Why did you enter religious life? What were some of the crisis points or times of change in your religious life? Or, to put that another way, how have you become the person you are today? And, finally, why are you still a religious?"

The women were interviewed because they have been nuns during a tumultuous time in history. But they are also women, and that was always in my mind during the interviews. So we talked about God and the vows and ministry, but we also talked about their mothers, about biological clocks, about cancer, about men and love and friendship. As I look back, I can see that the interviews that come alive are those where the woman, whatever her accomplishments, spoke personally, in her own voice, about how change happened in her life.

After the interview was completed, the tape was professionally transcribed. I edited the transcripts, making only those editorial changes required for the sake of clarity or because of constraints on length (most of the transcripts ran more than 50 pages). I removed some digressions and repetitions and verbal false starts like "Well" and "You know." I then gave each woman whose edited transcript was to appear in the book an opportunity to review her history. I allowed corrections only for mistakes of fact or for clarification. Occasionally, in a follow-up phone conversation, a woman asked to elaborate further on a certain point. Where I included the addition, it is set off and called "Afterthought."

For the second edition I attempted to contact all the women whose narratives appeared in the 1996 edition. For those who had died or were unable to converse with me, I spoke to archivists from their communities and read obituaries. For all who wished it, I offered a phone conversation or an e-mail exchange in which they could give me an update on their lives since we had last spoken in the early 1990s. I suggested that they talk about their ministries or their interior journeys or their current understanding of religious life, recognizing that these contributions would be necessarily brief. These communications were all completed in the first half of 2010.

In addition, I conducted new in-person oral histories interviews with seven of the women from the first edition. These interviews, running longer than the updates, followed my standard oral history procedures and are noted in the text. All updates and new oral history interviews are preceded by my contextualizing comments, also following the format from the first edition. To allow room for the updates and new interviews, I deleted four interviews that appeared in the earlier collection. I chose to make that difficult decision by leaving out one woman who had left the convent and all three anonymous narrators.

As in my original encounters, I found the women once again refreshingly honest and deeply connected to their spiritual roots and to their communities. While we did not dwell on the Vatican investigations that were in progress as we spoke, almost all the women reflected in one way or another on how they felt. They expressed shock, sadness, anger, and resignation, but also pride in the women they had become. Perhaps Sister Joan Chittister expressed the complexity best: "I pray [the result of the Apostolic Visitation] will be positive, that somebody would finally say, 'These are our beloved daughters in whom we are well-pleased.'"

In 1995 when I had begun to struggle with arranging the oral histories into a book, a friend advised me, "Weave the basket and place the objects in it as you choose. It will be up to others to view the arrangement as they choose, each piece individually or as a whole." I followed her advice. Clearly, many of the women could have been placed in any of several chapters. Sister Florence Vales, for example, who appears in Chapter 9, could also have been included in Chapter 7 because she is a member of a cloistered order. I based my selection on the thrust of each story, as I perceived it. As I arranged the chapters, the focus is, first, on changes from the past to the present, moving from a highly visible aspect of nuns' lives, their evolving ministries, to more subtle interior considerations, their changing attitudes; and second, on changes from the present to the future. I did not change this arrangement for the second edition.

There is, to my mind, progression. But there are also parallels and echoes and the occasional ironic twists that I hope will move the reader back and forth among the stories. The theme is change; the narrators are women who happen also to be nuns; and, in the end, it is the oral histories of their lives that matter.

A note about the selected bibliography at the end of this edition. At the same time as communities of women religious have aged and grown smaller, their archivists have stepped forward, professionalizing their holdings, sharing them generously, and helping to keep the stories alive. Since 1996 when this collection first appeared, there has been an explosion of books written about women religious. Some of these have been journalistic; far more have been academic. A new generation of scholars, many of them historians, has been attracted to the accomplishments of women religious in past centuries. Women religious, scholars themselves, have published significant historical, theological, and sociological studies of their lives as well as memoirs and essays. It was not possible to include anywhere near as many of these works as I would have liked. I have retained books that the narrators mentioned as significant in their lives, even those that now seem obscure, and added several newer works—some overview texts and others, by women religious themselves, that add to a collection of contemporary voices.

I note, in particular, the highly respected work of Sister Sandra M. Schneiders. In the interlude since the first edition, she has become one of the most prolific and articulate explicators of lives of women religious. Two volumes of *Religious Life in a New Millennium*, her three-volume study of vowed religious life, have been published. In addition, she has published numerous essays more accessible to the ordinary reader. Theologian Richard McBrien has called her 2009 essay, "The Past and Future of Ministerial Religious Life," "the best, most compact, and most significant study of the biblical and historical foundations of ministerial religious life available today." In my updating conversations, several of the women mentioned studying her work and relying on her insights as they continue their improbable journeys into an uncertain future.

Habits of Change

Part One

FROM THE PAST INTO THE PRESENT

1

IN THE SCHOOLS

SISTER BONAVENTURE BURKE

At the time of the interview, Sister Bonaventure Burke lived in St. Bernard's Convent, a four-story brick building in Nashville, Tennessee. The grass on either side of the driveway was uncut, the parking area was empty, and several of the windows on the chapel side of the building had been replaced with plywood. The week after the interview the building was to be closed, and the few Sisters who remained were to be moved to a new retirement home on the far side of Nashville.

Unlike most other Sisters of Mercy, Sister Bonaventure, 84, wears a short black veil on all occasions. She spoke with a gentle Southern accent, and laughed gently, too, most frequently at her own expense.

I was born in Harriman, Tennessee, a very small town. My mother and father are Canadians. They came south for his health and he was going to South Carolina, but someone told him that there was a little town in Tennessee that was just beginning and it had five railroads and manufacturing and that it would be a wonderful place to raise a family. So they changed their course. Now Harriman, Tennessee, was a little town. There were no Catholics—well, very few, let's put it that way.

However, my mother was a very good Catholic. So was my father. And she talked to us about Sisters quite a bit, and she had pictures of Sisters around. My father went to the Christian Brothers. And so I had that atmosphere, that ideal, and then I came over here [to St. Bernard's Convent]. I just transferred that idealized notion of Sisters, and I wanted to be a Sister.

I entered here and I received my name here. I didn't choose [my religious name]. It was given to me, and so I don't have too much devotion to Saint Bonaventure, but I have great respect and admiration for him. He was a great philosopher and theologian back in the thirteenth century.

At first it was grammar school I taught. The fifth and seventh grades and eighth. And those classes, you wouldn't believe it, but those classes were very, very large. I remember one class particularly was 72. And it didn't bother me at all. Well, everybody had large classes.

Sister Bonaventure Burke consults with the pastor of the Cathedral of the Incarnation in Nashville, Tennessee, in 1962. Sister Bonaventure was for many years a teacher and a librarian at Cathedral High School, which was staffed by the Sisters of Mercy until it closed in 1970.

Then one day I came home and saw my name on the bulletin board and it said, "Sister Bonaventure, this summer go to Peabody [College]."

"What?" I thought. I already had my degree. In education. I'll tell you this little bit. The first day the teacher asked us, each one, to identify himself and to tell something about why [we] were in library school. And the lady just before me was very dramatic. She says, "I am in the library because I love children. I love children from the first grade through the twelfth, and I thought the best thing in the world for me to do was to become a librarian so I would have contact with all of them."

I thought, "What am I going to say next?" So I said, "Well, I went home and saw my name on the bulletin board. It said, 'Sister Bonaventure, go become a librarian.' And here I am." Well, of course, everybody was so relieved after that dramatic explosion we'd had. That was why I was there. I went because I was told to.

So I became a librarian—a teacher and a librarian—for a long time. I was librarian at the cathedral school for half a day and taught half a day. I taught French, history, and English. And then I went to Knoxville and I did pretty much the same thing. And then later on I was in Memphis, pretty much the same. And then I came back to the cathedral school. French, English, and history—and librarian half a day because that's all that was necessary. You didn't have to have a librarian full day until the school had over 300. The Catholic population of Tennessee is very small.

The thing that hurt me, that really got to me, was the changing of the habit, putting aside the habit. I've tried to be as conservative as I can, as you can see. But many of the Sisters are out of the habit completely. All the younger Sisters are. I love the habit. I felt that it wasn't so much that it distinguished me as the fact that it was a witness. People would see me, they'd know that somebody is trying to serve God to the best of her ability. And it would make them think that somebody still is trying to practice Christian values. That's why I kept it.

One day I was up in the mountains and I was sitting beside a stream with this friend of our family. Way up high on the road was a little boy with a fishing rod over his shoulder. And he yelled, "Hello, Sister." He didn't know me. I didn't know him. But I was a Sister. He had gone to a Catholic school. He was very much at ease with Sisters. And so many places I've met that. People feel at home and at ease.

And then I was in the airport in San Francisco, going to see a niece. And a strange woman said, "Oh, it's so good to see a Sister of Mercy. I'm a Sister of Mercy." And I thought, "Oh. You'd never know."

Well, now I have a great deal of freedom [since I am retired]. When I was younger, I was very busy all the time. With those classes you would know how busy we were. And we did all the work in this house, I mean all the Sisters did. And for many years while I was here we burned soft coal which made a great deal of soot. That took a lot of time to keep that soot down. Then gas came in and it wasn't so bad.

But anyway, there were the classes, and I was really very busy. I thought, well, someday I'll learn how to pray. I never skipped prayers or anything like that. But now I try as much as I can to pray. When I first retired, I said to this priest who had been a Trappist monk, "I want to spend my retirement, Father, in learning how to pray." And he said, "You've been in the convent 60 years, and you don't know how to pray? I am appalled."

It shook me. So I thought, "Well, you learn." And so that is my greatest challenge right now. However, I have charge of the sacristy still. I fix it for Mass. I do not clean because they've got somebody else to do the cleaning. But I am responsible for the sacristy. So I do that and then I visit with the sick upstairs. I try to get up every day just to see those people.

As a novice, we had 30 minutes of meditation every morning. And sometimes I was so tired I slept through it. I was young. Now I have a priest, the priest I was saying who was a Trappist. He has helped me a lot, just by giving me ideas on what to do with the time.

I said, "What about the distractions?" And he said, "You've got to stop them."

You can only go so far, there are distractions. But I am learning not to try to put prayer into words, to feel God's presence, to know he's there, and to listen to what he has to say. And sometimes, with my imagination working as quickly and easily as it does, I find that a little bit difficult because I can think of all the things that I want to do or I haven't done or started to do. And I put these things in words. But I would like to learn to sit still and listen to what the Holy Spirit has to say. I must really work on that. I'm sorry I didn't work harder on prayer. I thought I didn't have time, but I did.

This entire building will be closed. It does break my heart to go. But I know, I'm being practical. This is too large for us. To do it over again would be very, very expensive. If we used the money to restructure this, it would cost more. The plumbing, the electric wires, the roofing, and the bricks themselves would have to be straightened out again. And it's too large for us. The chapel is a luxury we could not afford.

So when I realized that the altar was going to be taken stone by stone out to the new church, the commonsense thing to do was just to go. The new building is a very nice place. They have more conveniences for the sick, you know, things that they would need. It's hard for me. As I said, it breaks my heart. But I know it has to be done. (June 1991)

Sister Bonaventure died on January 9, 2003, at the age of 95.

SISTER GLORIA PEREZ

Sister Gloria Perez is the principal of an inner-city high school in Paterson, New Jersey. From the windows of her office you can see a few sparse trees, a cement parking lot surrounded by cyclone fencing, and high-rise apartment buildings. Through the open windows you can hear the universal sounds of teenagers— laughter, shouts, loud music.

During the interview Sister Gloria, 50, sat away from her desk, but her chair faced the door and she interrupted herself often to talk to students, a parent, a police officer, the football coach. A Sister of the Presentation of the Blessed Virgin Mary, she was an animated conversationalist, gesturing, pointing, snapping her fingers to illustrate a story.

My mother died when I was four and a half years old. And that to me is a very significant reason why I entered religious life. I did not enter religious life for all the most wonderful holy reasons. What I really did was, I entered to find a mother.

My father, even in the 1950s, was petrified that I was going to be corrupted if I went to public high school, so he put me in a Catholic high school. And I met the nuns. And I fell in love with them. They were wonderful teachers; they were caring women. I think it was the first time in my life that I looked at women as women. They were just so good at everything they did. I wanted to be just like them.

I entered in 1959, very much wanting to be that perfect teacher, and wanting to be surrounded with these mother figures. But I was so untypical. First of all, everybody in my community practically was Irish by background. Light hair, fair skin, light eyes. And I walked in with this black hair and these dark eyes and a more olive complexion. I always felt different in religious life for a very, very long time. And personality-wise I was very different. I am very outgoing. I talk all the time. I came from a Spanish family where we were all verbal, and we were lively. We moved a lot. I could dance, and I sang, and I did all these things that were not part of that Irish community. All those rules of silence and demeanor were just not me.

It was very hard. And to be very honest, I felt for a long period of my religious life that I should leave. I don't know why I never did. I always chalked it up that I just didn't have the guts to do it. When I look back, I really believe that God had a plan for me. For some reason God wanted this crazy Perez with all these Irish women. At that time I painted myself a coward. I always painted myself a misfit in the community.

All those 1960s years were not terrible years for me. I kind of floated through. I was one of the first ones to change the habit. I sew. I make all my clothes. I was always getting into a little bit of trouble, but not enough that I got in a lot of trouble. We were allowed to wear solid colors but, of course, when I bought the fabric, I'd get a gray with a little something in it.

We were not allowed to take our veils off. I went out with a bunch of friends and we went to a movie. I took my veil off. And of course, in those days, everyone was telling on everybody—you know, all this nonsense of religious life. So I was always in a little bit of trouble. As one of the superiors once said to me, "Your problem is not that you don't care; it's that you're not very prudent." And I wasn't prudent. I was 17 or 18 for a very, very long time.

I felt very responsible as a teacher. I felt very effective, I felt very good about what I did. But the private part of you, the part inside that you touch, always felt like I didn't belong, that I was being a phony. I was fooling everybody and they thought I was okay, because I was a good teacher. You know, when you're good at what you do, people think you're terrific.

I went to college, got my master's, did the whole thing. I had said I wanted to be in high school when we were going to college, which you never said in those days. All the young Sisters started with the babies, and then when you were seasoned you went to the upper grades. The high school teachers were like the queens, you know. Right away I said, "Oh, I want to work in a high school. I want the older kids." And I was told by the older Sisters, "Shhh, you can't say that." I was five years in elementary school and then I went to the high school.

We only had two high schools at the time. Those were the days where you didn't go outside of your high schools. You worked within community commitments. After teaching there [for several years] I became the assistant principal, the dean of discipline. I moved into an apartment with three other Sisters in the Bronx.

One of them became the principal of the high school. She was teaching biology in another school and they brought her in as principal. I was very hurt by that because I would have liked to have been the principal. It put a very bad strain in our relationship. She also, I felt, did not handle it very well. She fired me. The faculty wanted to petition my community to keep me and get rid of her. She was sick a lot of the time and not there, and I literally was running the school.

One day after Easter she came to me and she said, "By the way, you won't be back next year." At that point I really felt my life had ended, because I never separated who I was from what I was. What I was, was an excellent teacher and a wonderful dean of discipline. And she fired me.

I really felt like I lost it all. Talking about it now, and I'm well over it, I could cry. It was such a painful experience to me because I felt that I was no longer anybody. Because up to that point I really had no self; I was good because of what I did. You took away what I did and there was nothing there.

Not only that, it was someone I lived with and I very strongly felt was a very good friend. She never sat and confronted me about it. She just, boom. At that time, we went through our growing pains as a community. We were trying to be very professional, you see. If your boss felt that way, she could do it and that was it.

I remember the president [of our community] coming down to me at the time saying she understood how I felt. And I remember flying out of a chair and waving a finger in her face and saying, "You don't know what it feels like until a friend betrays you." I wouldn't talk to anybody in the community about it.

I went and got myself another job as a dean of discipline. And I called the community up and I said, "I have a job."

They said, "Well, you can't do that. It has to be approved."

I said, "You don't understand, I have a job. Now you go do whatever communities do, but that's where I am working." And I moved out of the apartment and I moved into a convent that was convenient to that school.

But what I felt like at that point was there was no Gloria anymore. I am this lovely shell that came across to everybody as being extremely competent, very secure, that I could be running IBM. But meanwhile all I felt like was a very thin egg, but an egg you already took the insides out of. If somebody really touched me I would crack and they would find out there's nothing there. That was probably the lowest point of my life.

I lost a tremendous amount of weight. I was not sleeping at all. I was so wired. I was scaring myself. I don't think I ever contemplated wanting to kill myself, but I knew that I had to do something. I knew that I just couldn't continue functioning the way I was.

At that point I went into counseling. I didn't stay with it long; but what it did for me was, I could talk just about me. I didn't have to worry about being the good Sister. I think what I did was, I emotionally threw up. I got rid of the loss and the anger I had for losing my mother. I used to think that was all a big crock. It was probably the first time in my life I cried because I did not have a mother and how much I missed.

I was always a very angry person underneath. But to be angry made you a bad little girl. So I always suppressed that. And you could not be a good Sister if you were angry and I was always angry. So I overcompensated by being this great worker, this efficient person.

The psychiatrist was totally psychoanalytic, Freudian. He spent the whole time going, "Hmmm, hmmm." Knowing my personality, the totally wrong person to go to. One day he said, "You know, everybody that seems to know you says you function so well. Can I ask you just one question? Why do you think you don't?"

Now that's such a simple thing. I walked out of his office and I said, "Well, he's right. This is how I function 98 percent of my time, and this is how people interpret me." From that day this empty shell was just filled up. I went back the next week and I said, "I don't need to come here anymore."

At that point I worked for nine years straight at St. Nicholas of Tolentine [a high school in the Bronx] with a lovely bunch of people, with the hardest kids I ever worked with in my life, inner-city, troubled kids. Kids who slept on benches, kids who were cocaine addicts, kids who came from very abusive homes, drug-addicted homes, alcohol-addicted homes.

I was strict with them. I mean, the word among the kids was, She's really nice but don't cross her. Because I used to say, "You think you've got a temper? You haven't met anybody 'til you've seen this Spaniard get crazy." And I would get crazy with them. I'd say, "If you want to come with a gun"—which they had done—"and you want to kill me, then you kill me, but you're going to do what I tell you to do. And I'm telling you because it's the best thing for you, and because I love you."

That was the hardest job I ever had and probably the most rewarding. I loved the kids there. Again I felt very highly successful. But I was ready, personally, for a change. And that's really why I left.

I was asked to speak at the National Catholic Educational Association. And somebody from this diocese was there. They called me up and said, "Our only inner-city high school needs a principal. Are you interested?"

I was ready to say, "I want to be the boss." I want to run the school the way I think it should be done for kids. There's not a kid in the school who will not tell you that I care about what happens to them. That's what so hard about working in an inner-city school. The streets teach children that you hit first and you talk later. I beat you before you beat me. I may have to shoot you before you shoot me. I want to show that there are alternatives. I put Martin Luther King's words right out there—"To walk and talk in the manner of love for God is love." He said that on the march to Birmingham. I want the kids to walk and talk in the manner of love. Because that's the only way the world's going to function.

I've always lived in a convent. And my strength very much came from my community. Since I live alone now, I even feel more bound to them. I belong to a prayer group which is composed of our Sisters. Some are in convents, some are in small group living, some live alone. We meet periodically to pray together. And we cook dinner for each other. It's really a fun thing as well as a prayer group. So I feel very close to them.

Some people say, "Oh, you live alone. How can you stand it?" But I'm rarely alone. I'm never lonely 'cause I'm not there long enough. I live across the street and the only thing I asked about the apartment is that it not face the school. It faces out the back. So when I go home I don't look at the school at all. I feel like I'm going to a different world. I am usually here by seven o'clock and I leave, depending, at five, five-thirty, six. I can go home. If I come back at night for a meeting, I have a space of a couple of hours where I can watch the news and eat or play some music or read something or pray.

I try to pray every day. I'm not very successful at it. My life is so crazy. But I feel now, and part of that is knowing who I am, I pray all day in a sense. Because when I talk to kids, I talk about God a lot.

I say this prayer every single morning: "Christ, look upon us in this city, and keep our sympathy and pity fresh, and our faces heavenward lest we grow hard." I think it's what I am about and I hope I keep to it. That's very much my faith. I am not a great pray-er, I'm such a restless soul. I felt very unholy most of my life. My relationship with God is "Hi, God, I'm here, I'm running, gonna talk soon."

I do not regret entering religious life. Some people have gone through very peacefully. I can never say that my life has been peaceful in that sense. I miss a heck of a lot of stuff that those vows say I can't have. I'm one of these people, if I make a promise, come hell or high water I'm going to keep that promise. I always felt I was so inadequate in so many other ways I better keep my promises. So my vows were very important to me and I kept them.

Chastity in my life has always been a struggle. Because of my personality, I think. I've had opportunities where I could have made other choices. One regret I would say is that I don't have someone who thinks I'm the best thing since sliced bread. Maybe many marriages don't work. But I look at my sister who has made a very successful marriage and has someone who deeply loves her. And I miss that. I really do.

I made a choice. And I'm not unhappy for my choice. But I wish somebody really thought I was the best thing since sliced bread. You know what I'm saying? And I also miss not having children. Again, that was through choice. I love children. I really adore kids. I look at my sister. My niece is 21, and she and my sister are like best friends. Who says mine would have worked? With my personality I'd probably be divorced and my kids would all be drug addicts or something.

Poverty is hard. I make all my clothes, so I can say what's on me I've made for five or six dollars because I get them off the remnant tables. Every suit I own, every dress, everything I own practically is handmade. But I would love beautiful clothes, and I would love real vacations, and I would love gorgeous cars. This is the first time in my life that I ever had a car for my use. And I feel like I died and went to heaven. When I want to go somewhere I get in the car and I go. Before, you went to a book and you signed out or you're all conniving to work with the one car among five of you.

I very rarely shop, because I don't have the money to buy what I would like. If you come to my apartment, everything is a hand-me-down. I crochet and I sew and I've made lots of very pretty things. People say to me, "Oh my God, your house is so pretty." But nothing there is new.

Obedience was always hard, because I've been a very independent person. We've become a liberal community in a lot of ways. We very much accept who we are. And we don't have silly rules that we impose upon each other. We have come to the point of being a group of adult women leading an adult life.

I love my community deeply. They are definitely my family. They're the women that I will live and die with. If I left tomorrow, if something happened to my life that I left, they have made me who and what I am. To me, being a religious has been a struggle, but it has been a happy struggle. I can put it that way. I feel it has enriched me, made me who I am, made me grow up, made me happy most of the time. I find God very much in my Sisters.

Do I every day say I pray for one hour? No. But I spend time to talk to my God. That is important to me. I hope what I do is a reflection of who he is in my life. I try very hard to love as the Beatitudes say, feed the hungry, clothe the poor. And that's what I do. I buy kids underwear.

I really believe that when it's all over, God's just going to say, "Gloria, were you good to the people?" (May 1991)

In 2002, at the age of 60, Sister Gloria moved from her ministry in inner-city education to social services for the poor. She became executive director of Eva's Village in Paterson, New Jersey, an organization that feeds the hungry, shelters the homeless, treats the addicted, and provides free medical and dental care to the poor.

I changed my whole life, but I continue to serve those less fortunate. I am blessed to love what I do.

SISTER MARLENE BROWNETT

Sister Marlene Brownett, 58, lives with three other members of the Society of the Holy Child Jesus in a center-hall colonial on a quiet suburban street in Summit, New Jersey. The side porch has been turned into an oratory—a place of prayer. She explained that for her the oratory was "nonnegotiable" when Oak Knoll, the private Catholic girls' school where she teaches, needed space in the convent and she was asked to move into a house off the grounds. Sister Marlene quoted often from Tennyson, Eliot, and Hopkins. Yet there was nothing pretentious about her; she frequently declared herself an ordinary voice.

I didn't enter [the convent] to be a teacher, but fortunately that's what I am. But that's not all I am; I'm not just a teacher. People used to ask, "If you were going to identify yourself, who are you?" My Sister and I would often talk about this, and I would say, "Well, I'm Marlene Brownett." "Okay," she would say, "That identifies you as a girl, and as a Brownett girl. What else?"

"I'm Marlene Brownett; I'm a Roman Catholic American."

She'd say, "Oh, you're not an American Roman Catholic?"

I'd say, "No, my Catholicism before my Americanism. All the time. And I'm a nun."

"Oh, you want to be known as a nun?"

And I'd say, "Definitely, absolutely, certainly, yes."

I have to remember often that I truly came to religious life not with the idea of being a teacher but of being a vowed religious woman who is a teacher. When I celebrated my silver jubilee, I tried to figure out how to integrate the students. We had a beautiful liturgy and the whole upper school sang and did the readings. [The girls] asked me about my religious life and how I became a nun. They were very, very interested. And I decided, "I'm going to try to tell them that I'm normal, that I wasn't born a nun." We had had a country home, and we were cleaning it out before it was sold, so I chose a lot of the pictures—pictures of dances and playing badminton, pictures from high school, from college, and from childhood—and we put them in the front hall. And oh, the questions those provoked. "Well, if you had boyfriends, why did you ever enter the convent?" I'm not like St. Augustine who led a wild life. I didn't. But I enjoyed life from grade school up through college.

So they really want to know what motivated me. [They ask,] "Are you happy?" And they often say, "You really believe, don't you? You really, really believe in this." I love the interchange with students. They're lively, and they keep you abreast of the times, and they want so much to know so many things. They keep me young. I think often we've cheated our students in these years. As a religious, and as somebody trying to give them values, I'm concerned that we [as educators] haven't always done as much for them as we should. I think they're thirsty for truth, I think they're thirsty for religion, but to find a way to give it to them is tough. In English you're able to do that without making it superficial, because it's so abundantly a part of literature.

Once in a while I get discouraged. Is it really worth it? Is anything going in? And I don't mean grammar. I mean anything of the real truth of what life is about. And almost every time something happens. I get a letter or somebody leaves something on my desk that says, "Keep at it. You're doing the right thing. You're a teacher."

I teach a course called the Drama of Human Courage, which I designed in 1980. At the time I had come back from Rome and I had been very influenced by Jean Vanier, the founder of L'Arche, which is a lay community to care for mentally retarded adults. I had met him and he spoke about the fact that the Church was entering an age of martyrdom such as it has never before experienced. And Oscar Romero was killed while I was in Rome. So that period of time influenced me to think about the drama of human courage.

We study *Murder in the Cathedral, A Man for All Seasons*, several plays about Joan of Arc, and then stories of the Holocaust. Every once in a while I [would wonder], "Is this stuff going in? Is this too religious for them?" And invariably— this year I got a letter from a student who is graduating from NYU, and she said, "I was reading *The New York Times* the other day. I couldn't help thinking of you. I'm going to get to this play on Joan of Arc." And she sent that review to me the week we were starting the Joan of Arc plays.

Another student said to me, "I don't pray too much; I'm not too religious." I said, "That's your choice, but someday you will be." She wrote a poem, her response to the course, called "There's a Cathedral in My Heart." She came to me yesterday and said, "My poem won first prize. I entered it in a contest. I just wanted you to know." Those are the little things. You can call them coincidence. They are; but I think God guides coincidence. I call it Providence.

Last week in the speech class I teach to seniors I had each of them choose a favorite passage from the Gospel or from the Old Testament, the Psalms; and I asked them to read that, proclaim it, to the class and then to deliver a two- to three-minute homily for their peers, not for me. And I must tell you that the sincerity of their approach, and the honesty of their comments, moved me to tears.

You spoke of obedience and the new freedoms we [religious] have. That freedom is a real incentive and also a stumbling block because today we have to use it well, to use it for self-growth, and to use it for the service of others, always keeping that balance. Life's a tightrope. You have to do a balancing act, and I firmly believe that we are made in the shape of the cross. Stand up and put your arms out, and you balance yourself. Friends have said to me, "Oh, sure, you have individual poverty and corporate wealth, you religious." It's an indictment of us. Maybe we do. Poverty is the big struggle, I think. Mother Teresa said there's no poverty like the poverty of America. And there's no poverty like the poverty of some of the rich. There are times when I envy Mother Teresa, but that's not what I'm called to. A lot of the Sisters have left teaching and have gone to work among the poor. Maybe some of my Sisters in the Society of the Holy Child are called to that, but I'm not, and to envy that is wasting time that could be spent beneficially in loving God and in serving His people.

I work in a very affluent school. Some of my friends say, "When are you going to start working for the poor?" But I do, in a secondhand way, because while I am here some people [in the Society] are released to work for the poor. My salary goes to the Society, and it helps to support our elderly Sisters and the people who are in apostolates that I'd probably not be good at.

I'm still pretty young. I would like to continue teaching until I recognize that the girls are not responding. I hope I have the good sense and the grace to recognize it; and if I don't, I hope somebody has the bravery to confront me and that I graciously accept it. I think I have a couple of good years left. After that I might want to go into a school on a part-time basis where I'd just be around if anybody needed me, teacher or student. I think there is something of the spiritual life of Cornelia [Connolly, our foundress] that I could help hand on to laypeople who are taking up the role. Our whole job is passing on that heritage.

In my early years I was a principal. I had the privilege of being a superior. I served in Rome [as Secretary General of the Society]. I'm not saying I've done it all or that I've worked as hard as I should. Cornelia used to say, "Never enough, never enough." I say, "Enough, enough." It would be very hard to be a leader in the school today. I don't have that kind of personality. A lot of people say, "Oh yes, you could do it." I don't know, but what I do know is that I'm a very good teacher. (March 1992)

Sister Marlene moved to New York City to live with her sister and care for her until her death. She has stayed on in the apartment to finalize her family's affairs.

"Once a teacher, always a teacher." If there's anything a real teacher knows, it's that we never stop learning. So these days I still teach and I still learn. I read, write, Skype, e-mail and blessedly have time to think, ponder, and even do a little penance. At 58, I thought, "I have a couple of good years left." Now, at 76 I'm convinced that I do.

Then, students kept me young. They still do, as alumnae who have happily surpassed their teacher as RNs, MDs, and PhDs, professional women, mothers, and grandmothers. I still enjoy public speaking on the life of our foundress, Cornelia Connelly, to anyone who invites me. As I delve deeper into prayer, it's good to have the time to pursue those words of my beloved poet [Hopkins]: "There lives the dearest freshness deep down things."

SISTER ROSEMARY RADER

Sister Rosemary Rader, a Benedictine nun, was in the midst of conducting a retreat for an abbey of Benedictine monks when the interview took place. We met in the lounge of the abbey infirmary—a quiet space overlooking peaceful rolling hills. Sister Rosemary, 63, did not disturb the peace; she spoke softly, and she sat quite still, hands folded on the table between us.

She has been a teacher in high school or college for most of her life, and recently served as prioress of her Benedictine community in St. Paul, Minnesota. She has also given numerous retreats. The fact that she is invited to offer spiritual guidance to communities of men reveals the depth of the changes that have occurred in her life—and also in the Roman Catholic Church.

When Sister Rosemary entered the convent, in the days before Vatican II, priests gave retreats—for each other, for the nuns, and for the laity. While nuns have for some time offered spiritual guidance to each other and to laywomen, it is a more recent development that they are sometimes invited to give retreats for priests.

I think I entered because I had always wanted to be a teacher. For women in those days, that was the only way you could be a part of service within the Church. And I loved being a teacher.

I taught for about seven years in primary school—first, sixth, and seventh grades. Then they needed a Latin teacher in high school, so they sent me off for a master's degree in Latin. One day while I was teaching at the high school, the prioress called me into her office and said, "One of your professors at the University of Minnesota called me and said he had told you to apply for a Fulbright grant to study in Italy for a year. And he tells me that you didn't think the community would want you to. What makes you think the community wouldn't want you to, since you didn't ask?" I said, "I just think I know the community, and we're hard up for money because we have this big debt on the new building." She said, "I want you to apply. I also want you to know that we may think of sending you on for a doctorate in case we ever have a junior college." So I applied, and I got the grant and I did study in Italy for a year. They didn't send me on for a doctorate right away. We had to wait until we had the building a bit more paid for. In 1972, I applied for several grants, and I took the one from Stanford [University] because it was the best.

There's a very personal thing that I need to touch on. I think the prioress picked up that I was getting discouraged, burned out. I was teaching high school. I was working hard in community, speaking up at chapter meetings, and helping to bring about some of the changes we needed. I was chosen president of the Minnesota Humanities Council. I was being asked to give talks around the state. And I think some of the Sisters were looking at me as somebody who was becoming a little too different from the rest of the community. I felt that, so I was trying to be very cautious, not even telling them the grades I got. I was underplaying my activities and turning down requests for talking because I felt that I would be seen as having privileges others didn't have. It sounds crazy, and it doesn't bother me now in the same way that it did then, but my going to Stanford gave me a brand-new lease on life, including religious life.

When I went out there, for the first time in my life, I had the leisure to learn. I got the M.A. and the B.A. while I was teaching full time and taking courses, going on Saturdays and summers. Stanford was like a heavenly blessing. I was 39 years old [when I started my Ph.D.], and it was wonderful. I see it as the turning point in my life, because had I not gone, I'm not sure that I would have stayed in community. I think I'd have died on the vine.

My field at Stanford was comparative religion with emphasis on the history of Christianity. It was an area where I could use all the languages I had: Latin, Greek, French, German, Italian. I had professors who were atheists by their own self-pronouncement, but had such a great respect for the monastic tradition. One summer when I wasn't going to go home, back to the community for a few months, one of my professors said, "Rosemary, you are a monastic at heart.

You have to return to the source." Here was this Anglican who had left the Anglican Church, a very wise friend, who realized he couldn't stay within the church tradition, but he saw that what was in me demanded I stay a part of that. And he was right. He also said something that has become for me a philosophy for people who are finding things hard in the church. Every once in a while when I'd leave his office, he'd say, "Well, so long, Rosemary. Remember, you keep the Church and I'll keep the faith." He was teasing because he knew I was finding things hard within the Church.

The institutional Church very often gets in the way of religion. And the Church, as an institution, can very much get in the way of an individual's faith. If one is going to stay within a tradition, there has to be a reconciling of those divisive elements. People have to find their own way of retaining sanity if they love the tradition enough to want to be a part of that tradition. And that's what I had to do. Stanford opened up my mind to a lot of truth about Christianity. I was finding Latin and Greek sources about women's roles in early Christianity that I had never heard of. I would go to this professor and I'd say, "Why didn't we hear about this?" And he'd say, "Why do you think you're here? Write about it."

I had to work through my anger—anger at the way women were treated and anger at the dishonesty I saw coming out of an institutional Church, out of a male-based hierarchy, which denied women's role. I had started to be aware [of the problem] back in Minnesota, in 1972 to 1975, when I was chair of the Archdiocesan Sisters' Council. Many of the communities of Sisters would call and say, "This is the problem we're having with the bishop. What could the Council do?" The Council is like a senate of Sisters; and after we'd talked about the issue, I'd be the troubleshooter for the Sisters to the archbishop. I began to see there were a lot of grave injustices. But I was always frustrated because I would say something to a bishop, and when he'd question where I had gotten my information, I couldn't always give the source. Once I started in Stanford, I began to find the sources. After that I was no longer afraid to stand up, because I was backed by knowledge. The historical data was there.

The first woman [I researched] who was a shock to me was Olympias. She was a deaconess in Constantinople in the fourth and fifth centuries, a good friend of John Chrysostom, one of the Greek Church fathers. I began to find letters to Olympias from him where he thanks her for going to court for him, for defending him. He was exiled from Constantinople, and he thanks her for helping to set things right in the Church and even for meeting with public officials and going to the Senate—all things we never realized women did. She kept the Church going while he was away, and she kept his foes at bay. I was astonished. I said, "Wait a minute. She was a deaconess? I can't believe this." I copied passages. I looked for other sources.

At the same time [as I was working on the historical data] there were women—Mary Daly, Rosemary Ruether, and a little bit later Elisabeth Schüssler Fiorenza—who began to work on the theological implications of the history. All of it began to come together for me in a way that I felt I could live within the tradition. What I finally realized was that I'm not good at being angry for very long. I decided that a creative anger would help me to write, and it did. I began to give talks around the area on women in the early Church. I began to do some writing on women in religion.

One of the summers when I went home to St. Paul, I did a workshop on women in the early Church, and that was received very, very well. The community began to realize, "What's she doing, giving all these talks to other people and not to us?" So they began to coax me to come back. And I was afraid because of the jealousy factor. The sad part is I worked through [those feelings] by not being in the community. I was 10 years, almost, in exile. But not really. I do see that community members were supportive because they knew I was off by myself. Many of them would come out to see me, and they made it a point always to be there when I came home. They were always writing. When I look back, the community grew even as I had. I did appreciate that.

After I received my Ph.D. I went to [a large public university] where they had established a new religious studies department, and they needed somebody in history of Christianity. They even wanted me to do a course on women and religion, which was my expertise at that time. It seemed the right place. I minded that it was so far away from the community, but it was the only place that had an opening in Christian studies. The community knew that we needed the money that came from my college teaching. Once they had trained me to be a Ph.D., they didn't want me to go back to the high school, because I was over-qualified; and we never did open a junior college.

I was at [the university] for seven years, with one year out to return to teach at Stanford. Then what happened is, I was denied tenure. I knew that there was something wrong because I had published more articles than the other person up for tenure in the department; I was the only one to get a teaching award and then not get tenure. I couldn't understand what had happened.

Normally, as a good nun, you'd walk away and say, "Well, it's meant to be. I shouldn't be here." Maybe I'm a fighter by nature, but I said, "Hey, wait a minute. If it's unjust, it's unjust." And men and women in other departments said, "You're fighting this, and we're going to help you. If you need help with money, we'll even contribute." I started [the appeal process], and it was going through channels. Then one of my students was so upset that she talked to somebody on the board of regents and the board of regents asked to see me, which had never happened before. They decided that denying me tenure was not justified, and after a meeting with them I received tenure, associate professorship, and money for a sabbatical in Oxford.

But in the meantime, the community elected me prioress, which was tough, because I really wanted to stay [at the university] to prove that I could teach and that I did have the support of people in the department. But the community said that I couldn't this time say "No" to becoming prioress, because I had turned down the nomination twice before. So I had to send in my resignation to the university. But it was worth the fight for tenure. At [that university] it was so bad that about 82 percent of men got tenure and about 13 percent of women. And I think I helped to change that. Even back in St. Paul, when I was prioress, I got calls from women who had heard, "Rosemary won tenure. You have to talk to Rosemary." So I told them what steps to take, where to go.

I was amazed that the community would bring me back after 12 years. So as prioress I tried really hard to get their input on what we should be doing. The first year we studied long-range goals and we discussed what we would do each year. We started on building projects; we started spiritual renewal efforts; we started bringing people in to [talk] about women's issues, about third-world poverty issues. And I found what was happening was we really pulled together as a community.

During the eight years I was prioress, I also taught at least two semesters each year at St. John's University in Collegeville, Macalaster College, College of St. Catherine—wherever they asked me. I loved teaching, and I was chomping at the bit to get back into that kind of dialogue with students.

I had to wait to go to Oxford until last year. Going to Oxford gave me time to come out of that mold of being prioress, where you had to be caretaker, general manager, and all of those things. That never became the full-time job I would have chosen, and I realized I was very tired after those eight years. It takes a lot out of you. For about the first two months I worked, but it was very slow. I took time to walk around Oxford, sometimes in a daze, because I couldn't believe I was there. Then I became very sick with pernicious anemia, and I think it was because I didn't take any time off. I recovered, but it shocked me into wondering what had happened between the ages of 40 and 63. I saw that time had gone so fast and somehow that developed into the realization that I was a workaholic and that I had to start slowing down.

I spent a year and nine months in England, doing research on St. Frideswide, the foundress of Oxford. A lot of people don't know that this monastic woman founded the whole City of Oxford! That became a chapter in a book, *Medieval Monastic Women*, that's going to be published next year. Now that I am back, I'm teaching a course this summer at St. John's, and next year I will be a visiting associate professor at Carleton College in Northfield, teaching six courses in Christian studies. I'm booked for teaching in summers until 1997. And I am working on a book on early monastic communities of women. There's a lot more information than we ever thought there was. I do think we can look at women's monastic histories and find little clues to the role of women in general at the time.

You must be a good teacher. Your excitement is evident on your face.

I do get excited—yes. And I have students say that. They also say, "You speak too fast. We can't take notes." I just say, "No, you're listening too slowly." (June 1994)

Sister Rosemary retired and is living with her Benedictine community at St. Paul's Monastery in St. Paul, MN.

SISTER MARGHERITA MARCHIONE

Sister Margherita Marchione, 69, has published more than 30 books, met presidents and popes, and received awards for her scholarly work from numerous organizations in both Italy and the United States. She began teaching in elementary schools and moved up to high school. She was then, for 19 years, a university professor. She has not stopped researching and writing. In addition, she serves as treasurer of her order, the Religious Teachers Filippini. Since the interview took place, she has published three more books; her most recent is Yours Is a Precious Witness: An Oral History of Jews and Catholics in Wartime Italy. *Sister Margherita wears the black habit and bonnet that all members of her community wear.*

I was a very determined individual. Inspired by my eighth-grade teacher, who was a Benedictine, I made up my mind that I would become a nun. She had told me about the motherhouse and made all the arrangements for me to attend high school there in September. None of this was discussed with any member of the family. I just made all my own plans.

Well, it so happened that in our town every three years we had confirmation. I was in the confirmation group, although I did not have to go to instructions because I attended a Catholic school. The Sisters who were teaching the confirmation class were the Religious Teachers Filippini. Bishop Thomas Joseph Walsh was to be officiating. The bishop loved the Religious Teachers Filippini; he had taken a special interest in them since 1920. This was 1935.

This was the first time in my life that I saw a bishop. A real bishop. With all his robes, with the crosier and the miter and everything. So I'm looking at him, impressed—I was 13—and he's talking. At one point he's looking at me straight in the eye. He used to go like this with his finger, you know, pointing. "And if there is any young girl of Italian extraction who wishes to become a nun, she *must* go to these Sisters."

Well, for me that was like God Almighty telling me what to do. Telling me what to do? I had not even told my parents. I had told no one. My sisters, no one, knew what my plans were.

After that I thought I could not go to the Benedictines anymore. So I told the Sisters who were instructing, "Bishop said I have to go to Villa Lucia [the motherhouse of the Religious Teachers Filippini]."

They informed me that the following week there would be an investiture ceremony, and they encouraged me to come. Of course it was a very impressive ceremony; so all the more I became determined that I would be like those girls. The mistress of novices told me to visit her when she had more time in the summer, and I did.

I was visiting a cousin, and somehow I had the courage—remember, I had never left home before—to get a bus from Newark to Morristown. I found out where Villa Lucia was and walked for two miles at noon in July, wearing my graduation

At the end of a papal audience in October 2008, Pope Benedict XVI pauses for a brief conversation with Sister Margherita Marchione as she presents one of her many books on Pope Pius XII. Sister Margherita has devoted much of the last two decades to researching and writing about the role of Pope Pius XII during World War II.

dress with a hand-rolled hem. By the time I got up the hill to the mansion door, the hem was coming down. I was exhausted. I rang the doorbell and began to cry because my hem was down and I didn't think it right for me to be in public with my hem going down. Before I could stop crying, one of the nuns had to come with a needle and thread and sew that hem. I was so spoiled.

The mistress of novices settled for me to come on September 2, 1935, so that I'd be ready to start high school with the other girls. I didn't say a word to anyone all summer long—just kept on living a normal life.

September 2 was Labor Day. Two days before, on Saturday, I went to confession, and Father Maxwell, who was the pastor, was there. I told him that I was going to become a nun and that on Monday I had to be at Villa Lucia. He said, "Oh, I'll take you there."

On Labor Day we were having dinner. I can still visualize my sisters, their boyfriends, my mother, and my father all there eating. At one o'clock I stood up and I said, "Excuse me, but I have to go get dressed because I am going to become a nun."

This was the first time anyone in the family knew of my plans. I went upstairs to change my clothes. They think I'm just joking. They had no idea how serious

I was. By 1:15 the car still wasn't there, so I called and a maid said Father Maxwell was out, that he wouldn't be in till the next day. It dawned on me then that he was only teasing me, but here I had taken him seriously. By that time I was a little indignant, and I picked up the phone and called up the mistress of novices and I said, "You told me to come today and Father Maxwell said he would take me and he's not home and I don't know what to do."

She told me to telephone the Sisters from the order who were in a convent nearby and tell them to get someone "to drive you here today." She still had not spoken to my parents. This was just between her and me. How she had the nerve to do that, I don't know. But I called the Sisters, and within a half-hour there was a car at the house. It was a big black limousine with a chauffeur—one of those funeral cars, you know.

One of my sisters looked out the window and saw the car and saw me all dressed up. I did not have a suitcase. Sister Ninetta had said, "You don't need anything. Come here and we'll take care of everything." I didn't take my treasures or anything [I loved as a child]. I had beautiful pearls from my confirmation godmother. I just left everything.

My sister said, "Ma, get dressed. I'll accompany you because certainly you can't let her go alone."

So my mother and my sister Marie came with me. We went into the mansion. When the mistress of novices saw my mother and my sister, she sent for some coffee. She was very hospitable.

At one point she asked my mother, "How many children do you have?"

And my mother said, "Eight."

She said, "How many girls?"

"Seven."

Sister just looked. "And you are not willing to give one of these seven girls to the Lord? You ought to be ashamed of yourself."

My mother had been crying. She was so shocked she stopped crying. It was something out of this world for her to hear someone talk to her like that. Sister sent me off to get dressed as a postulant with the black dress and a veil. Of course I came down all pleased with myself that I had won the battle. My mother said, "We'll let her stay for a few weeks and see what happens."

There's a little hallway that leads from the mansion to the chapel now. At that time the chapel was just built, and I remember standing in that hallway practically every day crying my eyes out. I was so homesick, and it was such a different life. I had never been away from home, and here we were, all these young girls living on the third floor of the mansion, all in one big dormitory because that was the only building.

I was still a spoiled child, the youngest in a family of eight. I remember sitting at the table with some of the older girls. When the food would come around, I would refuse to eat certain things. The first Friday I was here we had sunnyside-up eggs. And I had never eaten a sunnyside-up egg. I didn't like the looks of it and I refused to eat it. The assistant mistress and the older girls insisted that I eat it. Well, I sat there. I remember everybody had gone and I was still sitting there. Do you know that to this day I cannot eat a sunnyside-up egg? That was in 1935. Oh, those were hard times for me.

In those days we never went home even for a day. At the time we were willing to follow regulations, and even not going home was accepted. Our parents were allowed to come once a month. Every time my parents came, my father would insist that I go home with them. I'd say that I was happy, that I had to become a nun.

I was a good student. I finished high school in three and a half years, really, because we studied during the summertime. I took additional courses in normal school which led to a degree from college.

When I was 19, I was sent to Baltimore, where I taught grades six to eight. Later on, when I came back from Baltimore, I went to Columbia University for an M.A. I was teaching, full time. In fact, I got my doctorate as a part-time student.

When I went for my M.A. in Italian language and literature, I was 23—very young for a nun to go to a non-Catholic university. The professor, Giuseppe Prezzolini, said, "I teach Machiavelli." I had practically never even heard his name! I didn't know what I was getting into.

He said, "I think you nuns ought to go sign up for something else."

We said, "Well, no, the superiors told us to sign up for this course."

Later on in a book Prezzolini wrote, he has a chapter on me and the Sisters. He says the whole atmosphere in the classroom changed. Prior to our presence in the classroom there would be snickering and all sorts of irreverent statements. There was none of that anymore.

Giuseppe Prezzolini was a great Italian writer, journalist, and philosopher. Columbia thought so highly of him that they called him to teach. He was in France with the League of Nations. He became a professor emeritus without ever having a degree in Italy or here. He was a self-taught man. A great man.

By the time I went back in 1956 for a Ph.D., he was no longer teaching, but he was on the campus. I had an official mentor, but Prezzolini was really my mentor behind the scenes. I was only there two months when they gave me a scholarship to go to Italy to interview Clemente Rebora, the poet I was writing about.

Until that time no one ever dreamed of a nun going around by herself. In the community it was unheard of that anyone would study in Europe or take a trip. To travel alone was a big problem. When I received the scholarship, the mother provincial wrote to the mother general [in Rome] and asked her if it would be all right for me [to accept it].

The mother general said, "Absolutely no. Ask the archbishop."

So the mother provincial asked the archbishop.

The archbishop said, "Oh, it's wonderful. Yes."

When mother general heard that, she said, "No, that's not sufficient. I'll have to ask the Vatican." Our superior in the Vatican approved. I was 35.

Prezzolini moved to Italy in 1962. Every time I went back and forth to Italy, I always visited him there, as well as in Lugano when he moved to Switzerland. In 1966 my publisher was able to arrange a private audience with the Holy Father, Paul VI, who knew Prezzolini. He had studied all his books before he even became cardinal and then pope. I said, "Your Holiness, I bring you greetings of Giuseppe Prezzolini. He was my professor at Columbia University, and he asked me to give you his regards."

He looked at me with a twinkle in his eyes and said, "Well, teach him how to pray." I looked at him and didn't blink an eye and said, "Your Holiness, if you didn't succeed, how do you expect me to?" He didn't realize that I knew that a few months prior to my visit he had had Prezzolini with him for three-quarters of an hour.

Then he said, "Well, you're right. We have to pray for him." I never saw the Holy Father smile like that. Paul VI was a very serious person.

Every time I went to visit Prezzolini and his wife, I was always their houseguest. I tried to keep them happy, bring things, and liven up the place a little. After all, I was 40 years younger than he, and I was like part of the family. I know they both loved me. I would clean out his files and straighten things up and do shopping. We'd go out for walks. I'd walk with him down to the center of Lugano, and he'd say, "If anyone asks who you are, I'll just say you're my niece." Because they all knew that he was considered an atheist and here I am parading the streets of Lugano with him.

But in 1982, when I went to Lugano [during one of my sabbaticals], I noticed a terrible deterioration. He was going to be 100 years old, and she was 80 years old. I calculated that I would spend three months with them. Within one month, his wife died. So I just continued staying on, taking care of him and arranging everything. Of course a woman would come in the morning and do the housecleaning. Another woman would come in to prepare some food; I would set the table. We had everything in fine style.

When I had to leave Lugano in June, I said good-bye to Prezzolini. He walked me to the door and he said, "I may not see you again."

I said, "You know I'm coming back. You saw my ticket. I'll be back in a few weeks."

Well, in the meantime he passed away. But I have such wonderful memories. I'm very grateful for what I learned from Prezzolini.

I was very independent as a child and went off on my own. Later on when someone would say, "I don't feel fulfilled," I would say, "Well, that's your own fault." No one told me to feel fulfilled. It's a matter of willpower if you want to achieve something.

I remember sitting in the bathroom as a young Sister, not to have the light on in the dormitory. I'd sit in there at night studying French and German. I was teaching full time all my life. After my novice days, then I was out teaching in schools for 15 years. I was in Baltimore. I was in Trenton. I was in Newark. I was school musician for all the plays, operettas, everything that we had. I was parish musician, responsible for church services. So it isn't that I neglected religious duties or other tasks that I had. I did everything that everyone else did. But I squeezed in these additional things because I felt the urge that I had to do so.

Who dreamed 30 or 40 years ago that I would have published 30 books and more? When I think of it, I can't believe it myself. That's why I say my life is just like a fairy tale. Because if you ask me how did I accomplish so much, I must say I don't know. I can't explain it. I can't even explain where I got the energy to do this kind of work. Certainly I'm healthy enough, but I'm not that strong. It's God's way of doing things.

Nobody has to tell me I'm a workaholic. I know I am. And yet I feel, why not do all I can? When the Lord calls me, I'll just be ready. I mean, I've got nothing to preserve of my own, so I'd rather do as much as I can. Even if it shortens my life, so what? (February 1991)

Sister Margherita, now 88, has continued to write and publish books about the legacy of Pope Pius XII. Her books have appeared in English and Italian and include scholarly work as well as pictorial editions and bilingual coloring books for children.

2

MISSIONARY
WORKERS

SISTER CARITA PENDERGAST

In 1991, at the age of 87, Sister Carita Pendergast, a Sister of Charity of Saint Elizabeth from Convent Station, New Jersey, published her first book. Havoc in Hunan *in a history of the years the Sisters of Charity spent in China. Her own missionary experiences in China, she said, left her open to the changes that would bring havoc to the lives of many women religious in the decades after her return.*

The interview took place in her office among her community's archives, not far from the computer she recently mastered.

When I was 21, I entered the community of the Sisters of Charity. They had been my former teachers, and they also educated my father, my uncles, and cousins. We knew them well. And they seemed to me the kind of community that I could best survive in. They educated their Sisters, and one of the things I wanted to do was be a teacher. There was a prayer book that a lot of us had at that time, and I always remember these words: "Those who instruct others unto justice shall shine like stars for all eternity." I'm afraid I wanted to be a star!

But when I was still in my teens, there was all this talk about China. I knew—I knew—that someday I was going to wind up in China. But I found that hard to reconcile with the Sisters of Charity, because they were a teaching community and they were largely centered in New Jersey, Massachusetts, and Connecticut. However, in 1924, five of the Sisters of Charity were sent to China. Well, you know, when you're young you think God is doing everything for you. I was sure that was a direct answer to prayer, because now I could be a Sister of Charity and I could go to China.

As soon as I entered, I petitioned to go to China, and the reverend mother said to me, "Come back again when you've made your vows." Well, when I made my vows I came back again. And she said, "We'll remember you when there's a need."

Finally they sent out a request for volunteers. And I wrote a letter, and I said in the letter, "I am 28 years of age. Strong. Healthy. Not easily scared." Everybody

Sister Carita Pendergast, in full habit, receives a trophy for winning the shuffleboard contest on board the S.S. *President Wilson* in 1951. The Sisters had just endured expulsion by the Chinese Communists from their convent and their mission in Hunan and were on their way home to the United States.

said to me, "They won't take you because your mother is still living. They don't take people whose parents are living." But I was one of those who were selected, and I went to China. That was 1933.

I spent 18 years in China. They were very difficult years because China was in turmoil all the time. Warlords. War with Japan. The communists. That was the background. Hunan is a very rural province in west central China. It's not at all like being in Beijing or Shanghai.

We had two missions. One in the city in Yuanling, and the other one was Wuki. [First] I was in Yuanling. China was at war from 1937 on, so I was there four years when the bishop began looking for a safer place for the children because of the bombings. Yuanling was bombed 32 times. In the end the Sisters' compound was bombed to smithereens.

I went down to Wuki with the children. That was a wonderful place. The word *Wuki* means *fertile creek*; the creek ran right at our door. It simplified a lot of things. You didn't have running water there; you didn't have central heating. The children could bathe in the creek and could wash their clothes in the creek.

Our relationship with the people there in the country was very good. We employed several of them. We had a cook for the children. We had a cook for ourselves. We had a woman who taught the little ones how to sew, how to make shoes, which is a cottage industry in China. We had a messenger to go over to the next village for mail and run errands and things like that. And we had a farmer. We had two catechists, one for the men and one for the women.

My work was chiefly at the orphanage and the school. Foreigners could not be principals, but we had a wonderful old Chinese gentleman who was principal. And foreigners were allowed only to teach certain subjects. Among them was mathematics, which the Chinese considered was their weak point. I taught mathematics in elementary school. And some of the children were hard to educate because they had been starved as babies. These were throw-away children, all girls.

We prepared the girls for marriage. We had a hard job holding onto them. They married very young in China, and we tried not to let them go before they were 18 at least, 20 even better. I married off so many girls that the other Sisters used to kid me and call me the mother of the bride. But it was always an agonizing experience.

A woman would come in—if she had a marriageable son—and she'd look over the girls and she would say to Rosalie, our catechist, "I've been watching So-and-So. I think she'd make a very good match for my son. Will you do what's necessary?" So Rosalie would come to me, and she'd say, "So-and-So"—let's say Mrs. Li—"has been looking at the Zong girl, and she thinks the Zong girl would be a good match for her son." So then the Zong girl would be called in. These little children had absolutely no caste at all, but we had tried to give them self-respect. It always amused me—the demands they would make of the bridegroom's family.

We had been brought up in the United States, where you think of marriage as a love affair. In China it's business. And I was always afraid we might be forcing a girl.

I remember one episode. There was a girl by the name of Audrey, always a handful. The night before the girls married, we used to have a kind of stag party for them. The bigger girls were allowed to stay up all night if they wanted, just to talk and reminisce. And I put the little girls to bed. This night, the eve of Audrey's wedding, I went upstairs and I put the little girls to bed. When I came down and stopped outside the room where the girls were having the party, I heard Audrey sobbing and saying in a loud voice, "I wouldn't marry this man at all if it weren't for that Sister Carita. She's forcing me to."

I nearly died. I ran into the room—now, I had been in China about 14 years at this time; I knew their customs—but even so, I ran into the room and said, "Audrey, it's not too late. If you don't want to marry that man, I'll send word over right away."

"Oh, no, no, no, no," she said.

And with that I heard a lot of laughter. All these little kids were outside listening, and they had burst into laughter when they heard Audrey. Anyway, she was married the next day.

We had another little girl by the name of Gemma. She was a sweetheart. She married a boy over in the next village, and the next morning at five o'clock in the morning there was somebody banging at our gates. So I went down and I opened the gates, and who's there but Gemma.

She said, "I'm lonely. I don't know anybody over there."

She was a new bride, you know. I thought, Oh my God, what do I do with this?

Our messenger was a very stately old man. His back was so straight that we named him Six O'Clock. I said to him, "What do I do in a case like this? This girl is married. We have to send her back. No two ways about it."

And he said, "Give her a present for her mother-in-law, and I'll take her back and I'll explain that she just wanted to let you know how much she appreciated all you did for her and that she's really just a child and she didn't know how to handle it."

So that's what we settled on. We got some stuff together—I've forgotten what it was—and Gemma returned with a lot of face and a nice present for her mother-in-law.

In 1951 we had to leave because the communists took over our mission. They took over our convent. They took all our work from us, and they tried to diminish us before the people. [The people] were forbidden to have anything to do with us. They knew the story, but in the end they went along because they would have been punished if they had not. They were beaten. In the end we knew we were hurting them by staying. They didn't dare look at us, or they'd be accused of being friendly.

So then we came home. [That] was heartbreaking because I had learned to love the people. I felt that what I was doing was worthwhile, knowing that I was helping people. In a foreign mission you get to know the people very well. It isn't a faceless crowd. You know the individuals; you know their history.

In 1955, I was appointed director of the Junior Professed Sisters. It was wonderful dealing with young Sisters—wonderful dealing with their idealism, their generosity, and so on. Many of them came right from high school. So when they came to me, they were in their early twenties; and when they got to know me and trust me, they would talk about their problems.

I thought I knew young people. I had taught in high school before I went to China, and I had just come from a high school. I thought I knew young people; but when I really got to know them, I saw that they had problems I didn't know about.

So then I decided, "I'll go into psychology. That's the way I can best help these young Sisters. Common sense isn't enough." I was afraid of my own judgment and the advice that I could give them. Then, part time, I went on for a master's in psychology, and when I finished that I went on for a doctorate in psychology. The whole direction of the studies that I would have done took a different direction because of the difference in the young people.

In the beginning I nearly died when they began to leave [the community]. I had these girls three or four years; they stayed with me until they had completed their education. I thought I had put too much emphasis on education and not enough on religious training. And for a long time I couldn't walk past that building. I'd take detours because I was so hurt.

And then we did a smart thing. We invited all the ex-Sisters back. I remember it was a beautiful day in June. These young women came back, and they had their little children with them—two, three, four, five years of age—and their husbands. Very often the husbands were ex-priests, ex-brothers. And I remember looking at those little children and thinking, "If your mother hadn't left the community, you probably wouldn't have life."

These children were beautiful. And they were children of well-educated parents—which promised well for our Catholic religion, because they would get a good Catholic education and they'd probably be Catholic leaders. From then on, it was easy for me. It didn't hurt any longer.

We have those reunions about once every two years. And as time has passed, the girls—the women—are even friendlier. Because now they have teenage children and they're looking at everything from a different perspective. They are very grateful for the opportunities they had while they were in the community. Sometimes they say they were too young, that they had made a decision to enter too young. And I think that might have been it.

But, however, as it stands now, I think that in the providence of God he was taking care of all this. We had very little to do with it. We were really educating the Catholic laity. These women, many of them, are very active in Church work, and they're doing all kinds of good. (March 1991)

Sister Carita died on March 17, 2002 at the age of 98. She had remained active until 2001, tutoring and mentoring young women from China, students at the College of Saint Elizabeth, which is located on the same property as the mother-house where she lived.

SISTER ROSEMARIE MILAZZO

Sister Rosemarie Milazzo, 60, appeared at first a very thin woman, worn and tired. Once she started to talk, however, her eyes glistened, sparkled, and burned, and she became energetic—gesturing, turning, rising from a cumbersome overstuffed sofa to illustrate a custom or execute a deep ceremonial bow.

The interview took place at the motherhouse of the Maryknoll Sisters in Ossining, New York. After the interview, "Ro," as she is known among her Maryknoll Sisters, showed me one of her favorite possessions: a piece of needle-work that now hangs on the wall in her office. The embroidered scene depicts everyday life in Bura, Kenya, her last mission. In the foreground a row of women—some carrying wood or cotton, some in colorful dress—are all moving toward one figure to say good-bye. The Swahili words are translated below on the lavender matte: "We the women of Bura will never forget our Rosemarie."

There's a lot of mystery in my life. I'd have to start right there. I didn't have a real knowledge of Maryknoll. I had seen their magazine, and the magazine always had pictures of people having fun doing regular things. Now, that appealed to me, because I didn't think I was going to be able to do big, spiritual things; but the regular things I thought I could handle. And that's what I saw at Maryknoll. I remember a Maryknoll Sister came once to speak at our parish. And she was so funny about the things that would happen and the way she adapted.

"It was so easy to sweep our floor," she said, "because we lived in a house that had slats; so we just swept and stuff went down, you know." She laughed, and I thought, "That's it. That's what I want to do." So it was really a stab in the dark. I wrote and asked for some information. Once I got a little more in touch with Maryknoll, I felt a real desire to get here. Maryknoll seemed to me to go beyond, and I wanted to go beyond.

Sister Rosemarie Milazzo, as a member of a Christian Peacemaker Team, visits a camp for internally displaced persons in Goma, Democratic Republic of the Congo, in early 2009. The children were amazed to learn that Sister Rosemarie speaks Swahili, and she has just finished singing a popular Swahili song with them. *Christian Peacemaker Teams*

By good luck I went to the novitiate in St. Louis instead of New York. [I had been] living in Brooklyn, going to school in Brooklyn, teaching in Brooklyn. I'd never been out to the country. And I moved out to St. Louis, and there was sky and big trees. I loved it. I loved the river down our valley, just outside our property. And so I got into the routine, which was a very, very traditional routine. We got up very early; we answered bells; we did all that. Some of it didn't make sense; some of it I really questioned. But I could get into it, because it seemed to me like it was moving on to something that I wanted to do.

A lot of the explanation was obedience. We hardly ever talked about anything else. You get an assignment and you go. They used to have a tradition here: A bell would ring sometime in May or June, and the name of each Sister was called and her assignment read. This one's going to Africa, and this one's going to Panama, and somebody's going to Japan, and someone's going here, and Rosemarie Milazzo's going to New York City—Chinatown. It was my first assignment. Yes, I was very disappointed. I was already 30 by then.

But once I got there to Chinatown—and I think this is part of the mystery—I really loved it. It was a very traditional school. This was the first time I had ever been in a Catholic school; I went only to public schools. I was just shocked when I walked in the classroom and the children stood up and said, "Good morning, Sister." And I thought, "Ohhh, my God, amazing." How do you answer? But we would finish teaching and we would go back home to silence and assigned work. We'd go down to the laundry and do sheets. We had a mangle—it's a machine you put the sheets in and it presses them out—like we had in the novitiate. And then we had common prayer. In the morning we took turns ringing the bell and meeting for meditation, and then we'd walk silently over to the church.

But [this was the '60s and] things were changing. And we moved along, changing in ministry also. By the time I left, it was no longer a little parochial school; it was a community place. One day this priest comes in with two women who were on drugs. And he says, "I'd like to know if you people who are Sisters would be willing to help these two women who are on the street." I thought, "My God, a whole new thing to be about." I was just shocked to realize that people my age were using drugs from the time they were 13. To meet a woman who's your own age, whose journey is so different because of some chance—or perhaps some choice she made, which I could easily have made—just absolutely blew my mind. I used to sometimes feel so guilty that I was living in a convent that was so clean and so pristine, and these women would leave, and I knew they had to go out and prostitute to get the next shot. So that group of women got bigger and bigger. I would visit at the prison while they were in prison; and then they would go into detox programs and I'd be visiting at the hospital.

After four years, again the assignment bell rang. And when you were out in a mission, a letter would come. And my letter came. I was just delighted. I had just come from a retreat, and I said, "Oh God, you've answered my prayer." And then the letter said, You will be principal of the school. Thank God there were a couple of friends with me, some Franciscan Sisters. Well, they had to hold me up. To stay and be principal! I never in a million years would have chosen administration. Oh, I wept, wept, wept. I couldn't believe that. That took a lot of faith. Anyway, there I was, so I ran out and started graduate work in administration and supervision. But I was afraid to do too much, because then it would be my job for life, you know.

The convent became a very nice open place—as it should have been, I think. People could come whenever they wanted. We had, in our first floor, a sofa that opened into a bed. Sometimes the women who came who were drug abusers were very strung out. I remember one young woman who came. That same priest brought her, saying, "I don't know what to do. It's Sunday afternoon. Where can I take her?" She was shaking all over. So I kept her, and I found that I had to sleep in that same bed because I was afraid that she would harm herself. The next morning we got her help.

What was nice about the school, if a woman was really stressed out, sometimes I would ask the first-grade teacher if she could spend the day in the classroom with her. I'd say, "Let her give out crayons, collect milk money, whatever." And the woman would be in the atmosphere with kids who are needy about crayons and milk and going to the bathroom. Why, she'd be real that day. At least one day, she had some normal feelings.

I was very happy then. [The '60s in New York City!] We were into public demonstrations for this and demonstrations for that. Oh, I felt like a million dollars. I felt the sense of community, of being able to do something. It was a solidarity that I longed for, and I could sense it. We were a lot of young people, all on fire.

Well, after six years I thought, "I can stay here for life. More doors open all the time, I'm meeting more and more people, more happening, more possibilities." But I kept thinking, "But you came to Maryknoll for a particular reason. Don't lose it." And I really couldn't lose it; it was at the bottom of me.

[After eight years] I wrote a letter and said I think it's time and I'd like to go to Africa. People said to me, "How could you ask for Africa? Why don't you go to Hong Kong? You've been in Chinatown; why wouldn't you go to Hong Kong?" But I never lost my dream. The Chinese people have so many gifts, but I still felt: Africa. And so when I asked Maryknoll, I asked for Africa, and they finally said yes.

I had thought, naively, that people would share this with me. Well, that was not so. They kept saying, "Why are you going? Have we done something wrong? Have we hurt you?" That was very, very difficult. I'm not poor, you know. I try to live simply. I can wear secondhand stuff, but I'm not poor. I think poverty for me again and again has been the constant good-byes. I often feel that Gospel passage where Jesus says [that] the birds have nests but I have nowhere to lay my head. And I think, yeah, I can put my head down here, but tomorrow it's going to be there, and next week it's going to be there. And I may never be back here. And all of the people and all of the life, I have to leave. And every time I do, I leave part of my soul.

Anyway, I left and went off to Africa in '71. I went to language school in Tanzania first. All of that experience in New York made language school extremely difficult. I kept thinking, "My God, what a jerk. I was on top of it. And I come out here, and I can't even say hello. I am a child again." You are a child in language school. However, the people of Tanzania and the people of Kenya were just so lovely. They would help you even with the first syllable and invite you home.

While I was in language school, a new bishop who had just been named in Kenya asked for Maryknoll Sisters to do teacher-training. Well, it was perfect. So I went to teacher-training college right after language school in a magnificent, magnificent town, Kitale, in Kenya. After a couple of years that college became a secondary school and the bishop asked if I would move on to another, which was about an hour away. I was still training teachers. In the second school I was the only expatriate woman; they were all Kenyan—very few women, mostly men. Women are on the staff but, at a staff meeting, hardly heard. But the women were smart, see; I was the only dope. The women would not try to say something; you'd see by their body language. Say you're the headmaster, and you'd say something and I didn't like it. I'd . . . [turns her head away from the interviewer]. And then you'd say something else . . . [turns her body further away]. Well, before you know it, all the women are sitting like this . . . [has turned her body completely away from the interviewer]. Every one of them was sitting that way, you know, and I'd have my hand up and be saying something. Well, nobody's paying much attention to me; it was the body language that they were hearing.

I am not an African woman, but we could laugh together, we could share together, and we could hope together. We visited one another and we celebrated. We would go out and supervise our students together.

The students would press what they were wearing, and they would carry little bits of paper and little sticks which were going to be used for charcoal, and little boards for blackboards; and then I'd get out there and the classroom was smaller than this [gestures to a sofa—perhaps six feet]. We sat under a tree once, and the morning dew was coming down. They would just do this [wipes off the sofa cushion]. And yet the teachers would go out to teach like they were going to Madison Avenue or Park Avenue. I was just filled with wonder when I'd watch it.

When it looked like there were enough Kenyan-trained personnel to do teacher-training, I asked the bishop how he felt about me doing pastoral work—because I was already going to the prison; I was at the hospital; I was visiting families; I was working with a St. Vincent dePaul group trying to get jobs for people. He said, "Good. I think you'd be great. Go ahead." Well, there was a misunderstanding. I, being American, thought "go ahead and do it" meant we were going to do the whole thing. And then the bishop calls me in and says, "Wait a minute. I will do all this." His great "Do it" meant "We'll look into it." So we struggled with that a little bit. Then my mom had a stroke, and I came home. She had had a stroke before and she was okay, but the second time she was paralyzed on one side. We're a big family—10 children— but everybody's married and has a home. So I said, "I'll stay." I didn't know how long that would be; it turned out to be three years. When my mom died, I went back [to Kenya] and I didn't go back to that diocese. There was a bishop in the northeastern frontier who said, "We're just desperate, we have no religious up here. It's brand-new; there'll be nothing for you, but we need people." Well, it was marvelous. They were going to reclaim the desert. The World Bank and the Kenya government were setting up an irrigation scheme; and people would get three acres of land, a home, a little house, and they'd grow cotton.

Some were relocated—homeless, landless Kenyans. The nomadic people had lived around that area for generations but the government was trying to settle them so that they would be agriculturists, too. The nomadic people and the relocated Kenyans from other parts of the country lived together in the villages.

Anyway, when we got there, because the people were just coming and we were just coming, I visited every single house and said, "We're here together. How can we live and work together?"

They said, "We want nurseries for our children, as we need to be out in the fields all day long." So Maryknoll Sisters started a nursery and trained young women to teach. Our doctor and nurse set up dispensaries and trained young people to do physical exams, give injections, etc. I was very eager to see how we could work with women to be more self-reliant and more independent. So I got started with women's groups. We also started literacy classes with the women, as most of them had never been to school and wanted to be able to read and write and do some math.

At that time, there was only one school in all 10 villages that were set up. The kids would have to walk maybe seven, eight, nine miles in the hot sun, their bare feet burning, as the temperature could go up to 130 degrees. The sun was here [gestures toward her shoulder]. I often felt like I was carrying it. It was hard to catch your breath. The women would come to the group meeting after they'd been working in the fields all day. They didn't know their neighbors even. You know, traditionally in Africa you live in a geographic area and every one in that geographic area is the same tribe. You share customs, traditions, and language, and food, everything. All of a sudden, they were uprooted; and some were Kalenjin, some were Luo, some were Kikuyu—all different tribes. There were so many different traditions, languages, customs. So our woman's group shared foods, special celebrations; we had all kinds of dancing. You know, the traditional dances are marvelous, simply marvelous.

It was a Catholic-Christian-Muslim community. The nomads were mostly Muslim. As they moved on, the people built their mosques—very simple little structures—and you'd hear the Muslim call to prayer five times a day.

The Muslim women had their own little group, and I'll never forget beautiful Fatuma. I used to visit her at home all the time, and I said to her, "You never come to my house." So one day she came. They have a little curtain for a door, so she was looking for the little curtain and she kept going around and around and around, and finally she screamed, "Sister Rosemarie, Sister Rosemarie, where is your door?" So I opened the door, and she came in. We had four walls, you know, but we had nothing—a couple of chairs, a bedroom each. But she couldn't believe that a house could have more than one room. We had tea together, and we talked, and then she said, "Now can you show me again where the door is?"

Anyway, we got to be really good friends, and Fatuma came one day and she hemmed and hawed and hemmed and hawed, and I knew she had something to say. It wasn't a usual visit. And she said, "They have sent me to invite you to join our church as a Muslim." Well, I said to her, "You know, I really admire what Muslim people do. I am so inspired by your fast. It's so hot and I'm thirsty, and you people don't drink and you don't eat. You're called to pray, and you're so faithful to it." But I said, "In the morning when I don't answer the door it's because I'm at prayer. And my belief in Jesus is my reason for being here." We talked about it a lot. They believe Jesus was one of the prophets. I said, "Jesus is the center for me, but thank you." It happened another time. Once a year they had the day when the women go to the mosque and the men pray outside, and they invited me. I went in and I prayed with them. I was so touched by that invitation and touched by that experience. And the next day the man who called them to prayer came and said, "Now you will be one of us; you have prayed with us, so we invite you." And I explained the whole thing again.

There were 250 families in each village in Bura. I'd say our village was maybe 60, 70 percent Muslim. The Catholics were certainly not the majority. We didn't have an established church there; it was like the early Church—we had to make our church. And as the Christian community came together and got to know one another, we met and reflected on our life together in this village. We really prayed and struggled together. We decided together that we wanted a justice committee.

Things were so difficult in the village. We had four years when we had no crop. People were getting poorer and poorer. So that's when you found things like drunkenness, which we hadn't had before. You know, traditionally, in Kenya, men and women are married when the families agree and the dowry is established. Then they live together as husband and wife. It may be many years later when they ask for a church blessing on their marriage. They would come to the Christian community to ask for agreement on this next step. In this community, women would sometimes refuse, saying, "I don't want to marry him in church." The man would say, "We're going to get married." And she said, "No, not until I know you're not going to be drinking and I know whatever money comes in is going to be used for the whole household and not just for you and your drinking." Well, that could never have been said before. That was between the husband and wife in their little place, and he made all the decisions. *Now* she could ask the community to support her, and he would be called to task. Finally, that voiceless woman had a voice. And she had a community to support her.

I remember one man had put his teenage daughter out. His wife had given birth recently and had gotten very ill and had to leave the village for help. He was left to take care of teenage kids, little kids, and also do the farming. He just had so much to do; he was becoming more and more abusive. In fact, one day, after an argument, he put his teenage daughter out of the house. She was sleeping out, you know. Well, the people in the village, especially the people in our community, saw this, and they said, "This is our daughter." And so the whole Christian community came together and sat together and asked the father why he did that, and then they scolded him, "You put your daughter out." And then they said to her, "And why didn't you come to sleep at our house? You're our daughter. Why did you go there and there and there?" So everybody got their little bit in. Then they have a common pot where they have the local brew, which symbolizes peace, and everybody took a sip of that. And that's reconciliation. There were many sacraments together.

We lived as the people did. No electricity, no water. We had all the struggles that they had. And like I said, they taught me so much. I have a bad back, and when there was water, you know, you'd fill a bucket, take it in. One day I picked up the bucket, and my back—whew! I thought, "Oh my, this is it." We used to have a magnificent liturgy on Thursday night, and I was trying to get over to that. But I couldn't get there. And people saw it; oh, right away, they ran over to the house. I had to stay in bed. All you have to do with a bad back is to lay flat, you know, so I just had to lay flat. Well, the people would come. I left my door open. "Hodi!" [they'd call]—How are you? Hello, I'm here. And I'd say, "Karibu"— welcome. And there would be water all the time, there was food all the time. My laundry was done. The nomads have marvelous history and traditions. They have done massage for years and years, so Mumina was massaging my back and my leg where it was so painful. I couldn't have been in a better hospital anyplace in the world than in that little village with those people taking care of me.

Sometimes the hot sun bothered me. But I used to think, Get on with it. I would not let myself think about it, nor would I ever rest in the afternoon. If you ever got in bed, you'd never get up, because you're soaking wet. And we didn't have enough water for two showers in one day.

We had much simpler food, much simpler, but sufficient. We often ate beans. This was our beans ritual. Sunday night we'd soak them. We did a lot of work with fuel conservation with the women to help them, especially when the crop failed. So we had one of these little outside stoves that was covered with mud so you wouldn't lose heat. We'd put the beans out there after soaking them. They'd cook in no time. So Monday we had beans. Tuesday we had beanburgers. Wednesday, if I had gotten macaroni in Nairobi, we might have beans and macaroni. Thursday we would have beans, maybe with a different something in 'em, a vegetable; and Friday we would have beans with all that was around. So five days on the beans, we wouldn't use that much heat, you see. We had a kerosene fridge at first, and then the bishop got us a gas fridge. You buy bottled gas.

For breakfast, when we'd go to Nairobi, I'd buy cereal. We didn't have milk; we had powdered milk. And sometimes there were bananas. At night I usually used to eat the same thing I ate for breakfast, except I always ate peanuts. Peanuts were good protein. You needed your protein. We had mangoes when they were in season. I was thinner, but I was quite okay.

When I think—we're so healthy in comparison, plus we have so many opportunities. When I had hepatitis I was in the teacher-training program; I was taken to a hospital in Nairobi for a month and got well. Then about 15 years later my neighbor had hepatitis, and I watched him die. There was no hospital in his village. It was the rainy season, and he couldn't get out.

The first time I had malaria, it was in Bura after 13 years in Africa. But I was flown out by the Flying Doctor Service; so I was taken care of. My neighbors would just die, you know. The children, especially the children. I found that sometimes the hardest thing in the world, to watch kids brain damaged from those high fevers, and then they'd live for eight, nine years without recognizing their parents. Our children here get care, you know. No matter how much we complain, we'd never go to a hospital here and there wouldn't be a doctor. I took a woman to the hospital once; she was having a baby. She had to have a C-section. The generator was not on; they couldn't find the anesthesiologist—he was someplace in town—and they had to find a surgeon. By the time all this came together, the baby was dead. It's a wonder they saved the woman.

It's that kind of lack of facilities that bothered me. We struggled for water so much; and when I first came home, I was at a workshop in Wisconsin. People were watering their lawns with these sprinklers. And it would water the lawn, but there was all this concrete. It was like they were washing their concrete every day; every day water was going on the concrete. I wanted to scream, having just come from that place.

Why did you come home?

Maryknoll asked me to come home. Every 10 years we give service [at the Maryknoll Sisters Center in New York]. I hadn't given it last time, because I had been with my mom; so in 1991 it was 20 years and I was due. Coming home is far, far more difficult than going. It's like I didn't know where I was. I would cry. I did all the things you do in transition. It was horrible. We have a lot of transition workshops right here because all of us are in the same boat.

I missed the people and the life, and I minded this life. I found this so luxurious and so peripheral. It's like being in between, but I don't feel that way anymore. I guess I needed to step totally into this. I'm still eager to go back—I will never lose that—but I can be here now. I'm doing vocational ministry for the community. I went down and got involved in hospice; and then one of the young women I taught in Chinatown was extremely abused as a child, and she struck back as a young adult and is in prison. So I visit her, and we got a group at the prison that I'm working with. So I think as long as I am involved and I'm working with people, I can now be here.

I'm thinking, What am I going to do in three years? I have so many places I could pick out right now. South Africa would be one. I would love to go to the townships, because there's been so much prejudice, so much hatred—just to walk with people as they heal, you know. We've been invited to Namibia. I think I would like to stay in Africa. However, I also keep thinking of areas around the Persian Gulf and eastern Europe. You know?

Sometimes I think, maybe in about 20 years, when I come back for my final mission, that I'd like to go to someplace in Appalachia, someplace out with Native Americans. Then I also think it's wrong for me to be thinking these things, because hopefully there's going to be a better world, there's going to be peace, and there's not going to be this kind of violence and prejudice. Then I don't know what I would do. I would dance along with everybody else, maybe.

I have a lovely, lovely story that I like to tell about the people in Bura. We had so many deaths in the village; we learned the tradition of death. In '88 my brother was walking in New Jersey, and he was hit by a car and killed. And I came home, but I had so much trouble afterward. My brothers and sisters seemed to get into the rhythm of their lives and seemed to be healing. I couldn't. So I thought, Let me go back to Africa. Maryknoll said, "Wait a while; you're not healed." My family said, "Wait." And I thought, Well, healing is not happening. Go. So I went. And I remember the people would come with an egg, saying "Oh I'm so sorry." Or they'd bring a little sugar, "Oh I'm so sorry." Or a little tea, whatever they could bring, "I'm so sorry, so sorry." And then I was walking in the village one day, and one man—a nomad—said, "You haven't been to our house since you came back. Come and have tea with us." So I went to this little hut, and he says to me, "What can we do for you? The whole village is crying. How can we help you?" And he takes 10 shillings, and he says, "We would like to pay some of the funeral, so take this money." Now 10 shillings could have bought all kinds of necessities, but they wanted to help pay for a funeral for my brother. I think what they taught me is that we never lose our dignity; that's our gift that God gives us, and no one can take it from us. And they have this dignity, this human gift, and they simply shared it. They healed me. We did it together, and I realized later how many times I'd done it with them. One woman once said to me, "You should not come to our wakes. You cry so much." I said, "Tell me how not to!"

It was most amazing. People say, "When did you most feel that you are a missionary?" It's those moments, when things that should happen happen totally differently, and you get another glimpse, a glimpse of God, a glimpse of the human family. It's the people sharing with me deeply. It's what we do together. That's why it's so hard to leave it. (August 1992)

When I re-interviewed Sister Rosemarie, we met again at the motherhouse of the Maryknoll Sisters. She is 77 now, but no less passionate about her ministry. We spoke about her missionary work during the past 18 years, but also about her plans for the future. In the fall of 2010, as she had hoped, she joined another Christian Peacemaker Team, this time in Kurdistan, Iraq.

I went back to Africa in 1997, to Tanzania. When I first went there, I asked the people in the village, "What is the biggest problem here?" And they said, "AIDS." AIDS was pandemic there. I remember one Christmas. One patient who was quite ill was going to be alone and one lady says, "Well, I'm going in the morning because I don't have anybody coming." When I got there late in the afternoon, she had already done her hair. She had already cooked a little food she'd brought. They were singing Christmas carols in this tiny hut. The whole idea was to bring people together [in a support group] as they journey. Help the children to survive, even though their parents were not going to survive. I got very involved with the orphans. That was the hardest part. [And there were] very, very difficult moments when we accompanied people as they were dying. We're all stripped at that moment. We have our God, and that's all we have. They found their God and they gave me glimpses.

I stayed six years. Again, I was called home and they asked if I would be personnel director for Maryknoll. So I said good-bye to folks and came back and did that for four or five years. Then I thought, "Hmmm, I could go back to Tanzania. I could go back to Kenya." And I was invited back. But I had been involved in the peace movements in the States, and felt that I needed to get more involved. Christian Peacemaker Teams really appealed to me. I went on a delegation to Palestine with them, and I liked the simple lifestyle. I liked their commitment to peace. So I applied and went for training. Then in December 2008 I went to Congo with them.

It was my first time in a war zone. And I'm with a peace team, whose goal is to get in the way of the violence with nonviolent methods. That was very new for me. The first thing I saw were the United Nations tanks and huge, huge truckloads of armed soldiers. The weapon of war there is rape, definitely the weapon is rape. There's a whole lot of shooting and killing but wherever we went, women told a story of rape. Every place we went, we talked to the people. The women can't go fetch firewood. They can't go to fetch water. They are in danger whenever they leave.

We worked with Synergie, which is a women's group that works with rape victims. They were finally able to convince one woman to go to court to tell what happened to her. She needed a place to stay because she lived way out in the village, and two women said, "We have room in our house. You can stay with us." Shortly after that, the two women were killed.

I can't just be a stranger doing a job in a place. In Congo, I got to know my neighbors very well. I found myself going to visit families. [The militia groups] started to target university students, and so at one of our neighbors, a young man was home studying, and he was shot in front of his family. It was a terrible time. I got there, and I looked at this child on the floor, and I thought, "What is this that our children can't grow up?" Well, I sobbed and sobbed and sobbed. I could not say one word to those people. And then I left. A few days later they came to get me, and they said, "Come here, come here. We want to tell these people who you are." And I said, "For what?" And they said, "This is the one who cried with us."

That's the cost of relationships. You're into their lives. They're into your life. We enter into the pain of people, and I guess for me it's become more the pain of the world. It's so deep. There are so many trouble spots and there are so many people who don't get a share at the table. I hope my prayers are deeper. I hope my walking on this earth is gentler and more caring and more compassionate. I also feel that I have met the people and they've told me their story. So what is now my responsibility?

It's almost like Rebecca, this beautiful young woman I met. That's not her name. We call her Rebecca to protect her. She says to me, "I was in my house with my children and my husband, and the militia came and killed my husband and forced me to lie down in his blood." And then 14 men raped her. She said, "I was unconscious. I was torn." She said she had a fistula. She said urine and feces leaked right out. She said, "Bugs would walk up and down my legs. Dogs would lick them. My family threw me out." She talked about how the Synergie group found her and took her to the hospital. She was there a month. Now her job is to help other women. She walked me to the bus as we were leaving, and I could see all these women coming over and greeting her. They all knew her. She's extending and reaching out.

I'm carrying the stories. I have to tell them. (January 2010)

SISTER NOREEN ELLISON

Things came together for Sister Noreen Ellison—her early love of the missions, her background as a teacher, her master's degree in religious education—when she accepted a position with the Glenmary Home Missioners, an order of priests and brothers who serve the poor in rural areas of the South. Her role was to travel from mission parish to mission parish helping the priests provide training for lay ministers and planning programs that would enrich the spirituality of everyone in the parish.

Sister Noreen, 51, began her itinerant missionary life with a partner, Sister Jacqueline Riggio, also a Sister of Charity of Cincinnati. For 11 years they traveled to Glenmary missions in rural areas of Texas, Oklahoma, Arkansas, Alabama, Kentucky, and Tennessee from a home base in Nashville. The day after the interview was Sister Jacqueline's last day in Nashville. She had decided to move to Colorado to help care for her aging mother.

Three years later, after serving almost 15 years with Glenmary, Sister Noreen also left Nashville. She moved to Berkeley, California, for a sabbatical year of study at the School of Applied Theology. In August 1995 she began a new ministry, working with poor women and children in Colorado.

I'll often be gone from Nashville for two or three weeks at a time. We stay with parishioners for the most part—people whose kids are grown and have moved, and there's an extra bedroom now; or with a widow who has extra space. We know all the good beds and bad beds along the way. We know where we can get a good meal and where we may have to be sustained on peanut butter and jelly or pizza for a day or two. People offer us the Gospel kind of hospitality, and we accept the hospitality of that place when we go.

The people with whom we're staying have become like family to us. For some of the women we've become like spiritual companions. We've had times to pray a bit with them or to share faith deeply, sometimes into the wee hours of the morning. That's not part of our job description, but it's become, I think, an important part of what we see as our presence in those places.

On the road, there's a constant presence. That takes a lot of energy—it's wonderful energy, but [you get] really tired and you need some space. Even though you may have a room in a house where you might go, you just don't do that in somebody's home. They want to sit and visit with you or show pictures or drink coffee or take you to meet So-and-So. A lot of times people take us to visit their sick friend. You know, they're Baptists, they've never met a Sister, they would like to meet you. And we go to visit with them. It's maybe just the beginning— helping people to know that we have much more in common than we have that separates us. We're part of the human family; we believe in the same God.

[One of the first times we traveled to Texas for Glenmary] we stopped at this little old-fashioned type of gas station, just a couple of pumps that the man had turned it into kind of a health food store. You don't find a lot of health food stores in the South. At least you didn't in 1979. The man told us that he was a Southerner, and after he had nearly died of a heart attack a few years ago, he had been in rehab and had found a whole new life in foods, in meditation and prayer, and just living a more balanced life. So we went on our way. Every now and again we'd pop in there. It seemed we always needed gas around that time, and I had an Exxon credit card; so we stopped there.

Well, the second time we came, he said, "There's something special about the two of you. I need to know you more." We were in slacks, just anonymous people needing gasoline. And he said, "What brings you back here all the time?" We told him, "We work in the Catholic Church." Still, he didn't know our names. And even if he knew our names, it probably wouldn't matter that much, because a lot of them don't even know what Sisters are. So we would tell him the kinds of things that we were going to do.

And he said, "Well, you know, really you're trying to do a lot of the same kinds of things that I'm trying to do. It's just that we have different approaches. I'm trying to help people by eating good foods, thinking good thoughts, and doing the best things for their body. You know, to be better persons for themselves and for the world and for God. And you're doing the same thing."

We said, "That's exactly right. That's what it's all about." So we went on our way. The third time we stopped—which would have been two or three months later—he said, "I have been wondering if you were coming by here. Look, could you come in for a few minutes? I want my wife to meet you. And she just made a blackberry cobbler."

So he put up a card table in the little store, and his wife came. She said, "Wait a minute. I have some fresh cream; I just milked the cow." She brought fresh whipped cream and the warm blackberry cobbler, and we sat there for 15 or 20 minutes in this little gas station store and visited. And when we left there, the two of us reflected that God was part of that meeting. And we said, "You know, we've just been to Emmaus. It may be called Jefferson, Texas, but we've just been to Emmaus." [An allusion to Emmaus has become an accepted way to describe the continuing presence of God. It is based on Luke 24:13–31; the verses describe two disciples on the road to Emmaus who encounter Jesus in the days just after his crucifixion. At first they do not recognize the stranger who walks with them. Jesus reveals his identity only after they have shared a meal.]

This is the place I've been the longest, and yet it's changed. It's changing all the time. That's why I'm still here—because it keeps being fresh for me. I have some apprehensions. I can't say it's exactly fear. This may be another one of those natural passages. When I'm totally alone, I know that place on the other side of the front seat is going to feel really empty. Even when there's another person in it, it's not going to be the same. [Sister Jacquie and I] were not only partners in ministry; we were—we are—really good friends. We are community, and we lived together for 11 years.

Community has changed. I can hardly remember living in a convent. Community then meant living together and doing a lot of things in the structured environment. Today community means sets of relationships that are supportive around a goal and a mission that is held in common. There are many ties that bind us, but the ties are not necessarily similar geography. We live in a neighborhood; we're not in a convent. So we're available [to people in the neighborhood]. We lead an ordinary life in lots of ways. And I think by nature I'm a homemaker. I have an ability to make a home wherever I am.

There have been times when I have wondered what it would have been like if I had married and had my own children. But I've tried to be faithful to the choice I made. Every choice that we make makes a lot of other choices not possible. But that's true for everybody—for married people, for single people. It's the things we choose that put other things aside, because nobody can have it all. That's how you come to terms with your choices.

Maybe a couple of times in my almost 34 years in religious life, I experienced desires for a life that wasn't mine, probably the longing for marriage and a family of my own. As I look back on it now—and maybe those desires are not over completely; once was in my twenties, once was in my thirties—they were more passages than anything. At the time I felt like maybe they were the beginnings of vocation doubt, and yet they didn't happen at hard times for me in religious life. It was during happy times when I was feeling fulfilled, when I had good relationships with people. And that's been a puzzlement to me, because I always think you should have crises or doubts in times that are not happy. It was just that I thought at that time I would like even fuller intimacy than I was able to know through this kind of life. Yet those times passed eventually.

I believe that if we are old maids, then we are not very celibate. Because for me, celibacy means that I live unmarried so that I can be life-giving in other creative ways. And all of us have the obligation to live chastely. So it's much more than chastity. To me, celibacy means to be able to be life-giving.

Celibacy is something that people who are not familiar with the Catholic Church have a hard time understanding. We were getting our hair cut in a little beauty shop in Alabama. An elderly woman was crying, and she said she had lost her husband that day. Anyway, we tried to talk consolingly with her for a few minutes. Then she wondered who we were, since we were new in town. We tried to explain, and we never—after 15 minutes of conversation—came to any understanding that she had the faintest notion of what it meant to live in community, of what it meant to be celibate, of what it meant to join a religious congregation. She could never understand that our parents weren't with us, or that we weren't married, or that we never had children, or that we would never have children, or that we didn't even go courtin'. And so we felt like with some people, well, they'll never understand.

If somebody said, "Would you do it all again, given the circumstances and the time it was?" I would say, "Yes, I would do it all over again." If I were 17 today, would I do it? I don't know. Because everything's different. There are many ways to serve the Church; there are many ways to be apostolic. But at that time I made the choice I knew. And I think each time I re-chose, I re-chose more deeply. When I was 24 and made my final vows—even when I was 18 or 19 and I made my first vows, we were taught we were making that choice once and for all, like the marriage vows. Young couples think that it's always going to be like this; it's not going to ever be different. But it's a daily choice. I can't say every morning

I think of poverty, chastity, and obedience, but every day I think of who I'm called to be and the life I'm called to live. (June 1991)

> *Sister Noreen remained in Pueblo, Colorado, for nine years, working to provide health and wellness services to the vulnerable elderly. When her mother in Michigan grew ill, she moved home and began a new parish ministry, serving at the National Shrine of the Little Flower where she is a pastoral minister and coordinator of outreach services. She visits the sick and accompanies the dying and their families through end-of-life times. She sees a direct connection to her missionary work in Tennessee. She reflected on the Emmaus story in her earlier interview.*

My mission still is walking with people, discovering how God is present in this person or these events. We are not literally breaking bread, but breaking the bread of everyday life. I feel that now I have a great opportunity for evangelization. My ministry around death and dying is often with people out of touch with the church. I can reignite the love of God and the church community in them.

3

IN HOSPITALS
AND CLINICS

SISTER MARY HEINEN

Sister Mary Heinen was educated by her congregation, the Sisters of St. Joseph of Carondelet, to be a nurse. She has worked in the medical field for more than 40 years and has lived through dramatic changes, not only in religious life but also in health care. In 1991, she was part of the team of Sisters who decided to sell St. Mary's Hospital, which had been owned by her community since 1887. The Sisters now operate several small neighborhood clinics in both Minneapolis and St. Paul and provide basic health care to the poor. Theirs was not an uncommon decision; many other religious communities are moving away from large acute-care facilities toward free-standing clinics.

At 59, Sister Mary is a busy, take-charge woman who tackles problems and conversations with refreshing directness. At the end of a long workday she offered to come to my hotel for the interview, because she had access to a car and I did not. She was then going on to two receptions.

I entered a community, the Sisters of St. Joseph of Carondelet, who have a reputation for being educators. So I knew from the time I entered that I would be going to college. There was never a doubt in my mind. And after I had finished a couple of years in the novitiate, the Sister Formation Movement was born, and that meant you continued college right after leaving the novitiate. Long before women went away to get educated, our women were educated in Europe; they were also educated in some of the large state universities [in this country].

I learned about [the congregation] from brochures and from a good friend of mine who worked in the hospital across the street from where I lived. I was attracted to becoming a nurse and probably teaching nursing. That was described in the brochures, so I thought, okay, that makes some sense. I didn't know a heck of a lot about vows. I knew just that the women lived together, they did these wonderful things, and they seemed happy; and I thought, I want to do that.

I was happy in the novitiate, and part of it is that it reminded me of college. Another piece that I very much valued in our novitiate experience: We had access to very good textbooks, to the theologians and the scripture scholars of the day. And we had people who were so attuned to the liturgical movement. I remember we were among the first in the area to experiment with the Easter Vigil. That was new in the early 1950s. Vatican II had not yet happened, but we were beginning to talk about some of those things, and so that was an exciting period of time.

I had mentors whom I looked up to. So I don't think that I ever felt in any of those years, I'm in the wrong place, this is not for me. I really liked the academic setting, and nursing was at a point where we were beginning to look at the theory and the science so that it wasn't just a lot of heavy work. I know I loved all of that.

And I know the focus on ministry was very, very important those early 10, 12, 15 years. I loved the profession so much. Before I entered the community, I said to the novice director—and it might have been bold of me—I said, "I want to be a nurse. Can I be guaranteed that?" And she wrote me a nice letter saying, "Maybe when you're in the novitiate you'll change your mind." It wasn't "Maybe we'll ask you to do something else," but "Maybe you'll change your mind." And I do know that throughout the entire period I was always asked what would I be interested in. I always felt that I could say no. I was asked to go into the field of anesthesia. That was not [a field I was attracted to,] so I said, "No, I don't think I could do well in that. I want to work with patients." And for those of us who chose nursing it was considered great, because the majority chose education.

Now I did participate in community. It was important for me to know who was the provincial superior, because somehow I always had the feeling that those people were in awe of the people in health care. I never lived with people, superior types who had what I would consider absolutely inane or foolish or ridiculous rules and regs. The stuff that you hear—my gosh, they'd give you a nickel to take the streetcar. That was never a part of our situation. I think from my earliest years in nursing, we were always treated as adults. There were certain assumptions. When you went to school you used your good sense. I did my graduate work at Catholic University. And those of us from the Midwest used to get together and say, "This is a whole new culture; we don't know what this culture is. Sisters here need to get permission to do the stuff we take for granted. We go to conventions, we go to conferences, we buy the books. Well, they have to ask permission." Permission? We didn't know what that meant.

I went away to Catholic University, '61 to '63, and I know that back home there was a lot of internal turmoil. And at this point in time I began to sense some of my own classmates, some of my friends, were having real difficulties. Some of them may have had 10, 12 years of experience with oppressive pastors who interfered in their classrooms. [Or they had] high school situations where they were being torn because of a new culture among the high school students. They began to question some of the stuff they were teaching, some of the disciplinary actions, etc. When I came back from Catholic University, we opened a community college which was exclusively devoted to the allied health fields.

There were four of us who were involved day and night. We'd find out that some of our best friends left the community, and it was a shock to us because we were not part of that conversation. We came to realize that those of us in health care had been set apart in a way that probably was not so healthy. So then I think we became more involved.

I'm very conscious of hearing this from my friends and yet not personally experiencing it. There were people in our province who I know have had some very oppressive experiences. A group in our province who I think suffered the most were the people who felt they were not college material, so to speak, who were put into housekeeping, maintenance types of activities. I knew that their work was not that satisfying. They couldn't come home from school and talk about the fun things that happen in the classroom or the wonderful experiences they had at a convention. A number of those people [as well as a number of our well-educated people] have become the avant-garde, protesting the social system, the Church, the Vietnam War, oppression generally.

I came to realize how difficult it was for me for some of my very best friends to leave the state of life that I so loved and I know they loved. There are people who I see a lot, and we talk about the times we had together. I wish that other Sisters would have had opportunities that I did to focus so clearly, say on health care, so that in some ways they could have ridden the tide.

I say to myself, I may be among the last to be in this state of life. And I've said to people, It could be as exciting to bring this to closure as it was for those early Sisters to start it. I keep thinking we have made our mark in history. And maybe [religious life] needs to go through a dying out in order for the next new life to come. I could not take on the hermit's life or the true monastic life, and maybe the next group who lives out religious life won't want to be encumbered by what they see as a style that worked for us in our period of time.

I'm not afraid of growing older or of death. I've sold buildings, I have phased out nursing programs, and I have participated in the closure of hospitals. There is pain, but there's also new life following that. I very recently made the decision to sell the largest Catholic hospital in Minneapolis. And I'll tell you it was very difficult for the Catholic community, the non-Catholic community, the health care community. St. Mary's was wonderful. It had a national reputation for chemical-dependency treatment. When my father needed good health care, he came to St. Mary's in Minneapolis. [St. Mary's] was on the banks of the Mississippi. I'd go to the University of Minnesota and look out their windows, and there was St. Mary's. But over a couple of years I studied what was happening and I could see that the services and the relationships we had hoped to continue with patients, with clients, and with personnel were changing dramatically. I was the province director, and I said, "I would rather take the initiative to say we are removing ourselves from that and putting our time and energy and personnel and finances into another ministry." We? The Sisters of St. Joseph. That meant bringing people together at all levels and talking and sleepless nights and then taking the statuary down and the signage off. Some of our long-term employees were pink-slipped. There was a lot of unhappiness.

The bright light was that we knew we could take those resources and open clinics for the underserved. And in many ways our roots were [there]; that's how we started. There are five clinics up and running now, and we're doing something that the larger entity could not do. We are providing health care for the women and the children who have no other way of getting it. And we believe that our resources are wisely used—not going to bricks and mortar, not going to pay insurance, malpractice, etc.

As difficult as the decision was, I believe we made the right decision, so I'm living with it. If we really want to continue to meet the needs of the people, I think we have to look at these tough questions. That was one of the most difficult ones. [There was] a lot of mourning, and that continues to go on. That continues to go on. I cry, I acknowledge it, I don't hide it. Every once in a while I'll run into someone who says, "All five of my children were born there." And there's a sense of anxiety and anger and frustration. How could it have happened?

I've come to accept that change is a way of life. I work with it, you know; I don't buck it. When people start reminiscing about things, I say, "Oh, I can romanticize about things [but only for] so long, and then I've got to get on with what's happening."

Now I'm with our Carondelet LifeCare Ministries—that's the organization that was restructured after we sold St. Mary's—as director of advocacy and ethics. We had a community meeting, and we said, "What are some of the ministries that Carondelet ought to go into once we're no longer responsible for the oversight of the hospitals?" And clinics for poor women and children were first. We have another ministry called Sisters Care, retired Sisters who work in the homes of the elderly. And then right after that we talked about advocacy, particularly in the area of health care.

[As to my future,] I assume I will continue in the ministry I'm in. At the present time, I'm loving very much what I'm doing. I'm into systemic change, into advocacy and working with lawyers and politicians. I really want to stay in the struggle with the women and the men in Congress over changing legislation so there's better health care for people.

I'm getting my nurse refresher courses up to date, and by December first I should have that completed. So that if there's ever an opportunity, if I needed to go back into a hospital situation, a retirement home, nursing home, or whatever, I'd be willing to do that. I like nursing. I want to keep it up. I'm not afraid to get right in there. (October 1992)

Sister Mary has been director of advocacy for St. Mary's Health Clinics, a network of free primary-care clinics in and around the twin cities since 1992. She has received an honorary doctorate, humanitarian and social justice awards, and an outstanding achievement award for her work. She tracks health care legislation at the federal and state levels and advocates for those who are uninsured or underserved. We spoke in March 2010, in the midst of the debate over passage of the federal health care bill.

What we lack now in our society is respectful civic discourse. We have lost it at almost every level. We're so far from biblical traditions and American values that we can't even discuss [critical issues]. What I think women religious can bring to the table is respectful civic discourse. We know how to have dialogue about things. Our voice is a voice of passion and concern expressed in respectful civil tones.

SISTER MARILYN AIELLO

Dr. Marilyn Aiello, 57, a Dominican Sister from the Sinsinawa, Wisconsin, motherhouse, arrived in Marks, Mississippi, in 1981. With her came four other Dominican Sisters, and together they opened the DePorres Health Center. There are now 12 Sisters in Marks, from five different Dominican communities, providing a range of health and social services to residents of Quitman County and the surrounding counties.

The interview took place in the evening in Dr. Aiello's office at the end of a day that had begun for her at 4:30 A.M.. At 5:30 P.M., after she had finished with her last patient and removed her blue doctor's coat, she had brought me home to dinner—to a one-story house about a mile from the Center, where she lives with four other Sisters—and we had then returned to the clinic. She was still alert and energetic, although she frequently removed her glasses and rubbed her eyes as we talked.

I admired the Sisters, but I didn't really have any very close friends among them, and I was not very happy about what I perceived as the call to religious life. As the oldest girl in an Italian family, I understood that I was to be married and have children. There was a cedar chest, and the trousseau was being collected. I didn't rebel against that, but there was this little voice that just persisted, persisted. There was a lot of objection from my whole family. You know, in an Italian family, you don't only have to deal with your parents; you have your grandparents, your aunts, and your uncles, everybody against you. My grandmother, who still spoke Italian, would say things like, "It's only when there's too many daughters that you do this. Or if you're too ugly to get married." So it was hard, but I had absolutely no doubt in my mind that it was right.

When I entered in 1956, it was the time in religious life when many, many young woman entered. In my group alone there were about 100 postulants. So it was very much like going off to college. We didn't know one another when we got there, but we did everything together: prayed together, worked together, studied together. I'll be honest. I was very happy. I felt I was where I belonged.

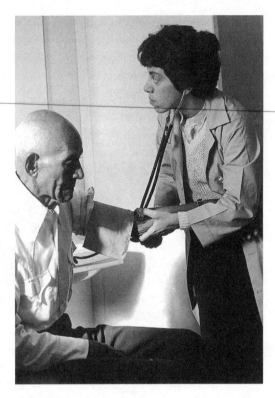

Sister Marilyn Aiello monitors the blood pressure of one of her elderly patients at the DePorres Health Center in Marks, Mississippi, in 1988. Dr. Aiello spent 16 years as a physician in Marks, where her interracial clinic attracted more than 50 patients a day, drawing from five surrounding counties.

I was two years at the motherhouse, and then I was sent to one of our two colleges. Right at that time they developed a new program at the college in medical technology, and they wanted to put a Sister into the program. The academic dean of Sister students called me in and proposed that I go into med tech. I said, "What is it?" They could have told me I was going to be anything. I entered because I felt called. It made no difference to me. So I said, "I'll do what you want me to do." But it was wonderful because science turned me on. I flourished. I became very academic. It's one of those turning points in one's life. You don't know why it happens, but it happens.

After finishing my med tech work, I went back to the motherhouse. My next step would have been to do my internship in med tech. But the mother general said to me, "We've decided that we're not going to need a med tech now." Fortunately, I had actually graduated with a double major in med tech and biology and a minor in chemistry. That's how I became a science teacher.

They sent me to the South in 1962, to Mobile, Alabama. I came right out of college and became the head of the science department and its only member. I taught all the sciences at Heart of Mary High School. It was an all-black parish. And that was another turning point. In 1962 even the Catholic Church was segregated down in the South. Separate parishes, separate churches, separate schools. The convent and church and rectory were on one side of a red dirt street in the poorest part of Mobile, with shacks all around us, and on the other side of the street was the grade school and high school. African-American children in southern Mississippi and Alabama who wanted a Catholic education—this is where they came. Heart of Mary was the only black Catholic high school.

It was probably the biggest single thing that affected my life in terms of forming my attitudes. The impact of having children that you came to love discriminated against only because of the color of their skin was just devastating.

We were one of four high schools in the diocese. [The other three] were all-white. Priests would get up at meetings and talk about "our three high schools," and we'd be there knowing we were not included. In May we had the crowning of the Blessed Mother in a big football field. The other high schools sat together in one part of the bleachers. Our high school had to sit with the black grade school children in the black part of the stadium. Our children were not invited to be part of the May crowning ceremony. All the other schools had representatives. These were things we had to confront. And we did. Other types of events—the same thing would happen. In parades we would have to march at the end with all the black children and not with the other schools. At communion services in the cathedral, blacks would have to wait until all the whites went to communion.

Our parish was right in the middle of the black community, on what they used to call "the Avenue." The Avenue was Davis Avenue. When the black community would want to have meetings, they didn't have a meeting place, so they would use our cafeteria. Well, there was an organization called Neighborhood Organized Workers, a group of black citizens who were trying desperately to get better jobs for the black community.

Now, two main events are nationally televised out of Mobile: One is the Senior Bowl, which is a college bowl; and then there's the Junior Miss Pageant. So this organization—ironically it was called NOW—decided that the way to get some kind of national publicity for the cause of jobs was to picket the Junior Miss Pageant. One of our Sisters who was black came home and said, "I'm going to be on the picket. The rest of you just have to stand in the park [across the street from the auditorium] to show your support." I thought, "Well, that doesn't sound so bad." So at the appointed time, she went off to man the pickets and we went to stand in the park. It wasn't very far, hardly five blocks away from where we lived. Actually, on one side of this park was the auditorium; on the other side was the bishop's house and the cathedral. We decided we would park on the church property instead of parking in the lot of the auditorium. So we walked across the street, going over to the park, and there's this policeman standing in the park. And he said, "You can't stay here." So we said, "Oh? All right. Well, that's strange." He said, "Now, you just walk around this park and go back the way you came."

But he told us to walk around the park. At that point, I still was very naive about law and order and police. So we started walking, and this big bus drives up, and this plainclothesman says, "Arrest all these people." And they arrested us. I couldn't believe it. That policeman set us up. I said, "Why are we being arrested?" "Don't ask any questions. Get on this bus." And they brought us to jail and they fingerprinted us.

The jail was hardly two blocks away. They dropped us off, and then they went back and they kept arresting people. At first most of the people they arrested were nuns because other nuns from other places were coming. And priests, a few priests. And then parishioners, all our parishioners. None of us knew what to do. We had absolutely no experience, and they wouldn't tell us what we had done. They put all the women in one big cell, and they put the men in another cell. After the pageant was over, they said, "All the Sisters come out." This big burly policeman said, "Now you know you've done wrong here. But we're going to let you sign your own bail and leave." I was scared stiff. I was ready to sign and run. I was not brave or anything. One of the Sisters said, "What's going to happen to all those other ladies back there?" Then he got mad and he said, "Just go back to the cell if you're not . . ." So we all marched back into the cell. The problem was that there wasn't enough money to bail us out. The bishop would have nothing to do with us, nothing. He was furious. There were some black lawyers, and some of the black people owned funeral parlors and things like this, and a few owned their houses—so they were able to scrape up some money. The lawyers decided that most of the Sisters should sign our own bail because they didn't have enough money to bail us out. I was right up there in line. But that was the beginning.

What they did was, they harassed us. We had to keep appearing in court. Finally, the charge was marching without a permit. Can you believe this? Marching without a permit. We had no intention of marching. I must say we weren't always innocent, but at that point we were definitely innocent. It deeply affected me. I'd have to say I grew up. I had no social consciousness, but these were people I loved, and so what they suffered, I was suffering. It was like another birth, and I don't think I've ever been the same.

That was the beginning of the civil rights movement in Mobile. Well, of course, the civil rights movement was spreading to the whole nation. The Catholic schools in Mobile did integrate early on, and we closed our high school because our children were very smart, and we felt that they needed to have the exposure to the type of society they'd have to face. We felt they were too insulated. We may have made a mistake. I don't know. But we closed Heart of Mary High School. Some of our Sisters went to diocesan girls' high school to help our children there, but I didn't want to go there. So two of us went to a poor all-black public school.

I was a very happy teacher. I loved teaching. I love that age group, their music, their sports. I enjoyed it all. But anyway, what happened was they opened a medical school in Mobile at the University of South Alabama. There was a lot of publicity about it in the newspaper. Two of my Sister friends and I were having breakfast. One was reading in the paper about the medical school, and she said to me, "Why don't you go to that medical school, become a doctor, and help these people?" When you're in a poor community, there are all kinds of needs, and certainly health care was one of those needs. So I said, "Are you crazy or something? What makes you think I can do that?" "Oh, you can do that. You're in science." They think you can do anything if you're in science. Fix electrical plugs, anything.

I said, "You don't know what you're asking." And I didn't pay much attention. But these two would not let up. They kept at me and kept at me. At that point I was 35 years old. I didn't have the slightest wish to be a doctor. They said, "What if God wants you to do this, and you're not even going to try?" Well, they hit that little button. I said, "Ohhh." And I said, "Look, I'm going to inquire about this now. The first sign that God doesn't want me to do it, you've got to forget about it."

The first thing I did was, I went to the Sisters at Catholic Charities—they were friends of ours, we had been through civil rights together. My first question was, "If I did this, could I be of help?" They said, "Oh, yes, that would really be a good thing." I had decided there was no use going anywhere but the University of South Alabama [right there in Mobile], so I went to the dean of the medical school, and I said, "This is who I am, and this is how old I am, and these are my credentials. Do you think I could be accepted at the medical school?" He said, "I think your age is against you. But why don't you take the test and let that decide what you should do?"

So I took the MCAT test. You get the results back and it's just a bunch of numbers. There's no such thing as pass and fail. So I went back to the dean with my numbers and said, "Now, what do I do with these?" He said, "Well, maybe you should apply."

At that point I went to my superiors. I told them the facts. Just like I'm telling you. There was no secret [about what I wanted to do once I was a doctor]. I was going to start a clinic right there on Davis Avenue, in that neighborhood I was telling you about, that we lived in. I even had the place picked out. I had every-thing ready. I just had to do four years of medical school and three years of residency.

So I started medical school at 37. I was the oldest one in my class. I actually went to medical school with one of the students I had taught. My classmates were very, very supportive. They would ask me, "Why are you here?" I told them what I was going to do, about opening a clinic on Davis Avenue. They said, "Well, let's do it now." I said, "How can I do this now? We're not doctors." They said, "Yeah, we can do it. We can get doctors to volunteer." So we started the clinic—my classmates and I, and the nuns of course.

An old black doctor, Dr. Franklin, had died, and the family told me that I could have the clinic. The Campaign for Human Development [a national bishops' fund channeled through the dioceses] funded us for three years, $30,000 a year. We had a salaried director and a social worker. Everybody else volunteered: the nurses, the medical students, the doctors. That clinic is still going. The government took it over, and it has expanded into many, many others. This weekend I'm going down there and opening a new family medicine clinic. It's going to be called the Aiello-Busky Clinic. Mr. Busky was a good friend and a member of the first board. It's wild. Nobody's been able to say "Aiello." I told them they could call it the ABC clinic, but that's what they call the liquor stores down there.

By the time I finished medical school, the clinic in Mobile was flourishing, so they didn't need me, which was wonderful. I went back to Chicago because my mother was still living and I had been away in the South for so long. I did my residency in family practice at Resurrection Hospital in Park Ridge.

When I was in my last year of residency, I felt that the greatest need at that point was in the rural South. So I wrote to different health agencies in the southeastern states from Virginia to Mississippi. I told them I was a family practitioner and I wanted to work among the poor. There was no end of need. I got bushel baskets [of responses]. That was another hard period of my life when I had to make a choice of where to go.

Throughout all of this, I had my friends, my Sister friends. I think I'm collaborative. I know I'm talkative. I can't keep anything to myself. So we talked, and I bounced things off them. And then they actually would come with me to look at these places. Probably I went to 10 places. We set up criteria. We said, "What are the things that are important to us? Which place has the most need?" On a scale of 1 to 10. I had to have something. Because I know what I had was a big headache. Everybody was pleading with me. I wished I were a hundred people.

For me it wasn't just being the doctor. It was the whole advocacy thing. I knew that if we served in a truly poor community, the medical thing was just a small part of the need—that the bigger needs were so many of the social needs. One place we went to, in Louisiana, was poor, poor, *poor*, dirt poor. But the Sisters were there already. I knew the Sisters would do something. The people had advocates. There is so much need everywhere that we've got to spread ourselves out. I was looking for a place where nobody had anybody. And that's how I found this place.

At that time the doctor of this clinic had died of cancer. The other two doctors in the county were very elderly. The white community here, most of them have cars and are able to drive to where the doctors are, but they realized that the poor people could not do this. So they desperately needed a doctor to help take care of the poor. Then the bishop of this diocese wrote to me. He said there was no Catholic church up here, no Catholic presence. The bishop was very, very supportive—he couldn't give us money, but they have let us feel trusted and free. They never breathe down our throats and say, "Are you doing this or doing that?" When we ask them to come, they come. They come and visit, just to be

social. That was important. I am a religious, and we are in a Church that is hierarchical. Sometimes that is difficult and stifling, and I needed to be in a position
where it wasn't.

Then I could not feel comfortable if my patients didn't have the kind of medical support they'd need. I went and visited Clarksdale, which is about 18 miles
away. It has a hospital with about 175 beds. There are surgeons and emergency
rooms and an intensive care unit. And Memphis is not that far away if I needed
a tertiary center. I knew that you couldn't say to your patient, Go here or go
there. You have to help them get there. I was going to be right out of residency.
I had to have some backup and support. If you're going to be a good doctor, you
can't be a good doctor in a vacuum. All those things were important. All the
pieces fit. That's how we chose Marks.

This is a very poor county. The Delta is the poorest part of the United States,
and this is one of the poorest counties in the Delta. In 1981 when I came, this
clinic was segregated. What was the black waiting room became our office. And
then we locked all the doors and left one door open. That's how we integrated.
Whoever wanted to come through that door, we would be glad to take care of
them, white or black. The other thing we did was, we instituted appointments.
They'd never had appointments before. The whites would always be taken; the
blacks would always wait. Well, the whites did not like it that we instituted the
appointments. The blacks loved it. Right away they started making their
appointments.

I heard grumbling about the appointments. And I'm sure there were other
grumblings. At first the whites didn't come in any numbers. But gradually they
did. I would say at this point in time my practice is probably 40 percent or more
white, and the rest is African-American. But, you know, the interesting and
beautiful thing is they all know each other. The blacks have raised so many of
the white children. And it's not unusual to see them embracing in the waiting
room, when they see one another after not seeing each other for a long time.
There's real affection. And there's real relationship. But the sad part is I feel that
the whites still feel that the African-American is somehow inferior by nature.
And that leads to a lot of other problems.

Like housing. They live side by side, but there's a railroad track in between.
I couldn't believe when one of the young women I hired said to me something
about the sewage in the street where she lived. I said, "What sewage?" She said,
"You know, what comes out of the toilet." I said, "You mean it's in the street?"
She was trying to explain to me like she'd explain to a child: "You know how you
flush the toilet, and then it comes out?" I said, "It comes out on the street?" She
said, "Yeah." They live in shacks, literally wooden shacks. One day a white doctor, a doctor I respect, said that this white man lived in a shack. He said, "No
white man should live like that." I said, "Well, black people live like that all the
time." It doesn't seem to matter that black people have to live in these shacks.
But no white man should have to live like that. On the other hand, I have seen

whites bring in blacks who are sick. I have seen whites bring flowers to the blacks in the hospital. I've seen them show real affection. But it's not an affection of equals.

Marks is the county seat, but it's in the southern part of the county. And it's very difficult for the elderly and the poor who have no transportation to get here. So after we were here one year, we found this little cinder-block clinic that had been abandoned in a town called Sledge, and we opened what we call a satellite clinic.

Right now I have 12,000 active patients, and the county is barely 10,000. We draw from a five-county area. We're averaging over 50 patients a day. More and more are coming because the old doctors are dying or leaving and the young ones aren't coming. It's a heavy load. Thank God I was able to get a Sister doctor to join me this year. I go out to Sledge one day a week, and she goes one day. Now there are two doctors, one nurse practitioner, a nurse, and a medical assistant on staff. I also have an HIV coordinator. In these rural areas what you're seeing is a lot of heterosexual individuals who are HIV-positive. A lot of multiple partners, a lot of venereal disease. No protection. I do prenatal care, but I don't deliver babies anymore. I'm getting older, too, but it's very high-risk care. Very young girls or older women. Their diets aren't good; they smoke. There's a lot of hypertension, a lot of diabetes. So I don't deliver babies anymore, but I do everything else. I do home visits, and I'm on staff at three nursing homes and two hospitals.

I get up at 4:30, and I leave the house anywhere between 5:00 and 5:30. I drive to Clarksdale, where I make rounds at the hospital. Then I try to go home and have a little breakfast, because 5:00 is too early to have breakfast. I try to be here at the clinic anywhere between 7:00 and 7:30, because I have to get two hours of paperwork done before I start seeing patients at 9:00. We see patients from 9:00 till 12:00, and then we break as soon as we can after 12. At 1:30 we start seeing patients again, till 5:00.

Will you stay in Marks?

When I came, they would ask me that question all the time. Every time a truck would pull up in front of the house, they'd think I was leaving. They don't ask anymore. I really intended that I would start the practice up, build it, and then someone would come, and I'd be able to go somewhere else and do this over again. I see now that that's not possible, for a lot of reasons. The whole medical profession has changed; doctors don't want to be by themselves anymore. So I can't just say, "Here's the practice." No one will take it. I don't want to make it sound like I'm a martyr here, because I'm not. I'm very happy. The people give me a lot of affection, a lot of support. It's a good place to be a doctor. In this community if there's anything I need, they'll all come running to do it. It's a safe place. I've taken up gardening; I grow tomatoes.

I never grew a thing until I came down here. Memphis is not that far away if you want to go to the opera or the theater. So there are a lot of very good things about being here. It's not a hard place to be. Being a doctor's hard all over. I see what other doctors do, and they all work very hard. But I'm in my fourteenth year here. I am getting older, and I have to realize that. I'm 57 now.

Sometimes I wonder. Being a doctor is like an indelible mark on the soul. I don't want that. I'd like to say I can rub that off and change and do something else. Because the important thing as a religious woman is the work I have to do. I want to say that my life counted. That it helped the people. I'm not so unusual. Most people want their lives to count. I think I'm very fortunate that I was educated, I was supported, I was nurtured in every way. This clinic has expanded so much, beyond what I ever imagined. If it could just continue after I leave, that's all I would care about. (November 1994)

Dr. Aiello remained at the DePorres Health Center in Marks until 1997 when she was able to recruit two new physicians to care for the clinic's patients. After a sabbatical year, she joined the faculty of the University of Mississippi's Department of Family Medicine, where she taught and supervised resident doctors and medical students for nine years. She lived in Madison, Mississippi, just north of Jackson, with two other Sisters. In 2007, at the age of 70, she returned to the Chicago area and now serves as the medical consultant for the 600 Dominican Sisters in her community.

I can tell you that leaving Mississippi and my beloved South was not easy after 44 years. But I was so enriched by my experiences and the wonderful people who touched my life that I feel they have not left me. I will always carry the South with me.

SISTER JUDY WARD

The interview with Sister Judy Ward, 55, took place in her one-bedroom apartment not far from St. Clare's Riverside Medical Center in New Jersey, where she works as a senior clinician in the alcohol-chemical dependency unit. The living room and dining area were filled with samples of her artwork and photographs of her mother, her twin sister, and her close friend Sister Daniel, another Sister of Mercy. During the interview, classical music played softly in the background and three scented candles mellowed the edges of the room.

Sister Judy is a recovering alcoholic. Her story is perhaps startling but not all that unusual. A study released in May 1995 by the Center for Applied Research in the Apostolate (CARA) at Georgetown University reported that 2.6 percent of women religious are alcoholics. Sister Judy reflects what the study calls a culture of recovery. But there is also within religious communities a culture of denial—a belief that "it can't happen here." For every woman religious who is in treatment, the survey reports, there are 13.7 women who need it. Sister Judy's history illustrates another aspect of the study: Alcoholics Ananymous (AA) has proven essential to long-term recovery among religious.

I grew up with my mother and my twin sister. My father left us when we were about a year old. My father had a drinking problem. I learned later on that he was an alcoholic. He came to visit us every Sunday, usually. He would take us to the local bar, and we would sit and have a soda and potato chips like most adult children of alcoholics. And pretty soon he would be unable to take us home. The bartender would call my mother, who didn't have a car, and she would find somebody to pick us up and bring us home. Most of the time, whenever I saw my father he was under the influence of alcohol. He died an untimely death when I was 18, in an alcohol-related car accident. By that time I was in the convent. My sister and I entered the convent together in September of 1956. My father died in October. My sister left the convent in February, and I stayed on.

Convent life in 1956 was extremely difficult and regimented. And I think the idea was [that] if I could become like everybody else, and not be myself, that

Sister Judy Ward combines a fine arts background and her interest in the history of the Sisters of Mercy with her new skills in computer graphics to create a variety of Mercy products. She says she finds this kind of contemporary art work "exciting, fluid, and instant!"

would be the ideal thing. I had this altruistic idea that I wanted to give up everything and be the good person. There weren't a lot of models in my life in 1956, and I have to honestly say in retrospect that the concept of marriage just didn't look good to me. I didn't want to go through what my mother went through. So [being a nun] looked like the best way for me to spend my life, no matter what it cost. The reasons I entered were not, of course, the reasons I stayed. Every crisis in my life, I take a look at who I am, and where I am, and why I'm there. The reasons for staying in the convent change as I grow and mature.

But then I was 18 years old and, as I said, very altruistic. I wanted to be the best of what I could be. I was artistic, and I thought there would be great opportunities for me—I have to say that. I probably didn't know what spiritual life was for a good many years, although I did everything they told me. I was very obedient. I'm a child of the 1950s. You didn't question; you just did what you were supposed to do. It was a very subservient position. When Vatican II came, you know, and different things happened, then I was allowed to be an individual and have different ways; I felt much more comfortable.

You know, I'm an alcoholic, and that really didn't show itself early in my religious life. I didn't have opportunities to drink. I would go home on home visits, and my cousins and aunts and uncles and everybody would say, "Have a drink." And I'd say, "Oh, sure. That's a great idea." That's probably how my drinking started, on holidays. Everybody drinks on holidays. I think in the 1960s when religious life was being so questioned, and I was as busy as could be, my drinking escalated a great deal. In the beginning I was in a habit, and it certainly was not appropriate to go out to a bar or even to go buy alcohol. So I didn't. But once in a great while somebody would give me a bottle of scotch, which I acquired a rapid taste for.

I think I have my drinking to thank for still being in the convent, because I might have been very rebellious. But instead I just drank away the problems, and got up the next day and did my work. I'm not real proud of that, but I'm very proud of being a recovering alcoholic.

I went to teach in a private academy at the motherhouse in '64 and I was there for 10 years. I wasn't an alcoholic when I went there, but I was an alcoholic when I left there in '74. I didn't know it, but I was one. Those 10 years were very hard. I started at the bottom of the ladder and worked my way up. By the time I left there, I was the senior class advisor, I was the yearbook moderator, I was the great artist, I was the answer to everything. And I was also drinking very heavily. These are the years of change. These are the years that most nuns left the convent. But I survived it all, and I might have Dewars to thank for it. But nothing happens by chance, you see, because I wouldn't be where I am today if I hadn't been where I've been.

About '71 or so, when I was 33 years old, I woke up one morning and I had a headache, and I said, "Something's wrong in my life. I don't know what it is, but something's wrong." I was really cool in those days. I had a black turtleneck sweater on and a black jacket with brass buttons—still wore a veil, though. I walked down to the art room and I said, "Get a model and do without me. I'm not going to be here." I went back to my room, and I sent for a friend of mine. I said, "I've got to get out of here. Something's really wrong. Don't bother telling the superior; I've just got to get out of here. I don't want to talk to anybody; I don't want to do anything. I need to be alone." Anyhow, they took me to [a monastery of cloistered nuns] for about seven or eight days. Everybody there really had such respect for what I wanted. About the third or fourth day I asked them if I could go to chapel, and they told me where I could go. I asked them if I could eat with the Sisters; they said yes. And then I had a couple of long talks with the abbess, and I told her I was drinking. But it wasn't obvious to anybody, if you know what I mean. I never recognized that the problem was alcohol, truly didn't. I wish someone had said, The problem is alcohol. But nobody knew it; I wasn't falling down drunk. I was very clever. If there was a big party, I'd have a couple of drinks in my room first, and I'd just sashay around with one drink, you know, and that would be cool. And again, I overcompensated and overfunctioned.

[After my time at the monastery] I made some serious decisions. I remember resigning from several immense jobs that I had. It was the beginning of my leaving. Then I made a choice to leave the motherhouse, and I went to [teach at] a couple of other schools.

I taught in a huge high school, boys and girls—2,000 in the school. My drinking accelerated, and I think that was the time my superior said to me, "I think you might be drinking too much." She's the only one that ever said it to me. I just looked at her. And I thought, I'd better be more careful. And then the next year my mother died, which was just the most traumatic thing in my life. They sent me to another high school, and I was so sad mourning the loss of my mother, it took me a while to get myself together. But I was there eight years, and I did an excellent job. I always did a good job, see. You know, I was supervisor of the art and music department, and besides supervising I taught. And did a lot of painting myself. In March in '84 I had a confrontation with the priest principal. I really was in the right, so I walked out of his office. I said, "The hell with this. I'll just leave and go figure out what's going on." I called the motherhouse, told the major superior. She came to see me. I said, "I'm resigning. I'm resigning from my job." So I went back [to the motherhouse] and then they said, "We're going to give you a leave of absence." I said, "God, you're being so nice to me. I can't believe this." They were giving me a sabbatical to watch me, and all of a sudden—zoom! They maneuvered a way to get me into treatment.

I was going to my own doctor for high blood pressure, which certainly was related to alcohol. Then they sent me to a doctor. And the guy says, "Why are you here?" I said, "I don't know. Those nuns want me to come here." And he said, "Do you have a drinking problem?" I said, "I don't think so." He said,

"How much do you drink?" I said, "Maybe a couple of drinks a night." He said, "Twelve ounces?" I said, "No. Don't be rude." So then I went for the blood test. Then I met Kathleen [the assistant major superior] and she said, "I have some bad news for you." I said, "What's the matter?" She said, "Your blood tests aren't too good." I said, "Uh-oh." And I said, "Can anybody make me do anything I don't want to do?" I had plans now to go on to school and become a career counselor. I was all set to go the next week. And she said, "No, I can't. But I can withhold your tuition." I said, "So that's it." She said, "Judy, it doesn't have to come to that. Please." I said, "All right."

So I went into treatment in September of '84. And I was in treatment for seven months. The place where I went was very severe. It was worse than the novitiate. Worse than the novitiate! That says it right there. You couldn't go up these stairs, you couldn't play with the dog, you couldn't do anything. And you didn't know when you were going to get out. It was always a secret.

Two weeks after I came out of treatment, my twin was taken ill and died 44 days later of cancer. I know all about trauma and grief. Oh, God Almighty! What more? You know what I mean? What more do you want from me? She had just bought a bungalow; so I had to bury her, have her dog put to sleep, and sell the house. But you know, I was with her every single day. God! What strength I had to do that! And I'm telling you, that strength came straight from God through AA.

I remember when I brought her [to our infirmary]. I went down to get her breakfast, and a nun said to me, "What are you doing?" I said, "I'm fixing Jean's breakfast." She said, "I'll do it." So she brought it up, and I went to feed her. It was a poached egg. And somebody else said, "I'll do that." I said, "Okay." Well, only in recovery did I ever let anybody do anything for me. So I just sat there. And then about three o'clock Jean went into a coma. But I didn't know it was a coma. So I remember talking to her and saying, "Jean, it's okay. I'm going to be all right," because she was worried about me. I kept saying that. And about 6:30 I turned to the head nurse, and I said, "I'm going to go out to a meeting [of AA]." She said, "Let me have the phone number where you're going." And I said, "Maybe I'd better not go." She said, "Maybe you'd better not go." So I stayed, and Jean died at 8:30 that same day. But I went to a meeting every single day while she was dying.

Then when I was in Jean's house, cleaning it out, Kathleen called me up and asked me if I were going to Mass every day. And I said, "No. I go over to the rehab if a priest is saying Mass over there. But I'm not going down the street to the church where Jean was buried." And I said, "Listen, Kathleen. Mass won't keep me sober." So she didn't say another word. I was going to meetings every day; that's a little bit more important. And then she said, "Judy, where do you want to go? Do you want to go to the motherhouse?" I said, "No way. That's where I did my heaviest drinking." She said, "How about the infirmary?" It's where Jean had just died, and where my mother had died, and I said, "Okay."

So I got there, and the administrator who was a friend of mine gave me a room for an art studio. I did some painting, did a lot of calligraphy. Somebody got me to start writing lectures on recovery. I was there two years, and then the superior said to me, "I need your room. You've got to go." I said, "Don't do this to me yet, please. I need more stability." Nobody listened. So I got out and looked for a job. I went to Sunrise House, a nonsectarian rehab [center], and they hired me rather quickly. I went to the superior, and I said, "I've got a job." She said, "Good. Where are you going to live?" I said, "I'll probably have to get an apartment." She said, "You can't do that. We just told five other Sisters they can't." I said, "What's that got to do with me?" Now! Now, my arrogance comes out! And she said, "We're not going to let you live in an apartment. We'll ask convents around there." I said, "Look, I'm going to work at one o'clock; I'm not coming home until 11 or 12 at night. I'm not going to eat with them, I'm not going to pray with them, I'm not going to play with them, I don't want to live with them." She was ready to kill me. I said, "You do what you have to do. But just remember I won't be blindly obedient to the degree that my sobriety's threatened." I think she was a little shook, but I meant it sincerely. So next time she came back to me, she said, "You can get an apartment." I needed time to get myself together. Besides, this is a physically and emotionally draining field. I want to come home, put my feet up. I don't want anybody talking to me, telling me their problems. I've had enough problems all day.

I started out as a counselor in training [at Sunrise House]. I became a primary counselor. Within a year and a half I was the Saturday supervisor. I was there three years, and by the time I left I was training other counselors. I left because I thought it was time to grow a little more. [I went] to St. Clare's Riverside Hospital, the alcohol-chemical dependency unit, and became a senior clinician. One of the most marvelous things about my job is that I consecutively get approved for doing good work, and I get rewarded for it. In the convent, when you teach, you get paid the normal religious salary. And you never get rewarded for working well. God's your reward and all that; but there's a lot of humanity in us, and when people are rewarded for good work, I think they work better. Since I've been at St. Clare's I've gotten about five raises. So I really feel good about myself and what I'm doing. I tell [my patients] about the wonders of recovery. They need to know they're good people, but they're very sick people. They need to treat the illness. They have a hospital band on their wrist that says they're a patient, and they need to be reminded of that.

There's a lot of shame involved in saying, "I'm an alcoholic," until you can begin to grasp the good things it has done for you. I can truly tell you right now, I'm a very grateful alcoholic. I wouldn't be where I am. I would never have had the stamina to do the things I've done. I wouldn't feel as good about myself as I do. I've had a lot of losses and I live well with them. I miss Jean terribly, but I don't have to be sad.

I have such a different concept now of religion and spirituality. I think spirituality is a very deep thing, deep within me. Spirituality is about my attitudes and values and beliefs, and religion is just something on the outside. I have probably the deepest spirituality I've ever had. I do give retreats, by the way, to recovering women and men. But for myself, I do a lot of quiet meditating. I have several books that I use. And most of them are connected with alcoholism. There's one little book called *The 24 Hour Book* that all alcoholics use. Another one, called *Each Day a New Beginning*, has a page of meditation a day. Very simple. Maybe I've gotten simpler.

The "prayer of acceptance" is the only thing that got me through my sister's death. Just saying the "serenity prayer": "God grant me the serenity to accept the things I cannot change, the courage to change the things I can, and the wisdom to know the difference." I think that's so profound. It all boils down to acceptance, not telling God what to do or making deals with him. That's where I have found peace. Another source of great strength has been [Sister] Dan, my best friend for over 25 years. In the "old days" they frowned on particular friendships. I don't know where I'd be without mine. She has always been there for me.

I may sometimes appear to be a little bit of a rebel, but I'm not really. I believe in my commitment to religious life. Even though I believe that the concept of religious life is changing before our very eyes, I still believe in what I am, and what I do, and the connection that I have with the Sisters of Mercy throughout the Americas. I love the history, and I love the older Sisters. [The community has] always been there for me. I feel the love and support, I really do. And now in recovery, even more. When people see me, they come up and say, "I'm really proud of you and what you're doing." I say to myself, Hey, it's not bad. (May 1994)

Sister Judy remained a clinician on the staffs of residential alcohol-chemical rehabilitation programs for 14 years. She then returned to the motherhouse of the Sisters of Mercy in Watchung, New Jersey, where she served as director of communications. When that ministry ended, she started Catherine's Legacy, a graphic arts service for anyone interested in Catherine McAuley, foundress of the Sisters of Mercy. She has combined her fine arts background with her computer graphics skills to produce prints, montages, note cards, and prayer cards. Sister Judy has been sober for 25 years. She doesn't go so often to AA meetings now; at 71, she does not like to drive at night.

4

SERVING THE UNDERSERVED

SISTER MARIE LEE

The Florence M. Lehmann Center in downtown Minneapolis is a dreary building; long corridors lead past numerous nondescript offices and classrooms. Down in the basement, a large industrial space hums with the sound of sewing machines. Two fabric-covered screens carve out a small office in one corner of the room. From there Sister Marie Lee, a Dominican from the Sinsinawa, Wisconsin, motherhouse, directs Project Regina, a nonprofit program she founded to help Southeast Asian refugees learn sewing skills and English.

Sister Marie, 75, is a small woman, straightforward, courteous, unpretentious. She was clearly proud of her students and her teachers, introducing each in turn. She wore a light-blue turtleneck, made by her students, and a blue floral overblouse, altered by her students.

When I was in fourth grade, somehow or other, one day I decided I wanted to be a Sister. And so I went home to tell my mother this great news. But, you see, she wasn't Catholic and she was really disappointed. That put me in a dilemma, because I didn't want to hurt my mother, but yet I had learned that a religious vocation was a great gift. And I didn't want to turn that down. So there I was. Then I came upon this fine idea. I decided I would pray that my vocation would go to somebody else. Then I wouldn't be refusing it, it wouldn't be lost, and I'd be off the hook. I think every day, certainly during grade school and well into high school, I prayed that my vocation would go to somebody else.

And so it came time to go to college. In those days, the university had a slightly shady name among some of the people in the small town. People had told me, oh, they'd heard of people who went to the University of Wisconsin and lost their faith, or they'd heard of a nun who went there and she left her order. Well, I began to think, maybe that's just what I need because I think this religious vocation thing has grown out of proportion. I've thought about it so much that it's bigger than it needs to be. So I'll go, and I'll get into other things, and it'll just go away.

I played in the band when I was in grade school and high school, and I really liked that. This thing about being a nun was always with me, so I looked around, and I'd never seen any Sisters who were band directors. I thought, well, somebody really should be. I began to think, you know, that's probably my job. And so I went to the University of Wisconsin for the purpose of getting rid of my vocation, but at the same time I went into music to learn to be a band director; so I was doing two opposite things at the same time. But [the attempt to forget about the convent] didn't work—it just never went away.

Now, I didn't enter right away. I finished college, and then, of course, I had some debts; so I planned to work two years and get that all taken care of. I taught music in White Lake, Wisconsin. But then my dad wasn't very well, so he asked me to wait two more years, because I was an only child and if anything should happen to him, I'd be there for my mother. So I did that. And then I entered the Dominicans.

When I entered, I was very docile in the community and I was ready to accept whatever [happened]. I like silence, anyway. I fit into the scheduled life, and it just seemed like I was supposed to be [in the convent]. And so I was never critical of anything, any of the practices that we had; I just took it all. Because it had been so hard for me to get there, you know, and I'd felt so bad about leaving my parents, it was a precious thing for me.

The neighbors told me that it was like a death in the family when I left. I know it was very difficult for my mother and dad, but they never begged me to come home; and as time went on, I think they felt much better about it.

[After a year teaching second grade in Chicago] I was assigned to Bethlehem Academy in Faribault, Minnesota. It was a high school, and they wanted to start a band. We had a wonderful principal, a very commonsense type of woman. She just said, "Well, it would be really nice if we had a band here, but I suppose that would be hard to do." That's all I had to go on; she never told me "do this" or said "don't do this."

Well, there I was. We didn't have any instruments; we didn't have any music. So I just sent out a note to the parents saying we were going to start instrumental lessons: we'd have ensembles, and maybe a band. But where anything was coming from, I didn't know. Well then, a couple of days later, two women walked into my room, and they said, "We're from the PTA, and we hear you're starting a band. Would you be willing to accept some assistance?" Well, of course, yes. So that's when it started. We bought a few secondhand instruments. Then we went to the PTA meeting and they proposed this, and somebody got up and said, "Well, we'll start this [project] and then she'll be moved and we'll have it on our hands." Then the pastor got up and said, "No; if you do this, we'll keep her here for 13 years." Guess how long I stayed? Twenty-three years.

AFTERTHOUGHT: After our conversation, I was thinking; and it seemed to me I hadn't answered some of your questions very well, especially about points of change in my life. So I prayed about that a little bit, and three things really just popped into my mind. It's like they stood out in neon lights. These three and none other.

The first thing was a scripture class that I took; oh, it was a long time ago. Probably before the changes in the Church. Up to that point I had only known about the literal interpretation of scripture, and I was having some problems with that. I couldn't reconcile some things. Anyway, I took this course called Literature of the Bible during the summer at our motherhouse. It opened up a whole new interpretation of the Bible to me. [I learned] the concept of literary forms and how there were other ways than the literal interpretation. Now that made so much sense to me that it helped me develop a love for the scriptures, but also I think it was a preparation for an open stance to other things.

And the second one was a retreat given by an Irish priest. I don't remember his name, and I couldn't tell you anything else about the retreat except that he talked about the "drawing power of God," and it's one of those times when you just say, "Ohhhh, yes!" It was something that had really been central in my life, but I hadn't brought it to consciousness. It reminded me of my experience in coming to religious life—why I stayed, you know; what pulls me back when I get lazy. That was a powerful line for me, and it has sunk down deep.

The third thing—and this was when the changes were just beginning—was a two-day workshop. Adrian Van Kaam was a teacher of spirituality, and he gave a workshop called Religious Vows in the Time of Transition. It was a real eye-opener for me. The one thing I remember specifically about it [is,] when he was talking about obedience, he said he thought of it being derived from the Latin word *obedire*, which means *to listen*. And he said that he thought of obedience as listening to reality and responding to it. That really struck a note with me. [Later] we heard that same idea as seeing the signs of the times and being in touch with the world around us, but that presentation was the beginning for me.

I had known for a long time that it was time for me to leave [Bethlehem Academy], because you get too attached to a place. I had suggested it a couple of times, but nobody thought it was a good idea. But then I was assigned to Regina High School—that's here in Minneapolis—to teach religion. I taught religion for quite a while, and then it seemed like it was time for me to get out of that, because I was getting older and it was harder to teach religion [to teenagers].

Regina High School was located in a middle-class neighborhood, about half black and half white. But our student body didn't reflect that. We didn't have enough black people to reflect the neighborhood situation. And we'd talked about that lots of times in our community: What could we do?

We did a neighborhood survey to see if community education would appeal to the people in the neighborhood and if they would come to classes. That also had allowed us to visit many of the homes in our neighborhood, and I got acquainted with some of the people. So we started this community ed. program, and I ran the night school classes: all kinds of different things, like typing or dancing or knitting or crocheting. And that seemed to work. It brought in some of the neighborhood people, and that's what we really had wanted to do. [Then] one of my teachers who taught basic knits and sewing—it was like how to make T-shirts—volunteered her time for one session for low-income people at no cost. Well, it was so successful I went around town and asked for some funding to enable us to do that again. And that worked fine.

So this one time, I think in 1980, we [were having] our first session in the spring for the basic knits class—we had offered afternoon classes, too—and I looked out the window and it was like a page from *National Geographic*. We saw these women coming across 42nd Street; they had come on the bus, and they were walking single file. Short people—shorter than I am—and they had long dresses and long hair, and we didn't know who they were or anything.

When they walked into our room, it was just an amazing sight. We could hardly believe what we saw. It seemed like another century had opened up and just poured its culture into our classroom. It was an exciting thing because it was a new adventure, something like a fairy tale coming true. We had worked with low-income people before—that's what we wanted to do—but this was something entirely new.

So they came, and they wanted to sew. They'd always get there early, and so we'd sit around and I'd say, "This is thread," and they'd say, "This is thread." And "This is red thread," and "This is red thread." And "This is blue thread," and "This is blue thread." And that's how we did it. And then we'd also talk about what you wear in winter; you know, they'd come in the winter without any gloves on.

We were very curious about them. We tried to find out about them, but all they could tell us was their names and the country they came from. So that's all we had to go on. But then we did some research and we learned they were Hmong.

As far as we know, or at least as far as I know, the Hmong originated in China, and for some reason they were driven into the mountains of the neighboring countries and mostly in Laos. They were not indigenous Laotian people, but rather they were a hill tribe living in the mountains, and their history is sketchy because they didn't have a written language. What they know of their ancestry is handed down by oral tradition; and when they first came to our project in 1980, we learned then that they had had a written language for only about 20 years and that a missionary had formulated their oral conversation into a written language; so they were a preliterate people having no reading or writing skills even in their own language. I tell you that so you see what obstacles they had [to overcome]. A few of the boys were sent down to the city to school, but in the time that we have worked with them I can think of only four women in our program who told us they ever went to school before coming to the United States. I think knowing this lets you see the tremendous handicap they face in coming to this country—not only culture but language and all. By our standards they lived in primitive conditions in Laos, like bamboo huts with dirt floors and candles for light and so on;

and the reason they came was [that] during the Vietnam War our army was not authorized to fight in Laos. So instead, [the Hmong people told me], the CIA subsidized the training of the Hmong to be soldiers and fight against the North Vietnamese army. And then when the communists took over in Laos, there was just merciless retaliation against the Hmong, and they were forced to leave the country. But thousands were killed in the process, so they had to escape through the forest and across the Mekong River. During the first part of this exodus period, the families could cross the river in a boat—just pay the man something and be taken—but later they couldn't. So they had to strap bamboo trunks together to make a small raft, and then they would tie themselves to this and cross the river with children strapped to their backs. Many were killed that way. So they have been through many hardships. And then when they got to Thailand, they lived in refugee camps until they were accepted by another country.

[The Hmong women] have a real native gift for needlework and sewing. They'd heard about Project Regina, I guess, and so they kept coming and coming and coming. And finally, so many of them came that we didn't advertise our night school anymore. It just became a program for the refugees. And that's what it is now.

Those first classes were only two-hour classes once a week. So you just did some very basic things. And then [a group of Hmong people] came and met with us and they wanted more hours. But we didn't have the money for that, so I would scurry around town and ask for money. So then we began to add a little bit more and a little bit more. Then they came again, they wanted five days a week. But we gradually worked it out so it's the 20 hours a week that they have now.

Regina High School closed, but Head Start moved into the building, and they let our project stay for two years; but then they needed the space [and we moved here]. This is a public school building—the community education people are in charge—and a lot of interesting things go on in this old building. It's not the beauty spot of the world, but it serves our needs very well. It's the headquarters for the English as a second language program, and so we're right here with them.

We have two sewing teachers and one Hmong person who is an aide. And we have an English teacher [furnished by] the community education people. We start out the day with an English class for an hour, but then the English teacher stays all morning and interacts with the students while they're sewing. And it seems to be a really good motivator for them to talk.

[We teach] a combination of things. It's industrial sewing; we also have alterations—simple alterations like shorten and lengthen, take in and out, and put on fasteners—and also home sewing. They've been making underwear, girls' and boys' underwear. We furnish the fabric and all, and then they can buy for 50 cents whatever they make. When we first started this program, they could just take home everything. But then we found out that there's a lot more dignity involved in it if they make it and then they can purchase it for 50 cents. And also, before we had to be sure that everybody got the same amount, but this way they can make as many as they want and as many as they purchase. They'll make underwear and slips and shirts and dresses and pants, slacks, just all kinds of things. Plus they learn factory skills—the way to sew in a factory. We do garment alterations once or twice a week. A lot of people come down here and get their garments altered. It's student work, so we cut the price in half. The students get the practice, and the project gets a little bit of income from that.

I was thinking about what our attitudes were toward [the Hmong at the beginning], and I think my attitude was somewhat patronizing, or maybe I should say maternal, because they were small people and they had many needs and they couldn't speak to us. I think my feeling was, "I will help these little people." So that's what we started with, a kind of adult–child relationship, from our point of view. But then when I got to know them as individuals and to learn about them and to hear their stories, you know, their stories were so touching that I could cry with them. But we couldn't hear their stories from them for a long time. Sometimes a man relative would come in and would tell us specific things about an individual. Like we had one woman who had crossed the Mekong four days after giving birth, and the child was strapped to another relative.

We started with an adult–child relationship; but as I got to know them, I began to shrink and they began to grow. When I saw the things that they had gone through and the qualities they had, the courage and the patience—and all the difficulties, I just began to look up to them. I began to learn more from them than they did from me.

I think I've learned something about compassion working with them, working side by side, and I think in general I've been able to see the poor or the fringe people through different eyes. Not looking at them, but in a way getting behind and under and looking through their situation with them. Those are things you know in your head. You say, "Oh, sure, I know that," but really experiencing it with individual people makes a whole difference in the way you feel. (October 1992)

After she retired as director of Project Regina in 1998, Sister Marie enrolled in a two-year course at the Center for Spiritual Guidance to enable her to do spiritual direction. She worked at that ministry for six years and then retired again. She is now 92 and living with four other Sisters.

Good health has been a blessing for me, allowing me to be quite active and energized by reading and study. Learning and evolving is certainly a lifelong process.

SISTER FRAN TOBIN

Sister Fran Tobin, 59, lives in a house on one of San Diego's hills, overlooking the ocean, with other members of the Society of the Sacred Heart. As a staff attorney at Catholic Charities, specializing in immigration law, she works long days, dividing her time between office and court. At the time of our interview, she estimated that

her caseload was approaching 150 cases. A Californian for only three years, she has
lived in Texas, Baltimore, Boston, Washington, D.C., Detroit, and places in between.

How did I end up entering the religious life? I remember people laughed when
I said that's what I was going to do, because I had had a checkered career. I even
had the great distinction of being put out of the third grade in a Catholic school.
I squirted water into the classroom with a hose, and that was not too good, especially when the nun came to the window because she got it on her habit. I was
asked not to come back. And I remember my mother, who picked me up at
school, saying, "I don't think that was a very wise thing to do, Fran."

I was not your church person. I preferred parties and sports. I played tennis
and golf, sailed a lot. I didn't really know much about God until I got to be a
senior at Manhattanville College. I remember going away skiing one weekend at
Stowe, Vermont, and being on a ski lift and seeing those valleys. There was
something about the beauty that said "God" to me. I had had boyfriends, and
I just thought, "One person isn't going to be enough for me. It's got to be the
world." That was the basis for my choice—it really was.

I was attracted to the Religious of the Sacred Heart. I thought, "Here's a group
of intelligent women really dedicated to what they're doing. They love life, and
they have fun besides." I entered the order in 1954, and was I surprised! It was the
closest thing to what you'd call boot camp. My watch went, the jewelry went, the
makeup went. Everything went, and there I was! And we had to do these things
that didn't make much sense to me. I don't suffer rules easily. I don't like rules.
We had a wonderful mistress of novices who read me well. Three weeks after I
entered, she announced she was going away to make a retreat. She called me
aside and she said, "Now, you may not leave until I get back." I looked at her
and said, "If I'm going to leave, I will leave when I want to leave." She said, "No,
you won't." And I said, "Yes, I will." And she said, "Well, my advice to you is wait
until I come back. It's only eight days." It was a battle of the wills, and I must say
I cooled my heels on that one.

What I loved [about being a novice] was the time to learn about God and to
pray. I guess I have to say I fell in love with God, and I'm still in love with God.
I can't say I liked all the things we had to do in community, because I didn't.
I thought, "God help us. This stuff is crazy. I'm going to miss the real purpose of
life by piddling around with all these little rules and regulations." And I was
right. That was the thing that shocked me. I was right! If Vatican II had not come,
I don't know whether I could have survived religious life. Enough of it was coming when I made my final profession that I thought I could say, "Yes."

During the early 1960s I was teaching middle school, grades five to eight.
I probably was very good with middle-school kids because I knew what trouble
they were going to get into, because I had gotten into all those kinds of trouble.
I had fun with them. And then in the late 1960s I was sent to Connecticut to a
high school for girls where I taught English and religion. The Vietnam War was

going on, and some kids were into drugs. I understood their frustration, but their frustration was coming not so much from the Vietnam War but from broken families. We dealt with several kids who were emotionally ill, which frustrated me. I knew that if I was going to teach religion and do counseling, I needed to prepare myself more.

At the time women religious could not get a master's of divinity from any Roman Catholic seminary. So I ended up in 1970 in the master of divinity program at Andover Newton Theological School in Boston. I loved the study; and I worked with a wonderful group of men and women—an ecumenical group, many of them ministers and priests—and developed some wonderful friendships, male friendships and female friendships.

I also had a terrible back problem. It was a year I would love to forget because there was also a misunderstanding among some of our Sisters and me. I was very much a Vatican II supporter, and some people didn't like that. I had been living in a convent situation, and I ended up living alone, because after my back surgery some Sisters said, "We really don't want you back in the house." I talked to an older nun, and I said, "This really hurts. It's so hard to forgive." She said, "It's not yours to forgive. God is the only one who forgives. You just ride along with Him." So I determined I would reach out to each one of the people I felt had hurt me. It was a struggle, but we mended fences.

I look back now and think, "Well, that experience was probably good for you, Fran." But it was a tough whack on the knees. The older I get, the more I realize that suffering is going to bring wisdom and insight or it is going to bring bitterness. And you have a choice. Luckily, I think I've had the gift to find the truth in my experiences and let go.

I graduated from Andover Newton in 1973. I then went and worked at St. John's Provincial Seminary near Detroit as director of field education, which is pastoral training. It was the first time a woman had had that kind of a position in that seminary, where all the priests of Michigan were then trained. These guys were used to being priests with collar power. You know, "I'm the father. Whatever I say, you do." And I thought, "No, no, no. You have to learn some things here." So it was rocky the first year. It got better each year.

That time, from 1973 to 1980, was a very significant time in the American Church. In religious life, in our lives, we had taken Vatican II very seriously, and we were loving it. We were dreaming; we were challenging. I had a wonderful time. My task at the seminary was to develop placements and supervisors where we could send young men and women to receive training in all kinds of ministry. I guess it was the last year of that, '79 or '80, that I was getting very tired, and I know I was getting a bit discouraged by the institutional Church's inability to understand that women and men were equal. It didn't bother me that they were priests and I wasn't. What bothered me was the Church's approach to women.

In the meantime, I saw so much poverty, and so much struggle for the poor in Detroit, that I knew that I wanted to simply walk around with the poor and learn.

In 1980 I had a sabbatical year. Halfway through that year I got interested in working with the Team for Justice, an organization that worked for change in the prison system in Detroit. And so I worked as a counselor to women in jail for two or three years.

I realized that women didn't have the rights I thought they should have. Now, that probably got compounded by the fact that I had been through the institutional Church. But when I saw it was also true in society, I wanted to do something about it. So I said, "I'll go to law school." I had a very wise provincial team in my congregation, who said, "We think you ought to test this out a little bit." So I tested it out by working with women in jail for another year. They were all young women—prostitutes and drug addicts—and some of them didn't speak English. I found myself going to court with them and being very creative. [I would say things like] "Judge, I don't think 30 days is going to cure the problem of prostitution. But I do think if we could get her into a program, and get her off drugs, and get her children cared for, then maybe this person wouldn't be a prostitute." A judge called me into his chambers one day, and he said, "When are you going to law school? Because you're doing what a lawyer does every time you come into the courtroom." This was to advocate. And I advocate well, I think.

So I went to Antioch Law School in Washington, D.C., a place that trained people to work with the poor. At 49, it was tough for me, but I loved it! I graduated on Pentecost Sunday, which I thought was very appropriate, and then I took the bar. Right after the bar exam I went to Guatemala, because by then I knew I wanted to study Spanish so I could work with Hispanic women.

I was in Guatemala for about two months. That was an eye-opener. At that time cigarettes were an addiction for me. I had quit smoking when I entered the convent and hadn't smoked for years until I went to law school. I remember the day this little Guatemalan girl had her hand out asking for money. And I had just spent my *quetzels* on cigarettes. I was confronted by a starving seven-year-old girl. I thought, "God, what am I doing? This kid is starving, and I've just bought cigarettes." And I quit. Cold turkey. Listen, quitting was something! I walked around those streets—it was a struggle. But I was glad I did.

Then I went on to El Salvador and then to Nicaragua. I spent a lot of time in prayer in those countries. I was by myself. I met people. I met some wonderful religious of different orders in those countries, and I came home saying, "Guess what? The best—the best—of the religious of different orders are in Central America." I mean, ours, the Charities, the Mercies, the Dominicans, and many others. They sent their best, and you could tell it. There were wonderful American women down there—wonderful. God!

I was interested in immigration law—which is federal law, so you can practice it anywhere. When I came back from Latin America, I went to Houston, which is one of the cities where our community is in ministry. There was a good opportunity to work with CARECEN, a nonprofit organization that did legal work for Central Americans. I worked there until I got asthma. The doctor said, "You've got to get out of Houston." He told me the kind of climate I had to live in, so I came out to San Diego and found a job at Catholic Charities as staff attorney for immigrant services.

Immigration law for me is representing undocumented people. Most of them are in deportation proceedings, and they are really defending their lives, because if they are deported, it means they must leave the country. I have to prove why they should be here, and that's getting harder and harder to defend, even though many of them left their country for legitimate reasons.

I have a wide variety of people I represent. One case, which I have on appeal, is a mother with three children who fled from Mexico eight years ago because of spouse abuse. Her husband continued to beat her and beat her children. She left her children with her parents because she knew that he wouldn't bother them if they were held by her parents. She found a job. She supported herself and sent money back, because he was not supporting the children. He was an alcoholic. She eventually got the children up here. That man came up here, found her, and started beating her and the children. It was after that that she was put into deportation proceedings, because when the police report came in, it was obvious that she had no papers. By then she'd been here seven years. There was a warrant for his arrest, so he went back to Mexico. Was I glad about that! But this woman really has suffered from post-traumatic stress syndrome, which is what you suffer from when you've been in a war-torn country.

We lost in court. We were asking for suspension of deportation, and I argued that it would be extreme hardship for her to be sent back to Mexico. She had no job there. She had no home. Her parents were very poor. Her children were becoming Americanized here. And in the place she was from was her husband. The local police never protected her when she was there, and they laughed at her when she reported him. The judge disagreed with my argument, so the case is now on appeal. In the meantime, I've gotten some counseling for the woman. The children continue to go to school. They probably speak better English than they do Spanish now. They've been here for a number of years. She's Americanized. That's the kind of person I think should stay here. Now, she didn't come with papers. But she's never accepted one cent from this government, not one cent. And she will never accept it. She doesn't want any money from the United States people. All she wants to do is live and not be scared to death that she's going to be beaten up. She's got scars on her body from this man.

We are very foolish the way we jump all over immigrants. I would be delighted if most of my clients lived next door to me and if they were citizens, because they work hard and they're very generous. They need lots of help, though, because they're the poor coming from poor countries. I would encourage the American people to keep helping people, regardless of what our government says. If somebody's starving and needs a job, and you've got something for them to do, let them do it, and pay them for it. As a lawyer I'm not supposed to say that, because that's unauthorized work. But as a human being and a lawyer, I would say I'll err on the side of being a human being. I don't apologize for it, either.

Am I changing the system? No, I don't think I'm changing the system. But I think I'm injecting a bit of humanness into it, which is important. I have a deep, deep care for immigrant women. And when we take cases, believe me, the immigrant woman with a child comes before the single male who's 24 and is going to survive. Because women and children are the ones who suffer the most, always. In the process of being their lawyer I've learned a little bit about compassion. Sometimes I honestly cannot do anything. There is no relief available for that person. So the only thing I can say is, "Look, you don't have any relief. But millions of people live in this country without papers. Good luck." I try to give them courage; I can appreciate the struggle they're going through. It's part of being a human being—it's part of being Christian. I think it's very much part of being a woman religious.

Obviously, you can see that I feel deeply about several things. I love my religious order, I love my Church, I love my life, and I love my vocation. They are all integrated for me. I believe that women religious today in American society are at a very interesting point. The facts say religious orders are diminishing. I think that's all right. I do believe that a form of religious life will continue in the Church if we religious pay attention to the movement of God in our lives. Religious life is meant to be prophetic. It's meant to ask questions. I don't think my life is about solidifying what others can solidify. That's one of the reasons why I'm a religious: to ask questions, to go to a place where other people maybe can't go.

I like edges. I love edges, as a matter of fact. I think they're great places to be. That may go all the way back to my childhood when I stood on a high diving board, and I looked at the water, and the water looked at me, and it was, "Well, are you going to join me? Or are you just going to stand there and look at me?" So I jumped. I think that's what we're supposed to do. And I think I've learned that God is not going to let me go.

What can I do today that is going to make life better for somebody tomorrow? That's a good question to ask. And if it puts me at odds with institutions, with powers—be it a political power, be it a Church power, whatever kind of power—fine. Your energy needs to be for the future, not for the past. Because behind is over. My feeling about the institutional Church today is that it always looks behind. Jesus walked along the road to Jerusalem. That's a good road to walk. But to walk, you have to put one foot in front of the other. That means your head is facing in that direction. It's not looking backwards. (March 1994)

Sister Fran retired as an immigrant attorney at the age of 70. After a year sabbatical, she began another new ministry—working on medical benefits for the elderly Sisters in her community in northern California.

The best part of these years has been walking with our elderly whose wisdom and humor and peace and prayer call me to a deeper delight in the little gifts of each day. I also find myself in a coalition of women religious to stop human trafficking. There is a strong connect with the immigration issues facing our country. Last year I celebrated 50 years since we took first vows. It was a joyful, poignant week. When I look back I realize I fell in love with God and because of God's goodness I remain in love on the good days and the bumpy days—and full of hope for the next generation.

SISTER JEANNE CASHMAN

Sister Jeanne Cashman seemed at ease in two worlds—the pleasant Wilmington, Delaware, neighborhood of the Ursuline Convent where she lives with other members of her order, and the not-so-pretty area of the city where Sojourners' Place is located. Sojourners' Place was once a factory; its 16,000 square feet have been transformed, under Sister Jeanne's direction, into a center for the homeless.

In the convent, where the interview took place during the afternoon, Sister Jeanne, 50, was exuberant, forceful, talkative—a visionary able to put her dreams into words. On a late-night visit to Sojourners', Sister Jeanne became a listener, a worrier, a consoler, a solver of ordinary problems: "What'll we use to clean the bathrooms now that the bleach has run out?"

I was a wild and reckless youth, shall we say, a kind of a devil-may-care type. I enjoyed life. I got terrible grades [in college]; nuns were constantly pursuing me to find out why I wasn't in class. It wasn't that I didn't care about learning, and it wasn't that education wasn't important to me—because it certainly had been in my early childhood. I think I went on strike against things at that time and was really into people.

However, one thing that was always serious was that I had a burning sense of justice, particularly when it involved a person or a group of people who were being oppressed. For instance, in college I was involved in the Catholic Interracial Council. I befriended one of the black students from Fordham [University] largely because he stood up in a group and said that he had gone down south and went to Mass on Sunday and had some trouble getting on line for communion, because some man was blocking his way, but anyway did get up to the front. And the priest said to him, "I cannot give you communion. The black church is down the street." I can remember being overcome with rage, hearing him say that and knowing that my Church had the nerve to refuse the body of Christ to a person who had every right to it. I said to him, "My God, that's horrible. I myself would have left the Church. I would have walked out of there making a big scene." It turned out I probably felt more strongly about it than he did, because he laughed it off when we were talking in private.

When I did graduate, finally, I remember lying on the beach that summer thinking, "Well, what am I going to do?" Around August 1st, I decided that maybe I would be a teacher. So I took myself into Fort Apache in the Bronx and talked to the principal of a school there, telling him I wanted to teach kindergarten. He asked me why, and I said, "Because I want to get these children in their first experience of school before they're ruined." He laughed and he said, "Well, you'll see how it is." He didn't have a kindergarten class; he only had a fourth grade, and I said, "I'm not interested." About two weeks later he called and said that the Board of Education had asked him to set up another kindergarten and was I interested? I said I was.

In those days in order to teach in New York City, you had to take a test to get a license. I had scored really high on the test. And I remember people—Mom's friends and other people in education—saying, "With scores like that you could teach anywhere. Why would you want to go to that school? I said, "Those are the people I want to work with."

I had never been in a public school before, and it was a shock. It was a huge five-story building. The floors, the walls, and the ceilings were all painted battleship gray. It was ugly; there were cages on the windows, and still somehow the windows managed to break. But there were 2,000 children in the school.

So I started there right after I graduated from college, in the fall of '64. The people in Fort Apache were considered the dregs. They lived in deplorable conditions. We were actually forbidden to visit the homes, because the principal would not assume responsibility for our safety, but I did anyway. I can remember going into tenement apartments with rats and mice and families of six and seven kids in one bedroom—a big dirty mattress spread out on the floor where everybody slept. When I was invited to sit in a chair, I didn't know how to react about the things that were crawling out of the chair. I remember being torn between [being] outraged and embarrassing [the mother]. Should I just pretend that I always sit on roaches? Or should I say to her, "You don't have to live like this." It still is a real problem for me, because I'm often filled with outrage when I hear or see how people are forced to live. But I don't want my outrage to come out in such a way that they get offended. I'm raging against the system that keeps people that way.

I was there for four years. Two things happened during my fourth year. One was that there was a teachers' strike in the beginning of the year. I think unions probably are a wonderful American institution. If electricians and plumbers strike, I don't have a problem with that, but when you're supposed to be witnessing to kids the values you want them to [learn], then striking is not one way to do it. I know there are other opinions on that. I was one of six people who taught during the strike, out of a faculty of 97. It was difficult teaching during the strike; parents of kindergarten children heard I was there, so they started sending their children. It was not just my kindergarten children who came; but eventually, by the time the strike ended, I was running into four rooms and getting kids started and having parents supervise, so that education, such as it was, could go on. And it was difficult when everybody else came back, because some people never again accepted the six people who had taught during the strike.

But something else was happening to me during that year. I [began to feel] there was something more I could do. And what made me finally decide to resign from teaching was, I thought to myself, "I could stay in this school for 50 years and still not address all the needs I see, no less the ones I don't see." And I suppose, when I look back on it, that was the beginning of thinking I should be doing something else with my life, although it was not at all crystal-clear [what that should be]. And so that year I finished teaching and went to Europe for 10 weeks with a friend from college and came back with no job. Then I went to California for a few weeks. In November I got a job as assistant director of public relations at a textile company. It was in that atmosphere, shortly after Christmas, that I suddenly thought, "Aha! Maybe religious life is what I'm looking for." And it made me laugh, because it wasn't my style. And it made most of the Ursulines laugh, too. "Oh, no," they said, "No, no, please no." But anyway, we all got over that.

In July I went to meet with the provincial, and I said to her, "Well, I can't come." And she said, "Good. Why?" I said, "First of all, my charge accounts are enormous—Lord and Taylor, Bloomingdale's, Saks. I'll never get to pay them off. The second thing is, I'm supposed to be a bridesmaid in two weddings." And [the provincial] said, "Suppose I tell you that you could go to both weddings? But I think we'll have to draw the line at being a bridesmaid. Will that be enough if you're at the wedding?" So I said, "Yes, I think these people would understand." And then we made an arrangement, too, for me to pay my charge account bills.

So I thought to myself, either this woman has not heard of my reputation or she's desperate. Nothing fazed her. [She'd say,] "We can work that out. Anything else?" "No," I said, "I guess I'll be there." And that was it. It wasn't until later that I looked back at the journey and thought, "I wonder why I didn't think of [entering the convent] sooner." But it wasn't an option for me sooner. I wasn't suited to the kind of life that people were living before that. I would never have made it in the old system. [In the four or five years since I had graduated from college] enough had changed that [convent life] suddenly appeared as an option, which it hadn't before.

I guess what happened is that I realized I could still do the important things. Some things that were superficial fell by the wayside. You can imagine—with all those charge account bills—I had an extensive wardrobe. One of my friends said, "What are you going to do with all those gorgeous clothes?" We did take our own clothes because we didn't wear habits, but I don't think they had enough closets for what I would have brought. So I gave most of my clothes to the nuns at the college, because they had just gone out of habit. For about five years I met myself everywhere, coming and going; the oddest people were wearing my clothes.

[When I was teaching in the Bronx], one of the things that kept surfacing in me was the growing frustration that nobody really cared about the kids. Even the people I liked, at three o'clock didn't want to talk about kids anymore. It was over. And so when the idea of joining the Ursulines became a reality, I thought,

"Well, that's good, because they care about what happens to people and they have the same values I have." I didn't think at all about praying together or about praying at all. That never entered my head.

[What] happened to me—and it happened so gradually that I didn't notice it myself until [much later]—was that I [discovered I] had a great desire to get to know the Lord, which is why people enter religious orders. It surprised me, and naturally that is what has kept me here.

I have taught every grade from prekindergarten through 12, except fifth; I never taught fifth. And I loved it all. I loved it in Fort Apache. I taught in parochial school; I taught in public school; I taught in private school, in cities and in suburban areas. People say to me, "What did you like best?" Well, I don't know. I liked the experience of getting to know new people every September and watching what happened to them by June. It's hard to explain that I didn't leave teaching. Something else happened and I segued, rather than moving up or down or away from.

[When you study history, there are] remote causes and immediate causes [of an event]. The remote preparation was all of the things I had been involved in years before. I was still wanting to change the world the way I did that summer day when I decided I wanted to teach kindergarten. The immediate cause for my segue was that I got a master's degree in creation-centered spirituality.

In simple terms [creation-centered spirituality] is an effort to reclaim what was lost by our concentration on original sin. It's not an effort to say there was no original sin, but it is an effort to reclaim what was whole and good and beautiful and came first. The master's program [established by Matthew Fox] focused on what he calls the "trinity" of compassion and justice and creativity. The third trimester [of the program] was a special time for me. It was the time when most of the focus was on compassion. We had to choose an oppressed group of people to work with. I wanted to work with a group of people whom I didn't know so much about. So I applied for two things. One was teaching poetry-writing in prison, because I hadn't done any prison ministry, and the other was working with the gay community. It was the latter I eventually chose.

And it was a good experience for me because I thought I was free from stereo-typical kinds of judgments. I somehow thought it was a gift I had, that I didn't put all of you "whatevers" into one [category]. But I found I did have a couple of images in the back of my head about gay people. One of the assignments I had was to help a gay church put together a coffeehouse for their congregation on Friday and Saturday nights. By about the fifth or sixth week of the coffee-house, I thought they all knew I was the "token straight." They called me the "token straight"; that was common knowledge. And this guy came up to me, and he was asking me about this medallion that I was wearing. I said to him, "Well, I'm a nun." And he said to me, "[What order?]" And I said, "Ursuline." And then he said to me so quickly that I almost went through the floor, "Well, are there many other gay Ursulines?"

I just stood there riveted. I don't think I've ever been as angry or hurt as I was for like 30 seconds. Then I just looked back at him and I said, "Not that I know of." I've often thought about that. You know how sometimes you wish you could have shown somebody you were right? Well, I've often had that feeling [about that conversation], and yet I feel good I didn't.

Because one of the things that has always been a part of my philosophy in working with "those" people, whoever "those" people are, is that you're not [there to] make them feel you're better than they are. Or even different. I think one of the things that helps you succeed in working with people who are different is to do what you can in their context and not be the great *deus ex machina* coming in to save the world. I don't pretend to be homeless among the homeless, but I guess I don't want to come off as well-housed as I am.

That year [1982] when I came home here on spring break, I found out the diocese was looking for a person to direct their peace and justice efforts. Another path opened up. And I saw an opportunity to use what I had learned and move out into the community.

When I worked for the diocese, I did a lot of work on the difference between charity and justice. Charity is an easier thing for most people to do. It involves writing a check or collecting a couple of cans or putting together your old sweaters and your kids' old sneakers and bringing them somewhere. It's something that makes you feel good because you've done something good for somebody else. But it may not be what they need. I remembered an experience I had as a child bringing canned foods for a Thanksgiving [collection]. I picked all the things I didn't like to give away. My mother was smart, though. She made me put them all back and take some other stuff. But I think that sometimes people do that. People bring clothing to Sojourners', and they'll say, "Well, it has no buttons and it's kind of frayed at the edges, but the homeless won't care." Excuse me; I care. I get angry. When people say that to me, I say, "If it is not wearable for you, then it probably is not wearable for a homeless person."

If charity is giving something that makes us feel good whether or not people need it or can use it, I think justice is realizing that, just by being human persons, people are entitled to certain rights and certain treatment, and that if they can't fight for it themselves, somebody else needs to do that. And I guess I see myself as one of those somebodies. At some point during those years in the diocese, I isolated the difference between making changes, which is the possible thing; and working for change, which is much harder and takes longer and you can probably die before it happens. But that was the thing that I decided to focus on. What you need to do is change the systems that are keeping people oppressed. One of the city council members [once] said, "You always give Sister Jeanne what she wants because it's the only way to keep her quiet. She rattles your cage so much that finally you give it to her." Maybe you do have to be relentless.

[After five years with the diocese I left that job,] and some Episcopalians, who wanted to do something about the homeless, approached me, wondering if I could help them put something together. Eventually we got the city of Wilmington to give us an empty firehouse to open as a shelter of last resort for people who had no place to go. The city assured us that, from their research, there were about 30 men on the streets; we went as high as 178. We had people hanging from the chandeliers. We had promised the city that, since they were letting us use the building rent-free, we would accept for shelter anybody brought there by a city employee at any time of the night. And so [after people were] arraigned in court at 3 A.M., they would bring them over. We were open for almost two years, and we learned a lot in that time. I will never do that again; I don't think that is an appropriate way to shelter people. I think that it gets people off the street, but it doesn't make any changes. And I'm into making change.

So I began working with a committee from these two churches, thinking about opening a shelter where we could provide in one place all the services we now know that homeless people could use. The services are available in almost every community, but they're so inaccessible for homeless people. Mental health workers would say to me, "She had an appointment here last Thursday at two." Well, you know, if you're a homeless person and they give you an appointment 10 days away on the other side of town, I don't blame you for not making it. It's just so hard to get yourself together. So I began using a lot of the contacts I had made over the years. I went to the State Housing Authority, and the director there agreed to give us the money we would need to purchase a building. I went to the Building Trade Union president and got him to commit the building trade unions to renovate free. And I got the state to agree to put in a drug and alcohol program on-site and also to provide mental health services. I went to the department of public instruction and got them to agree to do a GED [general equivalency diploma] program four days a week on-site. And we have a contract with Del Tech, which is a community college, to provide job training.

We officially opened Sojourners' Place in March of '91. That name [came] largely because of the biblical concept of the sojourner as a person who goes from place to place and is given hospitality and whatever they need to continue their journey. And that's what we want to do here: to provide hospitality, yes, but also whatever you need to get on with your life. We have at this point sent 125 people out into the community with jobs and housing. And that's pretty good. At least it's enough for me to know that it was an idea whose time had come. Of every person we've accepted into the program, our success rate is about 64 percent—which doesn't sound wonderful, but you have to realize that some of those people only stayed for a few days. One guy stayed for an hour and a half. The staff person said to him, "Where are you going?" And he said, "This ain't for me, man. God only had 10 commandments. You guys have three pages of rules. I'm out of here."

Sojourners' is not yet two years old. First I was the dreamer; now I'm the executive director. I often have short nights; and I have a beeper, so I often have interrupted nights. I never get enough sleep, and I have to admit I feel tired almost all the time, but I still have energy to do what needs being done. And I think one of the reasons I have the energy is that I feel very present to the Lord. If I didn't have a space in my life where I could focus on the person I'm living this life with and for, exclusively, I don't think I could do it. I need at some point in my day a time to be with that Lord. I guess there are people who can do good things without that. I just am not one of them. One of the things I pray, when I pray consciously in words, is not that the Lord will stay with me—because I feel that the Lord is always with me—but that I can stay with the Lord through the day. Not "please be with me today," but "please keep me with you."

I see religious life as a gift. And like all gifts, it comes to you when you least expect it or when you don't have any expectations at all. I like the surprise element. Naturally, there have been times when I've been frustrated. As a matter of fact, two or three nights ago I remember saying to somebody, "Well, no wonder nobody's entering this order. Who wants to live with somebody like that?" Because it's not always easy living. I have no doubt that everybody in this house and in this province is trying to do the same thing I'm trying to do. But coming together on the nitty-gritty is often painful. Those are the times you say to yourself, or to anybody who'll listen, "I think I'll get my own apartment. This is ridiculous."

But it blows over. I remember when I was very much younger coming upon two people who were fighting over the car list. (We have to sign up to use a car.) And they were making such a big scene about it, I thought, "I'll be damned if I'll be damned over the car list." The really big things have not been a problem. It's the [little things]. From what I know from my friends and relatives, marriage is like that, too.

I am a rather positive person. About two weeks after I entered the order, one of the nuns from the college saw me and said, "I still haven't gotten over the shock of seeing Jeanne Cashman entering the Ursuline order. With all the mischief and all the trouble you got yourself into, I did think you were much smarter than this." I said, "What do you mean?" And she said, "It never occurred to me that you were the type of person to join a sinking ship." I was shocked. I often look back on that moment. I remember exactly where we were sitting when she said it, and I've always tried to figure out if she was pulling my leg or if she meant it.

Sinking ships are not my thing. We have this joke around here: If I'm the last person, I'll turn out the light. The fact is, there are three people who were finally professed after me and I was finally professed 15 years ago. In 15 years we've had three people. So I know that at some point there are not going to be very many of us left. People today have found a lot of other ways to live a full spiritual life; there weren't so many options in other years. I had a friend, a priest who died this summer, who had a theory. For many years the religious held the Church in trust for the laypeople [he said], and now that the people are better educated and are beginning to take over the Church, we should calmly hand it back to the people we've been keeping it for. I can resonate with that. (November 1992)

Sister Jeanne is still executive director of Sojourners' Place, a shelter for the homeless that offers its residents time and guidance to work out their problems and get their lives back together. As it begins its twentieth year of operation, the shelter maintains its 65–70 percent success rate and has more than 1,100 graduates living and working in the community. It is a non-sectarian effort.

We function because of the interfaith communities. More than ever before, there is very little that can be done alone. If the world is going to be saved, I believe it should be saved by all of us. One of the things that keeps me from getting tired is the people themselves. They are so grateful. They say things like, "You saved my life." I've worked every Christmas morning since we opened. The people are filled with awe. They say, "Someone did this for us?" Would I do it again? Definitely.

SISTER PEG HYNES

Heart of Camden operates from a two-story renovated building on a reclaimed street in one of the bleakest areas of downtown Camden, New Jersey—a city that has become a cliché for "urban decay." Sister Peg Hynes had come into her office on a holiday so that she could block out two quiet hours for an interview. Although it was October, geraniums still bloomed in her windowboxes.

Sister Peg, 61, a member of the Sisters of St. Joseph of Chestnut Hill, is tall, with reddish-brown hair and blue eyes. She was born, she said, in an Irish ghetto in Philadelphia, and grew up a Phillies baseball fan. The day of the interview, the evidence was there: She wore an Irish cardigan and she served coffee in Irish mugs. After the interview she was going home to work on her budget and watch the Phillies play in the World Series.

I'm one of five girls, the second-oldest. My third sister, the next one to me, is a Sister of Mercy, but she entered first, and it tells you a little bit about my personality. She was a real go-getter kind of person. I got good grades, but I never was really aggressive. I finished high school and I kept putting off this idea of being a Sister. So I got a good job. My sister graduated a year behind me, and, of course, she said right away she wanted to go to the convent, and she went. I remember thinking to myself, "Well, I guess I'll wait another year."

The day my sister entered, in September 1952, was the saddest day of my life. I felt so cut off. I remember our house was like a morgue. [My two younger sisters] were just eight years old; they didn't have a sense. But my mother, my father, and myself—all we could do was cry. I went to work and got over it. Two years later I pulled the same thing. And I remember thinking, Can I put my mother and father through that?—because it was hard for a long time.

I told my mother first. And she said to me, "Don't you want to go where Jody went?" That's my younger sister. And I said, "I don't feel close to the Sisters of Mercy." My mother knew the Sisters of St. Joseph, and she said, "Well, wherever you'll be happy." So I said, "Will you tell Dad?" The following weekend I'm helping my father paint the back of the house, and I'm on a ladder, and in this sweet little brogue he says, "Peggy, I hear you'll be leaving us." I almost fell off the ladder. So then we chatted, and the tears are coming down, and we're painting the back of the house, you know. But they were very, very encouraging.

I was sent out to teach, and my mother died the year after I went out to teach. She was only 53, and I guess one of the biggest regrets for me is that I was not permitted to go to the cemetery. Now you say that's a little thing. That was a big thing. It was a big thing for my family. Just getting to see her when she was sick was not easy. I remember getting permission to visit on the feast of St. Anne. She knew she was dying, and she said, "Now the twins are going to need winter coats." My youngest sisters were only 14 years old. She was telling me all the things that would have to get done. I did exactly as she said. I went into town right after we buried her. We got their winter coats. Even for me to get permission to go into town with them was something. Anyway, the day of the funeral, I wasn't permitted to go to the cemetery. My Mercy sister was permitted to go with her companion. My sisters just told this story at a family reunion—how hard it was to pull away in the hearse and leave me on the pavement. What was the sense of that? There was no reason.

I went back to the house—that's where they were coming after the cemetery for a little bit to eat. I was going to pitch in. My mother's best friend said, "Peggy, go upstairs for a few minutes. You don't have to do this; we want to do this." I can still remember going upstairs and crying my eyes out. When they all came in from the cemetery, my sister's companion brought me a flower, and she said, "I put a flower in the grave for you."

Then a couple of years later, my youngest sister was married. We weren't permitted to go to weddings; neither was my Mercy sister. The reception—forget it; we didn't need to go to the reception. But to witness the sacrament? It just didn't make any sense at all. They were probably the two hardest things for me—my mother's death and my sister's wedding.

In the 1960s [our community was] growing by leaps and bounds. We were getting 112, 120 girls, and they were decimated once changes started to come about. It started with moderate habit changes and things that probably might not mean much to you. We were permitted to drive in the mid-1960s, and once we started to drive things really opened up. Until that time the people would come and take you wherever you had to go, or you used public transportation. You always needed a companion.

I guess everybody thinks the same about themselves, but I think I entered at the right time. I worked for three years, so I was 21 when I entered. I knew what the grass was like on the other side, and I had made a choice. The other thing,

I think, in my favor was that there were 54 of us in my group. I really enjoyed the companionship I had with girls my age. I was already professed at the time of Vatican II. We weren't young things; we were rooted. The people who entered in the 1960s never got that rootedness, and I can't help but think that the discipline was good for me.

Meanwhile I had a very good education. Our community is noted for the education it gives its Sisters. We have been generous to a fault. Once I finished my degree [at Chestnut Hill] I went to Boston College for a master's in education with a specialty in religious studies. The summer program at Boston College brought in the best teachers in the Church in those years. I had Richard McBrien, Charles Curran, Bernard Cooke, José Hobday, Tom Groome, Anthony Padovano, Paulo Freire. It was an exciting place to be.

A lot depends on where you are when things happen. I started [in that program] when I was at St. Athanasius, an inner-city school in Philadelphia. That would have been '76, so I myself was 43 years old. That was a rich community. We would talk about important things. That was my first time where what we consider minorities were the majority and the white kids were in the minority. That was a wonderful eye-opener for me. I was the principal, and I worked with a pastor who was bigoted and prejudiced—he's gone to God, so I can say that. He gave me a hard time; everything was a fight. That's why our faculty and our Sisters were so close, because we were fighting this man who was wrong. I have a great understanding of black culture as a result of my exposure at Saint Athanasius.

I continued my studies, and by the time I was finished I was in Washington. From '80 to '86 I was there, and that was probably the most exciting place to be. Had I remained in Philadelphia, I probably would not have grown as much as I did in those years in Washington. Spiritually, a lot of good things were happening to me. We had Sisters from other communities who didn't have a house in Washington living with us [in our convent]. One was studying law at Georgetown; another was doing philosophy at Georgetown; another was studying at Catholic U.; another was at George Washington University. Can you imagine the cross-pollination that was occurring with us? Dinner conversations were unbelievable. People loved to come to our house. I was the superior in that house, and we could have said we don't take visitors. That was not what we did. We opened our doors, and we were the richer for it.

I taught eighth grade in a parish where social justice was important. It was on the grounds of Georgetown University, but it wasn't elite people because it was a parochial school. The kids you were teaching really needed a good education if they were going to make things any better for themselves. I was able to take what I had learned and sift it and apply it, and so I was maturing. I think I was probably a very late bloomer.

I celebrated my twenty-fifth anniversary as a Sister of St. Joseph in April of 1982, and it was a wonderful celebration with my family and friends. A month later

I discovered a lump. I put this all in perspective, because everybody was at that jubilee and they were so shocked when they got the message a month later. I had the examination; the doctor said, "Oh, I think this is early stages, but I'm glad you came." A week later I had the needle biopsy, and I was so confident. This doctor said, "Everything looks good, but we'll know in 20 minutes." He gets the call back: malignant. He was shocked. He was one of the foremost lumpectomy doctors in the country, when lumpectomies were not really being done very much. Anyway, he said, "There's no rush. This has been growing for some time. So do what you have to do before you schedule the surgery." The kids graduated the 7th or 8th of June. I went into surgery the Monday afterwards. They removed the rest of the malignant cancer, and I went through 30 radiation treatments. The lymph nodes were not involved so I didn't have to have chemo, and I dreaded that.

I was very, very lucky. I happened to be in the shower, and I could feel this under my heart. It wasn't painful, and I'm not a hypochondriac either, so I don't know why I ever followed through. But maybe I do have a little fear of cancer, because my mother died of cancer. My Mercy sister had had very, very serious cancer five years before I had my breast cancer. So in light of what she had been through, mine was nothing. She did have to have chemo; she was out of school for months. But she has survived. [Now] we try to make our appointments with the radiologist the same day, and so we have a cup of tea together. He laughs at us, but we are survivors.

At the end of that six years [in Washington] I wanted to do something different before I got too, too old. In '86 I was 53 years old, and I had just come through cancer. I'd been teaching for 31 years; so I thought, well, I'd really like to move into something different—maybe a back-burner, low-key kind of thing, just to get myself together. I interviewed for this job; and at that particular time this was a housing corporation, and they needed someone who would take care of the finances. I was a math teacher for eons, so I thought, that seems like something I could handle. It's probably fitting, you know, [that] you live out your days at something like this.

I came here, and I could have been overwhelmed the first week. My first night I almost picked up a prostitute. It was a September night, misty, rainy. I had a blue jacket on with a short haircut, and I was making a night visit. I'm going very slowly down Winslow Street, and I had memorized where the street [I needed] would come in. I turned. There's a girl on the corner. She thinks I'm trying to pick her up. She comes over, she puts her hand on the door, and I look at her and I'm scared to death. And I went like this to her, no. She dropped her hand, turned away. So I gathered my things together, and I got out of the car. Her skirt was this wide and her heels were that high, but she turned around and she said to me, "I'm very sorry if I scared you." All of a sudden, I thought, I am doing my work and she's doing what she has to do to survive. It was a very good thing to happen the first night I was here. And then on my way home I saw a drug deal a block away. And I thought: This is it; this is what you've been trained for.

Heart of Camden was incorporated in 1984. It really began when Father [Michael] Doyle, [pastor of Sacred Heart Church], was on *60 Minutes* in 1980, and he talked about this area and what they hoped to do in housing. [Heart of Camden] buys houses, rehabs them, and sells them to low-income families, families who would never qualify for a mortgage. They're no-interest mortgage payments, so it's the best deal in town, as Father Doyle would say.

As I said, I came in '86, and there were eight houses here. The intent then was to buy a house, rehab it with a small band of volunteers, and maybe do one or two a year at the most. Well, in '87 we came across a house right down the street here that was abandoned for 16 years, and it was more than what a crew of volunteers could do in years. So Father Doyle turned to some friends of his in a suburban parish. Then I had to go and speak to the parish council, and they decided that they would do a house. That parish was the first outside group to do a house. Today we have many outside groups who help us.

[My job when I got here] was to manage the houses, but as a house would come up, we'd bring it to the board, buy it, start to rehab it. Then another one came along, then another. A Presbyterian church took on a house, and Rutgers University took on a house. So it was growing. I took it in stride; didn't think anything of it. It was no big deal, until maybe at the end of the year we would sit down and see what happened during the year and say, "Oh, my goodness gracious." Last Saturday there were probably over 100 people working on houses in this area. We're working on 12 houses right now. But we have 10 more houses we could start tomorrow if I had groups to work.

Besides housing, we have a counseling program. The parish has a food distribution program for emergency food for the last 10 days of the month. The parish also has a medical clinic—which was one of the seeds I sowed, because I had seen a dental clinic and a medical clinic work successfully in an inner-city parish in Washington, D.C. We have two doctors and nurses who give their services every Thursday afternoon and every Saturday morning. We're working on a youth center right across the street, and we're also doing a family resource center. We've been responsible for the playground that's being built at the end of the street here. And we deliver 1,000 food baskets at Christmastime.

I work here, but I don't live here. My pastor lives here. And it's tough for him, really hard. When he goes home to Ireland in the summer, he can't come back during the day; he has to come back at night and ease into it gradually. Now people say that's exaggeration. It's not exaggeration. To be very honest, I couldn't do that. I need to be energized; I need to see trees and flowers. I've done my best to do that around here, but I would be so depressed if I lived in this scene all the time, and maybe even frightened. I'm not frightened, but if I were here at night I would be.

You have to look at it with a sense of humor. We got an award from Fannie Mae [Federal National Mortgage Association], down in Washington, the first year they gave these awards, in 1988. They gave awards to six people doing low-income housing throughout the country, and when we went down there, the other five were high-power groups. Now we're still wet behind the ears, but we were even worse in 1988. We were the only ones who brought any of our people with us. It was our people who explained the program, but I did have to give a talk. I can still remember: We were in this big building on Wisconsin Avenue in this lovely foyer that had these wonderful ferns, and they'd throw a slide [of our program] up on the wall, and there's not even a patch of green—not a tree, not a flower, just these ticky-tacky houses. I said, "Well, I'm grateful for this award, and on behalf of our people I'd like to thank you." And then I said, "It's wonderful that you brought the flowers and the trees, because you can see by our slide that we don't have any." They laughed, but it was true.

In 1986 when I interviewed for this job, if anybody said, "This is what you'll be doing," I would have said, "Oh, I'm not qualified to do that." Now I would say that one of the strengths I have is I will not try to be something I'm not. I'm very quick to say I really don't know how to do that. I find people respond; they help me. It's not a virtue—it's just that I'm trying to be honest. And I do get overwhelmed. The other thing is that I am gentle in my approach. I said to you before that my name used to be Sister Francis de Sales, and I carried that moniker for some time. Francis de Sales was the apostle of gentleness, so I really did work at that. But maybe I had that kind of a personality, too. In my own home I wasn't aggressive. My sister would run circles around me.

I'm not the same as I was before I went the cancer route. I'm not quite as lighthearted; I take things a little more seriously. We lost three Sisters this summer who were my age. One had such an aggressive cancer, she was dead in three months. And those kinds of things say to you, "You are very lucky. Live every day with that gratitude." My mother died at 53; and when each one of us in the family passes that [birthday], it's like a hurdle—we made it past that age. With my work, it's one step forward and two backward. You have a kid who gets in jail, a marriage that splits up, a death or whatever, people fall behind in their payments; and you're trying to figure out what's going on with them. The disappointments come, and if you don't remember the step forward, it's going to make it really hard.

Do I regret coming to do this work? No. Because this is missionary work, as far as I'm concerned. Sometimes harder. It's not as glamorous as maybe working in Peru. Do you know what I mean? This is tough. (October 1993)

Sister Peg died in December 2002, at the age of 69, when the car in which she was a passenger was struck head-on in Cherry Hill, New Jersey.

SISTER MARY ROSE MCGEADY

The headquarters of Covenant House are in a startling white fortress-like building on West 17th Street in New York City. Inside, from a third-floor office that is both personal and businesslike, Sister Mary Rose McGeady, 64, presides over an international agency that has endured despite scandal and hard financial times.

In 1990, Father Bruce Ritter was forced to resign from the agency he had founded to protect runaway teens, after he allegedly had sexual relations with some shelter residents and improperly loaned Covenant House funds. The agency's tarnished reputation led within a year to a drop of more than $20 million in financial support, most of it from individual donors.

The board of trustees chose Sister Mary Rose, a member of the Daughters of Charity, to lead Covenant House out of its crisis. A large woman who wears her order's long-sleeved navy habit and a short veil tucked back at the nape of her neck, she spoke with enthusiasm and confidence. She laughed heartily and smiled often but offered a rather solemn view of the world and the Church today. She had just returned from a trip to the Covenant House in Tegucigalpa, Honduras.

I was a very happy child. And I guess that reality is even more emblazoned in my thoughts now because I deal with so many unhappy kids. The earliest memory that I have about having a sense of vocation was when I was in the fifth grade, and the readers we had—I think they were called the Cathedral readers—had a story about a Daughter of Charity who took care of this little girl who was sick in the hospital. I don't remember the story, but I remember the impression the Sister made on me, and the impression she made on the little girl in the story. That stuck with me.

Then when I went into high school, you know, the idea that the Daughters of Charity served the poor—that just had an attraction for me. And see, I have a very deep conviction that this is all in God's plan for us. One of the things that I could say has characterized my life is the conviction that there are no accidents in spiritual life, and that God has a plan for every one of us. While we're living it, we don't have a sense of that. But in retrospect, I can just put my finger on so many events, so many people, so many happenings in my life, and I get what I call the "Ah-*ha!* reaction." You know: Ah-*ha*, that was the Lord preparing me for this. Even the friendships that I had with Sisters were to me all part of the links in this chain.

I left home in September 1946. I think we entered the community at a very interesting time. It was right after the war. I remember the night I told my parents that I was going to enter. My father said to me, "Well, I hope your brother is home from the Navy before you go." I actually left before he put his foot in the house; but within a few weeks he was back home. So it was after the war. There was a real feeling of euphoria in this country—that right and justice had won the war, and we were the good guys. We don't feel like that in the nation now.

Sister Mary Rose McGeady examines the handiwork of a young boy at Casa Alianza, the Covenant House site in Guatemala City. More recently, Covenant House has reorganized its work in Guatemala to focus on combating human trafficking for sexual exploitation and labor. *Covenant House*

I was a postulant for about two months in Philadelphia at a children's home. You see, it's just one more link. Then I went to the seminary—we call our novitiate a seminary—for a year. Then I was sent to Boston as a young Sister to teach fifth grade in a children's home, which was really like an orphanage. I loved it. I still remember a lot of those kids I had the very first year. After a short time the congregation had me register at Emmanuel College in Boston, and I finished my degree there. I didn't study very hard, because I was on duty all the time, in charge of a group of high school boys. So I used to do only the homework that I had to do. It's always been one of my major sins.

Then in 1957, I was missioned to Rhinebeck, New York, to a psychiatric treatment center for seriously disturbed children and to start my graduate work in psychology at Fordham [University]. It was a wonderful two-pronged learning experience for me. Because what I was learning in school in clinical psychology, I was experiencing every day in the staff meetings and the work with the children. I was in charge of a group of about 12 children as their group mother. You did everything a mother would do. You got them up in the morning, and you got them washed and dressed and prepared for school. I really saw myself as an effective instrument in helping to heal very hurt kids. And I was good enough at it that I liked it. It's the kind of work that you either love or you hate, because these kids are tough, hard to handle.

In 1963, right after the Vatican Council, the habit changed. The Daughters of Charity had worn the cornette [an elaborate white linen headdress with large white wings on each side, commonly worn by women, and men, in the fourteenth century]. But on the same day—the 22nd of September, 1963—45,000 of us took off the cornette and put on the blue veil. And it was okay, because we were in the era of change in the Church and wanting to be more relevant and rid ourselves of any trappings that would prevent us from being relevant to the modern world. Well, some people resisted it, but I didn't. I loved new things, I loved change, and I considered it great that the community was on board—you know, that we weren't going to drag our heels because we're the largest women's congregation in the Church. But it was an enormous shift for us, and I guess it was the beginning of difference in thinking in the community. Up until that point you came into the community, and you came into a culture that was very well established. We lived on schedules; we lived on routines—and then all of a sudden *change* became the most important word. And some people found that very, very difficult. Some people loved the old and resisted the new, and some people loved the new and were glad to be rid of the old. And for the first time in our lives we were free to think different thoughts. It was a bit of a shock being challenged to think things through. I was never one that was upset with the practices of the community. I was very happy with the prayers that we said. But I wasn't the kind who sat and cried because somebody wanted to change a prayer.

I would say that in terms of service, I was in the forefront [of change]. The Daughters of Charity take a fourth vow of service of the poor, so that even when I was young—maybe 32, 33 years old—I had been asked to speak at national meetings of our community, usually on, What does the service of the poor need to look like now that we're in this modern era? Child care changed, and rightly so, because the needs of the children had changed.

Then in 1971 the biggest upset of my life occurred. I was asked to come to New York, to Brooklyn, to work in Bedford-Stuyvesant in a parish run by the Vincentian Fathers, who are our brother community, and to start a community-based service there.

Five of us went; and, I tell you, it was really one of the most interesting experiences of my life. First of all, I moved from a fairly countrified atmosphere in the suburbs, from a big institution on a hill where it was a quarter-of-a-mile walk to the nearest neighbor; into Bedford-Stuyvesant in Brooklyn, where 400,000 people lived in 90 square blocks.

I went down ahead of time, about six weeks before the group was coming, to talk to the pastor about where we were going to live. And he was trying to buy a house for us. The house that he had his eye on was only one block from the church, but the diocese told him not to buy it because it had a very bad roof. So we actually arrived there on the first day of September, 1971, without a place to live. He had arranged temporarily for us to stay with five Sisters of St. Joseph in the next parish.

The third day I was there, the pastor said to me, "By the way, Sister, I can't afford to pay you. Nobody ever discussed this with me, so I never told anybody. But you know, we're a very poor parish; and the parish doesn't pay the priests—the order takes care of that—so I'm assuming that your order's going to take care of you."

So I called the provincial, and she says, "Well, then you'd all better come back. We hadn't anticipated that." I said, "Oh, no, we can't come back. I can't repack." So I said, "Let me get a job." I went and talked to the director of Catholic Charities and asked for a job. And again—it was just in the plan of God—fortunately, they were looking for a director for a program for exceptional children.

So I went out to work every morning, and the other four stayed in the parish. The diocese was paying me $25,000 a year, and that was enough to support the five of us. The priests were in this great big building, and I said to them, "How about giving us a little space to live there?" So they did; they moved over and around, and we went to see the bishop to see if it was okay for priests and Sisters to live in the same building, and the bishop said, "Sure." And so we began living in the parish building. These buildings were actually the faculty residences of St. John's University, which started right there, and so there was tons of room. At one point 80 men had lived in those buildings. There are still 7 Vincentians and 14 Daughters of Charity who live there. I'm still living in that place.

We suffer from all the realities that poor people suffer who have to live in poor neighborhoods. We are very aware of the dangers of being broken into and attacked. And we live in the world with a lot of keys and locks and security precautions. But we also have the wonderful experience of knowing what it is to live in a poor neighborhood, and to share that with the poor. I remember when we had only been there a short time, I said to one of the parishioners, "What do you think would be the most effective thing for us to be doing here?" And he said, "The fact that the Sisters have voluntarily come to share life with us in this poor ghetto is the most important thing that you do." And that made a big impression on me. So we try to be present and visible to the people. We go to the parish church, and we do wear the habit, which is a great protection for us in areas like that. And the work that the Sisters are doing right there is wonderful, wonderful work. I think St. John's Center is known in the community as the place for services, that it's not just a place to pray.

We have an excellent community life. I guess now there's five or six of us that go out every morning. Oh, I couldn't exist if I didn't live with my community. We have two houses here in Manhattan, but they're small communities of five Sisters each. It's better for me to be in a big house, because I'm away a lot. I'm going to Washington after our interview, and I won't be back until Thursday. The Sisters at home won't see me until Thursday evening, because I'll come right [to the office] when I come back into the city. But it's still home. And that's what community is all about. You just hope that somebody's going to be sitting in the kitchen and you can have somebody to talk to, or that people are watching TV and you can get your shower and get ready for bed and just kind of collapse. It's a very accepting house and a very comfortable home for us. And that's doubly important, I think, when you're doing the kind of work we're doing. Because all of us are working with very poor people, very needy people; we don't get a whole lot of acclamation for what we do. So it's very important that we have a family life. We pray every morning together, and one evening a week we have a house meeting and a prayer meeting together; so we try to enrich each other spiritually and psychologically, just by presence.

Covenant House found me. After I finished my term as provincial in 1987, the bishop of Brooklyn invited me back. The director of Catholic Charities asked me if I would become the associate executive director with responsibilities for all the programs in Queens. I was working that job, and one day the phone rang, and it was a gentleman who introduced himself as a member of the search firm looking for a new director for Covenant House. He said, "We would like to know whether you'd be interested in applying." I said, "Well, no, thank you. I appreciate that, but I have a very nice job." He didn't take that. He said to me, "Could I come and talk to you?" So he came, and he spent three hours in my office. And then he asked me if I would come over for some interviews with some of the board members, which I did. I actually had eight separate interviews with board members, because they had been through a grueling experience and they wanted to be as sure as they could. Meanwhile, I had talked to my provincial. She left the decision up to me, because she knew it was going to be a tough job. And I have to tell you, after about a month of this I felt like the hand of God was on me, and that it wasn't my decision. It was really like a call from the Lord. Finally, the chairman of the board said to me, "We have 120 applicants. You meet our criteria more completely than any other applicant."

I'd been reading the papers, and I knew that it was going to be an uphill climb. I knew it was a big organization, an international organization, and I knew that the kids were really very upset, tough kids. I was 62 years old, and I said to them, "Can't you find anybody that's 35? I don't know if I can do it." And they said, "Well, we would like you to try." So on the 9th of July, 1990, the board offered me the position, and I said yes. I had spoken to my spiritual director, my friends, and my coworkers. Peter, one of the guys I worked with in Brooklyn, said to me, "Mary Rose, your whole life looks to me like it's been a preparation for Covenant House. You've been working with the mentally ill, with street kids, with homeless kids all your life." And that kind of capped it for me.

So then I went away for a few days, and I prayed and asked the Lord to guide my decision. All my life I've taken on things that I didn't feel ready for and really turned to the Lord and said, "If this is what you want, then I'll give it my best shot. And if you want this place to survive, then my best shot will succeed. And if it's not what you want, then it won't, and that's okay. But I will have given it my best shot." And that's how I came into Covenant House. The day after they offered me the job, they put my name, my picture, and my age on the front page of *The New York Times*. Mary Rose McGeady, 62 years old.

People began saying to me, "I think it's good that it's going to be a woman." But I don't think it's valid that the board set out to find a woman, and I know they considered some Brothers and some priests and even other Sisters who applied for the job. But I think after it was all done, people were saying, Well, it creates more psychological distance having a woman. People have been wonderful to me. It's a tough job. We live from day to day, because we're so dependent on donations. Our budget is $70 million a year, and part of my responsibility is helping to raise that $70 million.

I found an absolutely wonderful group of people working for Covenant House. When I came on board, the exhausted staff had just been through 67 days of negative media. People don't work here to get rich. People work here because they're committed and they really believe in the mission.

We're a $20 million smaller agency than we were two years ago. We've cut out a lot of things that weren't absolutely necessary. Our staff is leaner. You know, we just got past the scandal when the recession hit us. So it's been an uphill climb. The hardest thing for me to do is to cut back, because I'm a natural developer. And I've tried to work hard to make sure that for people who were being terminated, it was done in the most compassionate manner possible. If we're really supposed to be a caring agency, we need to care for our staff, not just for our clients.

We're going to make it. We still have some donors who are so angry about the Father Ritter story that they've left us. But about 75 percent of our donors came back on board, and we've tried to be very, very straight and honest with them.

I see my role very much as the purveyor of the mission, constantly calling people back to remember who we are, why we're here, and what our mission is. When I was 15, 16, and 17, I was preoccupied with where we were going ice skating on Friday night, and where we were going bowling on Saturday night, and what movie we were going to see. These kids are trying to figure out what they're going to do with their drunken father who beats them or who sexually abuses them. Or they're kids forced into prostitution to have money to buy their schoolbooks. What a different world it is! What it does, it just whets my appetite for what we do, to try to give these kids the second chance they need to get started over again.

People will say to me, "How can you do that work all the time? Don't you begin to feel overwhelmed by all these kids?" And I always say, "Well, we see enough success to keep us going. And the only way we can make a mistake is to stop." Some people don't think about that, you know, that the only time the Church fails is when it stops being a caring community.

By nature I don't get discouraged. I never worked so hard in my life as I'm working now. Maybe that's not true, either. There were many times when I was young when I was tired to death, but it was always a good tired. I guess these are the most frustrating times I've lived through, because I'm basically an idealist; and I would think after working 40 years at this that our American people, our nation, would be a more sympathetic, giving, understanding nation. And I honestly believe that these are the worst times I've lived through for children. As a young Sister, you know, when I was 20 years old, I went to Boston to care for these kids whose families had fallen apart; but death or mental illness had taken their families away. Now it's drugs and alcohol and abuse. I guess from that point of view, it's the hardest time of my life.

I told the board that I would give them five years and then we would see. We would just evaluate when I'm in my fourth year as to whether they think we should start looking for somebody else for this job. And I guess a lot depends on how my health holds up and how I feel, and how the agency is, you know. I know that I have done a lot to preserve and to keep the agency alive, but I know I'm not the only one who can do that. And the Lord must have somebody out there that he's preparing for this spot.

I've been thinking lately that when I was young, after the war, we went through an era of great prosperity, and the 1950s and 1960s became like the golden age. It was the golden age of religious life; we had more vocations than we had ever had in history. The Church was prosperous, and there was this great era of expansion. And then we had the Vatican Council, which created a real euphoria in the Church. We had the courage to look at ourselves and we had the courage to ask the hard questions, and the courage to bring the Protestant churches into dialogue with us. And then we had about 15 years of real excitement in the Church. Now it seems to me like it's all fading away. And I think it's so sad that we haven't been able to maintain that energy. You know, God is still God; the Church is still the Church. I guess I would be happier if I saw that kind of dynamism and energy in the Church today, because our young people are really not turned on by the Church. In the 1960s and the early 1970s, young people were turned on by the Church and just loved all that was going on, and we had a lot of young religious and young priests who kept that going. I see this roller coaster. We were high, and now we're low. I see it in the Church, I see it in religious life, and I see it in our society. Our society today is a much more depressed society than the society that I grew up in, and that was part of my young days as a Sister in the 1950s and 1960s.

I sometimes wonder if this is all part of God's bringing us to a deeper reality of sin and evil, and calling us to personally commit ourselves to truly live the Gospel. Maybe in the good days, it was too easy. And that to really understand the Gospel and the paschal mystery, we have to live the pain and the days of suffering in order to know what resurrection is. I'm sure the people who stood on Calvary on Good Friday wondered, "God, I put all my energy into this Jesus, and now look; he's up there dead." But then there was the resurrection. So I think that spiritually it's very important for us now as a people and as a Church and as religious, to keep in touch with the fact that God is in this, just as much as he was in the expansion. I don't think that's just a rationalization. It's harder to live in these times than it was to live in the easy time. Now, of course I was young in the easy times, and it's always easier to live when you're young.

I guess hope and confidence in God have always been dominant themes in my life, and trusting, trusting, trusting. But retrenchment is really hard. I often think, "Well, okay, God, you gave me the good years and they were wonderful and I thank you for that. Now I've got to love you just as much in the tough times as I did in the good times. And believe that you're still there and that you're still part of this and you're still expecting something." (September 1992)

Sister Mary Rose remained at Covenant House until 2003 when, because of her health, she returned to the motherhouse in Albany.

My heart was broken at leaving Covenant House. My body was also broken. I have to be in a wheelchair now because of injuries from falls I had while visiting some Covenant House sites. No matter how hard we tried, the number of homeless kids increased so much. All over the world they wanted us. "Come here . . . Come here . . ." I went around the world talking about the needs of these homeless teenagers and people responded. After I came here, five women from the Lutheran church asked me to help them establish a shelter for homeless mothers with children and it awakened in me a sense of what I had been doing. So I've been working at that for five years now. I'm 82. There's always something else to do.

5

PASTORAL WORK

SISTER MARIE GILLIGAN AND SISTER KATHY QUIGLEY

Sister Marie Gilligan and Sister Kathy Quigley live in a brick house just behind the tiny green stucco building that is St. Helen's Catholic Church in Amory, Mississippi. The parish priest used to live in the house; but after he retired in 1992, Sister Marie—a Sister of Charity of Saint Elizabeth from Convent Station, New Jersey—became one of very few women in the American Roman Catholic Church to serve as a pastor. (Approximately 10 percent of the country's 20,000 Catholic parishes have no resident priest pastor. Nuns serve as pastors in only 12 percent of those parishes.) Sister Marie has worked in Amory and the surrounding areas of northeastern Mississippi for more than 20 years; she is now 66. For the last 14 years, Kathy Quigley, 49—also a Sister of Charity—has lived and worked with Sister Marie, serving both the white Catholic parishioners and the larger, poorer black community.

The interview began in Sister Marie's study and continued over dinner, when Sister Kathy joined the conversation. It was a Sunday evening, and a weekend meeting of the Southern Gathering, a group of Sisters of Charity who have ministries in the South, had just ended.

SISTER MARIE

In 1973, the school where I was teaching was going to close, and I was going to be looking [for a place to work]. A friend of mine was the principal of a grammar school, and at the same time she was getting her M.A. After six years she felt as though she was on skates and needed a change. She read in the NCR [*National Catholic Reporter*] that Glenmary Home Missioners were inviting Sisters, Brothers, and priests into poor areas in the South. The priest was very outgoing and dynamic. He invited two Sisters to come to Mississippi; so we came down and visited and saw all the needs. He got a nice house for us in Smithville, which was in between Amory [where the parish was] and Fulton, which was the mission church. People in New Jersey asked us where we lived—What was our address? We said, "We live in the pink house behind the garment plant." That's

Sister Marie Gilligan receives the keys to St. Helen's Church in Amory, Mississippi, from Bishop William Houck, bishop of Jackson, on June 1, 1997. The ritual is part of the traditional dedication of a new church; as Resident Pastoral Minister for five years, Sister Marie had overseen the raising of funds and the construction of the new parish church.

where we lived, in the pink house behind the garment plant. And we paid $75 a month; that was our rent. If we worked in the garment plant, it would have been $50.

That first night we arrived in Smithville, it was about seven o'clock, and we decided to call our families to let them know we were here safely. So we walked down to a gas station that had a telephone. We walked in the middle of the street because there were no sidewalks, and a police car came in back of us. The closer it got to us, the slower it got, and it finally stopped, and a policeman got out. Oh, my goodness! He came over to us, and asked who we were. He said, "Well, what did you ever do to get sent to Smithville, Mississippi? They roll the sidewalks up here at six o'clock." We told him we chose to come. Well, he just laughed, and we laughed with him.

The priest here had so many things going that you felt part of a church and of a mission. He wanted us all to work together. That was the spirit: What can we do together? Because there were so few of us, and there were so many needs. After the first year, we went home in the summer. My friend was going to stay home because her mother had a bad heart. But I didn't make a decision. I just felt my life down here wasn't ended. The superior said to me, "You're not going to go alone, are you?" Well, there wasn't anyone else to go with. So [in August]

I made my reservations, and I came down. And I came down with the attitude that I would say yes to whatever I was called to do.

I was living alone and, as a matter of fact, I was the only Catholic in Smithville at that time. There was a black community there, and I was driving down the road and a black woman and her daughter were walking. I stopped. They were looking for a ride to take the little girl to the doctor. So I took them to the doctor. I went back to their house, and I discovered they were living in a shack. I had never seen shacks. The roof was leaking, and the windows were out, and they didn't have any plumbing in the house. Eventually, I got to know this family. There were three women, and they each had three or four children, and they all lived in this house. There was a grandmother, too. One of their boys had soft bones; and when he was in first grade, he broke his leg. I took him to a doctor, and they put a cast on it; but when the doctor took the cast off, he still couldn't walk, so I took him to the next town to get therapy. And then I got involved with the other youngsters in the family.

The grandmother, Miss Olie, had nine grandchildren, but she would leave her house and baby-sit for a large family. I said, "Miss Olie, how old are you?" She said, "I'm 65." I said, "You should be getting Social Security." "Well, I don't know. I don't have no birth certificate. They didn't give out birth certificates then." She said it was written in a Bible, but her house burned and she couldn't prove she was 65. I said, "Did you go to school?" "Yeah, I went to school." So I went to the superintendent's office in Aberdeen, and I looked through the roll books. I found her name and her brother's name. She was in school in such-and-such a year, so she must be 65. They accepted that. The white people she had worked for had to pay back Social Security. So she was able to get a Social Security check every month.

It was the people here and their needs and their warmth and their faith that I felt comfortable with. I got involved with encouraging them to go to the Welfare Department for food stamps. I encouraged them to send their children to Head Start. We started a Girl Scout troop, and out of that troop four girls are in college. I did adult basic education. I felt I was responding to needs, and good things were happening in those families. They would invite me to their houses, and they would say, "Y'all want something to eat?" And I would accept it. And one of the women would say, "Sister Marie, white people never eat in black people's houses. And you make no difference between people." That's how they expressed it. "You make no difference between people."

I didn't have any business hours. I was always available. I kept that same outlook year after year. I never really said I'd come here for 5 years or 10 years or whatever. I came with the idea of one year at a time. And every year there was some improvement; there was some change—in the town, in the people themselves. There was always growth happening.

The priest who was here was the kind of person who thought the Catholic Church should be reaching out to those in need. He used to say, "Hang loose." I would support whatever he was doing in the parish, too. Nothing specific—more as a presence and an encouragement. There were as few as 17 families in the parish at first. All white, mostly middle class and above. Our main thrust was to help the Catholic community be aware of the needs of others.

In 1992 the priest who was here retired. The president of Glenmary came and spoke to the people in the parish. He said, "In the next four years, we may lose 10 more men, and we don't have men to replace them. So we will hire somebody as resident pastoral minister—and it may be a layperson." The people said, "Why are you looking other places? Sister Marie knows us and we know her."

Glenmary advertised, and several people applied. Some Sisters, some laypeople, even a married couple. I put my résumé in with the others. They had an interview committee and arranged for interviews for all of us on a certain day. The next day was Palm Sunday, and all of those who were interviewed were going up to the mission church in Fulton. After the Mass, one of the interviewers sat down in a pew with me, and she said, "I want to talk to you when everybody else goes." I said to myself, "She's going to break it to me easy. She doesn't want me to react in front of the other people." That was my whole feeling. But when I went in to see them, they said that I would have the position.

I would be responsible for all the pastoral activities of the parish. The only things I could not do were say Mass, hear confessions, and anoint the dying. There are codes in canon law that allow a lay minister to take on this kind of responsibility. Our diocese also anticipated [the shortage of priests]. There is a job description for the resident pastoral minister. A priest would be assigned as a sacramental minister responsible for Mass and the sacraments. Another priest serves as priest supervisor.

Our sacramental minister came every Sunday last year, but this year he can only come once a month. I called the Benedictine monastery in Alabama, and the prior there is able to send a priest the first Sunday every month. So we have Mass the first and third Sundays. And the other two Sundays we have Sunday worship, which I lead. We have 52 families in the parish. On Sundays the church is crowded—about 70 or 80 people crushed together in the pews. We have 10 pews—five on each side—and then two rows of chairs. Right now we're in the planning process for a new church.

Do you wish you could be a priest?

Not necessarily, I'm responding to the need at this particular time. I can sympathize with those who feel called to ordination, and I say they should be allowed to be ordained. I'm just doing what I have been called to do at this moment in history. My role is well spelled out according to the job description and what canon law allows.

I've heard people say, "You're a pioneer." And to be able to do this kind of a thing is a road that has not been traveled. On the other hand, you're in a position where you can do this but you can't do that, and people say, "Isn't that terrible?" Well, it is terrible, but I just think it's important for me to continue doing what I'm doing. I can't get caught up in whether I should be doing more, or isn't it terrible that I can't be ordained.

The point is, if you don't communicate to the people the necessity of worshipping together on Sunday, you will lose your congregation. They won't come. We try to make Sunday worship as meaningful as we possibly can to let them know that if the faith is valuable to them, they need to continue gathering on Sunday. I see it as keeping the Catholic faith alive.

When I came to Mississippi, I came to a personal awareness of my own self-worth, my identity as Marie Gilligan, a Sister of Charity, and a Catholic. I was those, but I never was consciously aware of that before. When you're in New Jersey, you are Sister So-and-So, and you teach. But when I came here, I had no position to speak of—no particular job description. So all the baggage I had was gone. There was no agency, no community, no one else to refer to. All there was was me, myself. Who am I? And what am I doing? The answer was lived out by my experiences. That to me was an insight—a revelation. I was here out of faith, knowing that there was something calling me, and I wanted to be open to that call. No one could do that for me and there was no routine I could follow. There was no direction. I walked the roads myself, and I discovered. Everything was a discovery.

SISTER KATHY

I was alive and well in New Jersey [in 1980] teaching biology, and I thought I was a good biology teacher. And I was very happy teaching biology. In the summers when we weren't teaching, I went off studying, and I had about had it with studying. At that same time our congregation said that some of us should work with the poor all the time, and all of us should work with the poor at some time. I had never worked with the poor at all. I worked with middle-class suburbia kids. So I volunteered one summer. A friend of mine was going down to Mississippi to work in a summer camp with this person, Marie Gilligan. I said, "I don't even know that woman. Do you think she would let me go?" My friend said, "Oh, yes. I'll write to her." She did, and Marie said, "Y'all come." So the two of us came down to work in the summer camp.

It was 106 degrees that summer, every single day. I was here three weeks, and I lost 13 pounds. We were sweating. The bugs were biting; the chiggers were biting. It was awful. But there was a deep spirituality in everything that Marie did. I didn't have it, and I wanted it. I knew it was really, really important. Wherever I would go with her in Mississippi, the people were so simple and so poor, and yet so wise and close to the earth and close to God. I knew I had to stay here. But I had to go home and get permission. I met the provincial at a funeral, and I said, "Pat, I have to see you." She said, "I know what you want." I said, "You couldn't possibly know what I want." She said, "I know what it is. And it's her fault," pointing to Marie. Pat said, "The door's open. Go." So I did. Within a month I was back here full time, and I've been here for 14 years.

When I came here, I was a nothing; and I was a nothing, I bet you, for three years. I'm not the follower type; but I had to be an apprentice, because the language was different, the territory was different, the work was different. I couldn't even understand the people. I felt like a little animal trailing Marie around. I didn't know what to do, but I loved it.

The first week I was here, Marie got the flu. She was in bed for a week. It was terrible. I'd get up in the morning, and I was used to going to school, teaching, preparing my biology classes; and I didn't have any of this to do. So she would make some suggestions, like:

MARIE: Go see Miss Oliver.

KATHY: What do I do when I get there?

MARIE: Just be with her and see what she needs.

So I'd go over to see Miss Oliver. She lived in this shack, and she had nothing. Oh! She was skinny and old, and the place was filthy. And there were bugs and animals all over the place. And most of the time she had no running water.

And then another day I'd say, "What do I do now, Marie?" And she would say:

MARIE: Go to Head Start.

KATHY: What will I do in Head Start?

MARIE: You could sing a song for them.

KATHY: Well, I can do that, but what else? Just go over and say, "Hello"?

MARIE: Yes, and see what happens.

KATHY: I don't know those people.

MARIE: Well, they'll be glad you came.

KATHY: Just go?

MARIE: Just go and play a song.

I would go over, and the Head Start teachers were very poorly educated—this was 14 years ago. I was this professional schoolteacher, and here you had these nice young women who were still learning about teaching. You always felt you could do something. And then you used your own creativity. We had a Halloween party, and we did a Christmas play.

MARIE: She would come back and say, "Now, let's dress up and be clowns and have a parade for Halloween." So I would have to dress up as a clown and lead the parade, walking through the streets of West Amory. I was glad to have someone working with me. My main concern was that a person would find something she liked to do and would be happy doing it. And eventually Kathy did.

KATHY: Marie would run around saying to people, "Sister Kathy's just come to town. Maybe she could help you." She'd come home, and she'd say, "Bob Taylor wants you to help him." I'd say, "Who's Bob Taylor?" "Well," she says, "he runs the group home, and he wants you to do some work on sex education in the group home." I said, "Marie, he doesn't even know me." "Well, no," she said, "but he knows me. Can you do it?" I said, "Of course I can do it. That's not a problem."

When she was sick in bed that time, the phone rang, and I answered it, and it was a little boy who needed to go to the doctor's. She said, "Well, you can take care of that." So I took the little boy to the doctor's. And when I got to the doctor's office, this doctor comes out and puts his arms around me, and he says to me, "Sister, you don't know me. I'm Dr. Stockton. I am not Catholic. I'm Methodist. Just know that the Sisters and priests who have come before you have set the path for you, and that you are accepted and welcome because of them. The work they have done in this community has paved the way for you."

But being a nun didn't really help. You had to earn your way into the community. And it takes a long time to earn your way in. Because of the people that went before me, I had a shoe-and-a-half in the door. But I still had to sit on my ways and styles and adapt to their ways. See, Marie's style is very unassuming. She's very gentle, and has a very quiet, gentle presence. Where my style is very outgoing and very talkative and very assertive—I'll say assertive. And they don't like that. They don't like outgoing women especially. They don't like northerners. And when you're a northerner who has a lot to say, who has an opinion, who is verbal, strongly verbal, then that becomes offensive to the Southern people. There was a group of musicians in our church, and Marie would introduce me to these women, and say, "Sister Kathy sings and plays the guitar." And they would just look at me, and then they would say, "Well, if you'd like, you might want to join our group." And my initial reaction was, "Join your group? I'm the leader! You know? I'm the nun."

MARIE: She'd come home and say, "I think they hate me. They're so sweet, but they hate me. I know they hate me."

KATHY: They did, too. Well, they did not care for a stranger coming into their group and their church with all the answers. They reacted to that, and I could tell. I gradually shut my mouth a lot more often. When we had gatherings, Marie would say to the priest, "After the opening prayer, Sister Kathy has a song." Marie has this wonderful way of bringing you in. So I would sing, and then the next week at the music practice, the women would say, "Could we learn that song?" I would say, "Well, if you want to." I would wait for them to lead me in. I had to learn the lesson Marie already knew naturally. It was not my style, and it was very hard. It went against my grain. I just wasn't like that. And I still blunder. But basically I'm accepted and welcomed, thanks to Marie's mentorship.

She's been trailblazing from the beginning—from the very beginning, 20 years ago. That's why we're alive. As time goes on, everything continues to be new and exciting in the parish, but at the same time, we have never let go of the other work, because the people don't let us. Like tonight, in the middle of everything, we got a call that a pregnant girl's water broke. She has no transportation; she's mentally retarded and also mentally ill; and she needs to go to the hospital. So we drop everything, and we run [to] take care of that issue, and then we come back home. It's a ministry that has incredible flexibility. The whole county is your parish. It's very exciting. (November 1994)

> Sister Marie and Sister Kathy left Amory, Mississippi, in 1999. By that time, the number of families at St. Helen's Catholic Church had grown from 43 to 70. During Sister Marie's time as pastor, the tiny parish had built and completely paid for a new church that could accommodate all its members.
>
> Sister Marie had served the parish and the poor in Amory for 26 years. When she returned to New Jersey, to her community's motherhouse, she did pastoral services for the Sisters for five years and then retired. In October 2009, at the age of 80, when the Sister who had replaced her as pastor needed a medical leave, Sister Marie returned to Amory, serving as ecclesial minister for eight weeks. She gathered the people for Sunday worship and had authorization to preach at liturgies on the two Sundays a month when no priest was available. She met with several women in the parish who had become Seton Associates, their way of carrying on the spiritual legacy of the Sisters of Charity, as they had seen it modeled in Sister Marie and Sister Kathy.
>
> Sister Kathy ministered in Amory for 19 years. She found re-entry into life in New Jersey difficult at first. After a few years of pastoral ministry, she was invited to teach at Marylawn of the Oranges, an all-girls Catholic high school where the students are primarily African-American from poor urban neighborhoods. She serves as campus minister and music director. While she was in Mississippi, Sister Kathy composed more than 125 scripture-based songs and produced seven recordings, always using the voices she heard around her. It has taken a while, she said, but she is back composing music in New Jersey and gathering new voices from the Marylawn community to join her on her next recording.

SISTER KATHY: The way I see it, and we often talked about it when we were in Amory, is that the Spirit of God moves where it will. The work of the Spirit might not be the same [for other women] as it was for Marie and me, but religious life is continuing. It is passed on to other people and they embody it. I think women religious in the Church are at our finest moment in history. I have no regrets about our lifestyle because we have matured spiritually, we have matured emotionally, and we've matured ministerially. We are working as hard as we can. Most of us are way over 60, and almost none of us is under 60, and yet we are giving 1,000 percent every place we go.

6

SPIRITUAL COMPANIONS

SISTER IRENE GARVEY

Sister Irene Garvey—a Dominican from the Amityville, New York, mother-house—lives on the third floor of an old stone mansion that has been a Jesuit House of Retreats for almost 50 years. Her hair is gray; she was once a vivid redhead, and she once wore the long white habit of the Dominicans.

More than her appearance has changed; at 64, she leads a life far different from the one she foresaw for herself. When she entered the convent, her current ministry—giving retreats and offering spiritual direction to anyone who seeks it, including priests, nuns, laymen, and laywomen—was not an option for women. Sister Irene is a full member of the Loyola retreat team, living and working in a community of eight Jesuits and two nuns.

I had the desire to be a Sister from the time I was a small child, but I think everybody is caught up in that. My mother kept saying to me, "Well, you'll change. You won't want to do that as you get older." I think I was attracted to the white habit, but I was also attracted because of the kind of women I met who were Dominicans. They were very joyful and very human and very friendly. I can remember saying to my closest friend at the time, "It must be so easy to be good when you're living in a convent where everybody's trying to be so good." That was my teenage idealism.

But then I went through a rather traumatic period. I was in high school from '40 to '44, and we were in the middle of the Second World War. My brother, who was two years older than I, was in the Marines, and he was killed. My parents had lost another son—not in the war, but as a child. When this son came along, he was the gift of God to replace that son. So when he died, it was just a terrible tragedy. My mother said to me, "If you're still thinking of entering the convent, forget about it. God took two of my children and he's not going to get the third."

After I had graduated, my mother said to me, "You really do want to enter the convent." I said, "That's what I want to do." And she said, "Well, I have no right to stand in your way. I did with my life what I wanted to do. I have to let you do with your life what you want to do." That was a tremendous grace for my mother. I think it's just a bit of the measure of who my mother was.

The amazing thing—to bring that part to some kind of closure—was that when my mother was older and began to fail in health, we were at a point in our religious life where the community was very open to allowing us to go home to help our elderly parents. So then my mother could say to me, "I never thought you would be the one who would be able to care for me in this way."

I was professed in 1946, when I was just past my twentieth birthday. After I was professed, I was sent to my first mission—that's what we called it—in a very poor neighborhood, and I had my first experience in teaching. I had a double grade—2B and 3A. Now if you had 2A and 2B, the music and the art and the nature study and all that stuff was the same. But if you had 2B and 3A, nothing was the same. Everything was different. Here I was, a new teacher. I thought I would go out of my mind with all those little kids. I had a big closet in my classroom. And every so often I used to go into the closet and I'd say, "God, I can't do this much longer. This is what I'm going to do for the rest of my life?" I was talking out loud in the closet! I would be so frustrated, you know. But then I would come out and talk to the kids.

I went from there to another parish, where I had the fourth grade, and from there to a school that was just starting, a brand-new school. The first time I went out to see it, the school wasn't finished yet and the convent was an old house up on wheels that they were moving from one block to the other. But I would say that in that school I really came into my own as a teacher. I was growing up myself.

In 1987—and that's a long time afterward—I got a letter from one of my students whom I had never seen after I left that parish. She had her doctorate, and she met one of our Sisters and she said, "I would love to know where Sister Joseph Paul is." [That was my name then.] So I got this beautiful letter from her saying that she had come to the school from a public school. She was frightened to death of the Sisters and the whole Catholic school [environment]. She said, "You made me feel so cared-for and so loved. You are the person who has had the most singular influence on my whole life."

It was a wonderful place to live—the neighborhood, the people, and everything—but the convent was very difficult. I was too young to recognize it at the time, but the superior was a sick woman. She was charming. She charmed everybody in that parish, but in the convent—you read about stuff like that—it was a whole different environment. Four of us had bedrooms up in this attic. We used to pray together. We made this novena every Tuesday night that somehow God would intervene and change the situation. Which God did not do while I was there.

I suppose as I look back on it many, many years later, that time was the most formative period of my religious life, because I had to really come to grips with this experience. Through prayer and direction I was able to say, "I didn't enter religious life to put up with this kind of nonsense. But it's not stuff that's going to send me out of religious life." Another thing that was very helpful was [that] I had begun college at St. John's University. That was like the oasis. You got out to study [on weekends], and then in the summers we went up to our convent in

Monticello [New York]. We had this lovely camp in the mountains. So you got these breaks. We all survived.

Then in 1955 I started studying for a master's degree in speech at Fordham [University]. I was teaching English in high school, and I coached the forensic league. It took a lot of time: You stayed after school; you went to the contests on Saturdays. The girls qualified for the national tournament, so I went to Florida and Pittsburgh and Colorado and Washington, D.C. I got to see the country, and this was a very broadening experience. It was just a great time in my life.

I had a year's sabbatical from '65 to '66 while I started my doctorate at Teacher's College at Columbia [University]. I was still wearing the habit, I was still Sister Joseph Paul, and people were wary about a woman having a masculine name. I was confronted on that several times. I said to them, "My brother was killed in the Second World War, and when we were able to choose a name, I asked if I could have that name in his memory." But homosexuals were beginning to come out of the closet at that time, and I was uncomfortable with the name myself because it was masculine. I had never ever thought of anything like that before, but when people started to question me, I could see the source of their questioning; so when we had the opportunity to return to our baptismal name, I did it right away. My mother was not very happy. But I explained to her what was happening and how people were questioning me, and my mother said, "If it's going to make you happy."

Then in 1966 I was sent to [teach speech at] Molloy College. I was chairperson [of the department] for a few years—I think it was three years, from 1970 to 1973—and then in 1973 I was elected superior general.

I loved being in leadership. We had come out of the old way of living religious life and being told everything to do, and go here, and move there. And now we were making all of these choices for ourselves. I was beginning to understand what it meant to be an adult. I was always so involved in the changes in the congregation, it wasn't traumatic for me. I loved it!

I think the focus for me [during my term as superior general] was that I wanted the Sisters to discern what their gifts were. I wanted the Sisters to be free, to discern those gifts, and to use them where they thought they could most be used. In ministry, Sisters were leaving education and going into other areas of ministry. I saw that as something very positive, because there were many teachers who did not like teaching; and if you don't like what you're doing, you can't do it as well. We began to affirm Sisters in doing soup kitchens, working with runaways, or in spirituality centers.

It was very, very hard to say no. You had to trust that they were committed to their vocation, and this was the way they saw it unfolding. Sometimes it unfolded right out of the congregation, but you had to take that risk. We began to formulate policies and guidelines in the congregation so that when Sisters petitioned for something, there was not just a personal decision. If you fit this criterion, you were going to get it. There were some Sisters who were very angry. You had to deal with them.

I think the whole experience in leadership changed me dramatically. People don't often think I'm an introvert—I am shy—but in leadership I had to go constantly to meet people. Whenever there was any kind of a gathering where I knew a bulk of our Sisters would be, I would be there. We were 1,300—I think I knew almost every Sister by name. I went to visit with them, to get to know what was going on in their hearts and in their lives, and I really feel that I began to listen better.

When I was in leadership, Sisters would come and talk and ask me if I would be their spiritual director. Of course I would say, "I can't do that in this role. After I left leadership in 1981, I took a year in our House of Prayer, and again Sisters started saying, "Are you going to do any spiritual direction?" I said, "I'm not trained for it." And some of them said, "Well, I don't care if you're trained or not." So then I went and got the training. It felt right.

My time was up in the House of Prayer in 1987. We could be there six years. I wanted to be in retreat ministry. I sent my résumés around to all the retreat houses and got them all back. No, we're not hiring. There was nothing. I knew there was an opening on the staff here, so I applied. I knew the place; I knew the staff. This is really what I wanted. And I got it. But before I got it, I have to say, the year 1987 to 1988 was the most difficult year of my life, because I loved what I was doing at the House of Prayer and I was told to leave all of it and make room for other people. I knew [the policy] was right, but I was so happy and so fulfilled and so affirmed in the ministry. It was like, "Why do I have to move on from here? You don't move people out of principalship in six years. You don't take people off the executive board in six years. Why this magic number [for the House of Prayer]? Why can't I stay here?" I was asking those questions of the leadership, and yet inside myself I was saying, "It's right. You should go. You can't stay here forever." So it was a time of turmoil.

I have to say I spent a lot of time crying. [There was] the sense of being uprooted from the ministry that I loved and not knowing where I was going. It was a real struggle in faith to trust that God would take care of me. The thing was, I had the feeling that I would have to live outside the congregation. That had started to happen to Sisters when I was in leadership, and I can remember saying, "I don't think I could ever do that—not live with my own Sisters."

I don't want to be anybody but an Amityville Dominican. No way. I am so sure of where I belong. That's a singular grace—I have never really doubted that. When I was finally accepted in ministry here, that was exciting; and yet it was tremendous upheaval. I asked the leadership if I could have a room at the motherhouse. I said, "I have to be rooted in the congregation." Now some of our Sisters who go away for ministry don't have that need. They don't have a place there that's called their own space. I needed to know that I belonged there, that I had a room that was my room, and that when I was free I could go back and be with the congregation. So that was the trade-off, and I came here.

I know I can't be here forever. So when my time is over, I will go back to the congregation. The one thing I did experience on a faith level in the two years that were so traumatic was that God will take care of me. I now believe that in the depths of my being, in a way that I never believed it before. And so my whole prayer journey from that time on has been a journey of trust. Really trusting.

Now this will be my last story. This is very significant. After I knew I was going to be in ministry here, I went to a workshop, because I had already arranged it. [The group was] gathered together in this great big hall before they started the procession down to the parish church. I was feeling very alone and still getting ready for this uprooting. This young laywoman said to me, "Do you want to walk over together?" I said that would be nice. She was also alone, and we were together for the readings; but all of a sudden I got separated from her, and however the procession formed, I was at the end of the line by myself. I was the last one. And I was so overwhelmed with the sense of separation and loneliness that I said, "I can't be here." I wiggled my way all the way up through that line until I got in the middle and was surrounded by people. It was very symbolic of where I was at the time.

They had this pool set up at the rear of the church, decorated with these absolutely exotic plants. It was just beautiful. And the man who was preaching said, "What I want you to do is either come to the water by yourself and pray—or come with a partner." And they were playing "Come to the Water," that beautiful hymn.

I stood there absolutely frozen and isolated. I said [to myself], "I cannot go up to that water alone. I can't do that." So I said, "Then ask somebody to go with you." And I started to lean over toward somebody, and someone else came. It looked like everyone else was paired. I was totally alone. And I was crying because I couldn't move. I couldn't move to that water.

All of sudden someone came and took my hand, and it was this young woman. And she said, "Irene, let's go to the water together." I felt like Jesus Christ had taken my hand and led me to that water. It was such a profound experience. I went through the rest of the liturgy in tears. (March 1991)

Sister Irene remained in ministry at the Loyola House of Retreats for another 11 years. For a while the Jesuits opened the door for women to preach at community liturgies and Sister Irene saw that as a wonderful opportunity to live out her charism as a Dominican—an ancient religious order for both men and women, founded to be preachers. She retired in 2002, at 76, and returned to Long Island. She now lives in an intercommunity house with other women religious. She wanted, she said, a small feminine place, something with a garden where the birds come. Harvest Grove realized her dream.

SISTER JANET RUFFING

Sister Janet Ruffing, 48, is associate professor of spirituality and spiritual direction in the Graduate School of Religion and Religious Education at Fordham University in New York. She not only serves as a spiritual director; she also trains others in spiritual direction. She has published two books and several essays on the subject. She is a Sister of Mercy from Burlingame, a Californian still getting used to life on the east coast. The interview took place at her apartment in the northern reaches of the Bronx.

I was seven when my father said, "What do you want to be when you grow up?" I said, "I want to be a nun." He said, "Don't you want to be a mommy and a secretary like your mother?" I said, "No," and I never spoke about it again.

And then the sense of calling reemerged at significant times. It came back again when I was maybe 13 or 14, finishing seventh, eighth grade. And I wasn't terribly interested; I really did want to marry and have a family. So there were long conversations about this with God. When I was in high school, I'd be in the middle of a dance and God would be so present, I could not ignore it. And I'd say, "All right, leave me alone. I'll come to Mass tomorrow morning. Just leave me alone now."

I didn't talk to nuns about this. It wasn't that I didn't want anybody to influence me. I didn't want to be treated differently; I didn't want to be singled out as the prospective nun by the nuns. So I just kept it to myself. In my family there's a strong Nordic temperament, a very strong reserve.

My mother was somewhat fragile in her health all of her life, so my father always did a lot that needed to be done. And as kids [my brother and I] had to do a lot of the work around the house. Mom was never cut out to be purely a homemaker. She was very brilliant, very creative. Both she and my dad were Depression kids, and they didn't have money to go to college. My mother started working as a school secretary when I was seven or eight, and while she was in the school, her principal encouraged her to start college. Now this was in the 1950s; middle-age women weren't doing this. She was 38 when she started college. She went straight through four years, graduated third in her class at San Francisco State. When she started college I was 11, and on my holidays I would go to college with her. I guess what I saw in my mother was that you could make major changes in your life as an adult. When I was 16, my mother asked me what I wanted to be. She knew; she's very intuitive. And I said, "Well, if I don't enter the convent I would like to be a college professor, and I would either teach philosophy, psychology, or theology." And she said, "And if you enter?" I said, "Well, then I don't know. I'd probably be lucky to teach high school."

I was 18 when I entered, right out of high school. I was acquainted with five different communities, so [selecting one] was a very conscious choice. At the time, the most I could articulate was [that] I was profoundly touched and developed spiritually by the Sisters of Mercy in the one year I had them. The Sister who had the Sodality taught us how to do mental prayer, and it opened a contemplative dimension that actually my second-grade teacher had opened, but I didn't know how to get back to. There was a deep biblical and liturgical spirituality that was part of the community that was more authentic and rich than the devotion I saw in the other communities.

I was very, very happy as a postulant. I liked the studies; I knew it was right. The postulant director was really warm and loving. The novitiate was terrible. We were completely isolated from everything familiar; all of our communication was controlled. There were 45 of us in the novitiate, and we had a novice director who was herself a contemplative, a very mystical person who did not understand teenagers and who was afraid of showing affection to anybody for fear of developing favoritism; and so she showed affection to none of us. So it was two years of isolation and total deprivation from any positive feedback. I was very close to a nervous breakdown in those two years.

After I made first vows, the juniorate director knew something had gone very wrong. She had apparently been the person who answered my letters when I was exploring the congregation, and she [had been] taken with my creativity and intellectualism and independence. She observed that I was a changed person, and she literally loved me back into life. She said, "Well, you were fine before you got here, so all I'm asking you to do is be yourself." And I couldn't find myself. I couldn't find myself. I did, I guess, about six to eight months of therapy. It took maybe three years—the initial working through in therapy, and then this Sister who just loved me to pieces. I was very clear that I wasn't going to leave the community until I was myself again, that I felt the community owed me that. After three years I said, "Well, I think we've undone it all." And it was at that point that I made the vocation choice all over again. I had a completely open question: "God, is this where you want me?" [The answer] was, again, an intense experience of "Yes, this is where I want you."

I was a postulant when we started getting the documents from the [Vatican] Council. So I read every single document from the Council as it arrived from Rome all through those years, one after another after another. I knew after three years that if a lot didn't change I couldn't stay. My juniorate director said to me, "If you can hang on for a couple of more years, then I think it will be all right. You will be able to be a lot more self-determining. I would just encourage you to wait and see." And at that point she relaxed as many of the regulations as she could on my behalf, because she knew that if I had enough freedom over my schedule, I would be able to function better.

By the time I started teaching—you can't believe how weird it was. I started teaching in 1968. I'd entered in '63. I had missed the civil rights movement. And I landed in a high school in which we had young teachers who had done sit-ins and the moratorium and all that stuff in college and then introduced it into the high school. So it was an incredible situation. I can remember the first dances I had to chaperone. When I entered, it was soft surfer music; and this was hard, acid rock and it hurt my bones.

And yet I was living in the motherhouse, so it was two completely incompatible worlds. There were funny rules. We weren't supposed to stay overnight with the girls or do late-night things with the girls. But the married women [on the faculty] were supposed to do that. [We said], "This is ridiculous; it's not right for us to ask our lay colleagues to do things we're not willing to do." Those were the years we began to change, so that none of the arbitrary regulations impeded the actual ministry we were doing with people. So that was going on at the high school. In the meantime we didn't have keys to get into our own house. We'd be up at school until ten or eleven o'clock at night, depending on what the school activities were, and then find that we'd been locked out of the house because, you know, nuns are supposed to be in by a certain time. We'd be throwing rocks at the windows, trying to figure out who we could get up to let us in. And it got so intolerable.

What happened was, there was a marvelous group of women who created a subcommunity among the people in the high school; so those of us who were newest on the faculty were welcomed into an already functioning underground community. There were 70 professed Sisters in the house, and we were a group of 25. So there was a sense of belonging and of caring for one another within this kind of impersonal house.

[After four years] I was changed to our high school in San Francisco, which was a very difficult place. There were a lot of tensions in the house. I am the last generation that had a long enough taste of everything old to understand everybody older than me in the community. Those who entered two years after me, because the Council had affected us so dramatically so quickly, never had an understanding of the rest of the community in terms of what their formative experiences were. So at the ripe old age of 27, I was told I was middle-aged and was sent with other people around my age to bridge the generational differences in the house. It was a terrible time for me. It was awful. Every year several Sisters moved out of the house or left the community.

I taught there three years and then was moved back down to Burlingame. In the mid-1970s, the very first programs in spirituality became available, and I discovered that I could study my passion. So I started a master's degree program at the University of San Francisco, which began with a 30-day Ignatian retreat. What was more significant for me than the prayer experience, which was profound, was the reawakening of my intellectual life. I came alive intellectually.

I have received some really nice mentoring in my community. I was still teaching high school in Burlingame when a Sister who had taught me in college and was on the general council told me about a summer program [in spirituality]. I said, "I'd really like to do this, but it isn't academic enough. What I really want to do is a year at the Jesuit School of Theology at Berkeley, in a renewal program called the Institute for Spirituality and Worship." But nobody was let out for a sabbatical; sabbaticals didn't even exist. So she, wise woman that she was, said, "Oh, Janet, if you write all that up, they won't say yes to you. So just apply for the summer program and after you've done that partway through, apply for this other." And it went through. Now, is that not help? Someone is saying, This is how the system works and, yes, I think you should do it, but try it this way.

So I got my year in Berkeley. I was in Berkeley one week—classes had not even started— when I knew that I should be doing a doctorate. It had to do with being in an academic environment in which I fit for the first time in my life, where there were more people who were like me than different from me. I had assumed—as a Sister, as a woman religious—that these two realities were incompatible. And when I was in the theological school, three-quarters of the people there were—guess what?—religious, men and women.

Classes hadn't even started yet. It was so clear; it was absolutely so clear. I can still remember Columbus Day. I go down to Burlingame, thinking, "I'd better tell the president of our community that I need to do doctoral studies. It's not fair to her for her to be surprised in the spring, that I don't want to go back to high school." Well, I was quite unprepared for her inability to understand and appreciate what this was about. She was completely nonreceptive. So that set off probably the worst crisis in my entire religious life, because I knew inside myself that I was never ever going to deny who I was again. I had already done that once. I knew I was still called to religious life, but it was really questionable whether I could continue in the community I was in. And I had some good friends in Berkeley who would say to me, "Well, if you ever find you need to leave your community, we would love to have you." At the same time, I knew no [community] was going to want a transfer who was demanding higher education.

I had broken all the "rules" about self-initiation. At that point there was no process for requesting full-time doctoral studies. You were supposed to wait to be asked. I was being uppity; I was wanting too much. While I was in such pain over the conflict with the community, I had another mentor—another Jesuit mentor, who became a colleague and a friend—who said to me at that point, "You would perhaps be happier if you became a feminist." Now again, this is the great irony. My feminist consciousness was mediated by Jesuit spiritual directors and teachers. By the time I got to the Graduate Theological Union [at Berkeley] it already espoused a complete feminist agenda. Jesuits in theology had written their observations on the 1976 Vatican declaration on why women couldn't be ordained, criticizing the arguments. They were absolute leaders in supporting women, women's ordination. So I was imbibing a Christian feminism while I was there.

So this priest friend, mentor, said to me, "I think you should read widely in feminism. You are extremely articulate about your experience. You think it's just your experience, but it's every woman's experience." And he said, "I think you would feel less isolated if you could recognize what part of your experience is primarily because you're a woman, and not because you're Janet. And you could do a great service for other people by articulating in those broader terms your experience as a woman." Well, that really gave me a clue. That's when I became a feminist.

See, I had not identified with feminism, because I saw an aggressive, harsh, strident side of the feminist movement. And in my family the gender stuff was very, very subtle. I had a brother and I was allowed, or effectively able, to do anything he could do. So there was a sense we were not unequal. My worst experiences [of discrimination] happened in the Church, beginning when I couldn't become an altar server. I had really wanted to be a priest, not a Sister, at age seven. And that was when I found out I'd never be an altar server or a priest. The summer I made final vows, '71, a priest who was in residence at the motherhouse at that point, who taught in the local seminary, asked me if I had ever wanted to be a priest. At that point he thought women were going to be ordained in 10 years, so he was already cultivating the call to ordained ministry. And that was very foremost in my mind when I went to study. Even when I was presenting my reasons to my president—why I should do these studies—I said to her, "We need to have our own theological competence. We need not to be dependent on male theologians for interpreting our lives for us." And I said, "I think I'm called to be of service to the Church in this way." And she said, "But nobody's asking you to do that in the community." I said, "No one's asked me to do anything but sew and arrange flowers. No one's asked me to use my best gift in this community. They've been using my auxiliaries." What she was trying to say to me was, somehow I didn't quite fit. The implication was, there was something wrong with me. And I said to her, "I think I would have better relationships with women in this community if there was a place for my intellectual life to live. It wouldn't insert itself in the chitchat, which is what annoys people."

[After I finished the year at Berkeley] I was assigned to a high school in San Diego, which is about as far away from the headquarters as I could be—which was fine—and asked to chair a religion department, and that was fine, too, because I could at least work with the kids. I had not been assigned to study. And there was no indication that I was going to be assigned to study in the near future.

So I went to San Diego. I decided I was not going to get depressed or sick, so I was living a very healthy lifestyle. I ran my first 10K race. I consciously decided not to get depressed because of the frustration and consciously decided not to take it out on the people I was living with or the kids I was teaching. In the fall of that first year, I was still pressuring my leadership [about doctoral studies]. I finally said to the president, "How do I get in line? Where's the line?" Well, it was very ironic, because I was elected to the secondary education advisory board, and the business of the first meeting was two other women who were requesting doctoral studies in theology. I was furious. One of them was five years younger than I was and had not made final vows. The other was two years older than I was, and she was given permission to start her studies because she didn't fit in high school. They wouldn't let me out because I did a good job. So I was very angry and I said, "You're punishing me." Well, that made them very nervous. As they said, it was very confusing to feel my feelings.

The great irony—and this was part of what galvanized my feminism—was that in November I was told [by the community] I was so essential to the school that I couldn't leave. In April the superintendent of schools tried to fire me and replace me with a priest. So I then called back the people [in my community] who voted against me and I said, "You won't believe this, but they don't think I'm necessary." So I then elicited the same women in a fight for women, and they all rallied around me to fight for this job.

The charge against me was that I could not work with priests. Well, the principal knew it was garbage. He said, "You've had 15 [of them] in here. As far as I can tell, the only priest you can't work with is the [associate pastor] across the street." He's the one who went to the superintendent. It took about six weeks before the decision was reversed. But the principal—his contract was withheld for two months because he supported me—was very good to me. It was just awful. It was very disillusioning, because the superintendent of schools did not care what happened to the kids; he did not care what was best for the school. He only cared about his own career. And I had never met anybody in the Church like that before. For me it was the first time dealing with somebody who was vocationally bankrupt. So anyway, it ended up that I kept my job. I had three priests who reported to me for the ministry programs for the last year I was there, and we had a really good year.

[In the meantime it had been decided that I would be approved for doctoral studies—after a two-year delay.] So the pressure was reduced when I knew I would be going. Now the amazing thing is that somehow all that has healed in the community. Really, once I started my doctoral studies, all those tensions disappeared.

I went for the doctoral degree in Christian spirituality to the Graduate Theological Union in Berkeley in 1980. And I was there six years. While I was there full time, the community was very generous. Once they gave us something, they gave it to us. So I had no financial obligations the first three years. I got all my course work in. Then after I finished my comprehensives in '83 I started working in the permanent diaconate formation program for the Diocese of Oakland and doing a lot of freelance spiritual direction, retreat work, and then wrote my dissertation on spiritual direction. Presently I'm associate professor of spirituality and spiritual direction, in the Graduate School of Religion and Religious Education at Fordham University.

Part of what I was asked to do when I came was to develop the program in such a way that it included specific training in spiritual direction. Basically, spiritual direction is a one-to-one pastoral relationship in which the spiritual director is helping the person coming for direction pay attention and respond to how God is acting in their life. What happens for the directee—and this is the major thesis of the book I wrote [*Uncovering Stories of Faith*]—is the creation of an oral identity. The identity that's being formed is the Christian identity of the self, and that's an identity that's not allowed in public discourse in our culture.

For me, people who come for spiritual direction are people who are conscious of God's presence moving in their lives. So it's people who have undergone a spiritual awakening and who have a desire to respond in some ongoing way.

At this point I have all women, which was never the case before I came to this part of the country. And I have mostly feminist women, and at least half of those are academic women, because they're the ones who have the hardest time finding someone who will respect both their intellectual lives and their feminism. I have also had some gay men, because gay men and lesbians have a harder time here. The religious culture is so repressive here [on the east coast]. If you don't quite fit standard vanilla, it can be harder to find people who are going to treat you well.

Rosemary Ruether said something at a public lecture in San Diego that stayed with me. She talked about her own knowledge of the history of the tradition, saying that leaving the Church never changes it. It creates a new group, but it never causes change in the group that was left. I understood that to be [a challenge]; I feel a real call to change this Church. What I do in the ministry of spiritual direction and in teaching is freeing people to respect the movement of the Spirit and to be faithful to their conscience. I think I'm doing a lot of "subversive" damage, creating pockets where renewal can happen. So I can stay [in the Church] because I do experience that real clear efficacy. I have a very meaningful ministry. I'm helping people stay in the Church.

I'm now 30 years in religious life. When I started to celebrate my own jubilee, I started trying to articulate what the life was about, because we're living in this very strange paradox. I look at people in my community, and for the most part we're vibrant, we're alive, we love what we're doing. Our relationships with one another are deep and loving and compassionate, nonjudgmental. So that's incredibly exciting. But what I'm beginning to understand is that the Church—and by that I mean most laypeople and the clergy—only identify religious life with the work we did in the Church, not as a lifestyle of total dedication to God. There's something about the very core of religious life that seems to be invisible. Anything we do, any layperson can do. So we can't be defined by the ministry. And here in the east there's still a lot of anger at religious, for oppressions of one kind or another. In the west, that's pretty much gone now. But I find absolutely no social support among clergy or laity for religious life at this point.

My understanding of history tells me that you get a thrust forward and a thrust back and a thrust forward. Until more of the Church is going in one direction, we're not going to get anywhere. Women who are in religious life right now, even those who are living it in the most faithful way they can imagine, are being conspired against by the disharmonies in the Church and the huge paradigm change that's going on the culture as well.

I think my own religious life will always be transitional. I'm not at all sure I'll see the new form. When one has to live a life that may not live on in the next generation, the validation all has to come from inside. It's not self-validating by virtue of public acceptance or social support. Each of us has to have the capacity to live our vocation with such confidence and spiritual rooting that we know, "This is what I am called to do, and this is what grace has been given to me." That's very hard.

What I found when I came to celebrate my jubilee was deep—profound—happiness, and I couldn't account for it. You know, I shouldn't be able to account for it, if religious life is a dying institution. I think religious life is supposed to be an icon, a window onto the sacred; for some people a relationship with God is so compelling that it requires a total focus. And that is healthy for the Church because it says something about God. It says something about what we're all called to do, even if we're not all going to do it in the same way. (November 1993)

Sister Janet continued teaching at Fordham University, earning tenure, becoming a full professor, creating a model program of spiritual direction in an academic setting, and mentoring generations of spiritual directors. While she has lectured and given workshops all over the world, she has responded to the particular needs of women religious in Asia, speaking to them about contemplation and spiritual direction in a structured religious life where there is no time for contemplation. In early 2010, she moved to New Haven, Connecticut, to join the faculty of the Yale Divinity School where she is now Professor of the Practice of Spirituality and Ministerial Leadership.

[Since our last conversation] the Sisters of Mercy have been on a wonderful journey. We have had profound conversations with one another and we've gone more deeply into the heart of our charism. We had already responded to social justice. We moved into an embrace of the new cosmology, a recognition brought to us by our Sisters in the Third World that the earth itself is among the poor. And we have embraced our own internationality. Our efforts on behalf of women have intensified. For whatever our experience of Church is, there is also a very deep love for the Church, for its possibilities and what it stands for. We have not only a love for the Church but a commitment to the Gospel message. We have not been living an unreflective life. We have been trying to respond to the needs [we see in the world] and then reflecting on them. That is so opposite to the way the Vatican is moving toward us.

This is a very rich and deep time for me. I grew into a kind of fullness in ministry that could really only be done in the academic life. I find the students are hungry for conversation about God life in the classroom. My courses are meant to be personally transformative but also equip the students to be ministerial people who can address the spirituality needs and desires of their congregations.

SISTER ANNETTE COVATTA

Women's liturgies are one of the most painful and divisive issues facing women religious. Many of the Sisters had strong opinions—pro and con—on the subject, but there was also a marked reluctance to share, in print, their personal experiences. Given their honesty and openness in other areas, this subject, so closely allied to the ordination of women, may be the last taboo.

Sister Annette Covatta, 64, was one of the few who spoke freely about partic-
ipating in such liturgies. She described the dramatic changes in her spiritual life
from the time she was a novice to her current work as founder and director of
Fulcrum, a ministry devoted to holistic spirituality. She now travels from Georgia
to Montreal conducting retreats and workshops for women. A member of the
Sisters of the Holy Names of Jesus and Mary, she lives alone in a small rented
house on a winding country road in upstate New York. Flowers bloomed just
outside her front door. A grand piano dominated the living room, testimony to
Sister Annette's past as an accomplished pianist.

I'm a funny person. On the one hand, I'm a wild woman with lots of creativity
and open to change and living boldly and wanting the fullness of life. Early on
in the novitiate, I was so struck by what Jesus said; "I've come that you may have
life and have it to the full." I could see this cornucopia overflowing with life.
And in those days it was pretty much the romantic, pleasant side of everything.
I since see that being alive is also struggling with pain, because it's part of the
human condition.

The other side of me is a very controlled person. I have "to do" lists, and I meet
my deadlines, and I'm always punctual. That part of me really got nurtured in the
novitiate. Everything was very prescribed, and I loved that. I liked the predictability
from one thing to the other. And I was totally caught up in the spirituality.

I accepted it all with enthusiasm, but every once in a while something
scratched at me. We had no freedom—that scratched at me. But then I said,
"Well, that's what the vow of obedience is." You see, the spirituality of that time
was perfectionism: You achieve holiness through being perfect. Being perfect is
a hard road, and so the more you suffer, the better chance you have to be perfect.
When you have a choice, choose the hardest way, because there's more merit in
that and you'll be closer to God. When I had a hard time as a human being and
as this person that had so much life in her, I said, "That's what I'm giving up for
this way of life."

What I believe now is that the way I live is intrinsic to what I do. That was not
an early belief of mine. We are an active community, and therefore the life of service or ministry was where you really got your sense of worth. I was measuring
myself on how hard I was working on the ministry. And, of course, the ministry in
those days was teaching in the schools. You were what you did. At least that's how
it felt. It was also very important to be a good nun. Early on, the spiritual life as
presented by the Church was very important for me. If life was too joyful, I held it
suspect. There was a lot of guilt. If I ever thought to say, "Life is a feast," well, I'd
be ridden with guilt. Life has to be hard. Jesus died on the cross, you know.

I let go of that baggage with the second Vatican Council. I believe that God is
everywhere. He's in that dirt where I put my tulip bulbs this morning. And God
is very much alive in you and in me. I'm not saying I'm God, but I do believe
that the divine passion, the divine spark, the divine spirit flows through every

pore of my being. If I lost my connection with the Holy Spirit within, I'd be terrified. Because it's the source of my life. Outside of that, I have close friends and I have a ministry of service and I have a religious community; but all of it doesn't make any sense without the intimacy with God.

The Eastern mode of prayer, which is the type of meditation that I practice now, is a centering meditation. In the Christian centering meditation, you gaze on the Lord and you listen and you're there in the presence of Jesus. I pray this way at times. And there are times when I'm simply in the presence of the flow, in the presence of the light. I try to listen to the "still small voice within," as the Quakers put it. I go inside my heart, inside my body. When I'm quiet enough, especially in my head, I experience myself as a vast ocean. I feel at one with the universe. It's a cosmic feeling, and at times I feel a love without boundaries.

What's also important to me now are women's liturgies. One of the women in our community left for Haiti this week, and we sent her off in the light of the candle, nurturing and supporting her with our faith and love. We used the powerful Christian symbols of bread and wine. These symbols were given to all of us, you know. There is a ground swell of feminine spirituality that excites me. I've met a remarkable woman up here. She's a healer and minister. When she brings women together, we use symbols of Native Americans, Africans, ecological imageries, and all kinds of different things. Are they Catholic? Are they Christian? I don't know. I just know that they touch the depth of me.

I am at this time in my journey more integrated than I've ever been. I feel that all of the gifts I was born with and my purpose of life is now in full flow with the way I'm living and the work I am doing. The charism of our founder is education in the faith, and that gets translated for me into working with women who have low self-esteem and very little sense of personal power. I know how to work with these women. When people touch into this power within, they say to me, "I have found God." And they have. The folks who take my workshops and retreats come from all different backgrounds: Christians, Buddhists, Orthodox Jews, atheists. They're all human beings, and they all have a soul.

It's a time that's very rich for me, very rewarding in all its dimensions. My community life and my life as a nun are part of it all, but in a very nontraditional way. I think religious life is unfolding that way. We're trying to find new forms. I'd like to be part of that effort to explore the new forms that religious life will take, but we're living with so many questions. So I just keep going and do what I do and participate in the community as I can.

The future? I'll be 65 next year. I want to continue teaching workshops and giving retreats. Currently, I am being challenged by God, by my inner self, to integrate myself more into the "we" of the global community. There's something there that's beginning to challenge me, and I'm not quite sure how it will configure. But I pay attention to these things that begin to well up. While I'm very impulsive, in my spiritual life I'm patient and I listen a lot. I want to surrender totally to the action of love. *Surrender* is a strong word. But I know that's ultimately what the spiritual life is about. When I'm alive in that, people say "My God, you're radiant." And I know it's not me. I think life is much simpler than we make it. It's filled with struggle and problems and ambiguities. But all of it is part of our journey toward the full awakening, and the full awakening is the bliss of being touched by the holy. So it is simple, if we can just see that it's all there. (September 1992)

Sister Annette continued on her spiritual journey, integrating Eastern and Western modes of prayer, using scripture, meditation, and journaling. She retired to live in Colorado.

7

IN THE CLOISTER

SISTER VILMA SEELAUS

Sister Vilma Seelaus, a Carmelite nun from Barrington, Rhode Island, has lived on the edge of the radical changes that have come to many cloistered monasteries throughout the country. She has written often on the subject.

She is one of seven cloistered women whom I interviewed in four different monasteries. (See also Sister Florence Vales, Chapter 9.) All the women honored the spirit of enclosure. I was genuinely welcomed at each monastery, although I was not allowed beyond a reception room and the chapel. The women were well-informed and articulate on a range of subjects. Sister Vilma, 70, turned out to be a formidable conversationalist, ranging from theology to organic gardening to psychology to physics to music.

I should really say that my earliest experience of God was connected with my mother taking me to church when I was maybe four years old. It's one of these very vivid memories that has deeply affected my life. It was a magnificent romanesque structure that had been written up in an architectural magazine. I was too small even to see the altar; I remember I had to stand on the pew. I think now about the rose window and the sun streaming through. It was impressive for a child, but it was more than that—something happened inside me. What happened was [that I felt] an abiding sense of God's presence, which has colored the whole of my life.

I continued to do other things. I played with my brothers. I got into rather small mischief by today's standards. Then I started studying the violin, which also had a very special influence on my life. By the time I reached high school, I played fairly well; and when I graduated, began to play professionally. I had a lot of orchestra experience, but I was invited at one point to become part of a string quartet. When you play quartets, you alone are responsible for your part, but you also must be in total communion with the other people. We started [to play], and all I can say, it was ecstasy. I thought I'd died and gone to heaven. When I got home that night, I had this sense of total fullness, and yet there was a part of me that was still empty.

Shortly after that an older sister [of mine] entered the Carmel in Lafayette, Louisiana. With her entering the Carmel, I began to think and read a little about

Carmelites. At first it was totally frightening. I read all the wrong books! I'm being somewhat facetious—they focused on the difficult things. But all of a sudden it came to me: If my sister can do it, I can do it. So then I started to be less and less involved [in playing the violin] because I wanted to see if I could live without music.

It was the time after World War II, when the monasteries were being filled rather quickly. There was a vocation surge. My sister had applied [to the Carmelite monastery] in Philadelphia, but they were filled. I didn't even write there. I did write to Lafayette, hoping that they wouldn't take me, only because I do not like hot, humid weather. They wrote back and said, "It would be better not to have two sisters in such a small community." But they said, "Newport is also a small community, and they need vocations. We will write and recommend you." They had met my parents, and at that time to come from a good Catholic family was the best recommendation you could get. So, sight unseen, they took me in Newport. Which would never happen today.

I entered in 1946. I was 21. And it's funny. I've never regretted that I didn't go to college. I entered the monastery, and since then I have been studying. I am a natural student. Some years back I was invited into a doctoral program by someone who knew my background. But I said to myself, "What do I need a doctorate for?" My commitment is to a life of prayer, and you don't need a doctorate for a life of prayer.

When I entered [I knew] that's where I would be the rest of my life. I would leave only for occasions that were life-threatening. I found what I was looking for, even though some of it seemed to me strange. There were the traditional kinds of penance. Some of the ways in which we lived could have been more sanitary from my perspective. You didn't take a bath every day; you took a bath once a week. There were other difficult parts, like not getting sufficient sleep. I'm someone who has always needed seven and a half to eight hours' sleep, but I was young and healthy and I managed it.

Silence was something I had to get accustomed to. We would be at recreation, but we couldn't speak until the novice directress got there. And sometimes she was late. We would have to sit there in silence, with our sewing, until she arrived. She would read stories to us; that was part of the tradition. One day, after I had been there about a year and a half, she was reading the life of this pious Trappist lay Brother, and at the end of it she asked a rhetorical question like, "Wouldn't you all like to be lay Sisters?" And I heard the words inside me: "I want *you* to be a lay Sister." Now [the voice] was so true and so strong that I immediately went to the novice directress and told her what had happened.

The lay Sisters at that time were the ones who did more of the manual work. I had entered as what was then called a "choir nun," which meant that we had to know Latin, be able to chant the liturgy—or the Divine Office, as it was called. In many communities the lay Sisters were often people of lesser intelligence who could not handle the Divine Office, who could not handle the so-called responsibilities of the choir nuns. The choir nuns were the ones who were part of the decision-making process of the community, and they were the ones who would be fostered and developed for leadership. The lay Sisters did not have active or passive voice, which meant that in community meetings they could not vote, nor could they be voted for.

I have always felt that [being a lay Sister] was one of the most wonderful things that happened to me, and I'll tell you why. It gave me the opportunity to find my own challenges, and I discovered I'm someone who needs to be challenged. I need to continue to learn. And those years as a lay Sister made that possible in ways it might not have been possible as a choir Sister. I had a certain freedom in the library, and I continued to read scripture rather intensively. We were a small community with lots of sickness, and I studied diet and nutrition. I learned to cook; I learned to bake. I studied organic gardening because I did a lot of the garden work. In a sense, the manual labor was what I needed in order to keep my own psychic balance at that young age. I needed to do more than be sitting in my cell sewing. One of the hard things was no longer to go to the Divine Office, because the lay Sisters didn't pray the Psalms. However, I do have to say that in the community in which I was, there was no sense that the lay Sisters were inferior. We were treated with absolute respect.

My community was always ahead of things. [Even in the 1950s] changes were gradually happening. [Sister Margaret,] the woman who was prioress at the time, was an unusual woman. She was constantly reading good theology books, and she placed great focus on the fact that we were Christians before we were Carmelites. We started to expand our concept of cloister. Traditionally, we couldn't go down to the beach; we had to stay within the enclosed area. [We moved from Newport to Barrington in 1957; the property here adjoins the beach.] One year Sister Margaret wrote to the bishop and said, "I'd like you to give us permission for the nuns to walk down the beach." And he gave it.

When she heard both the Church and the order saying the Sisters need to be better educated, she immediately acted on it, and she began to incorporate the whole community in the decision-making process. She wanted the lay Sisters to become part of the chapter because the Vatican Council was saying that there should be only one class of Sisters in a community.

The Council ended in '65, and the interesting thing was that in '68, at the first chapter in which I had active and passive voice, I was elected prioress. I used to say the only things I knew how to be were cook and prioress. I was never anything else in between.

After I was elected, I never sat in the prioress's seat. In our choir the prioress and the subprioress sat in the back, and then you'd have the choir benches [facing each other] where the Sisters sat and chanted back and forth. I sat with the community. I stopped using the title *mother*, and I asked to be called *Sister*. I remember that about five years earlier I had said at a meeting, "Why do we call the prioress *mother*?" You'd think I had said, "Let's shoot the prioress." People said, "Oh, we've always called the prioress mother." But by the time I changed it, the community was very willing.

I was prioress for a couple of years when in '69 we had a meeting in Woodstock, Maryland, of all the contemplative communities around the country. Prior to that I had had the thought that there ought to be an association of contemplative Sisters in the United States. In the 1950s, Pope Pius XII had written *Sponsa Christi*, an encyclical for contemplatives. It was after World War II, and many of the convents in Europe were starving. And he was saying, "Unite as groups and help each other out." I was still a lay Sister when I read that encyclical, and all of a sudden I had this understanding that contemplative life could have a different expression. Nothing had ever said to me before that it could be different, because that's the way it always was. But I had a vision that it was okay to change. It was important, as a matter of fact.

That meeting in Woodstock ended up founding the Association of Contemplative Sisters. We had our first organizational meeting a year later, and I was elected the founding president. I was still prioress of my community. It was toward the end of my first term, and there was every indication I was going to be reelected; but I knew I couldn't handle another three years, so I resigned [as prioress]. The community was furious at me. They were absolutely furious. They felt they needed me for leadership, but they didn't. Someone else who they might not have expected turned out to be a good leader.

I served two terms as president of the Association of Contemplative Sisters. We found out that all of us [in our separate monasteries] were thinking along the same lines. We all continued to see prayer as our ministry, but we all saw that enclosure needed to change. [*Enclosure* or *cloister* refers to the part of the monastery reserved for members of the community.]

Here [in Barrington] we do keep enclosure. Even though we go out for various things and we meet people in a more natural way, there is a part of the monastery that is still private. You may come in only by invitation. And so if you take away the grilles and the bars and the "never going out" concept, there's a sense in which what *cloister* traditionally means is still here. Most of my life is spent here in the monastery, even though I get a lot of invitations to speak. For most of them I say no, unless it appears that the contemplative dimension to the Church's life should have some visibility.

People who enter Carmel have a need for solitude and space. It's certainly been part of my own need. If I do not have the time for prayer, nothing comes out right. Relationships degenerate. I can't write. I need to be in my own hermit space.

The hermit part of Carmel is probably more part of my life now than it was before [we made some changes]. We have weekly hermit days. On a hermit day, the only thing we come together for as a community is for Eucharist. We have no cooked meal. If you're hungry, you're on your own. We have two hermitages within the cloister, and any member of the community can use them. We also have individual prayer rooms that look down over the sanctuary. We try to make the hermit day one in which the focus is on solitude and prayer. For me it's often a day when I have blocks of time for writing.

My life story is in my writings. Everything I write about is connected with prayer, with living in the presence of God, and then trying to help other people to do that. One of the most popular articles I've ever written was "Meditation on the Compost Heap." I was an organic gardener and we had—we still have—a compost heap where we'd take all the garbage and manure and leaves. You throw them on this pile, and you turn them over. They may get a little smelly at a certain point, but when the banana peels and such get really quite black, a bacteria within the compost starts to break it down, and in the end you have the best organic fertilizer for your garden. And that became a symbol for me of my own life. I began to see how the dark times were part of life. In the article, I tried to show how the breakdown periods are really the dark nighttimes when God is most present, and that if we can be open to them, like the compost heap, new life will emerge.

I am by nature a perfectionist, and I was always looking for life to be perfect. I had to learn how I could live through the dark and messy times. I learned to live with people who were different. And I learned that things are not going to be perfect. Certainly as prioress initially I wanted to please everybody; I wanted to send everybody to bed feeling happy. And you discover you can't do that. People are not going to be perfect; community life is not going to be perfect. There are tensions. People will leave; people will die.

I had a hysterectomy in my early thirties. Thirteen years ago, when I was 56, I woke up one morning and it was like I was having a period. When you have a complete hysterectomy, you don't have periods, so I was petrified. I was giving a talk down in Connecticut, and I didn't see how I could go, but I did. I came back, and I called my doctor and he checked me. He couldn't find anything, but of course by then I'd stopped bleeding. So for about a year and a half every time I would have bleeding or a vaginal discharge, he could never find anything. Finally, whatever was there, he found it. He did a biopsy, and I was in the hospital within a couple of days. They ran all kinds of tests. It was vaginal cancer, but they weren't sure how far it had spread. It could have been rather invasive. I had to make the choice between radiation or surgery.

I have a very dear friend who is a psychiatrist; his wife is a psychologist. He called me every single day. He would say, "Ask the doctor this." He helped me to take charge of my life, so that I didn't have to be a helpless victim. I made the decision to have the radical surgery, which I'm very glad I did. I healed well. The doctors were amazed. I've since found out that the score on vaginal cancer is not swift, and most people die. I didn't know that at the time.

That brings us close to the present. [About five years ago] I was elected prioress again. It was the fourth or fifth time I've been prioress. I'm not sure. We had been through three years of construction because the roof was deflecting and we were living in a third of the monastery. Two members of the community died within those three years; one was 54, one was 91. And I had had it. When I was reelected about two years ago, I just sat there and cried. I had moved all my writing stuff to an office upstairs. My books were up there; all my plants were blooming up there; I was really settled. It took me several months to accept the election. I guess by personality I am a harmonizer. It is very difficult for me to confront people, to deal with issues. I'd rather pretend they don't exist. But when you have community life and you have differences, you have to deal with them.

My deepest pain at the moment is holding together our worship. My community is very conscious of women's issues in the Church and in society. We've been sensitized to inclusive language [in liturgy]. Contemplative communities should be places where women can find worship, not in feminist liturgies that would be separate from the life of the Church, but where Church worship is something they can be comfortable with.

But in our community we have people at different places. We have people for whom the official prayer of the Church is very important. They may recognize the value of inclusive language, but for them the approval of the Church for whom they've given their lives is important. On the other hand, we have at least one person who is almost militant that the face of God is feminine. She finds it very painful to hear God as Father, or God as King, or God as Lord. I happen to be someone who is comfortable with any God language. So I would say how we speak about God is the immediate struggle. And it's going on in many communities.

Contemplative life will have a struggle, I think, almost comparable to the time right after Vatican II. At that time we knew things had to change. We were intent on the changes, but certainly the heart of the tradition was kept through the changes. Now there's a whole different struggle, and it has more to do with theology, with the heart of contemplative life—how we envision God. Prayer has never been questioned. The language of our prayer and our worship is a critical issue because it touches what is deepest within all of us, our religious experience. And God does not speak to everybody in the same way.

I think also the whole concept of cloister will continue to be a struggle. How far is it revisioned? I believe the tradition of Carmel will last. I really do. About eight years ago now, a group of Carmelites formed the Carmelite Forum, and I was part of that. What we are trying to do is to keep the heart of the tradition alive, but bring it into a contemporary setting. The question I ask myself is, "Can Carmel only exist in sixteenth-century Spain?" I was dressing like a woman of sixteenth-century Spain. And I was living in many ways like a woman of sixteenth-century Spain. And that's what has been disseminated throughout the world as Carmel. I don't believe it, but we have to be careful in changing that we keep the tradition.

I'm somewhat respected when I speak about the future of contemplative religious life. So I will continue to do all the things I need to do: to write, to speak about the tradition, to pray about it. But the other side of that is that this is God's ballpark, not mine. When I get overintense, then I know that my ego is in there. And I need to keep remembering that. Because in the end the tradition belongs to God, to Teresa of Avila, to John of the Cross, the people that energized it. So I need to be a little more relaxed about all of this. (January 1995)

Sister Vilma is 85 now. She has continued her writing and until two years ago traveled extensively to speak about Carmelite spirituality. One of her books, Distractions in Prayer: Blessing or Curse? St. Teresa of Avila's Teaching in the Interior Castle, *is being used as a textbook for teaching spiritual guidance and has been translated into Korean. She is at work on a new book to be published in 2011. The future, she says, is in every passing moment.*

8

ON THE CUTTING EDGE

SISTER MARGARET TRAXLER

Over the years Sister Margaret Traxler, a School Sister of Notre Dame, has battled government and church officials as well as members of her own order for a variety of causes in which she believes. Most frequently, those have been women's causes.

The interview took place in her office in a South Chicago neighborhood. The office was once the front parlor of a rectory; upstairs is the convent where she lives with three other Sisters. Across the street is Maria Shelter, a residence for homeless women recently released from prison, which Sister Margaret founded and still runs.

Sister Margaret, 69, is an imposing woman—strong, square face; blue eyes; short gray hair; a firm handshake. Her smile was slow to surface, but when it did, it transformed her face. Most remarkable was the range of her voice—soft and caressing when she talked about her family or the women and children in Maria Shelter, thundering and severe when she talked about what she sees as pervasive arrogance among the Catholic clergy and hierarchy.

My father and mother were extraordinary people. Here they were living in a small town, and they were all things to all people. Utter charity toward them. When I was young, it was just at the end of the Depression, and no matter what people did in life, they felt it. We felt it naturally in our small town. I saw how other children in school had shoes that had holes in them. I was only seven or eight years old, and I saw some of my friends with their parents lining up behind the trucks that came to town with what they called "government commodities." Maybe it was grapefruit; maybe it was a case of apricots. That made an impression on me. It's really interesting how one considers afterwards what were apparently minor details in a childhood.

My father and mother—a simple country doctor and a nurse—would deliver a baby at night, and they'd come in and say, "We've got to find a blanket." They would go through our things and get a blanket and then take it back. I would be eating my breakfast. Those things impressed me, even though I don't suppose I knew what to do about it at the time. But my parents did.

In 1963 Sister Margaret Traxler wears the full habit of the School Sisters of Notre Dame, the same habit she would wear during civil rights marches in Selma, Alabama, in 1965. But she was already absorbing a feminist identity, which would come into public view by the end of the decade.

They were utter kindness, those people. I never heard my father put down the phone but what he would say, "I'll be right out." He wouldn't put down the phone and say, "Darn! They haven't paid their bills for years." No! He said, "I'll be right out."

Now, there were no Jews in our town. And I remember my father used to say, "As a country treats its Jews, so God will treat that country." I've thought of that even now. I think that's really true. Look at history. I'm sure he didn't grow up with Jews. He grew up on a farm. It was just the goodness of his heart. There was a young tradesman and his family who came to our little town and opened what in those days the kids called a Jew store. It was a clothing store, filled with fresh leather goods and so forth. I said to my mother, "I want to go down to the Jew store." And she said, "Never call it that. Never call it that. We don't call Dempsey's an Irish store." And I learned from that. Another time there was a man in our town who had an artificial arm up to his elbow. I said, "Mama, I saw a man and he was walking sideways and he had a black glove, and the kids said it was a wooden arm." My mother, unlike her, abruptly said, "His name is Bill Murray. He gave his arm in the service of his country, and I don't want to hear anything about walking sideways."

So I got what I would call an embracing attitude from my parents. My baby sister, Kitty Jo, [recently told the rest of us that] when she was preschool, the only one at home, my mother used to take a basket of sheets and towels and food, and they'd drive down behind the shoe shop, and mother used to climb up those outside stairs to take care of Bill Murray when he was dying. And then she would come down again, and she'd have this basket full of the used sheets. Kitty Jo said, "You know, Daddy once said to mother, 'Mother, I don't know who's taking care of Bill Murray. His sheets are changed, his face is shaved, and the dishes are done.' And mother said, 'Mmmm-hmmm.'" Kitty Jo said, "I've remembered that all these years. It was mother who was doing that charity." And she never told even her own husband, who was so good and who would have understood.

When I finished high school, it was 1941. The opportunities for a girl in 1941 were not what they are now. One wouldn't think, I'll be a doctor or a lawyer or an engineer. We didn't think in those terms, although I remember my father would say, "Don't cut yourself short. Do anything you want." [He had] five daughters, and he never made us feel that he wanted a son or that somehow we were half his expectations. You grow toward the end of your teens, you have to make choices, and so I made a choice. I went to high school with the School Sisters [of Notre Dame] and I admired them. And so I naturally entered them. My parents said, "Try it, but always feel that you can come home." For 30, 40 years, my mother always said, "You can come home, remember."

I haven't been disappointed. You see, one can be disappointed if you make up your mind to be. But I made up my mind, no, I will not be. Over here [in Maria Shelter] we have some women who have what the staff calls an "attitude." That means everything's wrong: the food is wrong, the bed is wrong, everything's wrong. It's an "attitude." I figured early I was going to have an "attitude" that was positive, and I've kept it even today.

I don't care what kind of theology people have, if they're friends and if they're loving, then you have enough nurture. [My formation years were] filled with friends. I would say that in my earliest years, though, our formation didn't have theologians. We had a very good priest. His theology was Council of Trent; that means about seventeenth century, but he was loving and good, and I find no flaw in him.

My early teaching days were days of severance. It was hard being way out in rather obscure rural areas. We were far from the mainstream, where even books were scarce. As I look back, I think [those early years] were very difficult. I had to steel myself, to tell myself that I could abide. I could abide for change, change in our basic life as a School Sister of Notre Dame. I knew it had to change. I knew that the habit had to change. I knew that the regimen [had to change]. We made retreats together, a couple of hundred Sisters with one man up there talking to us. To me it was profane and obscene that a man could tell us how a woman should respond to her three vows, how a woman should respond to community. He wasn't a woman, and he didn't have our vows and our rule.

That was in the 1950s. But we always had a little underground of friends who believed in the same things. When I came down here to the National Catholic

Conference for Interracial Justice [NCCIJ] in '64, I began to meet people from all over the country. They didn't all believe as I did, but I found enough who shared my thoughts.

[At NCCIJ we tried to] bring about an understanding of the importance of intergroup relations. What it really was, although we didn't say it this way, was to teach about racism. We had a program, which we called Choice. More than 400 nuns who had been educated and received Ph.D.'s [as a result of] the Sister Formation Movement would go down and teach for a year in [one of the 112] black colleges on a semivolunteer basis, so that the black teachers whose places they were taking could be freed to finish their Ph.D.'s. And then we had about five nuns with Ph.D.'s—economists, sociologists, theologians—teach the theology of race and the history of blacks. These teams gave over 112 workshops all over the country.

I went to Selma twice, as I recall. [The first time] was in March of '64. It was cold, and I can remember a Maryknoll priest asked if he could borrow my coat because he was cold. I remember giving it to him because I had a habit on. Oh, there were a lot of times before the march when we used to go out from the Baptist church, and we would sing the songs. Because we were in habits, they would line [us up in front], and the state troopers were about six feet away. Well, they put us there, and I didn't mind at all. I wasn't afraid. When I think of it, I wasn't afraid of anything. The summer of '64 was a civil rights summer that was thrilling, exciting. A lot of people who come in and out [of Maria Shelter] tell me they're from Mississippi, and I always say, "Where in Mississippi?" The very names [of those towns] are precious to me.

One day when I was the executive director of NCCIJ, the late Marc Tannenbaum, a rabbi, came to my office with two other local rabbis. Now, this was '71, and he said, "Would you ever think of joining with us in what would be an interreligious task force on Soviet Jews?" They knew Jews in Russia were suffering. That was an age-old problem. But that was the first time in history that they got the idea religions should join together and say, "Enough already!" He later told me that I was the only head of a Catholic organization with the name "Catholic" in it who they thought would join them. I asked our board, and they said, "Sure. We know what it means to be oppressed and discriminated against." That's why we did it. That's what triggered it, but even before he asked, my heart was in it.

There are certain things that hurt. About 1973, three elderly Sisters from my motherhouse asked me what in the world I thought was consistent with our rule in what I was doing with regard to Christians and Jews. Such ignorance on the part of elderly, experienced Sisters! They were serious. My mother was with me at that time. We were around a picnic table up at our motherhouse, and my mother gave the most learned treatise on why the Jews are important to Catholics today. I didn't say a word. But later I did say, "Mama, you were great! You were just great!"

Sister Margaret Traxler speaks in Chicago at one of the nationwide "Women Strike" demonstrations held on August 26, 1970, the fiftieth anniversary of the ratification of the nineteenth amendment that gave women the right to vote. Sister Margaret said: "I personally will do anything which will further the cause of women."

I suppose I'd have to say [my feminism began] in '63 with Betty Friedan. But long before that, in my files—I didn't call it feminism, but I had files on "women in society," "women and the Church," "education of women," and so forth. Way back into the 1940s. In 1969, I and some others started the National Coalition of American Nuns. I felt it was time for women to speak up and defend themselves. We had bishops telling nuns what time they could get up, what time they had to get to bed. No man should run our lives! That's the mistake of churchmen. They begin to think as the feudal men used to think of us, that we were their property. [The Coalition was] the first to tell men, priests, to leave their hands off the renewal in Sisters' orders. Out in California the IHM Sisters were being oppressed by Cardinal McIntyre, an arrogant, irascible man. We were the first ones who said to Cardinal McIntyre: "Leave those IHM Sisters alone." And, you know, it was just like electric. So many Sisters said, "We believe you! We believe you!" And they joined the National Coalition. In 1970, we were the first group to call for the ordination of women. Now, something like 64 percent of the laity believe in the ordination of women. Oh, it's got to change! We've got to have ordination of women so that we can get out and reach the people.

Back then I just about got killed for it. My provincial called me and said, "We were worried about you. That you would say a thing like that." And I said, "Well, don't you agree?" "I certainly do not!" See, they were so inured in their obedience to the men. And actually what it is is they were afraid of the men.

You have to understand—the first 25 years of my life as a Notre Dame, I was not wholeheartedly supported as a School Sister of Notre Dame by other Notre Dames. I lived with this metaphor. I was of them, but not of them. At first it was very painful. Terribly so—1969, those were the early days in my aloneness. After that I crossed a threshold, a threshold where I always thought, What will people think? What will the Sisters say? After that it didn't matter. It was part of life, you know, the yin and the yang.

I can see now how God drew good out of it. But those days were hard. All those nights—before I went to bed, I'd visit the Blessed Sacrament, and I used to say, "God has not called me to abandon me." I said that all the time. Because I did feel abandoned. But, see, in my life as it developed, God did not call me to abandon me. He called me to fulfill me and give me the opportunity to fulfill what I wanted to do. And what I wanted to do has, very happily, turned out to be another charism of the School Sisters of Notre Dame. Right now the charism is caring for children and women. And I would say that I am committed, dedicated beyond every breath, to women and children, especially poor women and children. But I was, long before it was identified as one of our charisms. In my heart it was our charism. I imagine to many nuns from my own province, I am a radical. And I'm sorry if they think so. But what they think really doesn't trouble me, because I went over that threshold in '69. My provincial right now is the first provincial in my religious life who trusts me. Can you imagine what it was like as a young nun not to be trusted?

But I didn't need that affirmation. Maybe that's it. I don't know. I was convinced that what I was doing was God's will and that it had merit and that it was within the parameters of my religious vocation.

Jeannine [Gramick] probably has talked to you about the time we signed that ad in *The New York Times*. [In 1984, Catholics for a Free Choice requested signatures for an ad saying that there is a diversity of opinion in the Catholic Church on the issue of abortion and calling for dialogue.] [The reaction from Rome] really did frighten our superiors more than it frightened us. But I must say about our superiors, they held their ground. They didn't support us, but they supported our right not to be dismissed for a statement we really hadn't made. They dug in their heels and said: "We find no cause." Fortunately, we had a very good general superior in Rome, and I think she really carried us through in a way which was least painful to us. I ended up being a good friend of hers. She is a good, good woman. I think that was what made the difference.

We were the only two [School Sisters of Notre Dame], and I said [to Jeannine], "You really want to stay?" And she said, "Yes." I wouldn't have cared had they said you couldn't be a member of the order any longer. Yes, I would have cared, but it wasn't something that was intense in my heart. That's hard to say, but, you see, my friends by that time were nuns from other orders and many other people. A woman whom we had gotten out of prison [told me] her grand-mother had left her a home, and she said, "I will give you the title and deed to the home, and you can live there if you have to leave your order." Now wasn't that something? I said, "Honey, thank you. I don't need a home. But I'll take your friendship and your love."

I was a faithful nun all the while. I have never knowingly been unfaithful. It's interesting. My mother had a few doubts sometimes, and my sisters would support me. My sisters would say, "Mother, she's right. She's right!" And my mother would call her friends and say, "All my daughters said Peggy's right."

All those years, had it not been for my own sisters and my mother, I couldn't have done it. My own natural sisters were the ones, primarily, who supported me. And what's so strange is that their lives were part of the Church culture that I was questioning. One time at a very beautiful Christmas Eve dinner—it was the days of ERA—one of my nephews stood up. "I'm going to give a toast to the Equal Rights Amendment and to Sister Margaret," he said. This is a guy who was very quiet and modest; he's since become a big banker. He looked at his sisters and cousins and so forth and he said, "I don't know how you can live as a woman in our society without fighting the way Margaret fights." Now how do you like that! The most modest of all my nephews. I said, "Well, Larry! Good for you!"

[In 1973 some friends of mine and I] went to the third world, really as kind of a rest. We went to ask women about their perceptions of their own role in their societies. We went to Iraq, to Iran, to Lebanon, to India finally. I learned much. I don't know if the position of women in society changed much since the Middle Ages in those third world countries. A woman in Iran, a marvelous woman, told me, "I'm a slave to my husband." Her 13-year-old son walked through the living room, and she said, "He's already turning against me because I am his mother and he's a man. He allies himself with my husband." And she said, "I'm as important to my husband as his cows out in the pasture." Women in our culture who've said, "I have never suffered discrimination" should understand that they must be committed to the welfare of their Sisters in the world. They just can't stand by and not protest. They must.

I came back in '74. Then we prepared for the Year of Woman [which had been proclaimed for 1975 by the United Nations], and that was when we started the Institute of Women Today. I talked to my friends, Protestant and Catholic and Jewish, and I said, "The first thing we can do for the Year of Woman is give some workshops and tell women of faith that they have much in common with one another, and that they mustn't let the women's movement set off without their dimension of faith and belief." Because in 1974 the women's movement was still frowned on. That first year, 1975, we had 50 very successful workshops over the country. Catholic, Protestant and Jewish women, lawyers, doctors, sociologists, speaking on what contributions they might make as women of faith to the women's movement. Fun!

During that year I met Jane Kennedy, who was in Alderson Federal Prison for protesting the Vietnam War. I brought her the Eucharist, and we read together, and we prayed. She said, "What are you doing now?" So I told her [about the workshops], and she said, "Oh! Bring one here." I said, "Oh, Jane, we couldn't do that." She said, "Why not? I'll talk to the warden, and you talk to the warden." So she did and I did, and we went down there, and it was wonderful. Down in Alderson, there were about 75 Hispanic women from Texas and those Southern states, and they couldn't talk English. One of our lawyers talked Spanish, and those women knelt at her knees. They knelt at her knees and pulled at her hands. Can you imagine?

The Institute of Women Today is founded to empower women—poor women, especially poor women who are incarcerated, and their children. We went to a lot of prisons—federal prisons, state prisons, and then city jails—with our work-shops and our teams of women lawyers, psychologists, and so forth. We used to go down to Westville, where about 200 women from Indiana were held. We always took lawyers there with us. One time this woman just grinned and she said, "I'm going home." I said, "How come?" And she said, "Well, that woman wrote a brief to my judge, and he said I was free." [She was pointing to one of our Institute volunteers, Sheila Murphy, a presiding judge herself and a good friend of mine.] I asked her, "Sheila, what did you do?" She said, "I just wrote a brief and told them something was unconstitutional." Can you imagine it? "I am going home." I'll never forget the thrill, the excitement [of those words].

[The women doing our workshops began to feel] that one of the gravest needs was to have a safe place for women to come to when they were released. And so that's why we started Maria Shelter in 1989. Women in prisons in Illinois—that's in Dwight, Kankakee, and Dixon—know that if they come here, they are our "preferred guests" and we will do anything we can within reason to help them get a new start. We're the only shelter in Illinois where they may upon release go pick up their children and come here to our shelter. They can stay four to six months. We don't let them go until they're ready. We have a staff ratio of one staff member to every four residents. We have a full-time clinical psychologist, a full-time nurse, a full-time caseworker, and a house manager. We hire women from the neighborhood. Four of our staff are former residents. Our house man-ager came in homeless, and her two sons, at 18 or 19, cried when they left their mother here. That was four years ago. We have 14 on our payroll over there, and they're all Afro-American. They're so loving and good and bright. So bright. When I think of what we have lost in the Afro-American community with bright, commonsense women! In 1990 we started Casa Notre Dame, which is the other shelter, a second-stage shelter for women who can stay a couple of years if they want. There are so many women who finish their four to six months here, and we see that all they have in front of them is another shelter. Then they can go to Casa Notre Dame and be somewhat independent.

I have invested my life in the Gospel, and that's Jesus—that isn't necessarily the Church. You see, when we were baptized we received the faith, but faith grows. One can believe in many parts of the Church. That's why you have what they call "cafeteria Catholicism." Oh, I surely am a cafeteria Catholic. I'm not going to believe in the infallibility of the pope—no, none of that. They split theological hairs, and that's precisely what Jesus said not to do.

I keep what I call an aesthetic distance from the official Church. At the present time in these years I have no close friend among the clergy. Some of them I admire, all of them from afar. I do sympathize with the peculiar position they find themselves in now at this place in history. But that's God's will, too, that all of a sudden they're not the favored strata. They've got to get used to it, and it's hard on them.

Now I think the reason all this clerical sexual-abuse suffering has come into the life of the Church is to help the hierarchy and priests get rid of their high-handed arrogance and supercilious superiority. I think that's why God has allowed it, so they'll get over their egotism, their false pride. The bishops call themselves the "magisterium." They named themselves, and then they keep quoting the magisterium. That's ridiculous. And the uniqueness of the male who brags that women can't be ordained because they're not made like a man. Such stupidity!

Now, next October there's going to be a Synod on Religious Life. A million women in this world are nuns. Not one nun will have a vote. Can you imagine? Enough already! And do you know some of the National Coalition of American Nuns are going to picket in St. Peter's Square? We're going to have street theater. We already have a nun that's going to be Pope John Paul.

I believe that divine Providence is going to call the Church into a new life, into a new structure. It might come through great pain, like what the priests are going through now. That humbles them. I hope it humbles them! So that through this mystery of anxiety, which comes with the humiliation, we will come to a new structure, a new sense of humility, an openness. I see it from afar as something that has to be. And miracles do happen! I believe in miracles. You know, the poet Maura Eichner says, "We walk in miracles as children scuff through daisy fields." And I think that's the kind of miracle that I've seen in my life.

I'm a very senior Sister. I'm 69. I'm going to embrace seven-o. I'm not ashamed of it. I've worked every year, every minute of every year. Whatever comes, God has been good to me. I'm looking at this little award up there on the shelf. I don't keep the awards around, but that was one of the last, so it's up there. I was chosen for the Hall of Fame of Chicago because of my contribution to religion. I thought at the time there probably isn't one priest in the archdiocese who would ever have dreamed of choosing me. But you see, Catholic, Protestant, and Jewish women of the city made that choice. God bless them. And I thank them.

I do not regret that I joined the religious life. I think many years were spent in a somewhat unprofitable ministry and, yes, I regret that. But I don't think of those who opposed me, I think of those who affirm me. That's what you've got to do.

I think the litmus test would be, would you advise your niece or nephew to join either the priesthood or the sisterhood? And my answer is no. While I am what I am—and I believe in what I am—I don't think it's the time for younger women to join. Just as I wouldn't advise a nephew or a young man to join the priesthood. It's all in a state of flux. A socially conscious young person must know that [the Church is] a sexist organization and it is not about to change, at least not right now. I wouldn't advise them to join. That's what I think. (November 1993)

Sister Margaret died in February 2002, at the age of 77, two years after suffering a serious stroke.

SISTER JEANNINE GRAMICK

Sister Jeannine Gramick does not look like a woman who would cross swords with the hierarchy of the Catholic Church—or with anyone else. She is a slender woman of medium height, her manner friendly yet reserved, her voice quite soft.

The interview took place in a small white bungalow in a racially and ethnically diverse neighborhood in suburban Maryland. As she filled mugs with tea in a tiny kitchen where a friend was making homemade soup, the conversation was casual, ranging from recipes to raccoons and wild turkeys. Upstairs in a small office-sitting room, a cat occupied one chair; we shared the sofa. During the interview Sister Jeannine, 50, sat quite still. At times her eyes filled with tears, but she regained her composure quickly.

Since the interview, Sister Jeannine, a School Sister of Notre Dame, and Father Robert Nugent, a priest with whom she has shared a ministry to the gay and lesbian community since the 1970s, were notified that their teachings on homosexuality were under investigation by a Vatican Commission. The initial written report of the commission was negative, but final recommendations have not yet been made.

I grew up as a child in the 1950s in Philadelphia, which was known to be a very conservative city. Philadelphia is the kind of city that is so Catholic that when you hear someone else is from Philadelphia, the immediate question is, "Oh, what parish are you from?" I went to a large diocesan high school—all girls, 2,500 girls—and graduated at age 18. Then my parents tried to bribe me not to enter the convent with a trip to Europe, and after the trip to Europe I entered the School Sisters of Notre Dame in Baltimore.

In those days [in the convent] one's life was controlled by others. That was the way we practiced obedience. After I had been in religious life about eight years, my mother was taken to the hospital with a brain tumor. I went to the superior and I told her that my mother was going to have brain surgery, and her reaction was, "Well, when are you going up?" I was very surprised, because I had expected her to tell me what to do. I expected her to say, "Well, you can go at such and such a time, and we'll make the arrangements for you." But she expected me to decide when I was going, how long I was staying, and when I was coming back. I was very surprised at the time, but I said, "Okay. Thank you." And I went ahead and made the arrangements. Reflecting on that incident years later, I began to see that was a turning point for me. That incident separated me from the old style of religious life and moved me into a new style of religious life in which I began to make adult decisions on my own and didn't depend on others to make the minutest decisions for me.

I went on to get my doctoral degree in mathematics at the University of Pennsylvania [which I chose to be near my mother]. My second year there, I met a young man, Dominic Bash, at a home liturgy. He was probably 25 then, and we became instant friends. After the Mass he began to tell me about himself. He was gay.

He told me that he had been in a religious community but that he left the religious community because he felt it was incompatible with his being a gay person. And he felt the Catholic Church really had nothing positive to say to him. All it did was inject guilt and feelings of self-hatred; and so he started going to the Episcopal Church, because they were preaching that God loved everyone, including gay people. And he knew that in his heart. Dominic never had a problem with God. He knows that God loves him and that God loves everyone.

So, anyway, that evening he said, "I have gay Catholic friends, and they don't feel that the Catholic Church wants them. They would love to come to Mass." I said, "Well, we'll have a Mass at your house for all of your gay friends." So we planned it, and I contacted a priest I knew. The first time I was very apprehensive. I really didn't know what to expect. What I found was that I was very comfortable, that the individuals who came—all men—were people who had grown up Catholic and who loved the Church, but hadn't set foot in a church in years. They were so grateful that a priest and a Sister would want them, and would be a sign that the Church would want them. It was just amazing to me that I could have that effect.

In those early days I had all of the myths and the stereotypes that anyone would have. I think I had heard the word *homosexual* once or maybe twice. I never gave it any thought, because it didn't touch my life. But here was a man who did touch my life. I had this myth that, well, they're nice but there's really something wrong with them psychologically. If it's a man, he just hasn't found the right woman; or if it's a woman, she just hasn't found the right man.

There has to be something that can help to change them. And I thought by my being friends I could help them change and become normal.

Then there was someone who was a great influence in changing my mind. She was a lesbian woman who worked for the ACLU. She was very intelligent, very self-assured. As part of her work at the ACLU she was a champion for the cause of justice. To her, "lesbian" and "gay" wasn't an issue; she treated it as a normal fact of life. And gradually I took on that mentality. There's nothing abnormal about this. It's different from the sexual orientation most people have, but it's no big deal. And so I just changed my way of viewing it, that's all. It was a gradual learning experience. And the learning came from being with people who were lesbian or gay, who were psychologically healthy; and I had to say to myself, "Hey, these people are as psychologically normal as anyone else. In fact, many of them are more psychologically healthy than a lot of people I've met who are heterosexual."

We began to have weekly home liturgies at Dominic's house or the houses of his friends. And I helped to organize a panel with a priest, a lawyer, and a psychologist to talk about lesbian-gay issues at the Newman Center, which was the Catholic institution on campus. One of the Sisters I lived with taught in a high school, and she asked me to come into her class to talk about this. So then I began to do a lot of reading. I had my experience in meeting these individuals and learning from them, but I began to do a lot of reading on my own. While I was at the university then, I had an informal ministry of education and spirituality and friendship. Then I left the university and taught at the College of Notre Dame, a college my community operates in Baltimore. I had heard about Dignity, which is an organization for gay Catholics; and I helped start the Washington chapter, and then I helped to start the Baltimore chapter.

And then I had an opportunity to leave teaching and to go into social justice ministry at the Quixote Center, which is a peace and justice center in the Washington, D.C., area. At the Quixote Center I was to develop workshops to educate the Catholic community about homosexuality with Father Robert Nugent, who had also had experience working as a Dignity chaplain. In 1976, this was still something that the Catholic community didn't know much about. We were just learning about it ourselves. After a while, Father Nugent and I left the Quixote Center and started our own center, called New Ways Ministry.

New Ways Ministry is an organization that seeks to promote reconciliation and understanding between the lesbian-gay community and the institutional Church by conducting educational workshops and publishing resources. Both Bob and I have written a number of books and articles. Well, it seemed that the archbishop [of Washington] didn't agree with what we were doing. We had one meeting with him which we thought was the beginning of a dialogue, but it became clear that [Archbishop Hickey] had already made up his mind that he wanted us to leave this ministry. He thought we were subverting the teaching of the Church. Now, the teaching of the Church in his mind is very narrow—at least that's my evaluation of it. He seems to believe that the teaching of the Church on homosexuality is that homosexual acts are immoral. That is the teaching of the Church on homosexuality, but he seems to think that's all there is to the teaching of the church. And there's much more. There's the teaching about human rights and dignity of the person. There's the teaching about homophobia and prejudice. There's the teaching on pastoral ministry. But none of that was important to him. He was only concerned about what we were saying in our workshops about homogenital activity. And it was his perception that we were telling people that you don't have to follow the teaching of the Church, that you can believe that homogenital activity is not necessarily immoral. Now, that was his perception. He never bothered to clarify it.

What we did do, and continue to do, is to educate the Catholic community as to what is the teaching of the Church in that area about homogenital activity; but we also tell people what moderate and more liberal theologians are saying, which is that in the context of a loving, faithful relationship, homogenital activity is morally good, if there's a committed relationship there. But we do not say it is okay to believe that. We try to enable people to make their own decisions. And going back to that superior I had who said to me, "Well, what are you going to do?" what I would say to a gay Catholic is that this is the teaching of the Church: Homogenital activity is immoral. This is the teaching of the majority of moderate theologians: In the context of a loving relationship, homogenital activity is morally good. And some liberal theologians or egalitarian theologians would go even farther than that and say, "Yes, in the context of a loving relationship this genital activity is good. But homosexuality is not a second-class status; it's just as good as heterosexuality." Moderate theologians wouldn't say that. But then I would also say [to a gay Catholic], "From your own prayer life, your relationship with God, you need to come to a decision, knowing the teaching of the Church, knowing what theologians are saying, knowing your own experience. If you have a spiritual director, talk things over with a spiritual director. But then you make your own decisions." And I think that's what it means to be an adult in the faith, that we take responsibility for our decisions, even if they happen to be in conflict with what official Church teaching is. Or they may be in congruence with official Church teaching. But the point is, we need to take responsibility for our own actions.

Well, at the meeting with Archbishop Hickey he expressed consternation that our workshops were open to the public. He said that if they were only for priests, maybe he could tolerate it. But they were open to the public, and he did not think that was wise. His mentality was: Laypeople won't understand this. They have to be safeguarded. They're not bright enough to get it. Now, that's as much as he said, but he went to our religious communities—to our provincials—and asked them to reassign us. That was in 1981. And they wouldn't reassign us. Then he went to our superior generals in Rome and asked them to reassign us, and they wouldn't do it. So then he went to the Congregation for Religious at the Vatican, and finally, after three years, the order came from the Vatican.

My community gave me a copy of the Vatican's letter, which let me know that the Vatican was requesting them to request me to [leave New Ways Ministry], but I didn't even put them in that position. My community leaders had been so good in supporting me, and at that point I thought they had done as much as they could do, so I said, "All right. Enough is enough." I agreed to leave New Ways. My provincial tried to find a diocese along the east coast that would accept New Ways Ministry into their diocese. She probably tried a half dozen of them, but no bishop would accept us into his diocese knowing that Archbishop Hickey was opposed. This is the political climate. New Ways Ministry had this cloud of disapproval.

I was allowed into the diocese of Brooklyn. The Sisters of Mercy took me under their wing. The diocese of Brooklyn knew that I was doing gay ministry under the umbrella of my congregation, the School Sisters of Notre Dame, but as long as I had an affiliation with the peace and justice office of the Sisters of Mercy, then they'd let me come into their diocese. I was essentially doing the same kind of work—giving the same workshops, the same kind of spiritual direction, writing the same things, saying the same things.

Does the hypocrisy of that bother you?

I wouldn't say it's hypocrisy; I would say it's part of the ludicrousness of life. It's politics, that's all it is. There's ecclesiastical politics, and there's civil politics, and on university campuses there's academic politics. What you can't do in one department in a university you can do in another. It's politics. You have to be clever and ingenious and find a way to do the work. I do get angry, but I hope my anger fuels me to be resourceful, to find a way to do the ministry, or to accomplish the objective. I don't want to get hung up on an anger that gets into a dead end of bitterness. That's unproductive.

So I relocated to Brooklyn, and I was there for five years. It felt like I was being banished. I have such a fierce sense of justice, and I was feeling that I was wronged because I wasn't even given an opportunity for a hearing. Even though I was still allowed to be doing gay ministry, I was uprooted from a place I loved and people I loved and thrown into a situation where I didn't want to be. I felt like I was in Siberia.

I had no sooner gotten to Brooklyn in September of 1984 when, in October, what comes across my desk but an announcement saying that Catholics for a Free Choice is going to place an ad in *The New York Times* saying that there is a diversity of opinion in the Catholic Church on the issue of abortion. It was a signature ad, to be signed by as many people as wanted to sign it. And so I read the one-page statement and I thought, "Yes, that sounds like what I believe in." It didn't take a position on abortion. In my mind the ad did not say "abortion is good" or "abortion is evil." All it was calling for was dialogue in the Catholic community, because there was a difference of opinion among Catholics about abortion. And I'm a firm believer in dialogue. So I signed it. In the beginning of December I was in San Diego giving a workshop, and I got a call from my provincial from Baltimore. Now anytime I'm on the road and I get a call from my provincial, I know it means there's been a complaint, a complaint from the Vatican.

So she said, "Oh, Jeannine, I just got a letter from the Vatican." I said, "Now what?" Because we had just gone through this thing with Archbishop Hickey and I had relocated to Brooklyn. So she told me it was about this ad, and I felt very relieved because it wasn't about homosexuality. And she told me that there was another Sister in our community, Margaret Ellen Traxler, who had also signed the ad, so our superior general got one letter naming these two Sisters in her community who had done this terrible thing. And I felt so good. I said, "Oh, I have company. This is wonderful." That might have been a unique reaction.

Twenty-some women religious out of about 100 people had signed the ad. And the Vatican wrote to the heads of their religious orders saying that the nuns who signed this ad had to retract, and if they didn't they would be subject to ecclesiastical discipline. Then they quoted a canon, which essentially meant you would be dismissed from your religious order. There was a meeting of all the superiors and the Sisters who signed the ad. It was good to get together with other women religious who were also confronted with the same thing. I learned the value of working in collaboration with people. I was in trouble, but I was able to talk about it with other people who were also in trouble—unlike my experiences with gay ministry, because no one else was doing that.

Ultimately, with the Vatican, it was a compromise. I wrote a clarification of what the ad meant or why I signed it—I don't even remember at this point—and I gave it to my superior general. I don't know what she did with it. I never had direct dealings with the Vatican. It was my superior general who negotiated with the Congregation for Religious at the Vatican.

[My current ministry still involves educating people about gay and lesbian issues.] Bob Nugent and I just had another book, *Building Bridges: Gay and Lesbian Reality and the Catholic Church*, published; and it's going into its second printing; so we're happy with that. And I'm working on a book called *Voices of Hope*, which will be an anthology of positive statements from Church leaders who support lesbian and gay ministry. The point is to show that there are leaders in the Catholic community who have very positive things to say about lesbian and gay people.

I'm on the road quite a lot doing workshops, one day or a weekend or an evening—educational experiences mostly to the Catholic community. In the last couple of years I've been doing a lot of work on Catholic college campuses with students and faculty. I would say most of my work is not necessarily with the lesbian-gay community, but with the heterosexual part of the Church, to help educate. I write letters of comfort and consultation to people who write to me. Parents. Lesbian nuns. I've given some retreats and workshops for lesbian nuns, and I'm trying now through a newsletter [to set up a network] for lesbian nuns.

I don't know where [the myth about all the lesbian relationships in convents] got started. I can see how people might think that, because it's a homosocial situation, a single-sex society; but it's a myth. According to Kinsey's statistics about women, which were published in 1953, about 7 percent of the American population of women were primarily or exclusively homosexually oriented. Now, that probably is a conservative estimate, because the data were gathered at a time when people were less inclined to acknowledge same-sex feelings. But at any rate, let's just say that about 7 percent of the American female population is lesbian. [I can't count as many as] 100 lesbian nuns. That's nowhere near the 7,000 there should be, according to Kinsey, given that there are about 100,000 nuns in the United States.

Now, my explanation of why there are fewer than the average in the American population would be as follows. I think, first of all, it's mostly heterosexual women who are drawn to religious life, because we have conceptualized God as male; and unconsciously I think a male God is more attractive to a heterosexual woman than to a lesbian woman. I'm not saying that a woman enters religious life with images in mind, but it's there in the subconscious somewhere. And so I think heterosexual women are much more attracted to religion or faith in general, because religion has been a patriarchal institution. Another fact operating here is that women religious do not really think of themselves as sexual beings. I've heard lots of nuns say, "I've never even felt any sexual feelings." So I think a lot of nuns are asexual. And then I think women are much more private about their sexuality in general. So women in religious life are going to be very private. Even if they do have sexual feelings—whether they're heterosexual, bisexual, or homosexual feelings—they'll be very private with those feelings and not talk about them.

The question we haven't covered is your own sexual orientation. Do you want to share that with me?

Very few people have asked me that question directly. I think almost everybody probably would wonder, but very few people have directly asked the question. And I guess my response has been—and is now—that it's not a question that is relevant to my ministry, because I don't want the ministry to focus on me; and it's much more important that people focus on or understand or know about lesbian and gay people, not that people know about me. Although I am a public person, there are parts of every public person that one keeps private. But I guess what I have found is [that] some people think I'm lesbian, and that's okay, because it helps them to think I'm lesbian. And then there are people who think I'm heterosexual, and it helps them. So I guess whatever people want to think is okay.

AFTERTHOUGHT: Your question about my sexual orientation caused me to think later on; and I mentioned to a friend that I had responded as I had, that I didn't say one way or the other. And then I said to my friend, "Well, I think I did that because I would like to live in (what I called to him) my 'preferred future.' In other words, a future in which relationships, whether they're sexual relationships or nonsexual relationships, are grounded in friendship; and that when you meet someone, the sexual orientation isn't important in establishing a relationship or friendship. Sexual orientation is important, but it's important in personal interaction. In the course of everyday living, there are occasions when one's sexual orientation or one's physical or mental health will become revealed to a person. But that always occurs very naturally and spontaneously and in the context of a relationship.

Right now sexual orientation is a label. But I think when the human race is much older and wiser, we will put sexual orientation in context, and it won't be such an all-pervasive or overriding issue. It is part of one's identity, but there are a host of things that make up one's identity. My hope is that we will arrive at a point where it's in equal place with a whole range of other features that make a person unique. Sexuality wouldn't be relevant to a public interview. It would be relevant in a private sphere in one's relationship with people you're close with.

As you know, to me religious life is very important, but in my preferred future I don't think it will be bound up with traditional notions of poverty, chastity, and obedience. But I think there will be a sense that religious life is a radical commitment to the Gospel, a commitment to a simplicity of life, a commitment to share the earth's resources, a commitment to a respectful sexuality that's not used to manipulate people, and a commitment to follow where God is calling you to go.

And so it could very well be that religious life would include people who are married or people who are single, heterosexual individuals as well as lesbian and gay individuals, lesbian and gay couples.

I have been a person, I think, who has gone where I felt God was calling. If you had interviewed me more than 22 years ago, I would have said I was called to the ministry of higher education, teaching mathematics. But then this young man intervened in my life—I should say, God intervened in my life through this man and his friends—and I felt called to do something for the lesbian-gay community because there was a need that wasn't being fulfilled by anyone else in the Church at that time.

I think my entire motivation in entering religious life was and is to draw more people closer to God, to be a catalyst or a conduit or a means whereby people would feel and know God's love. And I hope I've done that. I hope I will continue to do that. It seems to me for some reason God has chosen me to have a special ministry to the lesbian and gay community. And I hope they would feel God's love as a result.

Dominic, the young man who was responsible for calling me into this ministry, is now dying of AIDS, and it's been very painful for me. I've tried to spend some time with him, as much as I can, and chronicle his story, too. Even now he tries to give comfort to people who are dying of AIDS. He tells them not to be afraid. "Nobody wants to die," he says. "I'm not afraid of dying. I just don't want to die yet." But he says, "Life is like a roller coaster; it has its ups and downs, but when you're dying, you come down on that roller coaster and you go right into God's arms."

While it's been painful to see him lose his dynamism and his energy, it's been a blessing, too, because I've come away from the times I've spent at his bedside inspired and exhilarated, because he knows he's loved so much by God, and I just feel so much closer to God when I leave him.

I really wouldn't have been able to do as much as I have done with as much energy without the support of some very close friends and my community leaders. Since I've been in this ministry, every provincial and general administration has supported me when the criticism has come—and, believe me, the criticism has come. If they had not supported me, I would have been blocked. I would have been stymied. I would have been halted. The ministry that one does on a private level seems to be unhampered; but as soon as you work in a ministry that is very public, then the rocks begin to be hurled, and my community leaders have been very good in catching some of those rocks so they don't hit me.

Ultimately I think my strength comes from God, from a prayer life, a strong relationship with God. God's grace in a human way comes to me mostly through my friends. And my parents. My dad, particularly now that my mom has died.

I am an only child, and entering religious life wouldn't have been my parents' choice, but they [finally] said, "Well, if that's what you want and that's what makes you happy, then that's all right." And that typified their attitude toward me as a child growing up. On the one hand, you could say I was spoiled; but on the other hand, you could say I was unconditionally loved. If I did something they didn't understand, they accepted it because they loved me so much.

I told you the story of meeting Dominic and then his friends and having Mass at his apartment? There was an article in the paper about the work I was doing. [My parents] saw me the day the article appeared, and they didn't know I had been meeting with these gay individuals on campus. My dad said to me, "What's this?" And I said, "Well, someone has to be present for this group of people. They've been alienated, and they're part of the Church, and someone has to reach out." And he said, "Well, let the other nuns do it." [Laughs.] Then he thought a minute, and he said, "You're not going to burn draft records, are you?" This was at the height of the anti–Vietnam War era. And I said, "Well, you know, I'm against the war in Vietnam, but I'm not that heavily involved in the peace movement that I would do civil disobedience. But what if I did?" He thought a minute, and he said, "Well, you know, that's against our country." And then he said, "But if you did it, that would be all right, because you're our daughter." And that sums up his attitude toward what I do. He doesn't understand it fully. He's of an age and a generation in which homosexuality was some aberration, but he's a very kind person, extremely kind. He doesn't understand the whole psychology of sexuality, but if I'm doing it, it's okay because I'm his daughter. To me that's unconditional love. (December 1992)

> When I returned to suburban Maryland, to the same small house where I had first interviewed Sister Jeannine, we began the interview in the living room and continued in the kitchen where we had once shared tea. A cat once again kept us company. Sister Jeannine, too, seemed much the same. But as she talked, it became clear that much in her life had changed during the intervening 18 years. Some of the story was captured in a 2004 documentary, In Good Conscience: Sister Jeannine Gramick's Journey of Faith.

Yes, the report from the Vatican Commission that examined us here in the States was negative. There were only three meetings of the Commission, all in '94, and we felt that we did very well in answering the questions, so we had thought we'd get a very good report. But it was very negative. Then we heard that the Congregation for the Doctrine of the Faith was sending us a series of questions. They centered around homosexual activity and homosexual orientation, and we answered them. We said, "This is what the Church says about homosexual activity and what it says about orientation." They sent us something back that said, "Well, you just said the teaching of the Church. You didn't say what you personally believe." They said, "We suggest you make a statement saying you agree with the teaching of the Church on homosexuality, that all homosexual activity is intrinsically evil and the orientation is disordered." I could not do that.

When the [final] decision came out in '99 that Bob [Nugent] and I should no longer be involved in this ministry and that we were barred from holding leadership in our communities, they made it very public. They put it in *L'Osservatore Romano*. It was in *The New York Times* and all over the world. I was getting e-mails from Australia. Friends were calling and I could not pick up the phone. I was numb.

You do feel angry, but I suppress my anger sometimes. [During those years] friends would ask, "Aren't you angry that this is taking away so much time from your ministry?" To which I replied, "No, this is part of my ministry." My ministry is not solely or primarily pastoral work for lesbian and gay Catholics, although I do that. My ministry is to engage in structural change, to engage people who are in leadership positions in the Church and get them to think. I think it was very productive for the ministry that this investigation occurred.

My community was not happy. They had supported me and the work over twenty years. While they had resisted before in the face of [pressure from the Vatican], this was a document signed by Pope John Paul II. They did not feel that they could resist it, and they asked me to go into another ministry. I said I didn't feel called to another ministry, but that I would discern. For about nine months,

I went around the country, telling my story of what had happened and about the investigation, elaborating on why I didn't think it was fair. And if [people] didn't think it was fair, would they write to the Vatican and ask for another hearing. So the Vatican got thousands of letters. In May of 2000, my superior general asked me to come to Rome. She said the Vatican had gotten lots of letters. She said, "This has to stop." She read me these formal "obediences"—I was not to speak about homosexuality and I was not to criticize the magisterium. I said, "You know, I just can't do that."

[I was] like the battered woman who finally has made a choice to get out of her situation and tell her story. I was thinking, "That's what this whole year has been for me. I've been telling my story and telling my story, and I've gotten more strength." Not that I was physically battered, but psychologically. I had made so many retreats. My provincial would say, "Go away and make a retreat." Okay, I'll go on retreat. It was always the same, that there needs to be a voice for the lesbian and gay community. It doesn't have a voice in the Church. So I said I couldn't do [what they asked]. She spelled out the consequences: dismissal from the community. I thought then of transferring to the Sisters of Loretto. I never thought of leaving religious life.

I don't know if the name [Sister] Mary Luke Tobin means anything to you. She was one of the women observers at the Vatican Council, and she was president of the Sisters of Loretto during the time of Vatican II. She was a big leader in LCWR [Leadership Conference of Women Religious] and responsible for a lot of the renewal [in religious life]. I remember as a young School Sister [of Notre Dame] hearing about the Lorettos. We all kind of had them up on a pedestal. Now I think some other communities are more progressive than we are, but the Lorettos did have that reputation.

I applied and I was accepted. I joined the Lorettos in 2001 and I made my final profession in 2004. It was understood that I would continue in lesbian and gay ministry. Cardinal Ratzinger had written to the U.S. bishops about me, [saying] "no retreats or workshops for lesbian and gay people." I said, "Well, that means I can speak publicly about homosexuality." The broader education issue was always most important to me because my view is that the only reason lesbian and gay people and their families have these problems is because the rest of us aren't educated.

[Our work] had caught the Vatican's attention. It put homosexuality on the agenda. In the United States, the whole movement in the Church for recognition and rights for lesbian and gay people and their families became a major issue. Change takes centuries in the Church. I'm grateful that I've seen change from 1971. In 1971 you never saw the word "homosexual" in any Catholic publication. Now, we have dioceses that have instituted ministries for lesbian and gay people. In the New Ways Ministry newsletter, we publish a list of gay-friendly parishes. We have 200 parishes in the country. Now it's a drop in the bucket, but that didn't exist [in the 1970s].

My work has three parts. The main part that takes probably 90 percent of my time would be lesbian and gay ministry. The next largest chunk of my time would be with the Loretto community. I'm a coordinator for the Loretto Women's Network and I'm also on our Racial Justice Committee. The other portion of my time is with the National Coalition of American Nuns. It's an organization of U.S. women religious who study and speak out on issues of justice in society and in the Church. We take public stands, make public state-ments. We went to the Vatican in '94 when there was a synod on religious life, and we had a protest in St. Peter's Square. We were carrying signs that said: "No Speaking About Us Without Us." It's a rabble-rousing group, but we're also thoughtful, reflective. We're very few, but we make a lot of noise. What does Margaret Mead say? ["Never doubt that a small group of thoughtful, committed citizens can change the world. Indeed, it's the only thing that ever has."]

In your first interview you said, "Right now I think sexual orientation is a label, but I think when the human race is much older and wiser, we will put sexual orientation in context, and it won't be such an all-pervasive and overriding issue. It is part of one's identity but there are a host of things that make up one's identity."

I still believe that. It's not something I will see in my lifetime. No. But down the line. What gives me hope is the great change I've seen in only my lifetime. And what gives me hope is reading history, and seeing that things do change. What gives me hope are the wonderful people I come in contact with who are working for change in society and in the Church. What gives me hope is my faith, my belief in the Resurrection. What gives me hope is, as Paul says, "to those who love God all things work together unto good." No matter how bleak it looks, it's all going to come out right. (February 2010)

SISTER ANNE MONTGOMERY

At the time of the interview Sister Anne Montgomery lived with three other Sisters in a rough New York City neighborhood called Hell's Kitchen. The tiny living room and kitchen of their apartment were on the first floor; the bathroom was out the door and down the hall; the bedrooms were upstairs. Light bulbs hung by their cords from the ceilings.

A member of the Society of the Sacred Heart, she was a teacher for many years before she became involved in the peace movement in the late 1970s. Since then she has taken part in civil disobedience actions, served time in prison, spent 10 days in a peace camp on the Iraqi border during the Gulf War, and, most recently, endured wartime conditions on visits to Sarajevo and Mostar in Bosnia. Sister Anne, 68, is thin and intense. She is single-minded, unwilling to spend time talking about her early years ("I've wasted a lot of my life") or on issues other than her commitment to peace. The afternoon of the interview, she was wearing a navy sweatshirt that read, "Resist Trident."

1978 is a key year. It was the first UN session on disarmament, and a whole lot of activity was going on in New York around the UN. Some of us got involved. I joined the marches and workshops and began to be educated in what the nuclear threat was, what militarism was, how it was connected with the poor. The first time I got involved in a civil disobedience action was toward the end of that UN session. It was a very simple introduction, because it was so orchestrated by the police. We marched across 42nd Street and sat down at the UN, and the police put us into buses and processed us right there. There's something about crossing that line for the first time. Because we're trained to be law-abiding citizens, it's a big step, even if nothing happens.

I was afraid. I didn't know what would happen. And of course in the end it was simple. I was with strangers, but the spirit was very nonviolent, very positive; so I found it a good experience. We went back that evening to The Catholic Worker, where we had done our training, to evaluate what had happened, and there they put us into regional groups. There were so few peace groups in New York City at that point that we were joined with the Baltimore and Washington groups; and there were people from Jonah House, where Phil

Sister Anne Montgomery is handcuffed, one of 62 members of Witness Against Torture arrested at the gates of the White House on April 30, 2009. The group demands justice for detainees at Guantanamo and other secret prisons.

Berrigan and Elizabeth McAllister live. That's how I got an invitation to go to [one of] their summer sessions in Washington.

In the meantime, Dan Berrigan had started a Lenten peace prayer group. We met once a week and reflected together. And at the end of that Lent—I think it was 1978—those of us who were meeting said, "We want to keep going." And that's the way our New York peace group started. It was a small group called Kairos, and eventually, as we went along, we said, "We can't just pray and reflect. We have to do something." And I think I wanted to do something. At first I said, "I won't do civil disobedience, but I'll go support something." But I got into it pretty quickly because of the spirit around me.

That summer [session at Jonah House] in Washington was a big help. You spent the first two days getting to know each other, [sharing life stories], forming community, talking about your spirituality, whatever. You spent the next couple of days [getting] input. We'd see films, and other people would talk about the arms race, which was very heavy at that time. And then after that we began to talk: What do we want to do about it before we go home? So people sat down and decided on a specific form of witness at the Pentagon: a dying-in, which is like street theater. [We'd] reenact a nuclear bombing, and then we'd all die—big scene. Of course, when we lay down and wouldn't get up again, they arrested us. I found that process very holistic. You go through community formation, you pray, you reflect, you get input, and then you do something about it right away. You don't wait. Also, that particular group that summer was very significant for the future, because a lot of us met each other for the first time, and a lot of us have been together ever since in one way or another.

I kept going back [to Jonah House]. They always had special things for the Feast of the Holy Innocents after Christmas and for Hiroshima Day. At Eastertime in 1980, John Schuchardt approached me, and he said, "If there was a chance to actually disarm a nuclear weapon, which would probably involve a long jail term, would you be interested?" I said, "Well, I'll think about it." So I went away, and I thought about it, and it was still scary. Then I didn't hear any more. So I thought, this is all off, I don't have to worry. In June I went to a weekend gathering with the Atlantic Life Community, which is a loose network of peace communities on the eastern seaboard. Phil [Berrigan] approached me. He said, "Let's go for a walk," and he brought this whole thing up again. I said I was ready to think about committing myself.

We met a couple of more times that summer. There were eight of us. We were going to go to the General Electric plant in King of Prussia in Pennsylvania, because the Brandywine Peace Community had been vigiling there for two years, trying to make a dent on the employees [by saying], "You're supposed to be working for General Electric, which says, 'We bring good things to life.' What are you doing making the Mark 12A missile, which is a first-strike weapon?" During those two years, [the Brandywine group] began to see that the security was pretty minimal and they got the idea: What if we could get in and actually take one of these things apart? Wouldn't it be wonderful? It would be something brand-new, and the peace movement needed something at that point.

We were trying to write a statement ahead of time, and I think it was Molly Rush who came up with the [verse] from Isaiah [2:4]: "They shall beat their swords into plowshares," which was a real inspiration. This is the scriptural basis; we are ordered to do this. If governments won't do it, well, it's up to people to do it. I think what helped me make my final decision was not so much that passage as the idea that if you come face to face with a dangerous weapon, you have to take it apart. It just seemed very simple.

We actually went into the plant on September 8th. We were absolute innocents. They thought we had inside information. We didn't. The plans we had were from a two-year-old company phone book. There was only one guard at the door, and Carl Kabat had volunteered that in his priestly garb [he would try] to distract the guard. He wanted a woman with him, to be nonthreatening. Molly and I said, "There are only two of us, and at least one of us has to be in on the final action." So we drew straws.

The [plan] was that Carl and I would talk to the guard. The others would zip through the door. Then I would try to follow, and Carl would stay there. [The guard] caught on pretty quickly, so he grabbed Carl. At that point, I snuck behind him and zipped through the door. So there were seven of us inside. In the meantime the others had found a door that said, "Testing Center." They opened the door, and there were two nose cones—of course they don't have any dangerous materials there—and everybody started hammering. It was a miracle. I mean, it just happened. So many of these things have happened that way. So we hammered on them for about two minutes and poured blood on them. Dan [Berrigan] poured blood all over the plans we found on the table. And then workers started to arrive. As soon as we saw them, we stopped what we were doing; we held hands in a circle so they'd see our hands were up, and we started to pray the "Our Father." Security arrived, and then finally the police. They escorted us out to the front entrance, and then nobody knew what to do with us. They took us to the police station, but we sat there all day. It was the first time anything like this had happened. Something exploded in the peace movement.

Of course that was a major moment in my life. Molly and I were put in the county jail and shifted all over Pennsylvania for 11 weeks. We'd agreed ahead of time that we would not accept bail. The men were all together in Montgomery County Jail, but as time went on Molly and I were split up. Finally the men [wrote], "We've got to get ready for trial, and if the bail comes down enough, would you two be willing to come out?" We wrote back and said, "We would if two men did the same thing." We were being very careful about the woman-man thing. So that was the agreement, and they drew straws. In the end the bond did come down, and my religious congregation put it up.

All our supporters were saying, "People have to understand what you've done. You've got to speak out in a courtroom." So we agreed. It was a very oppressive trial, my first experience of anything like that. I gave the first opening statement, and I'd get interrupted because I was trying to say things [the judge] didn't want me to say. And finally it got to the point where we met between sessions and said, "It stops here. We're going to turn our backs on the court." We did that, and many people in the courtroom, our friends, stood up and did the same thing and went into silence. At that point, the judge went wild, and he called on court-appointed attorneys to speak for us. They [said], "We don't know these people. We can't speak for them." And they sat down again. The prosecutor summed up his case, and of course we were convicted. The appeals went on for 10 years, and finally in 1991 the conviction was upheld in the appeals court, but the sentencing was overturned. What [the judge] did was to give us all time served.

So that was that case. But in the meantime none of us had stopped. We felt that this kind of symbolic action had to continue, because obviously the arms race was not stopping. This was during the Reagan-Bush years. Since [that first time] I think there have been 49 Plowshares actions. Some in Sweden, the Netherlands, Germany, Australia, and, of course, many in this country.

In 1982 several of us went to New London. We called ourselves the Trident Nine and we split into two groups. One group got on board a Trident [submarine] and hammered on the missile on it. The rest of us went into the yard in New London where they had the sonar spheres, which are the eyes and ears of the Trident, and we damaged those. The next time was during the years the Pershing and Cruise missiles were deployed in Europe. A group of us went down to Martin-Marietta in Florida. Four of us went to a launcher—which we thought was a Pershing launcher, but it actually turned out to be a Patriot launcher—and hammered on that. I was in federal prison, Alderson Women's Prison in West Virginia, for almost two years as a result of that. That's the longest time I've been in prison, from 1984 to 1986.

You learn a lot in federal prison. They are deadly places. You're not suffering physically so much. You have a bed and three meals a day. You have to work, but usually I was able, after doing some time on KP, to do some tutoring as my job. What you find out is how oppressive women's prisons are. Very little real education for women. And then the jobs. Basically, the jobs were cleaning. I felt that there you were getting the other side of the arms race. It was like warehouses for the poor. Women typically got longer sentences than men, less opportunity for furloughs or any of the goodies that came along. There were few college courses they could take. You hear about these wonderful men's prisons that are like country clubs. It wasn't like that. Alderson was in beautiful landscape, and you could walk outside when you weren't required to do something else. Being outdoors just saved me. The library was very poor.

I tried to keep the discipline of prayer even in the noisy county jails or city jails. Typically, the TV's on all the time, and it's a constant noise. You can't get away from it. I found there was a way of letting the noise go over you. In Alderson, after a year I got a room. I'd go outside and pray. And then after work I'd spend a lot of time writing letters. You planned your time. If you're disciplined, you could do it.

[Being in prison] is part of the action. It affects you, even though you're not aware of it at times. I came out; physically I was not too well. That is part of breaking the cycle of violence. You accept the violence—even if it's just this kind of institutional violence—on yourself rather than hurt somebody else. Not that you want to go to prison. But you accept it. You don't run away; you don't go underground. You wait to be arrested. You admit to what you've done in the courtroom. You accept the consequences.

When the Persian Gulf War was in the making—after the sanctions were placed on Iraq, and we knew the war was coming—the Gulf Peace Team had the idea that if a group could form a peace camp on the border between the two opposing armies before a war started, to try to stop the war, this would be a very nonviolent thing to do. Finally they were given a camp [in Iraq] about two miles from the border of Saudi Arabia, which had been a way station on the road to Mecca where pilgrims stopped and laid down their arms, which is sort of symbolic in itself. The agreement was that the campers would stay inside the fence, and the Iraqis would stay outside, and [the camp] would be neutral territory. It was just this bare cement area with a tin roof over it.

By the time we went, it was early January. At that point you could still fly into Baghdad. We stayed [at a tourist camp outside of Baghdad] for three days. While we were waiting, we visited a children's hospital, and we were immediately impressed with the fact that the war was already on because of the sanctions. The doctor said, "We have 40 children dying daily in this hospital." This is what we saw.

The Iraqis would shuttle us down to the [border] camp, which was about five hours from Baghdad. The peace team had put up big Bedouin tents under this tin roof. They brought in portable toilets and showers, and we actually had running water and electricity, because there was a generator for the border guard outside. It was cold, the desert in the winter. We had our sleeping bags and some mats and wool blankets, but it was freezing at night.

So we settled ourselves there 10 days before the war started. By the time the war started, there were 73 of us—17 different nationalities. We put out a statement saying, "We do not want to be rescued. No matter what happens, we don't want to be rescued."

The war started at night here; it was early in the morning there. The way we knew the war had started was at two in the morning we heard the planes go over. And at that point all communication was totally cut off.

So there we were. We had nothing to do. We had to keep the place clean; we had to cook; we had to ration the food. We were on two meals a day at the end.

Some days we only had rice, and some days we only had vegetables. The soldiers had nothing. Of course we went through community building. With 73 people—17 different nationalities, everybody from atheists and anarchists down to people who were very religious—there was conflict in the beginning. We managed to get ourselves together. A lot of friendships formed. I felt by the end we'd really started to do peace work in that community formation.

We knew that eventually the Iraqis were going to take us out. They were very protective, even had an ambulance outside the fence. And it wasn't just propaganda. I think they really had a sense of hospitality. We were their guests in one sense, although we were insisting on neutrality. I guess it was about the 20th of January, early on a Sunday morning, again about 2 A.M., we heard the buses arrive. And we knew that was it. They said, "No choice. You're getting out of here." They'd brought a trailer truck down and they said, "Take everything." So we piled up all the blankets, all the food we had left over, and all the cooking equipment and piled it on the trucks. And they took us back to Baghdad to the Al Rasheed Hotel. They had moved all the internationals there because it had a bomb shelter and was the safest place. It was absolutely black. Here was this luxury hotel, and you couldn't see. You had to feel your way up the stairway. Of course the elevators weren't working. We were on the sixth floor. They said, "We will turn on the water for one hour." So we all rushed into our bathtubs, and then we filled up everything, including the wastebaskets. We were always hungry. But you knew that everyone else was starved.

Through this whole experience [the Iraqis] never treated us like enemies. They loved the idea that we would stand there, trying to protect them as well as everybody else. And we said, "We really want you to take us out and show us the bomb damage. Because nobody at home is going to believe you, but they will believe us if we've seen it with our own eyes." There's something about the Iraqis. They're very reluctant to admit damage. It's pride; it's morale; I don't know what it is. We never really saw too much. They did take us to the milk factory. It was a baby-milk factory, and there was absolutely no doubt about it. The milk was ground into the floor, into the dirt. You saw the raw materials for the milk. There were packages of powdered milk for babies. We took it back and tried it. If that had been a chemical factory, we'd have been dead. And it was just a twisted mass of metal.

We were there for five days. Then they said, "We're going to send all the internationals to Jordan. We can drive you across the border to the first town on the Jordanian side. We have to leave you there and return. We can't go any further."

I've been back to Iraq four times since that time. We went back the next summer for about 10 days. We lived in a cheap hotel, we ate in our rooms, and we traveled on public transportation. We walked the streets, we walked the bridges, and we went places by bus. Everybody says the rationing is fair. But it's not enough. If you don't have money to buy on the black market or elsewhere, you're stuck. You don't see milk; they save it for the babies under one. You see some in hospitals. But the medicine—even though it's exempt from the sanctions, they can't buy [it]. The pharmaceutical factory, which used to serve one-third of their needs, cannot get spare parts, because anything that could possibly serve a dual purpose is not allowed in. They can't get any raw materials for medications. They can't get chlorine to purify the water; same reason. The sanctions are not hurting the government. They're getting what they need. They have enough food. It's not hurting the rich, because there are rich people in the luxury hotels in beautiful clothes, playing tennis. It is hurting the poor. It's hurting the children.

I don't start these things myself. I'm not a good organizer. But if somebody else has started something I think is good, and I feel I could be of help because of my nonviolence training and experience, and the fact that I'm free of a family and can do this kind of thing, I try. You do what you can, even if it won't work, and you have to do it nonviolently.

I think that's really all I want to say. Except that the help I have received through contemplative prayer is very important. And I think it's a gift that as religious we have to offer. [We also have] our experience in community. We in the Plowshares Movement and in the Atlantic Life Community are very strong on community. If you're going to be nonviolent, it should come from community. Unless you can get along with each other, what's the point? As Ghandi would say, "The means contains the end." (May 1994)

A few days before Christmas, 2009, Sister Anne and I spoke at a sunny kitchen table in a New York City apartment at the far western edge of Harlem, which she shares with three other women religious. She had encouraged me to come quickly because of an arraignment scheduled just after the New Year for her participation in the Plowshares action at the Trident submarine base near Seattle, Washington. In an indictment unsealed on September 3, 2010, the five activists were charged with conspiracy, trespass, and destruction of property. On December 13, 2010, a jury found the activists guilty of all charges. Each defendant faces up to 10 years in prison.

I joined Christian Peacemaker Teams in '95 and for some time I was very careful about risking serious arrest situations because it would interfere with that work. I had been going to Iraq for a couple of weeks every year because I had fallen in love with the place and I was distressed at what was happening. So I would take time off from working with Christian Peacemaker Teams, go to Iraq, and then come back again. We were trying to bring back the stories of what the sanctions were really doing to [the Iraqi] people. We were also trying to say to the people, "We care about you, even if we can't do much." I was in Amman, Jordan, trying to get into Iraq [on March 20, 2003] when the second Gulf War happened.

Right after the war, I went back to Baghdad with a Christian Peacemaker Team. We tried to get into one of the American detention camps near the airport.

We couldn't get in, but families saw us there and asked for help: "I don't know where my father is." "I don't know where my brother is." Some of the imams in the mosques would call us and say, "We have some good people you want to interview. So-and-so has gotten out of prison. You want his story?" Word spread and that became our work—finding out what happened to prisoners and getting their stories. Nobody paid much attention to our stories about the prisoners until the Abu Ghraib scandal.

I changed teams [in 2005] because I wanted to go back to Palestine. In the West Bank we lived in Hebron in the old city. Much of our work was on the street. People would come to us, or they would phone us: "My son is being held at the checkpoint." [We witnessed to] the house demolitions. [The Palestinians] would have half an hour to get out of their house. The soldiers would go in and throw everything out in the mud or whatever. Families out there weeping, you know. I can't tell all of the stories.

I resigned finally from Christian Peacemaker Teams last spring [2009]. I had resigned several times before, and then had gone back. [Laughs.] In the meantime, a year ago last summer [August 2008], I was invited to join a Free Gaza Movement trip to open the port of Gaza. They wanted somebody from a religious community with them. We were publicizing the Israeli blockade imposed on the Gaza Strip. Two ships sailed from Cyprus and I went in on the converted fishing boat. The Israelis decided not to stop us. When we entered the harbor, half the population was on the rocks waiting to greet us, young men swimming out and boarding our boats. It had been 40 years—40 years and nobody had been able to get into Gaza through the port.

The other thing I want to tell you is that in December 2005, I went with a group called Witness Against Torture to do a 70-mile walk from Santiago, Cuba, to [the U.S. Naval Base at] Guantanamo. That was a defining experience for me. It was like a pilgrimage. At first the Cuban [officials] were afraid of us because they saw we weren't really tourists. Even though we had come in on tourist visas. It was very primitive. You walk all day in the heat, and you camp at night when it's cold and very wet. We walked in silence, mostly single file.

From Havana [people from the government] said, "We'd better find out what's going on here." They came down and followed us around in this rickety old bus. At first they were saying, "We'll take you up on a hill where you can see Guantanamo in the distance." We said, "No, we want to get to the final gate on the Cuban side." Finally we got within, I'd say, a day's distance of Guantanamo, and [the Cuban officials] sent for us to meet with them at a resort place. They let us camp on the tennis court. I spoke. A Catholic Worker and others spoke. They listened. And they got the message that this was an act of faith, that we weren't challenging the Cuban government. They said, "You can go to the gate, say your prayers, and have your press conference there. Then come back." So we got all the way. We hung our banners [saying "No Torture" and "Close the U.S. Base"] on the fence facing Guantanamo. People were crying.

This November, I was part of a Plowshares action on a Trident submarine base called Kitsap-Bangor, just west of Seattle, where more than 2,000 nuclear warheads are stored. The Trident submarines are the most dangerous weapons on earth, and we wanted to get to the bunkers that hold the weapons. [They're] in the center of this complex in this forbidden zone, a shoot-to-kill zone. We decided, well, this is an impossible place to get to, but we're going to try. So [on November 2, 2009] at about 1:30 in the morning, we cut through the fence around the base. We walked for four hours without anybody questioning us.

We were three women and two men, two Jesuits. Bill Bichsel is 81 and Steve Kelly is 60. Lynne Greenwald, who's from Seattle, is 65, Susan Crane from Jonah House in Baltimore is also 65, and I'm 83. Of course, we were in work clothes because we had to have protection against the blackberry bushes, which we considered the greatest danger. [Laughs.] Thorns like this and they were all over the place. This is a forested area. It's enormous. Because of our clothes, I guess, and the shift change, nobody paid much attention to us. We carried sunflower seeds as a sign of hope, and scattered them, because they are the universal peace sign. We had our own blood mixed together in a baby bottle to show what's happening on the other end of these weapons.

We all got through. It was amazing. We cut through the last fences and hung our banner—"Disarm Now." At that moment the sensors went off. The Marines came. It was a shoot-to-kill zone and they have the right to shoot you. We knew that. So you take great precautions. Two of us held a banner, a peace sign, and walked very slowly. A security van came and a Marine got out. He never raised his gun. He said, "Stop." We stopped and knelt down before he told us to. "Put your banner down." We did.

They separated us, put us down, handcuffed us behind our backs, face on the grass. Thank God it was grass, but it was cold because it was wet. Sunrise came just as we entered. They hooded us. That's the first time that's happened. Three and a half hours we were like that. [When] they interrogated us, the NCIS, the Naval Criminal Investigative Services, they treated us decently. They gave us coffee and let us use the restroom. We were there all afternoon. Finally they gave us "ban and bar" letters and a summons and took us to the central gate and left us. We are going back on January sixth [2010] for our first arraignment.

I have been doing Plowshares actions since 1980. The heart of violence is there. [These weapons] are totally illegal under international law and our own Constitution. What's the purpose of these weapons? To kill people. It's a horror and nobody pays attention. [But] it's very difficult for ordinary people to do something. They put them in prison for years. What have I got to lose? Somebody has to do it. I think the body of Christ is a good metaphor, the way [Saint] Paul talks about it. People contribute in different ways. Those of us who feel called and have the support of our communities should be willing to take some kind of risk. (December 2009)

9

ENCOUNTERS
WITH JUDAISM

SISTER ROSE THERING

Sister Rose Thering, a Dominican from Racine, Wisconsin, has devoted the major part of her life to Jewish-Christian relations. Between 1970 and 1992 (the year our conversation took place), she made 43 trips to Israel. In 1988 she took early retirement from the faculty of Seton Hall University to become the executive director of the National Christian Leadership Conference for Israel, a position she held until her retirement in 1995.

We spoke in her small upstairs apartment where the tiny study, living room, and hall were filled with plaques, awards, and photographs. Dominating the living room was a large fabric painting of Jerusalem given to her by Golda Meir.

Sister Rose, 71, remains a professor emerita at Seton Hall University, where there is now a Sister Rose Thering Endowment for Jewish-Christian Studies. She is also a trustee of Kean College of New Jersey and a member of the Governor's Commission on Holocaust Education.

The work I'm doing I think goes all the way back. I am in the middle of a large family; we are 11 children. My mother's still living; she's over 100. I would say it was a very religious family: morning prayers, evening prayers, the rosary kneeling next to a chair, always studying our religion lessons. And I remember, distinctly, finding in the Benzinger history books that the Jews were never going to have a home. First, who are the Jews? Why weren't they going to have a home? And I got the same answers that were in my books—that the Jews killed Christ and, therefore, they had to wander about the face of the earth without a homeland of their own. This was very disturbing to me. You see, we did not have Jews in the area. Probably in today's jargon you'd say I came from a disadvantaged area—Plain, Wisconsin. It was disadvantaged because there were no Jews, no black people either—all white. Almost everyone in the area was Catholic.

In my little Bible history I would find out about Abraham, Isaac, and Jacob, and Sarah, Leah, Rachel. And they seemed to be wonderful, good people. Well, where are they going to go? These answers never were given to me. But interesting that I was asking those questions then.

Sister Rose Thering, center, on one of her more than 40 trips to Israel. She traveled for conferences and to receive awards, but mostly, she wanted to bring groups of Americans to Israel as a way to break down anti-Semitic stereotypes.

I went to the Catholic school at St. Luke's in Plain. It was sort of natural, I guess, that I wanted to become a religious, give myself to God. And I wanted to do it as a Dominican. I suppose it was because I had Dominicans in school; but there was also the fact that I really wanted to teach, and the Dominicans were a teaching order—that I knew.

I was a born teacher. There is such a thing as a born teacher. I loved it. But even when I went out to teach religion, those "false teachings"—I'll call them now—were in the books. I remember when I was principal. Little Arthur came from first grade down the hall—at the end of the hall we had a large crucifix— and he said to me, "Look at what those bad Jews did to Jesus." So again, you can see that the type of instruction we had been giving all along was not accurate. Arthur was only in first grade, so it was a bit difficult to try to explain, but I knew that something had to be done.

And then when I went to St. Louis University to get my doctorate in education—I was there from 1957 to 1961—[one of the professors], Father [Trafford] Maher, saw my transcript and said, "We are studying our history and literature books to know how we teach about other faith groups, other racial and ethnic groups. And you're equipped to do this research. Would you like to do it?" I told him the problem was in religion. And I said, "It needs to be done." So I examined the religion teaching materials most widely used in secondary schools.

I remember one incident. We had an education day, and we invited the superintendents of [Catholic] schools, all monsignors, to come to St. Louis, all expenses paid, for a presentation. We had Protestants, Jews, and Catholics coming together talking about our religion textbooks. However, in order for us, for the Catholic Church, for the Catholic university, to accept it, we did history and we did literature and we tiptoed into religion.

The night before the presentation I said to Father Maher, "You put me on last. You know what's going to happen. I'm going to be the one that's tarred and feathered." And he said, "Oohhhhh, don't worry!" Well, that's exactly what happened.

There were two other researchers. Sister Linus Gleason did the literature, and Sister Rita Mudd did the history. I gave my presentation after lunch. I told them what we understand by prejudice and ethnocentrism. It's impossible to find out, you know, whether a person is really anti-Jewish, because everybody would be saying, "No, I'm not." I said, "But let's take a look at the teaching materials. What are we teaching? What kind of a picture are we really giving?"

So I gave examples. I knew that the backlash would come after I'd finished, and indeed it did. One said, "Rose Thering said Pope John XXIII inspired her because he took the word 'perfidious' out of the prayer we used to pray on Good Friday. But I want Rose Thering to know that he hasn't changed the Gospel, and he never will."

And it kept on like this. Finally, a bishop who was the editor of one whole series got up and said, "If we have things in our books as Rose Thering said, they've got to go." Another bishop said, "I hear a lot of prejudice in this room. I think you priests should examine your consciences. Why are you saying what you're saying? Why are you so opposed?"

When we finished that meeting, I went back to my room. For a few weeks I didn't go near the university. What am I going to do? I was frustrated. Not only frustrated, but I was sure that what research I did would be on the Index [a list of books Catholics were forbidden to read]. You know, we still had the Index then. [It was established in 1557 and repealed in 1966 by Pope Paul VI.] I got a call from Father Maher. "Rose, I had a number of calls. They'd like to have your lecture, the talk you gave, for an article for a magazine." I said, "Oh no, no. Thank you very much." And then he said, "Rose, would you let me publish it under my name?" I said, "Yes." That was the time that women, and especially nuns, could not publish. What did nuns know as far as priests are concerned? And they were the ones who were going to read it. Okay. So it went out in *Religious Education* under his name.

You had no problem with that?

No. I'll tell you why, though. It was so important that it get out. That's what was most important to me. And that leads up to the request for publication of my dissertation. And again, I agreed that it be published. I said, "I tell you it will not be accepted by those who should read it if it's by a nun. But I know it has to get out." And then I suggested Father John Pawlikowski of Chicago. So *Faith and Prejudice*, written by John Pawlikowski, was published by Paulist Press. He gives me credit in the book. However, it's a priest who's telling it, which at that time was acceptable. The women's movement would be horrified now if they hear me say this, but it's true. But the findings had to come out.

The title of the dissertation was "The Potential for Developing a Healthy Self-Concept." Even there we had to hide what we were doing. Then, however, I found that my dissertation was taken to the Vatican. A summary was shown to the people who were considering *Nostra Aetate (In Our Times)*, the document of 15 Latin sentences that indicates what our relationship with Jews and Judaism should be. That document almost didn't come out, because there was so much anti-Semitism among the cardinals.

I had finished my dissertation in '61, and really, I would say in lots of ways it was a changing point in my own life because you cannot possibly be engaged in that work without becoming a better Christian. It just gave focus to many, many, many things. Why am I religious? Okay. I wanted to give my life to God, and I was doing that. I wanted to do His work, but I didn't know what His work was going to be. And all of this fell into place. I knew that my main area was to work in either biblical studies or Jewish-Christian relations.

People didn't really move until the Vatican document came out. Now they had both; they had *Nostra Aetate*, and they had the research on what's wrong with the books. All the books I studied, over 100 textbooks, were coded. But I decoded them for the publishing companies, and I sent them a copy of the dissertation. These are your books; clean up.

So many, many book companies would come to me with their manuscripts. "Please, would you read this?" When Benzinger Brothers brought their new text to me, they were just so happy and so was I. There was a whole chapter in there devoted to the study of Judaism. I was thrilled. I opened it, and the editor was sitting across the desk from me.

"Oh!" I said.

"What's the matter, Rose?"

"I can't believe this. You have here the Jews *were* loved by God. Were? Are they not now loved by God?"

"Is that in there?"

"That's got to go."

After I finished at St. Louis, I came home to Dominican College in Racine. My community had asked me to get my doctorate so I could head the department of education, which I did from 1961 to 1965. Then I went to Chicago and worked at the Catholic Adult Education Center. We were deeply involved in black studies, but also in Jewish studies. We brought in all these wonderful speakers. Then the Institute of Jewish-Christian Studies at Seton Hall University had an ad;

they wanted a program director. In 1968, I went to Seton Hall. I worked at the Institute with Monsignor [John] Oesterreicher, holding Menorah Studies; and I taught in the College of Education.

My first time in Israel was in 1970. I went to Israel for 30 days with a group from all over the United States—a very, very wonderful study trip. And I could see that something like this would even be better than studying at a university or a Menorah Studies program. You need the knowledge that comes from praying, working, talking with Jews. Prejudice is not only something that's intellectual; it's also emotional. And to uproot prejudice, or to uproot this anti-Semitism that we've absorbed or been taught, you need some type of experiential knowledge to shake us loose emotionally.

And so in 1972 I led 30 Catholics to Israel, and it was a wonderful trip. In 1973, I said to the dean of the College of Education, "Don't you think it would be great if we could design an annual study tour of Israel?"

And we've been doing this every year—three-week tours for students and teachers. Something can really happen to individuals when they do this. It changes people. I'm convinced—to be born a Christian, or to be a Christian, is to be anti-Semitic. And you're that until you get ahold of these ugly things that you've been taught or that you've caught. Each time I take a group, I see it. I hear it. I feel it. On one trip, somebody said to a nun, "Oh, where'd you get that beautiful necklace?" She said, "I got it in the old city, in East Jerusalem. I jewed 'em down."

I was sitting in front of her, and I heard her. I turned around and I said, "Did you hear what you said? Where did that come from?" So that's what we talked about the rest of the bus trip that day.

[In 1978] I got a call from Rabbi Irving Greenberg. "Rose, we're going to hold a demonstration outside the United States embassy to the United Nations." George Bush was then our ambassador to the UN. It was the time that the Jews of the Soviet Union were paying exorbitant amounts to get out of the Soviet Union. The rubles that they had to pay were more than they ever could earn in a whole year. So he said, "We're going to ask that no wheat be sent until they take off this tax." And he said, "We probably will get arrested." Well, I came down the steps from my office at Seton Hall, and I said to Monsignor Oesterreicher that I would like to go in for this demonstration. "You know I'm afraid," I said; "I might get arrested." He said, "Sister Rose, would you do this in the Soviet Union?" That's all he had to say. Because there I'd be locked up in a gulag. I went to New York. We chained ourselves to the United States mission until Mr. Bush came down to talk with us. We didn't send the Soviets wheat, and they removed their tax.

That was one incident I will ever remember. The other one is in 1986, when I protested Kurt Waldheim's inauguration as president of Austria. I went to Austria with a group, a Committee of Conscience. When I called my motherhouse to say that I'd been invited to go, the immediate response from my people at the motherhouse was, "Of course. We'll be with you; we'll put up a sign; we'll ask for prayers. Rose, do you need some money?"

We were in Austria for a week. And we went right from the airport to the police station to get our permits to demonstrate. We came on Thursday, and Friday was shabbat. And I remember we set up our table and our prayer books and sabbath candles, and we prayed the Psalms. They were praying in Hebrew; I was praying in English. And people would stop at the table: What are we doing? Why are we here? We had a big sign up noting that Waldheim should not be president. And we had a real picture of him in Nazi uniform. The Jews were kind of sneaking over to their synagogue; you had to hide to be Jews in Austria. Okay. What I want to say to you is that we met about 500 people.

We were there Friday night, then all day Saturday. The next day is Sunday, and I had gone to St. Stephen's church. We moved near the president's office. There wasn't much traffic that day, because they're all Catholics. Everything's closed. A few tourists were coming through, and, yes, they believed we should be doing what we're doing. Next day is Monday. We were given a certain place to protest. I have never in my life experienced such overt anti-Semitism. The Austrians would like to have killed us. "We didn't kill enough of you." "We'll come back tomorrow and hang you from the lampposts." These are things that they were saying. Some would take out their billfold and show that they were in Nazi uniform, they were in the army—Hitler's army. One said to me, "You're not a Schwester; you're a Jew." Policemen finally had to make a circle around us. We were on benches because the president was going to pass right where we were. When that was over—the police weren't there anymore—one tore the Magen David right off my lapel, and the police then came out again and guarded us back to our hotel.

But one other thing I wanted to tell you. On Sunday, we also moved to the front of the president's hotel. We lined up on the sidewalk. I was getting frustrated and cold and tired, and I said to Rabbi Avi Weiss, "I'm going to go to the car." So I went over, and as soon as I got in, I heard a knock on the window. "Schwester Rose? I have a letter for you from my mother." I was sure she was telling me to go back home and pray my rosary. Okay. I opened it. He said, "I just came back from Munich. I'm going to the University here in Vienna, but I was at home with my mother, and she sent you this letter." And I said, "Well, you'll have to help me read it." It was in German. And the mother went on to say, "I read about you in the newspaper. Thank God you're doing what you're doing. We should have done this during World War II; then it wouldn't have happened." Very lovely letter. I said, "You've given me courage. I'll go back out now. You come with me and help me." So he came with me.

Another of the good things that happened was that a priest came up to me on Monday. And he said, "Schwester Rosa?" He took out his identity card and he said, "I'm Father So-and-So. I'm from Augsburg. I should be where you are, but

I don't have the courage to do that." And he said, "My parish is so anti-Jewish—my parishioners." And would I pray for him.

Afterward, Rabbi Weiss left for Holland. He didn't eat anything, even though we were fasting for two days. He just left. Father David [Bossman] and I stayed overnight and left the next day. We got to the airport; we were going through security. I walked through; I didn't hear any bells go off; somebody shoved me into a booth. I didn't have my purse, because it had gone through the security, nor my carry-on bag; and all I remember was there was this woman inside. There was a bunch of bananas in a bowl on a table. And she takes hold of my jacket and she says, "Remove. Remove. Remove." She strip-searched me. I was so horrified and angry. I had everything off, and there she stands. And I felt, at least help me get dressed now. No, she doesn't. She stands there. I get out. David said, "My gosh, what took so long?" I said, "I was strip-searched. Weren't you?" At the time I thought, well, maybe everybody was. And he said, "No."

Okay. I said to David, "You know, we experienced the screaming and the hollering the way Jews do—the anti-Semitism—but in just a little way I experienced what the women did during the Holocaust. They had to strip naked."

All the way home here, I'm thinking about it. I was supposed to call somebody at the airport. I didn't. I took a bus from the airport over to Newark. I was supposed to call somebody from Newark. I didn't. I took another bus from there home. And I got here, and the first thing I did was call my mother to tell her I was home. I called the motherhouse that I'm home. I told my superior that I was strip-searched. And then I called the airline and I said, "Do you have a practice of strip-searching people for security reasons?" "What? What? No. You have to call in the morning at nine o'clock; I can't answer that." About midnight I get a telephone call; it's Avi Weiss. "I just got home from Holland. How was your trip back?" I told him I was strip-searched at the airport. "You were *what?*" We talked about it, and then he said, "You know, we are having the press conference tomorrow, and we're also going to see the Austrian ambassador at the UN."

The next morning at nine o'clock I called the airline, and "No," they said, "We don't do that. That's the Austrian police."

We got to the ambassador, and I told the whole story. And they listened, and I was thinking they were believing me. And then I got real brave and I said, "How much teaching about the Holocaust do you do in your schools?" The older man, the one who was really the ambassador, said, "Well, I don't know." And the younger man said, "I can tell you. We don't teach anything." He was really honest about it.

That was all good. Avi Weiss wrote to the ambassador in Washington, and he called me and told me about the letter. News reporters were calling me so I gave them the message. All of a sudden I get a call from the ambassador. "That was a private matter." Why had I to tell? I said, "It's about me. I was strip-searched." And he said, "We have checked it out. And no one was strip-searched the day you said you were." I said, "Mr. Ambassador, I'm the victim, and I know I was strip-searched." And he said, "Well, it's your words against his." And that was it.

I don't have that much longer to live, really. When I say that, I mean I see how much there is to be done for people really to understand Judaism, and Christianity's rootedness within Judaism. There is so much anti-Semitism yet. So, so, so much. I just hope and pray this is what I can do so we will be better Christians. (February 1992)

> *The documentary* Sister Rose's Passion, *the story of Sister Rose Thering's lifelong battle against anti-Semitism, was nominated for an Academy Award in 2005. Despite her failing health, Sister Rose was still able to enjoy some of the festivities that celebrated her achievements. She died on May 6, 2006, at the age of 85.*

SISTER FLORENCE VALES

> *Sister Florence Vales spent 23 years as a Sister of Charity in Cincinnati before joining the Monastery of Saint Clare, a convent of cloistered Poor Clare nuns in Bordentown, New Jersey. Sister Florence, 55, is slender with light-brown hair and expressive brown eyes, which were particularly luminous when she spoke about her experiences in Jerusalem and about her study of Hebrew. In addition to her prayer life with the community and her share of domestic duties, she has three jobs—archivist, librarian, and vocation director. She also writes poetry.*
>
> *On the day of the interview she wore a white turtleneck sweater under her brown habit. We spoke over lunch, which she served in a small reception room just inside the front door of the monastery.*

The Jews have a saying. Three things keep your memory alive. One would be to have a child—which I, of course, don't. The second is to plant a tree—which I did—and the third is to write a book. And so I feel that telling you my story is like being in memory and going on in life, even though I do believe in the resurrection.

Well, this is a long story. I really wanted to be a cloistered nun first; but my mother was very sick, and my father said, "That will kill your mother, because she'd never be able to see you again." I desired so much to give my life. That's all I can say. I had a good time in life, but there was something more that I wanted. I knew that life was very, very fragile and disappeared. I remember my dog being run over and being hurt, and my father had to shoot it. I remember I played up in the attic. I must have been about 10, and I remember looking out over the street and thinking then how short life was.

That's why I wanted to be a Sister, because life was so short and there must have been more. So [in 1951 I went] to the Sisters of Charity in Cincinnati, the Sisters that taught me; but after I started teaching my first year, I went to the local superior and I said, "I really think I want to be a cloistered nun." And she dis-

Sister Florence Vales works in the garden at her monastery in Chesterfield, New Jersey. As a member of a cloistered community, Sister Florence gathers for prayer with the Sisters seven times a day; chores, gardening, and other pleasures must fit into whatever time remains.

couraged me. I felt because she discouraged me, that was the will of God for me. I put it in the back of my mind. Then as I went on, it kept coming back. And so I asked another friend of mine, a Trappist, and he told me to stay where I was and be happy.

When I was out in Denver, Colorado, teaching, a Sister told me she was going to the missions in Africa, and she said, "You know, I always wanted to do this; and if I don't do it now, I never will." I thought, it's the same for me.

When I told the provincial, she told me to go to a spiritual director. And I did. The whole process was very painful, because he wasn't much interested in anything. He was leaving the priesthood to get married. So after I had confided in this person, he said, "Well, do what you want to do." Which left me again wondering if I was going the right path. And I chose this man purposely because he was hard, and I wanted someone to be hard with me. I had a friend who was a Jesuit, and I felt that he would just say, "Oh, yeah, go ahead." And I wanted the truth: Was I trying to escape, or what? Finally, I went to the Jesuit; and he was very good in the sense that he let me talk through this whole thing but never once told me to do it.

The last three years in Denver, I was teaching in a day-care center because I had received my master's [degree] in early childhood [education]. There was a tension in my life between teaching and prayer. It seemed like I never had enough time for prayer. And then as the active orders became more liberal in a sense, there was less prayer together and less community together. That's why I wanted to look at it. Did that frighten me? I don't think so. I really felt I wanted more prayer. Not that I couldn't have done it there, because I think that prayer comes from within a person. But I think also, for my personality, I needed support with a group that prays together.

Someone told me about this [monastery]. I looked at other places, too, and then when I came here because they wanted to interview me, I fell in love with this place right away. The whole spirit was different from what I saw of [other] cloistered Sisters, contemplative orders. [St. Clare's] seemed to really fit me. The Sisters were warm, very warm and welcoming, and very much themselves. That was in '73. And then I came in June of '74.

In 1985, I was going through a difficult period, and the abbess said to me, "Maybe you ought to go away for a little bit." I said, "No," because I didn't want to run away from anything. I wanted to work it through.

It was just that I had to refocus myself or something. I felt that sort of cabin fever. They were getting on my nerves, or I was getting on their nerves. And I was not beginning to think clearly about it. As hard as it was, I wasn't thinking of leaving. It was little things. I couldn't see where it was so important that the washing machine had to be wiped out so perfectly. That was getting to me, you know? But, on the other hand, if it's bothering some people, then that's really their problem and I don't have to take it as my own.

A priest friend of mine in Detroit had asked me two times if I wanted to go to the Holy Land. He was going to pay for the whole thing, because he was taking a pilgrimage. I said, "Well, that's out of the question. I'm a Poor Clare nun, cloistered, I can't go." That was before the abbess said to me, "I think you ought to go away." And so I thought to myself, if Father Bill calls again, I'd say yes to that now.

It was funny—he did call, the next day. He said, "This is your last chance." And I said, "I'll go, Bill. I haven't asked the abbess yet, but she did say to go away." I really thought it was right. So I went to the Holy Land, and it was a very moving experience for me.

I've heard them say, "Oh, you go there and it just moves you." It did move me; that's all I can say. I began to see that Christianity's roots are really in Judaism. And that our religion, Christianity, is very, very short compared to the Jewish religion. And I also began to realize Jesus was a Jew, and if I understood Judaism, then I would understand Jesus.

It's as clear to me today as it was then. I'm crying now. There was the church, the Holy Sepulchre, the spot where Calvary was. It belongs to the Greek Orthodox in one part, and I think the other belongs to the Catholics; and you walk from one part to the other. Underneath the altar was the stone, and you could touch the earth where Jesus was said to be crucified. I know they say these are just spots. But the thought that I was kneeling there just brought so many tears to my eyes. I didn't want to get up from the spot, because everybody was there and they would have seen I was crying. So before I got up, I put on my sunglasses because it was such a private moment.

It moved me so deeply; it seemed like my whole life came together. The rabbi asked me once, "What was the most touching moment in your life?" He expected me to say when I made my vows. I said, "When I was in the Holy Land." That moment. That was what my life was about.

[After I came back] one of the Sisters had to go out for shoes, and she asked if I would go with her. I said, "You know, someday I'd like to stop and see that new rabbi and ask him if he has a book about the Semitic mind." So we were coming back, and she stops right in front of his house and says, "Go ask him." I didn't know what to do. She says, "Go ahead, go ahead. We're out." So I went up to the door, and his wife answered. This was Rabbi Steve Tucker, and he had a little boy, Samuel. It was a Saturday, and they were just sitting around enjoying the sabbath. So I said to him, "I'm Sister Florence from—" And he said, "Oh, from across the street, the Sisters of Mercy." I said, "No, down by the monastery." He said, "Oh, I don't know about that place." And so I described a little bit about what we were and how we don't go out, but why I was out. And then I said I really was interested in a book about the Semitic mind. Well, he enjoyed that. He thought that was really funny.

I told him the whole story about the Holy Land, and that I felt that if I knew Judaism I would know Jesus. He said, "You're right, absolutely right." He's a lovely man. So he said, "I don't know if you can do this, but I have an adult ed class, and that's what we're taking now—the holy days in the Jewish religion. If you understand that, you understand the holy days in the Gospel." And so I came back, and I told [the abbess], "You know, Mary, this is important to me." We do sometimes go out for workshops. So she let me do that.

It was at seven o'clock, just down the street here. When I went there, I didn't know he was [also] teaching the group Hebrew. I said, "Oh, I really don't think I want this." And he said, "I'm going to have you reading out of the Hebrew Bible." It was so hard. But then it came to a point where I began to like it, and he realized I was going ahead of the group. So then he came here, and I didn't have to go out anymore.

It's just been such an enriching experience for me and a spiritual one, too. It makes me understand God's love. Sometimes we think God was harsh in the Hebrew Bible. I always had that idea that love didn't come until the Christian part. In the Hebrew there are a few words for love. One word is *hesed*, which everybody knows, and they'll say *mercy*, but the Jews will say *loving kindness*. *Mercy* is so flat, you know, it doesn't give you [what] *loving kindness* [does]. There's also the word *ahav*, and that is our love for God, our love for others. Then there's a word that God uses for his love for his people. That's *ruhak*, and that is also the root for *womb*. So what the Hebrew mind is trying to say, and

God is trying to say to us, is that his love for us is the love that a mother would have for the child of her womb—which I think is just beautiful. As a mother could never stop loving her child, God loves us that way. So when I pray, I think of that.

I also have the New Testament in Hebrew, so that gives me another flavor. And one day we were reading the story of Zacchaeus. He went up in the tree—you know the story—and Jesus says to him, "Come down and I will stay at your house." Well, the word *stay* in the Hebrew translation for the New Testament was *shabbat*. The same word you use for sabbath in Hebrew. What Jesus probably was saying was that he didn't have a place to celebrate. You can't walk on the sabbath. You have to have a place to go and light the candles and have the shabbat. And so it gave me a whole new flavor of Jesus, when he would stay at different people's houses. He probably was celebrating the shabbat.

I've been studying six years; I've gone through three rabbis. They just came here for two years because they were students, and then when they're ordained they get a job with a bigger congregation. Now we have another rabbi here; and I thought, to make my life a little more prayerful and [take] less time out, I would do it only once a month, because I can do a lot on my own now. And so she comes once a month rather than once a week. It gives me more time for my own reflection.

I love [the Hebrew] for the Psalms. See, that's the reason I wanted to do it, because we use the Psalms seven times a day. And I wanted to know what these Psalms were in the Hebrew language. While we're reading, I have the Hebrew on my lap. We do a choral reading. One side [of the choir] does a stanza and the other side answers, and then we have a period of a minute in between to meditate. So while I'm waiting [I read the Hebrew]. I prefer that to meditation, because it tells me a lot. It is my meditation.

I realize I have an active mind. And I've come to accept that that's my contemplation, too. Early in the morning I go and pray, and I don't use any books at all. I love that time. And then we have another period of time at four o'clock in the afternoon, again just contemplative prayer time. But I don't pin myself down to any special way of praying. I pray as I can for the day. I always had this image of a contemplative sitting very still and just [gazing] off into the. . . . That's my ideal of a contemplative. I don't think I match that, but I'm beginning to accept that that's okay, that's how it is.

Our prayer life here has to have some fruit in the world. I know that the world is suffering and there's a lot of pain out there. And I want to do something to help that. Sometimes it's easy to pray and be kept in an ivory tower. I don't like that image for myself. I don't think any of the Sisters here do. There is something I have to do besides just say my prayers. I listen to this one priest on the tape, and he'll always say, "Unless the rubber hits the road." He's very much for action and contemplation going together. I don't believe in it that much, or I wouldn't be here. But I do feel that to make my prayer real, I have to extend myself the best I can.

To write a letter takes time from something else I could be doing, and so I want to be able to give that time to something I feel is important. I do believe peace begins with myself. To be gentle in my own life and to try to bring that gentleness to others is what I strive for. Even my letters that I write to the senators are not aggressive.

One issue was the Persian Gulf War. I begged that we wouldn't go to war. I wrote to Christopher Smith from New Jersey, to Bill Bradley, to Senator Nunn. All those three answered me. I wrote to Joseph Biden; he did not. [I wrote] to the president of the United States. I wrote to Barbara Bush, hoping she could influence him. I called the toll-free number at the Senate. I called the UN. I wrote to the UN president. I wrote to Saddam Hussein, and that came back [marked] "temporary embargo." But then I sent it on to the ambassador—the ambassador of Iraq here in the United States. I wrote to our ambassadors. I wrote to the ambassador in Saudi Arabia.

I spent a lot of time on that. I did write to Christopher Smith and asked for the list of those that died. And to this day, each day I take one of the names and I pray for them and their family. Because I think we take life so fragilely, and it's wiped out. That pains me, enough to tears.

One of the issues I know we struggle [over is] women's ordination, and I don't feel called to that at all. I don't feel oppressed as a woman. I feel that my job is to nurture people as a woman. And I feel very satisfied in that. Out there in the world, a lot of women feel they've been oppressed. But I don't. I feel free to speak my mind, and I feel that my role as a contemplative is liberating.

There are certain constraints. It's a little bit like a classroom situation. Somebody looking from outside says, "Oh, there's discipline there." But that class could be stimulated by learning, and it's because of the discipline that learning is happening. So whatever discipline is here, it's only so that the contemplative aspect can happen. I accept those restraints so that I can have what I want.

We have, naturally, a schedule which we have to follow. That's really not [what] I or anybody here would consider obedience, real obedience. That's just following rules. Anybody could do that and not really be giving their whole self to being an obedient person. [In] the Hebrew again, they don't even have a word for obedience. It's listening to the voice. In the Hebrew Bible, those two come together, the word *voice* and [the word] *hear*. Many times the prophet would come and say, "Hear the voice of the Lord." And I think my obedience is just that—listening to the voice of God and listening to the voice of God through what my Sisters here are saying.

Like coming to prayer, for instance. Not just being there, but [recognizing] that this is the time the Lord speaks to me, speaks to us. To do that seven times a day can be draining. It's the support of my Sisters—that they're so faithful—that calls me to be faithful, too. When I go [to prayer] sometimes I'm surprised that something will jump out from the text and take on a new meaning, and I'm so happy I was privileged to be there. One of the Psalms says, "Harden not your hearts." I like that for myself. My obedience is part to my Sisters here and to my superior, but it's also to God. It's listening to the word. In relationship with others I have to always call myself back to that youngest one or the one I least want to listen to. That could be obedience for me, too, at that moment. We're not asked to do a lot of things we don't like. We do things in consensus within the community. But I can go into a meeting and have my mind set that I want it this way, and then after we go around the room and everybody talks and I see their thinking, I sometimes change my mind. Then when it is accepted, whether I liked it or not, [I have to] accept it in my own life. I have found [that] when I accept it right away and not try to fight it, I'm much more at peace. And I think, well, I want peace, I want happiness. So I try not to fight anything, because you're only really fighting yourself.

A lot of people have talked about monastic life being a desert experience. And I relate to that very well, because there's nothing out there in the desert. I had seen the desert in the Holy Land. And when the Persian Gulf War came, I remember one soldier saying that he understood why the prophets went out to the desert, because you don't have anything out there. You just have yourself. And that's this life.

Oh, we have food on the table, we have clothes to wear, and things like that. I have more than I need, I would say. But essentially it's you and God. You find out a lot about yourself, and you have to face yourself, and sometimes that's a little frightening. You have to be able to face that, and then see where God is working in your life. I don't know if I have really done that well yet. I'm working on it.

I think people need a desert experience in life. I know I need it in my life. The desert experiences I've had here have only made me grow. I wouldn't be the person I was today if I didn't have those. I don't [handle those times] very well. I'm like a rabbit caught in a net trying to get out. I think if I knew I was going to get out it wouldn't be painful. It's because I don't know I'm going to get out that it's helping me. Even my squirming. All the shame of not being who I really should be. Here I am, with all my degrees, and I don't have it all together. That's very humiliating. People here see all that. All of us see each other's dirty laundry hanging out. So [in the bad times] you just wait and do what you can. I think though, [you have to be] faithful to prayer, even in those times. You don't go to bed early; you don't close your door and say I've had it. You don't give up. You just go on and on and on.

I love this community. I feel like I belong here. [It's] a community that I can laugh with. That is a joy to me. They tease me and I tease them, and I love that. It reminds me very much of a family, because what I remember is that my family teased me, and there were a lot of jokes in the family. When I went down to the Jewish synagogue, there was a lot of bantering back and forth, and I liked that.

There's a part of me that would say maybe I'd go to the Holy Land and be a Poor Clare there. But I know I wouldn't do that. For me personally, I want to continue searching for God. And I feel I haven't found him in a sense. It's always a very elusive thing. I think he found me. I know I am loved. And so it's that whole adventure daily of coming back and being more faithful to it. That's the only future I see.

It seems like I have to make a break, a leap, to go forward and not count on myself. I sense that now, and I feel a little frightened by that. I feel like I'm at a point in my life, at my age, that I'm ready to move forward. I want to get to this point, and I can't. It's like I keep pulling myself by my hair, and it only hurts. So I know I have to let go, just let go. I'm at that point in my spiritual life. That to me is the future, where I will go. (December 1991)

In 2001, the Poor Clare nuns moved from their large urban convent to a new monastery in a rural area of southern New Jersey. At night, instead of street fights outside their windows, the nuns hear the unfamiliar sounds of neighboring wild-life. Sister Florence delights in the greenery that surrounds her. She continues to write poetry. Now 77, she maintains the monastery's Web site, has a Facebook page, and has learned to blog—all to communicate the charism of the Poor Clare life and draw young women to join them. The monastery celebrated its 100TH anniversary in 2009.

10

THE CREATIVE DIMENSION

SISTER IRENE MAHONEY

Sister Irene Mahoney, an Ursuline, came to her current career as archivist for her community after making a success of several prior careers; she has been college professor, biographer, and novelist.

The interview took place in her office, which is now in the Bronx, midway between the College of New Rochelle campus—where I was one of her many students—and the small cubicle at the New York Public Library, where she researched and wrote two of her three widely praised biographies. The first, Marie of the Incarnation: Mystic and Missionary, *took 13 years to write and was accepted by a publisher in three weeks.*

Sister Irene, 70, with a gentle demeanor, a keen sense of the ironic, and a passionate love of music, is also the author of All That I Am, *a play about women forgotten by church historians, which has been performed around the country.*

Since the interview, Sister Irene has written a history of the Ursuline order in Taiwan, traveling to Canada, China, and Rome for the research; has edited a collection of Ursuline narratives; and has written another play, Off with Their Heads.

I don't think I ever thought of changing the world, or making it a better place—all those things that you read about in *Lives of the Saints.* I think I had a profound need for God. And, in a way, it was quite wonderful, because it didn't have a lot to do with organized religion. By the time I finished high school, I so hated my high school and hated the nuns that I remember thinking to myself, "I don't want to hurt my parents, but when they're not around, I'm never going to go to church again."

But somehow or other, I could keep God quite pure and loving. I think I probably had a lonely childhood. I was an only child, and I lived in an area where I really didn't have children to play with. I had older parents. I think I developed a lot of inner resources. I developed an imagination which has stood me in good stead. But somehow or other I had this grace of feeling that indeed there was this personal God, who was close to me and protected me and loved me. And nobody could infringe on that. That's been wonderful.

And that's been true in my own religious life. Even though there were dark and stormy times when we felt the institution itself was harsh, that obedience was almost unjust, and I know that a lot of people would say, "This is all too much and I'm getting out," somehow or other there was this loving and pure and merciful God, and you weren't going to take that away from me.

So when I thought about entering a convent, I look back now and I think, "Oh dear, how did they ever let me do it?" Because I think I gave them all the wrong answers. I didn't really think about living in community and supporting other people. I was such a patent individualist. I was a hopelessly shy adolescent, hopelessly shy. Just to open my mouth was dreadful. I never thought I could be a teacher.

They didn't let me enter right away, I must confess. When I finished college, I wanted to; and I was told to wait awhile and work, which was wonderful advice. I certainly have never regretted spending a year and a half doing something else and sort of coming to grips with myself. Then I went back knocking on the door again, and this time they sighed and said, "Oh, well, give it a try."

I found [the Ursulines] understanding and well educated. There was a lot about the novitiate that I liked, and probably not for the right reasons. It was a very protective atmosphere. It was quiet. I had time to reflect. I not only had time to pray, but I was given instructions in prayer. All of those were wonderful things to me. And somehow what was hard didn't unstring me. Well, yes it was hard, but that was all right. And I didn't go through some of the troubles that I know some of my companions did. I was not homesick, and I think that's a very real problem for people. They're suddenly cut apart from everything that's represented normalcy to them. And if they come from a very large and loving family where there's always been a lot of happy interaction, that can be very painful. I didn't have that, so that was one thing I didn't suffer from. I didn't suffer from not having a lot of outside activity. I like quiet, so there wasn't anything wonderful or virtuous about it. It was basic to what I was.

I think what frightened me more was the thought of this stupendous commitment that I was making. The night before we made our first vows, I can still remember almost not being able to catch my breath. And I was terrified of teaching, absolutely terrified. Everybody was so happy because they were going out and getting into the real world and doing real work. If they had asked me to stay and be the cook, I would have been very happy.

My first assignment was awful. It was first grade at a large parochial school, with, I think, 58 little girls in first grade. I had never had anything to do with school until then. I didn't know what on earth to do with them. And there were a great many of them. I must say they never learned any arithmetic, but they got to be wonderful storytellers. We had show-and-tell all the time. But just as I was getting used to that and thinking, "This isn't so bad; I think I could do this by the end of the year," I was told that I would go and do a master's in English. I guess I should have been very happy at the thought, but it was just another enormous change that took my breath away. I had tried so hard to do well in this setting where I thought I was going to be for an infinity of years, and then all of sudden, presto chango.

I taught at college until '52. Then I went down to Catholic University to do a doctorate in English, which I did not want to do. If I'd wanted to do anything, I was dying to go to writing school someplace. And the woman who was president of the college at that point really went to bat for me. Well, not everybody went to writing school, but she did her best to convince people that it would be good for the college and it would be good for me. But it didn't work; it was too bizarre.

After I had made my final vows—I guess in 1949—we had a wonderful provincial. Oh, goodness, she was alive in every muscle in her body. And she had asked me to do a small pamphlet on Marie of the Incarnation, the first woman religious to arrive in North America in 1639. So, a woman of some prominence. Also someone who left a lot of letters and diaries.

I was thrilled, of course, and I started to [write a pamphlet]; but the material overwhelmed me. So I just kept writing, and it turned into a book. But it was between 13 and 14 years before the book actually materialized. During that time I was teaching a full schedule in college; and also I did not have superiors who took me very seriously. So I was just never given any time to do it. It was a triumph of perseverence that it ever came out.

Religious women were great contributors, you know. [They ran] hospitals, schools, orphanages. But I think the thought of doing something creative— being a painter; or being a poet; just *being* a musician, not playing the organ in church, you understand, but *being* a musician—these were thought of as dangerous because they would be selfish and self-centered. And they weren't making the kind of social or religious contribution that religious women should make. I shouldn't say just religious women. Look at poor Gerard Manley Hopkins, who tore up everything before he entered the Jesuits. And found it simply didn't work. He just about went mad if he wasn't able to use his creative gifts. But I think he always had this feeling that he was a failure because he was a bad schoolteacher, and that he was an impossible preacher, and that he wasn't good at discipline with the boys, and what could the poor wretch do? He could write the most beautiful verses.

So it was in the atmosphere, I think. I certainly absorbed it. I think for most of my life I've suffered from at least a minimal kind of guilt that I'm a creative person. I find myself apologizing for it. I know now that that is not true. And I'm very fond of truth. So that helps very much. But there are [still] times when I'm at a community meeting, for instance, and others are talking about the people they serve at the soup kitchen; and I'm sitting there thinking, "What am I doing?"

You know, nothing succeeds like success. So once there was really a book published, and people—not just nuns, but other people—were saying, "This is very fine"; then somehow or other it took a little different turn. I think some people thought I was just engaged in busywork. And then things were changing.

Marie of the Incarnation came out in '64. Vatican II was already on its way. And I think what nuns expected of themselves and what society expected of them was different. It was the beginning of something else. But I certainly can remember saying to a superior right around the time I had taken my final vows, "In the summer when we have vacation and we have a little free time, do you think I could write some poems?" And she said, "Well, will the subject be religious?" And I can still remember being angry, and I wanted to say, "How do I know what the subject is going to be? What a stupid question." But, of course, I didn't say that. So I think there was always this, "No, no, no; come back into the mainstream. We don't do that."

In 1957 [when I was back at the college], we received what we were told was a great privilege. And that privilege was that our vows were to be solemn vows, that our cloister was to become more controlled than it had been. Before then students could come into your room—not in the convent proper but [in the dormitories]. After 1957 the nuns' rooms were cloistered; and if you saw a student, you had to see them out in the hall, which was really a travesty.

[The rule was] very strict. We couldn't go home even for the illness or death of our parent. My own feeling is that many of us are still feeling repercussions of not being able to be at our parents' death or funeral. There just wasn't any space permitted for grief. I was talking to a contemporary of mine the other day. She comes from a big family, and we had just been to a talk on death and grieving and how important it was to have this period of grief and to be able to express your feelings. And I said to her, "I almost feel as though we need a ritual for those of us who never participated in the death of our parents. We need a communal ritual." Part of me was exaggerating, but I still felt something. And she said, "I don't have that experience, because I came from a large family, and immediately after, my brothers and sisters came to see me. We've talked so much about what it was like and what it was like for me not to be there." She felt she had exorcised a lot of that.

But as an only child, I never had anyone to talk to. [When my father died] my mother was totally alone. So that was like a nightmare. I don't want to escalate it into some Freudian thing. But it was damaging; and, in a way, I think it's something in my life I've never put to rest. In a sense it was never real to me.

Writing freed me up a lot. But then there were lots of other changes that I found extremely difficult. When you went into the convent, it was a silent place; it was a place for reflection. To move from a monastic kind of life where, except for your teaching, there was a great deal of silence in your life into a sort of small community situation where everybody talked at breakfast, and you met people in the hall and they said, "Hi, how are you?"—that was very hard.

And again, don't let's make it virtuous. I just like silence. The older I get, I realize it was the way I was brought up as an only child with older parents.

My parents were not antisocial, but they were not great social people. The thing they valued was reading. I also found the transition into trying to find a life of prayer in this new order difficult. For the first time we were going from meditation—which one does alone—to group discussions, coming together, and sharing the Gospel. There were things that, when I look back now, I realize I forced myself to do because I thought they were part of this new order, and I thought so much of that was good. But it took me a long, long time before I realized that I don't profit from this kind of thing and I don't help anyone else. I'm not good in discussion; it takes me too long to process things. By the time I have something to say, they're off on the next tangent. I've lost it again.

I think what happened was that in the old days, when professionally you didn't have so many responsibilities, a monastic rhythm was wonderful. But when you took that whole thing and then added to it the responsibilities for a fairly sophisticated professional life, it was destructive. I can remember being so tired that I didn't know what I was doing. If you sat down, you fell asleep.

So what was my complaint? I clearly recognized that it had to be changed. I didn't know what was the matter with me. I knew that I was uncomfortable. In the mid-1970s, I was out in the Midwest doing some work, and a Sister I knew mentioned a place down in Texas on the King Ranch where she had gone to make a retreat, a hermitage. Somehow or other that said something wonderful to me. So I called. It was right around Christmastime, and I asked if I could come; and they said, "Well, yes, but you wouldn't want to be here at Christmas, would you?" Well, it was either Christmas or not at all. So I said, "Yes."

I had some other business to do in Houston, so I went down there, and then I borrowed a car and I drove down into Brownsville. It was like country I'd never seen in my life. You come to a sign that says, "Be sure your car is in good condition and you have sufficient gas because this is private land for the next"—I don't know—"500 miles." It was very frightening in a sense, but it gave me a feeling that I was entering a new country. And spiritually I responded to that. It was like a metaphor to me. And sure enough, this group of people had established a little hermitage community. There were probably four down there at the time.

There wasn't a hermitage for me, which was probably just as well; I would have been scared to death. But there was a room for me in the big ranchhouse. They told me that I could go and get spiritual direction from a brother who was living there as a hermit. I thought, "I don't want spiritual direction. I just want to be left alone." But what could I say? I couldn't ignore this man. And I can still remember the Sister who ran the house saying to me, "Now be careful when you walk across the pasture to Brother Louis. If it's a sunny day you may run into some rattlesnakes." And that all became part of a metaphor: that I had to do something unusual, which might even seem dangerous, to get to this place. To get to him. Although I didn't want to get to him. Anyway, I went. He was just an extraordinary person, and I don't even know why I say that, because he wasn't particularly articulate. But he affirmed something in me that I had lost. So I stayed there for about six days. And when I came home, I knew that I had regained my place, some sense of being a contemplative person.

And everything that I had been so busy about—being articulate in a group and all of that—wasn't bad, but I needed something other than that. My anger was at myself for somehow playing false to something in me that had always existed and that I knew was very precious to me, and that I suppose in some way was the reason why I had entered the Ursulines. And when I turned away from it, there was this terrible kind of panic and emptiness.

I remember a Sister I know: We were talking one day, years and years ago, right after things had changed, and she was saying how wonderful it was. She said, "I used to absolutely dread college to be over, because it was so terrible in the summer having those months of quiet and really nothing to expend my energy on." And she said, "The worst of it was you had an eight-day retreat, and that was supposed to make you feel better." I remember that conversation very well. And when I looked around, I thought, "There are a lot more people who feel the way Mary does than who feel the way I do."

Once you've seen what it is that's calling you and that it represents the truest part of yourself, it doesn't seem to me that there is a problem doing it; it simply happens. I guess I'm sorry it took me so long to accept myself. But I suspect that's a regret that we all have at some point or another.

Any thinking religious finds an enormous amount of ambiguity in the way the life is lived. Maybe that's just the period we're going through. And I think to short-circuit those ambiguities by either leaping ahead into something else or trying to leap back into something else would be catastrophic. But it is like a theory in stasis, isn't it? Clearly nothing much is happening. We keep living as though there is no end, and yet the signs around us are all telling us there's some kind of an end. I look around here, and I look at all those documents, which are dear to my heart; and at a tradition, which is wonderful to me, even in strictly human terms. Just to see women that were as courageous and hopeful and dedicated, even if you're not talking about them as religious people, if you're just talking about the triumph of the human spirit!

If vocations do not come in any more than they've been doing, in 20 to 25 years what will this mean to anybody? Who will be here? I keep saying I should at least get a system in order so that someone else can take over. And I think, who? And what value will they find in it? That's a rather terrifying thought. Not one I give in to very often, but I have my moments.

You have to have the personality to keep going. It's not going to do anybody any good if I just trash all the documents and lock the door. Or if I stop praying. Or if I embezzle some money and go on a Mediterranean cruise. [Laughs.] I think I've always had a long view. I've always felt sort of maverick about it, but once you become an archivist, it's your professional task. So you're not just being an eccentric anymore, you're being paid to do it.

I'm not simply talking about "let's keep alive a dead tradition," or "let's keep venerating our ancestors." But it seems to me that in the words and deeds—this sounds like a speech—in the words and deeds of these people, our future direction lies. That must be true, in some way I don't understand. I think it is. Here we have these wonderful letters from our foundress from 1535, 1540, saying, "I will never desert this company; I will be with you." If she is our foundress, and if she is a saint, as I believe, then I can't believe they're just words. There must be some kind of truth there. (July 1991)

In the years since her earlier oral history interview, Sister Irene continued her work of telling the stories of Ursuline missions. She went to Bangkok and Chieng Mai to research the work of the Ursuline Sisters in Thailand; she went to Montana to study their work with Native-American nations. She used her storytelling skills, evident in her earlier novels and biographies, to craft three books from the letters and archival documents she studied.

In early 2010, Sister Irene published her twelfth book and first memoir. Encounters is about what she had always seen as her dual life: the writer and the nun. In the "Introduction," she writes: ". . . it became increasingly clear that what had absorbed me throughout my adult life was this insistent double vocation I had struggled to live for over sixty years . . . The wonder was that everything 'fit'. . . . There was no need to choose. It was all one, as I was one."

SISTER HELEN DAVID BRANCATO

Number 1345 46th Street, on Philadelphia's South Side, is a narrow inner-city row house with peeling paint and steps that are slightly askew. The building, the Southwest Community Enrichment Art Center, is the domain of Sister Helen David Brancato, a member of the Sisters, Servants of the Immaculate Heart of Mary, Philadelphia branch. Sister Helen David, 51, was an art teacher in high schools for more than 20 years; she is now an artist with an international reputation as well as director of the center.

She runs the center from a tiny, cluttered upstairs office where the interview took place over a foil-wrapped turkey dinner sent from the soup kitchen next door. It was mid-December—and downstairs a Christmas art show and sale, featuring the work of neighborhood residents, was in progress.

Sister Helen is short and round and cheerful—given the season, it was hard not to think of Mrs. Santa Claus. She wore a mid-calf-length navy skirt and a red sweatshirt, over which she wore a denim apron stenciled with Christmas designs. The navy skirt is part of the habit she must wear; the red sweatshirt covered the bodice of the habit. She said she tries never to wear the order's requisite bonnet.

Sister Helen Brancato is surrounded by children in the after-school art program at the Southwest Community Enrichment Art Center in Philadelphia where she worked for 14 years. "The children felt safe here," she says. "They could give visual voice to their hopes and dreams."

I come from an Italian and Irish background. It's a hot combination. My father's Italian. The name Brancato means "a handful." My mother is from a Scotch-Irish background. As a child I had an awful lot of energy, and my mother didn't know how to deal with that. She could never catch up with me. I would zoom out the door. Even when I was a little child, I would never sit still on her lap. She expected this little girl to be quiet and love to dress up. I loved to get dirty; I loved to run. I think I inherited some of my father's athletic ability. He was a baseball player by profession; he played shortstop for Connie Mack's [Philadelphia Athletics].

[Entering the convent] was something that I never thought of until my senior year in high school. Midway through that year, I went to a day of recollection, and I met some young Sisters. There was one novice who had gone to the same school as I had who used to belong to a motorcycle gang, and I thought to myself: If this girl can do it—she's so normal—maybe I should think of this. I really had a very powerful experience, where I almost felt compelled to do this; and I knew that if I didn't do it at age 18, I would never do it. I would become an artist, and I would enjoy that life, but it was so profound an experience I knew I had to act on it. Part of that religious experience, part of that call, had to do with the love I received from my mother. My mother and I had this wonderful friendship. I think my relationship with God has an awful lot to do with that mother image, always feeling you could say anything, being very comfortable.

I entered in 1961. And it was a shock to my system. I went from being stylish to almost feeling like a child again. It was hard to wear that dress. I minded eating with a hat on. I hated the bonnet from the very beginning. I blocked out those three years of my life; that will tell you a lot. I began to reject very quietly what we were being told and held onto my family values.

I thought I could get through formation, because my real reason for entering the convent was to serve the people of God. That was always my reason, to show love to the people of God, wherever that may be. I didn't think too much about church. I didn't think about teaching. So if I was being taught something that was contrary to what I believed, I would just negate it. But this is what my mother says about those years: She watched me regress. She said that she saw a maturing young woman enter the convent, and for three years something happened to retard that growth because we weren't exposed to news, to all of the normal things. Instead of fulfilling that wish to serve the people of God, we were removed from everything.

The leadership of the Philadelphia IHMs in the early 1970s did not respond to Vatican II, unfortunately. And that was a real disappointment for me, because I loved John XXIII. I loved everything that was happening—these new changes in the Church. At that particular time, the leadership was not open to that type of change. There was a fear, an insecurity; and because our Sisters had been docile for so long—used to listening to other people, letting leadership make their decisions—not many people questioned. At least the women who stayed didn't question. We lost a lot of Sisters who did question, who wanted change. This was when the Philly IHMs were plunged into darkness. [During those 12 years], I was angry; I was like a madwoman. My good friends were leaving in droves because they couldn't stand this kind of regimentation, of being lumped together with this group that was rejecting Vatican II, and sitting by smugly, letting everyone else plunge into the water, making all the mistakes, and learning so much. We were sitting back in judgment.

[I stayed because] the call was so powerful that I knew it was of God and that I shouldn't tamper with that until I received a sign to move on. But my life as a Sister of the Immaculate Heart has been against the grain. I think everything I am as an artist, as a woman, has put me in the position of being in tension with the community—needing solitude, being on the margins in my thinking, not always going along with the majority of Sisters. It puts me in a position of constant tension. Now, I don't consider that necessarily bad. It's a creative tension. And it's only within the past few years, let's say after the age of 40, I began to develop an inner freedom. You stop blaming other people for your struggles, and you create your own freedom. I think maybe it's given more substance to my artwork as a result.

[In 1988] after teaching art education 20-some years in high school, I pleaded for some time off where I could begin to fill myself up again. I had given so much of myself after those years of teaching, as an artist I wasn't getting any time to paint. My studio was my bedroom, and my art table was my bed. I would be working late into the night.

So all this was bottled up. And [the community] finally gave me permission to have a sabbatical, two years of study at the Tyler School of Art, which is Temple University's art school. There have been miracles in my life, and that's one of them. It was a tremendous time for me. I just poured out everything that was inside. Artists work in isolation. They really do. So to be able to sit down at lunch and talk about art—which is life, which is religion to me—was tremendous. It was like stopping at a gas station and getting refilled so there's plenty of gas for the journey. I have about 100 canvases to show for those two years. But more than that, the creative energy, the healing, that took place during those two years, I can't even describe. It was wonderful.

Then [just after I finished studying at Tyler], I went to Haiti. [That happened because a few years earlier] the editor of *Maryknoll* magazine saw an illustration I had done, and he called and said, "Can we use this? Would you be interested in doing more artwork for us?" And then eventually he said, "Would you come up for a summer?" It was the beginning of this relationship that I had with the missionaries and the people who come to that summer program at Maryknoll. So I began to be aware of the poor in a new way. A priest friend of mine said to me one day, "You can really do more with an image than I can ever do with words. Why don't you direct your talent to peace and justice?" I took him very seriously, because I always read the signs; and I began to do just that, to take in what people were telling me and then put it into visual form, to make people aware of what other people are suffering. So when [the people from Pax Christi, the international peace organization], were trying to get a group with different backgrounds to come together and experience what the people had to say in Haiti, [I was asked to go]. I came back with a folio of 75 sketches and then converted those to paintings. That was in August of 1989.

When I got back, I went the very next day into teaching high school again. After getting two years of total freedom and expressing myself, I received an assignment to go back to high school. Everything seemed superficial to me after that experience in Haiti. It was a clear sign to me, the very first day, that I couldn't go back, that I was being led to something else.

[The something else also goes back to Maryknoll.] My five summers at Maryknoll, doing artwork and being exposed to liberation theology, had opened my eyes to this whole world beyond life right here on the east coast. I was thrilled to be part of that, to hear people's stories. And I really plunged into the experience. But after the richness of that background, I had said to myself, now I have to go back into the city and begin practicing some of this theology.

I had some friends, some IHM Sisters, who had been tutoring in the summer here at the Southwest Community Enrichment Center, which was founded about 25 years ago with the idea of empowering the black community [in Philadelphia]. So I joined them, and I introduced the art element. What I saw, and what the staff saw, was the children's response to the art, that they were hungry for the art. After three summers of my volunteering, the staff proposed the idea that maybe I could be released to work full time. They said, "Not only the children but the adults are starved for this kind of experience."

I said, "There's no chance [I will be allowed to come full time], but if you want to try, go ahead." So they sat down and wrote a proposal. Even though they didn't have the means to pay me a salary, they said they would. They outlined it in such a way that the proposal was tremendous. What I had to do then was go into the motherhouse and sit down with them and say, "This is what I'd like to do. This is my dream."

I met with a member of the council, who was second in command then, and she played devil's advocate. She asked me all the hard questions she knew the mother general would ask. The biggest issue, I guess, was stepping out of teaching at such a young age. You know, the high schools really need art teachers; and if you do this, what will these students do? And where will you live? Will you be safe? And what will happen if we say, "No?" And I said, "I'll do it anyway." I felt that strongly. I believed God in his providence was calling me to this. I think that the council understood my commitment to these people, and communicated that in some way to the mother general. I don't know the inner struggle that took place, but they approved it.

The people purchased a third row house to house the arts center. And this was a real risk, because when people are very poor, art isn't always a priority. And yet it's given a lot of life to the neighborhood. I've seen people change because of the art.

Ida Mae Sydnor is a 73-year-old woman who had the misfortune to be the victim of our system of mental institutions and was put in an orphanage right after her birth, because her mother died giving birth to her. She was misdiagnosed, and then went from one institution into another, and eventually found herself in Byberry, a mental institution up in northeast Philadelphia, for 18 years, being drugged with thorazine. She has this wonderful creative spirit. You can imagine how stifled she was for 18 years.

When I first came to the center, Ida Mae was this little lone maverick, walking around the streets with her Sony Walkman on her head. She loved music. You could hardly understand what she was saying. She couldn't read or write. And yet the artwork that comes from her fingertips is like nothing you've ever seen before. She has the ability to portray the world within her. And it's this magical world where her figures are floating through the air. She has one of Eve being banished from the Garden. A little tree is down at the bottom of the canvas, and Eve is up at the top as a little primitive woman. And then there's this magical world. When you talk to Ida about it, she'll express the fact that, well, things were kind of wonderful after the banishment. There's a real pure spirit inside Ida Mae.

There's nothing slow about Ida. I call her a savant. Her work shows a knowledge of symbols that can be traced back thousands of years. I don't know how she knows them, but her work reveals all this. I also think she's a shaman. Her work has the power to heal other people. They respond to Ida Mae's paintings because she has a universal theme of struggle and of celebration. She portrays somebody's insides as well as their outside. She did a series called "Shedding My Skins." She sees the snake as a very positive symbol, the symbol of resurrection.

I try to learn from Ida Mae. We run this center like a workshop, and we sit down side by side and learn from each other. It's a very comfortable way of operating. What's more important in the center is the process, the socialization, the way people come in and just sit and talk over their problems, or what's happening day by day, as they work. So it's a place of welcome and warmth and comfort.

Monday and Tuesday after school the children come in. About 8 to 10 teenagers will come in on Thursday. They're the hardest group to reach, because it's not cool to come in and do artwork, especially for the boys. Adults have the freedom of coming in early morning and staying straight through. We try to take trips to Washington, to New York, to visit galleries. We went to see the Picasso exhibit. And when I asked Ida Mae how she liked it, she poked me in the arm and she said, "Child, I can do better than this." She has this belief in the dignity of her work and of herself.

I'm as much on the margin in my community as the people in this community here. Right now, at this point in my life, I feel I have been led to this place, that I wouldn't be here if I hadn't allowed providence to take me through those years and to refine me and purify me and chisel at the hard edges. I feel strongly that this is where I was led. I was oppressed as a woman, as an artist, for many years. So it helps me deal with people here in the black community who have gone through, I'm sure, a much deeper form of oppression. It helps me to relate, to empathize. My own work has become much stronger, much bolder in color. I feel that the only reason it has strength now is because of my association with the people; that the more I plunge into this experience, the stronger and deeper my work will be. My art has saved me, like it saved Ida Mae. It was the one true thing. And when I say "art," I'm automatically implying that art is of God. I'm talking about the spirit of God when I talk about the gift of art.

My spiritual life has always been very much bound up in what I paint, what I draw, and the people I serve. I meet God every day in this neighborhood. This is my spirituality. The fact that they welcome me as a stranger is a sign of Eucharist and being part of the body of Christ. I think for a lot of people the Eucharist is a private party. They never realize that we have to put the Eucharist into action. My mother was my first model of living the real eucharistic life, even though she never spoke that way. I watched my mother put her faith into action. I watched her with neighbors. I watched her with children, I watched her with us, in our own family. Her actions were always very deeply religious. And usually

I am drawn to people who live out what they believe—not because they say it or verbalize it well, but day after day they live the Eucharistic life.

I think women are much more in tune with ritual and liturgy, which should arise from the people. From the time of the crucifixion, it was the women who stayed. It was the women who were the first to be given the message of resurrection and carried it to the men, who wouldn't believe until they ran there themselves. The women are in tune with what's happening. And from the very beginning of the Church, I believe they celebrated Eucharist; they were the presbyters, the deaconesses—they were very involved. And the men wrote them out. So I believe, I hope, we'll come back full circle, that it will be men and women who are celebrating liturgy together. We set these barriers up for ourselves. Jesus didn't mean for any of this to be an obstacle.

My definition of "Church" is "the people of God." And that enables me to stay within the Church, because I have such a love for the people. I try to disassociate myself from the trappings of power and politics in the Church, because I think that many, many of the people [in Rome] are out of touch with the struggles of the people. We need nurturing women in this day and age in religious life. We need loving women who are in touch with the feminine. The people don't need all the education in the world. They need this loving presence, this woman who is compassionate and understands the problems and walks with them on the journey.

I've never been as happy in my whole life. I feel I'm learning so much from these people. I thought I could never "become immersed in the life of the poor." But I'm realizing that I can do that because the poor are so welcoming. They wait with open arms each morning. They don't see color when they look at me, and I don't see color in exchange. We're just friends to each other. They care about my life. I care about them, and we try to share as much as we can. So this is a real fulfillment. It almost scares me that I am so happy. (December 1993)

When Sister Helen left the Southwest Community Enrichment Art Center in 2004, after 14 years, it was a difficult departure. She did not want to leave; she took a six-month sabbatical, a "grieving time," and was then offered a position on the faculty of Villanova University, where she now teaches drawing and painting. In one of her courses, "Art as Agent of Change," which is clearly connected to her earlier life, she presents the students with the works of 10 transformational artists, women and men like Kathe Kollwitz, Diego Rivera, and Judy Chicago. Sister Helen then adds a service component to the course: students volunteer to work with children in inner-city Philadelphia schools one or two days a week.

Sister Helen has no time now and no place to pursue her own painting. Although she was offered university housing, she had to decline. She must, by her community's insistence, live in a convent. Still, she is optimistic about religious life, believing new forms will emerge.

After the earthquake in Haiti in January 2010, Sister Helen's painting, "Haitian Crucifixio," created after her 1989 trip, appeared on the cover of America magazine.

This climate will force women to take more risks. It could create more strength—cause a birthing of new forms of religious life. Remember how the IHMs struggled against Cardinal McIntyre? They pulled away from the hierarchical church and formed a noncanonical group that is still doing wonderful things. I think there are some essentials that have to stay part of religious life. Reaching out to the poor. The poor have the secret. We need to be flexible in how we do that. The arts work. It's about ministry, being present. Community is important, but it's for support, to provide a bond. Not for rules. I'm not much for rules.

The artists I teach give me hope. There are strong transformational messages in their work. When someone asked Dom Helder Camara [the archbishop in Brazil during military regimes who was an outspoken advocate for the poor] how he kept on so courageously, he said that these times act as a catalyst to hope. That really helped me.

11

TWO AFRICAN-
AMERICAN VOICES

SISTER MARY ALICE CHINEWORTH

At the time of the interview, Sister Mary Alice Chineworth, 75, was superior general of the Oblate Sisters of Providence, a religious community founded during the nineteenth century specifically for black women. Her office in the mother-house, just outside Baltimore, was filled with photographs of her family and the eleven African-American bishops, most of whom she called by their first names.

She is a large, grandmotherly woman, light-skinned, with iron-gray hair. During the interview, she sat comfortably in a wing chair, often placing her elbow on an arm of the chair and her hand at her chin. It was a pensive posture, but not at all imposing. She has an easy smile and a loud, genuine laugh that surfaced often.

For their habit, the Oblates have a choice of four colors (black, white, navy, and blue), which they may combine any way they wish. That summer day Sister Mary Alice had chosen to wear a light-blue dress and navy veil.

Well, I have a British name, but no British blood. I've looked up [the name] in the genealogical section of the Library of Congress. The Chin family on the River Worth [in England], that's where it originated. Now, I've got no British blood, because my grandfather was enslaved in Madagascar. He was a very little boy; and even when he was freed in 1865, at the Emancipation Proclamation, he didn't remember his tribal name or anything. It was stamped out of him. So he took the family name of his master, which was Chineworth.

My grandmother would never let us ask him about his slave years, because she said it was too painful. So I know only that he was from Madagascar. I knew my mother's family for three and four generations back, and it hurt me that I couldn't go back on my father's side.

My mother, who's a native Minnesotan—all her siblings were born in Germany—came to Nebraska with her parents. My mother's father was a dealer in livestock. He and his partner were a very well-known firm in town. And my father's parents had moved into the same little Nebraska town. My father and my uncle [my mother's brother] worked in the same place. So when my mother and uncle were planning a party at her house, and they were

In a Christmas 2009 photograph, Sister Mary Alice Chineworth displays her pride in both her African roots and her Catholic faith by wearing a pendant in the shape of Africa with a crucifix imposed on top. Sister Mary Alice purchases the pendants directly from the artist and strings each on a leather thong with beads of African colors and offers them for sale at the gift shop in the motherhouse where she lives.

making out the guest list, he said to my mother, "Do you know anyone else you want to add to the guest list?" My mother was a telephone operator, so she said, "Well, that Alec has such a charming voice. Let's invite him." My uncle—my German uncle—said, "Oh, sure, he's a nice guy." You can see the color blindness of them. So oddly enough, my mother met my father in her own father's home.

And they began courting. [My father] was such a romantic. We always used to say, "Daddy, tell us how you proposed to mother." He said, "Well, we were riding on this bicycle built for two, and I said to your mother, 'We cycle well together, don't we, honey?' And she said, 'Yes, we do.'" And he said, "Will you cycle through life with me?" Isn't that darling?

When my mother told her father that she wanted to marry my dad, he said, "Well, I love Alec. He's a nice man. But I don't know what it will do to my business. So go over across the state line into Iowa and get married." So they went across the border, got married, and the marriage license reads, "Alexander Ross Chineworth, Negro; Victoria Schlicker, white." And then I guess the clerk said, "That's not right." So he crossed out the "white"—you can see all this on the license—and then he overwrote, "Negro." Over the "white" he wrote "Negro." When I was getting my passport and I needed it, I said to my mother,

"You know what they did to your marriage license?" She said, "What?" And then she said, "Well, you want to get it corrected?" And so I thought: You know what you are, and God knows what you are, so what difference does it make? I didn't need to correct that.

My father was going to set up a business in Chicago. On the train from Iowa they met Dr. Davis and his wife, who were newlyweds. They had just purchased a house, and he was going into practice in Rock Island, Illinois, and they persuaded my father to stop with them in Rock Island so they could share this house together. You know, a double house. So they did. On the spur of the moment they decided. So I grew up there instead of Chicago.

When people fear interracial marriages, I say, "Well, don't fear them, because if the love is strong enough to jump a racial barrier, it's strong enough for children." I had the most wonderful parents in the world. We wanted for nothing. We weren't rich. By no manner of means. My father was in business, and through the Depression it was a struggle; but we had a very comfortable home and a very happy childhood. The four of us and the two Davis children, the doctor's children, were the only African-Americans—"colored," in those days—in a whole school of 600 whites. I was educated by the Sisters of Charity of the Blessed Virgin Mary [the BVMs] from K through 12. They knew that I wanted to be a Sister; I got my call at four years of age in kindergarten.

My kindergarten teacher was helping me weave a paper mat—those little strips of paper that you go in and out—and she bent over my table and she guided my hand; and in my baby way I said, "I want to be a Sister and be kind to little girls." And when I got home that evening, I said to my mother, "I want to be a Sister." A four-year-old—who's going to pay any attention to that? But from that moment I've never, ever wanted to be anything else. Ever. Isn't that something? It was a very strong call, and a very great blessing, because if I lived a thousand lives I'd want to live the life I did. I would never make a change.

When I went to high school, the senior with the highest general average automatically received a scholarship to Clarke College, which was the BVM's college in Dubuque. And, oh, we were getting near June, and nothing was said about this; and I said to my mother, "I wonder why. Aren't they giving this scholarship?" So she said, "Well, why don't you ask Sister?" And, you know, I was shy. So one day Sister said, "We thought you wouldn't be very comfortable in the dormitory with the girls, so we're giving Betty the scholarship." Betty was my classmate, who had a sister in the order, in the BVM order. I was crushed. And I really felt bitter; but I didn't realize how deep-seated that bitterness was until about 10 years ago, Clarke College had a terrible fire, burnt down, lost records and everything. And something welled up from deep inside of me and said, "Aha, *my* records aren't there." Deep, deep down. Isn't that something? The psyche is something marvelous.

In my senior year in 1935, my counselor, who stayed a friend until she died, said, "You never speak about being a nun anymore. Have you given up the idea?" I said, "Oh, no." She said, "Well, what order are you entering?" I was aghast and I said, "I only know one order, the BVMs." Well, she began to cry and she told me that because of my color, they couldn't take me. But she knew of an heiress out of Philadelphia who had started an order for the education of colored and Indians. And she would give me the address and I should write to Mother Katharine Drexel, which I did. Mother Katharine Drexel wrote me back and said they don't receive us either. But she gave me the names of the three black orders. So I wrote to all three, and I liked the answer I got from the Oblates best.

When I came home and told my mother what Sister said about not being able to enter the order, my mother said, "Well, the Lord will show you a way." She was a very faith-filled woman; she didn't say, "Why did I marry your father?" They loved one another so much it never dawned upon her.

Some people are made for the convent. I guess I'm one of those fortunate beings. From the time I entered the gate on Chase Street, I just felt I'd come home. It was a change because my education and upbringing were Eurocentric, definitely. However, we as an order were Eurocentric. There was no emphasis on black pride or anything. That was 1936.

I spent my novitiate out here in the original house that was on this property. But all the rest of the two years and two months I spent in town, [in Baltimore], the inner city. After I was professed 10 days, I was sent into the classroom to teach Latin—which was my major—and English.

[The academy we ran] was for very well-heeled girls, you know, because it was a boarding academy. All black [students], but international. They came from Cuba and the Caribbean island nations. Life in those days was extremely humdrum. I loved teaching; I loved every one of my students. But we had the kind of life that you taught from 8:30 until 3:00, then you went to the convent, and you led a strictly cloistered life in the convent. There was no interchange of ideas. We couldn't read the paper; we didn't have television; we didn't have radios.

I enjoyed preparing my classes, and I enjoyed the children very, very much, but I can't say anything stands out as a highlight. It was all very, very pleasant; yet when I left teaching I didn't miss it.

In 1958 I was called home to do public relations, and in the interim I had gotten an undergraduate degree and had started work on a master's part time. They used to tease me in the novitiate. We'd get these assignments, and they'd say, "You always get what you want." And I'd say, "Oh, no, but I want what I get." I enjoyed whatever I was told to do; so when they told me to do public relations, well, I didn't know what that meant. Public relations, I found out, is whatever nobody else wants to do. In the meantime I was asked to be registrar at the two-year college for women [we had] here. Then I taught psych, because my second degree was in psychology. And I suppose I taught until I became president of the college.

[In 1967] a Mercy nun from Pittsburgh, Martin de Porres Grey, started the National Black Sisters Conference. So I was caught up in that, and I achieved a certain pride in blackness that I didn't think I would ever feel, because there was a certain degradation in blackness. It's all-pervasive in our culture. It's pervasive everywhere. "Black as sin," you hear in the catechism. So when this black pride began to blossom—I guess that's the single most exciting thing that happened to me in that period of my life.

I was very close to Martin de Porres. I felt that if the National Black Sisters Conference was going to speak for black Sisters, then we ought to know what they're doing. The NBSC was made up of black women in an all-white order. All these white orders had by that time opened up and had let [them in], and they gave them a terrible time. Oh, the racism in those orders was terrible. And that's why Martin de Porres Grey got them together.

[Those of us in black orders] felt no need. We were the majority; we had very few whites. [The Oblates] had only three white Sisters at that time. [The white orders] had maybe one or two—three at the most—black Sisters in an all-white order of thousands. We didn't have the same need, but some of us still felt that we had to be there. But the three black orders just turned a deaf ear to them. Martin de Porres Grey came all the way here to the motherhouse and begged mother superior to send some of us to their conventions each year. Only a few of us have remained [active]. I was out of it for 18 years, and I went back when I got this office [of superior general], and I have been warmly received in spite of the 18 years. It's a wonderful thing to be a part of, because they have extreme pride in their African ancestry.

What's it like to be a superior general these days?

Perhaps we can make an analogy here. [Ross] Perot, God bless his funny little heart, thought that he could change the country and probably the world. When you're president, your hands are tied, whether you're president of a religious congregation—which is what most of us are called—or president of a country. Your hands are tied, because you have a council to deal with; you have the corporate body. The president has the Congress. So I think leadership probably resides in your ability to do just that—to lead. You can't legislate alone. I can't say, "Well, I want to build a nursing home out here." I do. But I'm powerless to do it unless my council feels the same way.

One little head used to hold all knowledge. That is the saddest thing that could have ever happened to anything. History will show that it was a sad day when one little head was supposed to hold all knowledge. It's sad because it's impossible. I love my council, and I try not to think without it.

We are very, very constrained financially because we do not have an adequate retirement fund. We have fewer and fewer Sisters on the mission, and the fewer [we have] on the mission, the less the tax into the motherhouse. I think probably vocations [are the other big issue]. The lack of vocations here is—oh, it's just distressing. We're so small, and getting old, you know; our median age is 68.

I find myself being concerned with the aging of our Sisters and what it does to their minds. People are living longer and longer, and you sort of identify with them. You see yourself. Ten years from now, am I going to be ill? I have a dear old friend who's 91. I play cards with her every night, and I see her losing her grip on a lot of things. It's a personal challenge for me to keep mentally active and as alert as possible, to keep my interest in people and events alive, so that I won't die above the eyebrows before I die below the eyebrows. I love cards. I'm the worst game player in the world. I like to win. I say there is no point in playing if you don't care whether you win or lose.

I like to travel, and I do a lot of it. I had the joy of going back to Madagascar last year, in October. When I was given the trip, I was a little reluctant at first, but I'm glad I [went]. It was an emotional trip, really, sort of a homecoming. I just knew that this is where my grandfather originated. Madagascar's an island country, and it was actually settled by Malaysians; so, of course, they have the dark skins from the African tribes, but they have long silky hair. They have a way of saying, "Was your grandfather's hair silken or crinkly?" And that's how they tell where you're from.

I actually wept when I left. I don't know; something in the African person-ality, I guess, longs for rootedness. You want to belong. I remember talking to a group of young Sisters from different parts of Africa who were there in class, and I talked to them about American sisterhood, and especially African-American sisterhood. And after I got back home, I got this beautiful letter from one of the young Sisters from Tanzania, and she said, "Oh, Sister, I feel so sorry for you because you did not have anyone to welcome you. But believe me, you can't say you don't have a family now in Africa, because next time you come, we will welcome you." (July 1992)

For more than 25 years, Sister Mary Alice has participated in the Baltimore Study of Aging, a longitudinal neurological study of aging. She is now 93 and until five years ago, she traveled around the country telling the mission story of the Oblate Sisters of Providence. She continues to direct the ongoing formation program for all the Sisters. The future for the Oblates looks bleak. Only three Sisters have joined in 10 years; there were 10 deaths in one year. There are 75 Sisters in the community, but almost all are old and sick and no longer contributing to the financial bottom line.

We are greatly diminished and very poor. We started to build a new infirmary, but we can't finish it. We built the first story and then stopped. The future? I'm afraid to think. It doesn't look good. The fact is that the acceptance of African-American Sisters into white communities has affected the black orders. These are grim times.

SISTER GWYNETTE PROCTOR

I returned to Baltimore almost three years after my meeting with Sister Mary Alice Chineworth to interview another African-American woman: Sister Gwynette Proctor of the Sisters of Notre Dame deNamur.

Sister Gwynette, 43, is one of only 10 African-American women in a religious community of 3,000. She holds two master's degrees and has been a teacher, a principal, a youth minister, and executive director of the National Black Sisters Conference. The interview took place at the dining-room table in her apartment, where she lived with another Sister of Notre Dame. Sister Gwynette suffers from severe arthritis; she has had 10 operations on her knees and will ultimately need knee replacement.

Arthritis has not curtailed her activities; she is currently executive director of Our Daily Bread, the largest soup kitchen on the east coast. She spent July 1995 in Nigeria, teaching at the university there.

My mom was a city schoolteacher, and my household was always full of students needing a little extra attention. You came home on a Friday, you met the first-grader, and you got on with life. She brought her students home for more than 25 years.

So for me there was that early experience of community and what it meant to look beyond your immediate family unit. When I was 10, the oldest of four in the family, my parents adopted Norman, and he came in the door with all the privileges of being the oldest brother. There were no distinctions between being adopted or not. I made the mistake one time of screaming in anger, "You're not my real brother." When I got out of my room—like two months later—clearly the message was delivered: That is unacceptable in this house. And that mistake was never repeated.

And then for a period of five or six years we also grew up with four foster sisters and brothers. We went to Villa Maria, which was a home for children who were wards of the state, to get one child and came home with four, all sisters and brothers. We were going to be a weekend family for them. We took bunk beds apart; we made pallets on the living-room floor. Weekends, summers, holidays. And the amazing thing is, we went from four [children] to five and then from five to nine, and none of us can recall ever having any less individually of Mom's or Dad's attention. So I had parents who loved us a great deal, but they were never worried about being our friends. There was no democracy in our house. We knew it. But we never doubted their love for us or their care for us.

When we moved into this neighborhood, Blessed Sacrament was the only [grammar] school that accepted us, although it wasn't necessarily a warm and friendly welcome. There were three Proctors and five Bagwells [our cousins] and two other black students, and that was it in the entire school. Every year the school trip was to a segregated amusement park, which meant we couldn't go.

One year our parents went to the school and said, "This is enough." Unfortunately, the school canceled the trip. Well, that didn't make us very popular in school. So that was painful, and those scars are still there.

In high school I was an athlete, and in my senior year I was vice president of student government. So I developed relationships based on common interests, not on color. But still, those hurts come out of the blue. I still recall to this day my conference with the [guidance] counselor. My grades were A's and B's, but I came out of that counseling session with nothing more than pamphlets to community colleges. And you know how in the school lunchroom, you compare what Sister said to you? And the pamphlets she gave? But my mother said, "Don't give it a second thought." So my parents took me on trips to colleges.

What I didn't find in school, what the dominant culture didn't provide for me, my family and my family network did. I had no doubt there were African-American doctors, teachers, college professors, because that's who came in and out of my house. Those were my aunts and uncles. My parents assumed the role of creating the nurturing environment that gave me the role models I needed. I didn't suffer from any doubt that we had the ability to be teachers. I came home to one every day.

If anything, those early struggles served me well, because I found a welcome with my God that was separate from the institutional Church and its practices and the hurts. I didn't see any African-American religious women in my 12 years of Catholic school; but I always knew that we could be Sisters, because I had three cousins who were [members of the Oblate Sisters of Divine Providence], one of the predominantly black congregations that came into being, because white congregations said no.

I'm clear that God directed me [to the Sisters of Notre Dame deNamur]. The story of St. Julie, our foundress, is one of the few books I've read cover to cover the first time I put it in my hand. Early on, she took on the institutional Church, and that for me was a woman with courage. Her story paralleled one of my other wisdom ancestors, Harriet Tubman. This was a woman I could learn from. My grandmothers were also strong figures in my life. My family had an early influence on the Catholic Church here in Baltimore. My grandfather helped build a couple of churches. And my grandmother would tell the stories about building those churches and then not being allowed in them or being relegated to the top balcony. There never was a moment of bitterness in her tone of voice. She just described it as it was. So my vocation meant immense things to my grandparents.

The biggest question for me when I entered, and still is today, has not been a struggle with the vows. It's not been a struggle with obedience. It's not been a struggle with chastity. It's not been a struggle with poverty. The question I live with is: Do I have what it takes to live in a congregation that's predominantly white? That's the struggle and that's the challenge for me. And that's where I find my greatest blessings and greatest pain.

I told this community when I entered that there were two things that wouldn't happen: I would not bite my tongue for a period of six years of formation, and all of a sudden they'd see a new me after final vows. Wasn't going to happen. They were going to see me right up front, so we would know early on if this was going to be a match or not. Secondarily, I would ask them never to put me in a position to choose between the congregation or my family, because I could tell them they were going to lose that choice. I felt there was room in my life for both, and I intended to nurture both. People needed to know that, so if they had a struggle with it or a problem, they needed to say so. The either-or model is a European-American one. African-Americans have functioned dualistically for a long time, and it works. It costs us a lot, but it works. Fortunately, they came to understand the importance of that—that I can do both, and that I was a better person. I was a stronger person. I was more content. I was more whole.

[During my formation years] I sometimes needed to get away from white people. I needed to be around and see people of color, feel the language, smell the smells—you know, listen to the music. I needed to get grounded again. Nothing major happened. It was that whole sense of the fish bowlness. It just got to me. [One time] there were about four or five of us in the shower—there's like a dozen stalls—and somebody stuck their head in the bathroom and said, "Gwynette, such and such and—" Just by my feet [they knew I was there]! They started talking right off. Fortunately, the key people in my life were not threatened when I said, "I need to get out of here, just get away." I didn't know if it was permitted. I didn't know if it was right or wrong. I knew what I needed. And it was okay. They didn't make me seem strange or act like it was my problem. So I [would go] to my mom's for a weekend.

I also had a need to associate with other women of color who were religious. In 1980, when I entered, I was only the second black in the history of the province. The congregation alone could not nurture my vocation. They simply couldn't. They could tell me about Notre Dame and St. Julie. But I needed to be able to see women who looked like me, who'd been around 40, 50, 60 years, doing the hard things in this Church and in their congregations. The other difficult thing about being in a predominantly white congregation is that you're judged by Eurocentric standards. I'm not Eurocentric. But if I didn't have African-American religious women involved in decision-making [about me], that's the only measure by which I was judged. My province realized I needed to have African-American religious women, who were not Sisters of Notre Dame, involved in my formation. And that's unusual, because formation is sacrosanct to each congregation. Each congregation lives and dies by their formation programs. But they were open to my suggestions.

One of the awarenesses the province needed to come to was that they assumed themselves to be far more progressive or aware or sensitive than they ever were. They had interacted with the African-American culture for a number of years, but always in very limited and very controlling ways. When they interacted with people of color, they were principals or teachers; and speaking to a parent, you have all the power under your control. You like to think you're as liberal as the next person. It was very different when I entered, when they had to see me as an equal and as a peer.

Some of our Sisters had bought into the stereotypes about people of color, particularly African-American males. I have three brothers. So when my brother would come to the door late at night, I saw fear in their eyes. They were uneasy about opening the door until I said, "That's Terrence." "Who?" "Terrence, my brother." "Oh." And then, of course, the anxiety goes way down. The other phenomenon that would occur is, whenever a black person arrived at the door, I got called. Some people walked into my final vows celebration; [some of the Sisters] brought them into the house, thinking I knew them. I'm opening my gifts at the time, sitting with my back to them. And I look up, and I'm like, "Good evening." They were utter strangers! They were Jehovah's Witnesses! So that was the phenomenon that goes on. Black person at the front door, and I got to be the expert.

When I first moved into this house, each Sister had a night to cook. There were five of us, and we all ate together Monday through Friday. And you had a night to cook. The understanding was that you only invited guests on the night you cooked. If I didn't cook on Monday, I wouldn't invite you to dinner if I ran into you during the day. That would be unfair to the cook. Well, this is strange to me. I come from a people who are hospitable, so I couldn't abide it. If I run into a friend, I'm supposed to say, "Oh, wait a minute. I cook next week on Tuesday. Do you think you could stop by on Tuesday?" rather than, "Come on by to dinner tonight." This is craziness.

I have a ministry to my Sisters of Notre Dame, because I'm their only immediate contact with the African-American culture, whereas they're not my only contact with white people. There's always a teachable moment, and I continually ask myself: "Do I take this stereotype on? Or do I let it go?" It depends on what the energy is on a given day. I have to find a way to respond if I'm going to take that moment to teach. The whole thing with food. It's not a matter of whether they're good cooks or not. It's a matter of it just tastes different. I feel like I'm always eating in another country. We season our food very differently than those in the dominant culture. It's not better or worse, just different. I never grew up on casseroles, and you folks like to make casseroles. I come home, and there's not one pot on the stove. All of dinner is in the oven in a casserole dish. Where do I draw the line so that I can stay whole and healthy and be nurtured? There was a time I would've eaten everything, anything, not knowing what it was I ate sometimes. But everyone else was eating it and enjoying it. So I thought I should, too. I have to make my rules now: "Please take no harm, but I will make a tuna-fish sandwich." They have to understand.

Paula and I have lived together for almost eight years now, in two different houses. She knows my family through and through. She's been over to Mom's house. She recognizes all my brothers. In fact, they're here sometimes fooling around with her when I come in. There were times in community where I needed to be home in order for any black friends or family to be there, because everyone else was uncomfortable. Paula fixes the vegetables where they're not crunching all the time. Our greens don't crunch for us. My mom always keeps greens frozen, and I will just run by there and pick up a couple of batches and put them in the freezer. If people will cook them longer for me, those are the moments of hope. Because I never look for the big, humongous changes. It's the little [things]—where somebody will take their greens out and leave mine on and let them boil up a bit. To acknowledge that there's another way to do it—not better, not worse, just another way.

But then as soon as we get a third Sister [here], that's going to change. I will have to relate to her in a way that's different. I have dynamic changes every time somebody moves in here or I move. I'm always somebody else's first. So I start over again in building relationships. That's the dynamic I bought into by virtue of living in this congregation. So we get down to [basics]. You know, they bump into my hair, and they touch it, and they realize it's soft, as opposed to whatever their impression was.

There's another side of that coin that makes it exciting—encountering new people and getting to know one another and working through the difficulties to some common ground and acknowledging that there's some places where we disagree. That's an investment that I like making over and over. Obviously—or I wouldn't keep doing it. As much as I know there are moments of pain and mis-understanding in my congregation, I know, too, that there are women out there who love me for who I am. Not who they want me to be, nor their perceptions of me as I should be. But they love me for who I am.

There's an interesting dynamic that we are aware of as African-American women in predominantly white congregations. You come in, and you're treated with kid gloves. Everybody's so afraid you're going to call them racist that basi-cally you can do anything you want. You know people aren't honest with you. They're not dealing with you straight up. I had to live through that phenomenon. Well, it was those handful who didn't let me do anything I wanted, who did risk putting themselves in that posture, but who said no to me. No, everything isn't all right. It's the "child loose in a candy store" notion. They risked my saying, "Well, that's mighty racist of you." It's those individuals that I see now, 15 years later, who helped me to grow and be nurtured. And I know that I have a respon-sibility to do that for others.

Remember I said earlier that the congregation in and of itself couldn't nurture my vocation alone? It has been the National Black Sisters Conference who provided the role models that I lacked in Notre Dame. Every year we have a conference, and we come together for a week. Most of us come from predomi-nantly white congregations; so for that one week the pressures are totally off. We can be for one another in a way that's familiar to us. We're not on show; we don't have to mind our p's and q's because somebody might not understand our loud, boisterous [behavior]. We come from our stressful situations, and we're able to mend, and put one another back together, and send each other back out there to do the work of the Lord. It's unimportant what your [order's] initials are, whether you're an SBS or an SSND or SND or Sister of Charity or whatever. Every year we celebrate our jubilarians. We lift up our elders as role models for us. Anytime I feel that this is too much, and I've had it, all I have to do is call to mind the picture of [one of them] and remember they have come through it, that I owe it to myself and to those who are going to come after me to do it, too.

I see the small signs of hope. That's what drives me. Because there are so many awarenesses that the dominant culture in our congregation has come to learn. There are probably 1,800 of us now in the United States, and there are 10 African-American women, but there were never any women of color who were delegates to our chapter meetings. I went to the chapter in 1990. We had to say, "You can no longer speak for us and our experience. You can speak about it, but you can't speak for us. You have no clue of what it's like for me to walk as an African-American in this country. You cannot represent us at chapter. We need our own representation." And our Hispanic Sisters said the same. People have heard that.

I live my life now so that my niece and nephew, who are 10 and 7, will experience a different world when they're 20. I know I'm not going to see ultimate change in my lifetime. But I'm not going to stop fighting for the small changes that, [for example,] will help our Sisters see African-American men in a different light. If it has to be my nephews [who serve as models], fine. I have one nephew who's a concert pianist, and another who is an artist and majoring in Chinese and headed to China next year for his junior year [in college]. These two were raised in the congregation, we say. They brought their bikes to whatever convent I was living in. So it helps for the folks to see them now.

Sometimes when I speak, I think I come off negative. While I speak freely and honestly about what troubles me, certainly I have also experienced a great deal of joy. I hope that has come through, because I would want my Sisters to know that. Even through the difficult times and the pain, I wouldn't have it any other way. I've become who I am—Gwynette Proctor, Sister of Notre Dame—by virtue of the experiences I've described. And I hope in some small way I have influenced people around me. But I know I have felt their influence.

One of the moments of grace that I experience often—and that tell me in a very quiet, settling way that I'm in the right place at the right time; and however hard it might be for me, it's good that I be here—is when a Sister shares with me a moment in which she has grown or come in touch with the racism within her. And somehow she's been able to tell me how I have facilitated that. And that's a big risk, because she has no guarantee what I'll come back with. So I know it's right that I'm here for now. I couldn't see myself as not being a Sister of Notre Dame. (February 1995)

Sister Gwynette remained in social ministries in Baltimore until 2002 when she moved to Massachusetts to become executive director of the Notre Dame Education Center in Lawrence. The center provides ESL and citizenship courses for new immigrants and teaches Spanish to doctors, nurses, and librarians in the area. Sister Gwynette also coached boys and girls basketball teams at Notre Dame High School, part of the Cristo Rey Network of schools for poor students in urban areas where there are few other educational options. In 2008, after she was invited to move into leadership within her community, she returned to Baltimore.

The American culture still wants us to divide. It promotes fear. I will not buy into that because I know different. Religious life is one place where we are pulling away from the culture message. We see differences as gifts not as divisions. There is a richness of life we're missing [in our culture] and we need to be intentional about changing that.

Have you seen changes in attitudes in your community?

Yes! I am blessed to have experienced heartfelt transformations. [In 1995] it was lip service. Now it is heartfelt. We realize that we need each other to do mission. To be an SND [Sister of Notre Dame] is the most exciting thing in my life. We stand with the poor. The call is still there. And the blessings.

12
STRUCTURES AND FISSURES

SISTER GERMAINE FRITZ

While most religious communities managed to stay together despite large numbers of departures, conflicts over ministries and finances, and their members' disparate lifestyle choices, some convents were torn asunder. In my research I encountered five separate incidents of such fissures. Following are two histories of a split that occurred among the Benedictine Sisters at St. Walburga's Monastery in Elizabeth, New Jersey, in 1971. The first is told by a woman who chose to stay; the second by a woman who chose to leave.

At the time of the interview in 1992, Sister Germaine Fritz, 57, had been prioress at St. Walburga's for eight years. She spoke with obvious pain of the troubles, both past and present, that the monastery had endured, but with great warmth for her Sisters. She is a tall woman with a presence that confirms her years as teacher, principal of an urban high school, prioress, and gifted musician. She plays both piano and guitar but is best known for her fine soprano voice.

In 1994, Sister Germaine was invited to record an album of liturgical music for Angel Records; Vision, *a collection of chants written by the mystic Hildegard von Bingen in the twelfth century, has become a worldwide best-seller.*

I always found community life very supportive. But those years [after Vatican II] were very difficult in community and probably started me thinking very seriously about a lot of things. Not so much in terms of my own call—I never had a question in terms of my own call. I found my own life deepening and deepening the longer I lived the life. But it was during those years of the 1960s that we began to lose large numbers of Sisters. And that was a very painful time. We had at one point 250 Sisters. But there was a period of time when we were losing 13, 14, 15 at the end of every school year. It got to the point that you didn't know how many it was going to be.

And there was a period in that time when a significant number of the Sisters of our community did not want to leave religious life, but felt that their interpretation of what it was to be a monastic woman was different from what they were experiencing in this community. So in 1971, 23 members of our community left and founded a new community. It's only in the last five or six years that [I have realized that] the loss was extremely deep, but I had never named it. And when I was able to name it, it was very painful. It was really difficult.

There's a big gap in our community because of the people who are in the other community, which is Emmanuel Monastery in Baltimore. They are the 40-year-olds, the 50-year-olds, a couple of older Sisters; but it's really the people who would be moving into leadership in this time. Not that there are no leaders in this community; but we lost a big chunk of people.

People reflect on the morning when they left, that last Mass when everyone was together. Many have memories of the tears. Others don't. And what I've learned from my own experience is, when something is very painful, you can block it out so totally that you have no memory of what you felt at that time. And I think that probably a lot of us did that. And I'm sure a lot of them did, too. It was not an ugly separation. The two communities can visit, go back and forth, a lot. As a matter of fact, when this chapel collapsed, those Sisters were right back here; their sleeves were rolled up, and they were here with us. They never missed a funeral, never missed an event, always came back. So there was a great desire to be with one another, but there seemed to be two different expressions of the same tradition.

So now both Emmanuel and St. Walburga are members of the same Federation. Let me just tell you a little bit about our Federation. There are four federations of Benedictine Sisters in this country. And each Federation has so many independent autonomous monasteries. We are one of 21 monasteries in the Federation of St. Scholastica. In 1985 I was elected to the Federation Council. And another Sister from Emmanuel, a person I had been close with, was also elected. So we would see one another frequently. We often said, "Would it ever be possible that we could be one again?" And we'd find ourselves dissolved in tears in that conversation. You can even hear it in my voice. It happens.

At a Federation meeting there was a theme of tradition, of going back to our roots. And the Sister who was a member of Emmanuel and I had been asked if we would be willing to speak of our memories of the separation of our communities. It was always understood, I think, that these two communities separated gracefully; but it was painful, because we deeply loved one another.

I remember very, very clearly sitting in a classroom, right down the hall here, with many Sisters who ultimately became members of the new group, and members of this community, who never became members of it. And there was a lot of frustration. How was this separation going to occur? And I remember a member of the community calling the question—a Sister saying, "Look, I think the first thing we have to do is to say who's going and who's staying." And I can remember sitting in that chair and knowing that I'd never seriously asked myself that question, and knowing that I didn't know how I was going to answer when it came around to me. It's like when I entered. I can't tell you that I experienced a bolt of lightning. I came because I felt drawn. I'd love to be able to say it was the silence; it was the contemplative life; it was the prayer. That's not the way the Lord drew me. But I can remember sitting in that room, and as each one was speaking, she was saying what she was going to do. When it came my turn, I heard myself say that as much as I loved every member of that group, somehow or other I knew it was not my call to go. There was no bolt of lightning. There was no crash of thunder. I just in my heart somehow knew that it was for me to be here.

And the thing I can remember saying in front of all those people at that Federation meeting was that, when that occurred, nothing changed in my relationship with those Sisters. The fact that my relationship with them never changed—even when it was very clear that would not be a direction I could go—made it very clear to me that they were following a call, that the Spirit was somehow in that call, that the Spirit was just as much present in remaining here.

It was a painful time, and it was a struggle, but it was a group of women who never, never behaved in an ugly or unkind manner to one another. At least that was never my experience. I guess there had to be some of that. How do you know you're that different? But at the same time, it was not my experience.

And so the time came when they left. I can remember being very peaceful about that. [And I remember much later] sitting up on kind of a stage and speaking about what it was like and the kind of growth that occurred, [and saying] I think that's how the Spirit enters into the Church. That's how new life is born. It's born in pain. Isn't this what childbirth is? There was great pain in the community, and it was out of that pain that a new community was born. This community continued to go on, and we have grown. It was difficult, but I think we learned a lot about accepting one another.

The one thing that used to be so obviously different to me was [that] when the Sisters went to Emmanuel, they went into contemporary dress. That didn't happen in our community until 1990. Many of us have asked the question, "Could we have accepted changes that might have made it possible for this community to remain whole?" I, for one, have stopped asking those questions, because I truly believe that God works in very natural ways with all people and all life. I'm peaceful with it. But to be at peace doesn't mean not to experience pain.

There's a wonderful exchange between the two communities. They visit here; we visit there. They had their first death, a terribly painful experience for them. This community was down there en masse. Antoinette entered in this community; she died at a very young age—early forties. And that was a terrible loss for them. We grieved with them. They were ours.

Benedict, his whole sense of community was this: When I commit myself to live with these women and my relationship deepens through the years, then trust grows. It is that trusting relationship that allows my vulnerability to show, allows me to be who I am, not to have the mask up here [gestures toward forehead]. Once the mask goes down, obviously I can be called forth. My Sister can call me and challenge me to growth. Being with the same community doesn't mean sameness. It simply means that the support of this community is always there.

I don't know how Benedictine life will play itself out as the centuries move on. But I do believe we will be here. Benedictine women—like all women, I think—have had to struggle in many, many ways. You know the prioress takes the place of Christ in the monastery. At this point in time I, as the prioress, am able to be the presider at a lot of things. But the central prayer is Eucharist. The prioress of the monastery can never be the central presider at that very unique and special part of our day. I really have to say that I don't feel I am called to priesthood. But I have a great sensitivity to many women who do feel they are. They are prepared and could go into seminaries, and just because they're female they cannot. I do feel that that will change in time, and it must change. But that would not be the general thinking of my community, I don't think.

We talk about those things. We are able to accept the fact that all 84 of us think differently. And the beauty of it, and the importance of it, might be characterized in something as simple and material as dress. It was not an easy decision for this community to move into contemporary dress. From the fall of 1989 to June of 1990, we talked about it. We talked about it one-on-one, we talked about it in small groups, and then we sat together as a whole community and we talked about it. The rule of Benedict and our constitution say that the abbot or the prioress will decide, so that's not something that I expected the community to vote on, and we understood that from the beginning. But I didn't want it to be a 50 percent or a 51 percent in favor. I really wanted to talk that through so that it wasn't going to be a devastating experience for anyone. I said we should all try to understand what another member feels and why she feels that way, and try to be open to both sides of the issue. Ultimately, 73 percent were open to it. With that kind of consensus, I made the decision that we would go into contemporary dress. The only thing I asked of the community was that we honor where each one stands on the issue. And I have to tell you that only 25 percent of the community have actually made the change. But there is a total acceptance of one another's choice.

We don't have to think alike. We don't have to be clones of one another. As a matter of fact, Benedict in the fifth century was speaking about responding to the individual needs. But the core of community life to me is the relationship that one has with the other, which says I can support you even if I can't do that myself. So that's why I can be with another Sister who might dress differently than I, and it doesn't make a whole lot of difference. That's an external, you know. The Sister who feels that this external corporal sign is a critical thing will want to wear that sign. Another person who interprets that monks of Benedict's day wore the clothing of the people would want to wear the clothing of the people today. That's what I believe. It's not the clothing that makes the person; it's how one reaches out to others, makes Christ present to others. I might not be immediately recognized as a Sister from a distance, but I'm very quick to identify myself as that person.

Right in the middle of that whole dress issue, there was a tragedy, a terrific loss. The chapel fell down. On the morning of March 2, 1990, at 8:30, the roof simply fell in. We had noticed a problem two days before; but it didn't look like a serious problem—it looked like there was some loose plaster. The next day when we sent someone up to look at it, they saw daylight where they shouldn't see daylight. The roof had detached from the wall. And they looked with a flash-light, and two of the big trusses had snapped. But they did not even recognize at that point what that could mean. We prayed downstairs underneath the church that morning and the morning that it collapsed.

One of the Sisters came upstairs with the priest who had said Mass that morn-ing. There was a big crack coming down the side. The building was groaning. Still, you'd never believe what was going to happen could happen. At 8:33, our seniors had just come over here for class, had just passed by the building. At 8:36, the whole thing went down, debris falling all over. The students had just passed by. We had a Sister in the church watching it happen from the inside. She stepped back outside of the church, and the wind impact blew her literally against the wall. It was just an astounding experience.

We had to evacuate this whole place. We had to move out totally. We didn't know if there was going to be a secondary collapse. The big steeple was still standing. And people immediately came. Emmanuel was here, moving the furniture, doing everything we needed to do. The support was unbelievable.

I remember the Sunday after it occurred—it happened on a Friday—many had gravitated together. It was freezing because there was no heat. I remember saying to them: We don't know the answer; we don't know the question. But we can only be willing to stand in this mystery, knowing that God's in the middle of it somewhere.

We had to evacuate Sisters of all ages out of their residence. Temporarily, the hospice took all of our infirmary people. And we were able within a week to move them back into a residence over here that we made into an infirmary. It was not easy. We had a 93-year-old who didn't get into a bathtub for a year, because you couldn't use a Hoyer lift in that kind of tub. The Sisters received wonderful care, but the staff had to work harder to do it. We moved our dining room into a hallway. We moved into the lobby downstairs for our place of prayer. The Eucharist is down the hall in the parlor. We've gotten accustomed to it. It's not ideal, and we look forward with great anticipation to moving into a real church again, but it's amazing how well we've done. [The new building was completed in 1994.]

But again, there was that acceptance, that willingness not to go haywire but to just get on with life and do what needs to be done. Change is not easy for anyone, and I think our letting ourselves talk about those kinds of things is what brings new life.

We're a kind of steady-as-you-go community. We are a very faithful community, and we will continue to move along, responding to the needs as we perceive them to be. This is not a community that walks the cutting edge, you know.

We won't be in the forefront of new ways of thinking. But we will be at the core of what's critical, namely, the deep prayer life and the community living, which allows members to move out into ministry to others. (May 1992)

Sister Germaine served one more term as prioress of St. Walburga's Monastery and then became president and CEO of Benedictine Academy, a four-year college preparatory high school for girls in Elizabeth, New Jersey. In 1997, Sister Germaine, working with composer Richard Souther and professional vocalists, recorded Illumination, *a second album of chants from Hildegard von Bingen.*

SISTER KATHLEEN MCNANY

Sister Kathleen McNany, 47, lives in Emmanuel Monastery, the Benedictine community founded by the 23 Sisters who left St. Walburga's in 1971. The monastery is now housed in a Tudor-style family home at the end of a cul-de-sac in a suburb of Baltimore.

Kathy, as she likes to be called, was a teacher until 1979. Since then she has been a liturgist and has worked on retreat teams and as a spiritual director.

When I entered [in 1963], nothing had changed. Everything was in Latin, even the table prayers we said—the grace before and after meals. You never really knew what you were doing. It was just all in Latin. Having gone to high school across the street, I was used to coming over and joining the Sisters when they were praying. I was really very romantic about everything at that age, and I just thought it was lovely and beautiful and all the things you read about in books. It didn't take long for reality to hit. I guess the changes in the community started shortly after I entered. The first thing to change were the table prayers; they went into English. Around 1967, I believe it was, the habit began to change. It changed quickly once it started. It seems like in that two- or three-year period we went from small changes to wearing basically a black suit, a white blouse, and a veil. And those external changes were just indicative of a whole lot of stuff that was going on internally.

A lot of people left. I remember asking myself, How come they're going and I'm staying? What happened in my own life is, we had a series of talks at the motherhouse. I remember coming home from [one of the talks] with the sense that my entire perception of this religious life had been turned upside-down. Up until that point, I always thought that to be a good nun all you had to do was fit this very well-defined mold or description. I didn't find that confining. It's how I understood myself. The mold was out here somewhere, and I had to somehow fit myself into that and my life would be fulfilled. I came home from that talk realizing that there was something inside of me that was wonderful and beautiful and was an image of God, and that to be fulfilled, to be happy, to be of service to anybody, simply meant bringing that to birth. I didn't have to try to be something I wasn't.

They talk today about paradigm shifts. It was that kind of experience for me. And I remember coming home and not being able to sleep and kind of pacing the floor. We still had night silence then, so you didn't talk. And I got up very late, and went down to the chapel, and one of the older Sisters was there. She knew I was upset. I don't remember what she said to me that night, other than patting me on the hand and saying something like, "If you're faithful to prayer, God will help you know what to do." But it was very helpful. It was like it's okay to feel what you're feeling.

At that point I began to understand at least why other people were leaving—because they just weren't able to be who they were, in the structures that were there. Some of my best friends left, best friends from high school. I was 24 at the time. When I entered, there were 250 people in the community, and it seems to me in 1968 there were about 150, and not many had died. So within that five- or six-year period, we had lost so many people.

I don't think the people who were older in the community really understood what it was like for someone who was young and saw her whole life ahead of her, and saw what could be. And from my perspective I didn't think [the leadership] was doing anything about it, or taking responsibility for the amount of people who were leaving.

I might get a little teary on this, [because the prioress] was someone I grew up knowing. She and my father were best friends. And I was very fond of her, so it was very hard to be on the other side. I've become more of a vocal and strong person in my later years, but I certainly wasn't then. I was kind of this shrinking wimp. Somebody said something, I did it. And I can remember, a couple of times, taking a deep breath and standing up for what I thought and finding it real difficult. It was difficult to be at odds with her, and then it caused me to be at odds with my family.

Basically, the things that were happening were, from my experience, similar to what I think's going on in the Church right now. Things were beginning to change, and it was obvious you couldn't put the toothpaste back in the tube. And so instead of going with the flow and seeing how you could deal with the changes that were inevitably happening, we began to pull back. It was almost like a Custer's last stand.

I remember that period of time being very sad in terms of the losses, and yet one thing stands out for me—and this is true in many of the critical periods of my life. In spite of the sadness, there was always this glimmer of life or excitement somewhere, which I guess is the reason I stayed.

The one point during that time when I really seriously toyed with leaving was the night before I had to renew my vows. We were in temporary vows for three years, and then we had to renew for another two years. It was 1968. It was the day after Robert Kennedy had been shot. It was the whole Vietnam scene, and a couple of people that I had gone to school with were killed in Vietnam, so it was not a happy time in history. And I remember thinking, Why am I doing this?

It doesn't make any sense at all. And yet, I knew it was [what] I had to do. Again there was this glimmer of there's something more than what I'm seeing, even though the sadness, the heaviness was very real. I mean, I can feel it now, talking about it.

I think [the whole situation] had a bonding effect on those of us who stayed. At that point the motherhouse had just been built in Elizabeth, and they had a roof that we weren't supposed to go up to. [Nevertheless] that roof became very sacred space. We really helped and supported one another through that whole period of time, talking into the wee hours of the night on the roof, talking and having a smoke. We learned how to pray there, too. I think when we talk about our memories, that's one of the things that comes up a lot. I guess up until that point for me, and people around my time, prayer was the Office and a kind of a stylized way of praying. When we got to the roof and began to talk about what was going on in our hearts, we really began to talk to God in a group. We began to pray together. That experience intensified as it became clearer that something [was going to happen] in the community.

One of the hardest things for me right before the split was the way we began to make decisions. While the prioress can make the ultimate decision, it's really based on the input that she gets from the community. What I began seeing was that on really major questions, like which mission we should close, the community was giving input, and then the decision was coming out quite opposite. And it began to get increasingly clear that there was a major difference in the way we were seeing religious life. What was out of balance was that it was too work oriented. There wasn't time to be a person, you know. All of your waking hours were going into supporting our [schools and a hospital]. That was all good, but it was too much of one thing. And I think, too, the other thing that was happening to me at that time was a liturgical awakening. I was becoming very involved in music and liturgy, and in the community I was experiencing a reticence to move in a direction that was more free in terms of liturgy and the way we worshipped together.

There was an explosive meeting that I wasn't at, and a group of people left that meeting really upset. They met with a friend who was a Benedictine abbot and also a canon lawyer, and just said candidly, "What would it take to start a new community?" So that's where the idea germinated; and then later that week, calls went around saying: If anybody is interested in getting together to talk about what seemed to be happening in the community, there was going to be a meeting. I went to the meeting, [and] I remember thinking, there's no way I want a split in this community. Now, this was the end of May 1970.

At the beginning of the summer, they called in [someone from the Federation], who interviewed each member of the community. I was at the beginning of the interviews, and I remember saying to her, "I don't want to split. I don't want to see this community torn apart." I think she had seen maybe a dozen people before me, and she said to me, "Dear, that's not going to happen, because everybody I've talked to has said the same thing. So don't worry about it." By the end of the weekend, when I came back to pick up some Sisters who were at the end of the interview line, that had all changed, and what she said, in effect, was: The best thing for you would be to look at forming the new community.

I was going to make final vows in August of 1970. They sent us away that summer for a program on the vows. They sent Germaine [Fritz], who was on the Formation Team, with us. [The experience] was wonderful, and at the end of the program we came back and most of us made final vows. To me that's one of the greatest miracles that ever happened in the midst of that mess. My sense was that to not take vows at that point would not have been true to who I was, because I knew this was the life I was called to. In a sense, the vows gave me the stability in which to make the decision. And a week after my final vows, we did have a community meeting where there was a vote: Should we investigate a new community? That was the only time I voted in the Elizabeth community, and I voted myself out.

Then they asked people who were interested [in joining the new community] to sign a paper. Now that was really hard, because you had to walk up the center of this room. I think there were about 43 people who signed that paper. From that point until the following February, we met monthly as a group. It was an open meeting; anybody from the Elizabeth community could come, and a lot of them came as observers. We talked about what our hopes were, what our dreams were, what our fears were. I think what we were really looking for at that point was a way of life that was open to the change that was obviously happening in not just the Church but in our way of understanding the world and religious life and the relationships between the two.

It was decided that if we were interested in joining the new foundation that we would need to have a letter in by February 28th of 1971, and I can remember I turned 25 in January of that year. My parents were not real happy with the fact that I was considering this, and my father gave me a trip to Puerto Rico during school break. We have friends in Puerto Rico, and it was a present for my twenty-fifth birthday. I mailed my letter on the way to the airport. That's how I remember the date. In retrospect, I think that the move, as hard as it was for both our communities, was really right. They certainly have grown and developed as they needed to, and we have.

We were still in habit when we were in Elizabeth. When we came here we were not in habit. We never discussed it. We never had a community meeting. We never had a vote. We just didn't wear habits when we came down here. I mean, it was a total nonissue. Our beginning years were, when I look at them now, very reactionary. We reacted against authority. We were highly individualistic in lots and lots of ways. In other ways, we were extremely dependent on one another. We were 23 people; we had one car. We were teaching in I don't know how many different places, so that the car pooling was horrendous. I don't know how we did it. We eventually got a couple more cars so that we could deliver everybody to work, you know. It was a crazy, crazy setup.

I guess we were in a survival mode, those first 10 years. While we fought well with one another when we needed to do that, we were very protective of one another, and we did a lot of things together. We worked in four or five different schools in groups of two and three. Because we weren't in habit, we were sharing clothes, so you watched your diet to make sure you stayed the same size.

Somewhere in the course of those years, we became a community. [The name of our monastery is] Emmanuel. The translation of Emmanuel is "God with us." We decided on that name because our experience had been that God has been so much with us through every step of these 21 years. And that's not just the name of the monastery. It's really become an identity for us.

The liturgy we have here at Emmanuel is a feminine model of liturgy. The priests who come and celebrate with us, celebrate *with* us. They don't preside over us. In terms of where the Church is toward women right now, I find it very painful and very hurtful. I do. Because most of my ministry right now is spiritual direction; I'm with a lot of people who are in painful situations in their lives, times when they really need to experience reconciliation. It's hard for me to have to withdraw. I would like to be able to sacramentalize those moments. I live with people who work with the elderly and dying, who are with them through all those final stages of their life. And then when it comes time for the anointing of the sick, they have to bring in someone else. That doesn't make sense to me—that just because you're not a man, you can't pray in this way with this person. And when things don't make sense to me, I'm kind of intolerant.

It's getting increasingly difficult to find places where I can worship and feel I'm included in the congregation. I can't listen to it anymore when we are all called "brothers" and "men," and I'm sitting there and I want to say, "Hey, I'm here, too." In my ministry I travel in the summer, and that's where I really experience the tension. I go through all this trauma inside. Do I go to Mass? Or do I not go? Because I love liturgy. It's in my bones; it's in my blood. I love Eucharist, and to make the choice to absent myself from that is very difficult. I don't think I'm a feminist, whatever that means today; nor am I a very radical person. But I guess I have an innate sense of who I am in relationship to God, and who other women are in relationship to God. And I can't worship in a setting that doesn't allow that to be. It's not worship; it's going through the rubrics of something. And then my presence there is saying, "I accept this," or "This is okay." It's becoming a justice issue, I guess, and it's not okay anymore.

There have been a couple of men who have been significant in my life, both of them priests. I met one back in 1968, and I went through a whole infatuation period. I knew I was falling in love with him, and it was right around the time of my own final vows. But his fidelity to who he was, and is, helped me to be who I am. We are still very, very good friends. The friendship has been a very significant part of my life.

And then [there] was a person whom I worked with on retreat teams here in Maryland. Our paths crossed back in the early 1970s and again in the 1980s, and we found that we clicked in lots and lots of different ways. And he was just a very, very good friend. He was diagnosed with cancer two years [ago] this past June, very suddenly. He had a brain tumor. He lived for two years and I'm still processing what happened during those two years. We became very, very close.

I had an interesting experience with him. I guess it's about a year ago now, after he'd gone through extensive chemotherapy and was really, really sick. I went over [to the nursing home] one day, and he was miserable. He was lying in bed, and he said, "I just need you to hold me. Could you hold me?" And I remember standing there thinking to myself, "I'm 45 years old. I don't know how to hold a man." The relationship I had with him was a free enough relationship for me to say, "I don't know how to do that. Show me. Tell me how you want me to hold you." And then when I was holding him, I wasn't worried about myself or him. I was thinking, "What if somebody walks through that door? What are they going to think?" But I eventually got over that. What was important was to be there for him.

He was sick for a long time, and his death has left a real void in my life. But one of the things that I'm realizing is, I must be a very fortunate person, because even the hardest things seem to open another door that I didn't understand. I've begun to develop a relationship with him beyond death that is as strong as the relationship that we had. He's one of the few people that I allowed to convince me that I'm good, that I can do things I can't do. For some reason or another, if he said it, I believed it. He had a way of being there for me and encouraging me and calling forth things in me that I never thought I could do. It hasn't stopped with his dying. That's what's been amazing. I've been working on some programs the past couple of days, and I have the sense of him sitting there laughing, saying, "See, you can do this." We used to learn as kids about the communion of saints. It's beginning to make sense to me, I guess.

There is the reality within me of what I don't know, of never having had a real physical relationship with a man; but I don't worry about it. I think part of it is I'm someone at home with my own sexuality. I don't have regrets about the decisions I've made about my life, but I have a sneaking suspicion that if I'd made a different choice, and I were married and I had kids, I'd probably feel the same way about that choice, too.

I'm not sure if religious communities, as we know them, are going to continue. I would like to think that they are. I tend to be a visionary person, so as awful and as scary as a time like this is for me, it's one of those times I was describing before. There's this little glimmer of life and hope over here. If there is a trend, if the Spirit is moving the Church and religious life in a direction, I have to believe somehow we're going to know what we need to do. There is a sense in me that we just need to respond to what the need is at the given moment. I struggle; we all struggle.

I guess some of my feeling is the same as it was when I left the Elizabeth community. If religious life doesn't continue the way I see it or know it to be now, I still don't see my life as fruitless or meaningless. I feel now that there's a real need for what I'm beginning to understand is the Benedictine charism, which has something to do with community and prayer and service or steward-ship, caring for the earth, reverence for life and people—all of that combined. There's something about that charism that I feel impelled to carry into the future. But if that doesn't get carried into the future this way, that will be okay. I prob-ably can say that only because the life I'm living today is so drastically different from the life I thought I was going to live when I entered. I can look back, and I can see there was a direction in all of that. God's not going to take you just so far and then stop. (December 1992)

Sister Kathy continues retreat work and spiritual direction. She has moved into programs in ecumenical spirituality, and she assists Benedictine monasteries around the country in their discernment for new leadership.

I truly believe the Spirit is doing something in this diminishing [of religious life]. We don't know what it is. Our small numbers are breaking down barriers with the laity. Something is emerging that is of the Spirit. There's definitely an ecumenical piece, an interfaith piece. I see everything so interconnected. It's not just a Church issue. It's beyond that. It's a world issue.

13

SUMMONED TO LEAD

SISTER THERESA KANE

Since 1979, when she publicly addressed Pope John Paul II on the subject of women in the Church (see page 216), Sister Theresa Kane—60, a Sister of Mercy—has become accustomed to newspaper headlines and television cameras. But at Mount Mercy in Dobbs Ferry, New York, where the interview took place, she was far from the spotlight; rather, she was immersed in the kind of hands-on managerial tasks she has been performing for more than 30 years.

I was 18 when I entered the convent, thinking my life was going to be the same all the time. I wanted to be a good nun, so I really did follow the rules very closely. I was only in a couple of years, and the Sisters came back from a meeting and said, "Well, we're going to make this change and that change." Little changes, but big in our eyes at that time. I was a combination of both wanting to be compliant and yet somewhat excited about changes coming along.

Everyone who entered with me was going to an elementary school to teach. I had done a lot of the business subjects in high school, and when I entered, my part-time assignment was working in the secretarial office. Then one of the Sisters said to me, "We need somebody in the hospital field. Would you be interested in the business office in a hospital?" So they trained me, and my first assignment was in a hospital finance office.

What happened is, the Sister who was the administrator [at the hospital] in Port Jervis [New York] had a stroke and died within two months. They didn't have anyone right on hand, and so they asked would I be willing to be the administrator pro term. So I said, "Yes, I would." I was surprised; everybody else was surprised. I was only 27, I think. So that somehow was a catalyst for my being known as an administrative-type person.

I was administrator of the hospital for two years—from 1964 until 1966, when I left there and came into administration for the community. They called us an administrative council at that time, and I was brought in as secretary to the provincial. I was on the council for four years, and then I was elected provincial [for the New York region]. I served seven years as provincial. At the end of my two terms, I went to the meeting down at our generalate in Washington and was elected president of the Sisters of Mercy, which was 7,000 Sisters in the country. I was just a little under 40 at that point.

That year, 1977, was a big turning point for our community. Major decisions were made at that meeting. One was to sell our motherhouse down in Washington, which we had had for almost 50 years. Another was the issue of ordination [for women] in the Church. Early in January, the first document [against women's ordination] came from the Vatican, from Pope Paul VI. The Sisters were very strong in saying we took exception to it; and we set up a committee of Sister theologians to look at that document, to take issue with it, and monitor any future documents that would come out. So the women's issue was strong. Anyone being elected at that time would have to be someone who was promoting ministry for women in the Church.

And then in 1979 I became president of the Leadership Conference of Women Religious [LCWR]. It's very much a PR role. You're the representative of the organization to outside groups—you meet with the Vatican, you meet with the bishops, you meet with the priests' organizations.

In the spring [of 1979] we had heard the pope [John Paul II] was coming. Early in June someone said it was definite. So the officers of the Leadership Conference were trying to get a meeting with him when he was here. He wasn't pope even a year at that point, but we knew he had already talked two or three times about Sisters being cloistered and wearing the habit. We said to the men down in Washington who were planning the visit, "We really think it's important for him to hear from us that that is not going to happen in this country."

So most of our energy was going into trying to set up a little conversation with him. Maybe two weeks before the visit, I got a phone call from the priest at the national shrine. All he said to me was, "The pope will be giving a prayer service to the Sisters, and as the president of LCWR, we would like you to give the greeting." So I said, "Can you tell me how long it will be?" He said, "Well, very brief, Sister. They're really coming to hear the Holy Father." And I thought, "Well, I know that." So he said two or three minutes. Now that was all the conversation I had with him. He said, "What's your name? We want to put your name on the program."

There was a real preoccupation by the planners at the shrine because they had heard that Sisters were going to do a demonstration outside. What are these Sisters going to do? Are they going to blow up the pope? Is there going to be a security risk? They didn't seem to know who was organizing it. They did call me, and I said, "Do you want to meet with them?" They said, "Well, do you think we could?" I said, "I'm sure the Sister who's organizing it would be glad to meet with you." So I called her up, and she went over and met with them.

So the only instruction I had [about my greeting] was it was to be brief. I knew immediately that I wanted to welcome the pope on behalf of the Sisters of the United States. I also felt that the Sisters didn't get enough official recognition for the work that they had done. They were always behind the scenes. So I wanted to somehow acknowledge what the Sisters had done in the country. And then I did feel that the question of women in the Church was a very important one. So those were the three things I had in mind. I called three or four Sisters that I worked with in LCWR, and said, "These are the three things I'd like to say." And they said, "Oh, that sounds good." I also called one of the Sisters who had been the president of LCWR, an older woman who I had great admiration for. She said, "This pope has really worked hard to have people more aware of the poor of the world. I think it would be important for you to say, 'We acknowledge your priority, and we're in solidarity with you on the poor.'" So I had my four points there.

Two or three days before I was to give the greeting, one of the Sisters who worked with me at our motherhouse in Washington said, "Are you going to say something about women?" So I said, "Yes, I am. Do you think I shouldn't?" "Oh," she said, "I think it would be great. But I didn't know if you were going to do it." Now that was the first inkling that I had that maybe everybody wouldn't say something about women and the Church.

I didn't know [the pope's talk at the shrine] was being televised extensively until maybe Friday or Saturday. Someone called from New York on Friday and said, "Sister, you're being televised live." Initially I thought [I was just speaking to] the Sisters in the shrine. I remember thinking, "It's a bigger audience than I thought. I wonder how they'll feel if I say something about women?" It was just like a question in my mind. It seemed very right to me, so it really wasn't a reservation.

The day before I was to give the greeting, we had been invited to the White House because the pope was visiting with [President] Jimmy Carter. Several of the other Sisters who were invited were talking with me about this. I gave them a copy of what I wanted to say. They looked it over and said, "That sounds good." It was very short, only one page.

So the next morning I went to the shrine very early, at 6:30. Sitting next to me was an older woman. She saw me reading my notes, and she said, "Are you going to say something about women?" I thought, "Here we go again." So I said, "Yes, I am." She said, "Good. I'm glad." She was an older Catholic woman, an attorney. She said, "When I was going through law school, I got no support from anyone except my husband." I remember thinking, "That is my clue."

I was a little nervous, I think, because of being on TV, which I thought was just Washington and New York TV. I didn't have any idea that it was being televised nationally until it was all over. The other thing that was a bit of an anxiety for me was when we walked into the shrine. The Sisters were all demonstrating outside. There was a big crowd of them, and they handed out leaflets, which I really didn't mind. I personally supported that. But when we went down the aisle, I felt there was tension in the church. And I knew that the two priests who were running it were very nervous. One came up and told me where to sit, and he said, "Now, Sister, when you greet the Holy Father, I'll escort you to the microphone. And then when you finish, just bow and go to your seat." So I said, "Well, I'd like to go over and say 'Hello' to him." "Can't do that! Can't do that!" he said. I mean, they were very nervous about everything. So I think it made me a little nervous, too.

I went right to the mike, and I gave the greeting. And then when I finished, the priest said to me, "Bow and go to your seat." I said to him, "I would like to meet the Holy Father." So I left him and walked over. He was really annoyed at that. I went over [to the pope] and started to shake his hand. But I don't think he understood what I was doing. So I just intuitively asked him for his blessing, and I knelt down. He gave me the blessing and seemed pleasant enough. And I went back to my seat.

I was told that he probably didn't fully understand what I was saying because it was in English. And when you're sitting way behind the person, you don't always hear it anyway. I think that was probably accurate. After I greeted him, he gave a talk; and then, at the end of the prayer service, he was escorted out immediately. [The priests and bishops] were scurrying around, trying to get the pope out, either because he was late or because of what I said—or both.

While I was still up in the sanctuary, I got a note in my hand that CBS wanted to interview me. And when we went to the front door of the shrine, there were probably eight or nine people—it seemed like a million at the time—from the media with their mikes. And they interviewed me on the top steps there for about 10 minutes.

I think the thing that got the media, and probably everybody else, was the surprise element. One of the men said to me, "We looked over the materials for the morning, and nothing was going to happen, so we all took early lunch." They wanted my text right away. I didn't have any extra copies. So I said, "If you call my office tomorrow, we'll have copies ready for you."

I had been slated to go to a TV studio directly from the shrine. Three or four Church people had been asked to be on a panel while the pope was having the outdoor Mass at the mall. So I sat in that studio all afternoon. It went on forever and ever and ever. My mother and my sister and my niece had come down from New York, because I had gotten tickets for both the White House the day before and to the shrine. So when I finished up in the studio, I went home and we had dinner together. And then I took them to the airport.

I always was pleased that my family was there. Three generations were there, and they could tell the story personally. Someone in the family picked them up at the airport, and they went by the newsstand, and my picture was in the paper. I called to see did they get home safely and my niece said, "You're on the front page of the paper! You should see my brother. He's out on the street telling everybody, 'That's my aunt.'" So that was always a nice thing for me. They would have been supportive, but their being there was such a wonderful consolation.

Initially I got much more of the negative reaction than I got the positive. For instance, the following Thursday, the *Washington Post* ran a whole page of letters to the editor just on this issue, and they were all negative. The Sister who was doing our public relations called them, and said, "Our only concern is that you didn't put any positive letters." And their response was, "If we had gotten them, we would have."

I think within our own community the reaction was mixed. I would say the same type of mix as there was generally, with maybe a little more intense feeling because I was a Sister of Mercy; I was the president of the order. It's hard for me to give you percentages. I would say probably it was like 60–40, more in favor than against. I've never had any bishop who either said or wrote really disparagingly about what I said. Several bishops wrote and said they thought it was done respectfully. They questioned not the issue so much, but the timeliness of it. I never found the reactions painful. It was almost like once I had [given the talk], it didn't belong to me anymore. I did what I felt I needed to do. It was a conviction I had. I thought [those things] needed to be said, and I didn't think the timing was inappropriate.

My community [turned out to be] very supportive. This was the fall of 1979. My first term as president was over in 1980; and in April I was reelected, almost unanimously, by the community. There were other candidates who took issue with what I said and didn't want me reelected. But there were Sisters who came from all parts of the country because they said, "I want to make sure you're reelected." They were also conscious the bishops were watching this. The bishops were saying, "Well, does she represent the Sisters of Mercy? Is this where they want to go?" And so reelecting me gave a message to other people, and that made the news, too.

Would you do it again?

Oh, yes. I'm sure I would.

Did it make a difference?

I think it did. When I read the letters that came in—we got almost 5,000 letters—it was amazing how the women, not only Sisters, not only Catholic women, but any number of Protestant women, said how much it meant to them that somebody did speak publicly. It was an inspiring moment for some women. I found that very, very consoling. That is worth any anxiety I went through.

When I came back from Washington, I took a year off on a sabbatical. I went to South America, to Guyana, and worked as a missionary for a couple of months. When I came back here, I was in our high school as the campus minister for four years. And then I was on a formation team for four years. One of the things I wanted to do was to study again, because I hadn't studied in a number of years and my studies were economics, finances, and public administration. Those were my jobs. So I completed a master's in women's history.

I'd like to be able to teach women's history in colleges or even in the last year of high school. I was supposed to do it last year, but I just wasn't able to. I'm the administrator of Mount Mercy now. We have 75 Sisters living here, and we have an infirmary. I'm responsible with a team for the maintenance of the building, for the guests that come into the building, for the hospitality, for the switchboard, for the kitchen—all of the services for the Sisters here. Our motherhouse is closing, and I'm winding down from all that. When I'm 60, I'm retiring from administration!

It's been a wonderful life, and it's only about half over. One of the nuns here—she's 85, and she said she wanted to die. I said to her, "Well, if it's true that eternity is going on forever and ever and ever, what are you rushing there for?"

And then I said, "I want to live to the year 2050."

"Oh, my God!" [she said]. "How old will you be?"

"A hundred and fourteen."

Well, you know, I don't want to be decrepit; but if I live to be 114, I'll see the middle of the twenty-first century. Wouldn't that be exciting? (August 1994)

Text of Sister Theresa Kane's greeting to Pope John Paul II at the National Shrine of the Immaculate Conception, Washington, D.C., on October 7, 1979:

In the name of the women religious gathered in this shrine dedicated to Mary, I greet you, Your Holiness Pope John Paul the Second. It is an honor, a privilege, and an awesome responsibility to express in a few moments the sentiments of women present at this shrine dedicated to Mary, the Patroness of the United States and the Mother of all humankind. It is appropriate that a woman's voice be heard in this shrine and I call upon Mary to direct what is in my heart and on my lips during these moments of greeting.

I welcome you sincerely; I extend greetings of profound respect, esteem, and affection from women religious throughout this country. With the sentiments experienced by Elizabeth when visited by Mary, our hearts too leap with joy as we welcome you—you who have been called the pope of the people. As I welcome you today, I am mindful of the countless number of women religious who have dedicated their lives to the Church in this country in the past. The lives of many valiant women who were catalysts of growth for the United States Church continue to serve as heroines of inspiration to us as we too struggle to be women of courage and hope during these times.

Women religious in the United States entered into the renewal efforts in an obedient response to the call of Vatican II. We have experienced both joy and suffering in our efforts. As a result of such renewal, women religious approach the next decade with a renewed identity and a deep sense of our responsibilities to, with and in the Church.

Your holiness, the women of this country have been inspired by your spirit of courage. We thank you for exemplifying such courage in speaking to us so directly about our responsibilities to the poor and oppressed throughout the world. We who live in the United States, one of the wealthiest nations of the earth, need to become ever more conscious of the suffering that is present among so many of our brothers and sisters, recognizing that systemic injustices are serious moral and social issues that need to be confronted courageously. We pledge ourselves in solidarity with you in your efforts to respond to the cry of the poor.

As I share this privileged moment with you, Your Holiness, I urge you to be mindful of the intense suffering and pain that is part of the life of many women in these United States. I call upon you to listen with compassion and to hear the call of women, who comprise half of humankind. As women we have heard the powerful messages of our Church addressing the dignity and reverence for all persons. As women we have pondered upon these words. Our contemplation leads us to state that the Church, in its struggle to be faithful to its call for reverence and dignity for all persons, must respond by providing the possibility of women as persons being included in all ministries of our Church. I urge you, Your Holiness, to be open to and respond to the voices coming from the women of this country who are desirous of serving in and through the church as fully participating members.

Finally, I assure you, Pope John Paul, of the prayers, support and fidelity of the women religious in this country as you continue to challenge us to be of holiness for the sake of the Kingdom. With these few words from the joyous, hope-filled prayer, the Magnificat, we call upon Mary to be your continued source of inspiration, courage and hope: "May your whole being proclaim and magnify the Lord; may your spirit always rejoice in God your savior; the Lord who is mighty has done great things for you; holy is God's Name."

Sister Theresa has again become a public figure, an outspoken defender of the lives of women religious and an advocate for the cause of women's ordination. She delivers her message to gatherings around the country, including Voice of the Faithful meetings, and, in 2009, in a keynote address at the 40th anniversary celebration of the National Coalition of American Nuns. In her talk she said, "In the Church today, we are experiencing a dictatorial mindset and spiritual violence . . . I have one chance, one life, and therefore I have a responsibility to criticize."

SISTER ANITA DE LUNA

At the time of the interview, Sister Anita de Luna was in the midst of a one-year interim appointment as Vicar for Religious in the archdiocese of San Antonio. She had just completed two terms as superior general of her community, the Missionary Catechists of Divine Providence, a community composed entirely of Mexican-American women. She had also finished her term as president of the Leadership Conference of Women Religious (LCWR), the first Hispanic woman to serve in that role.

Sister Anita, 46, bilingual since early childhood, speaks English softly with the lilt of someone whose "language of the heart" is Spanish. In September 1995, Sister Anita moved to Berkeley, California, to begin doctoral studies in Hispanic spirituality.

My father died when I was seven. And so I was raised by my mom, in the Rio Grande Valley. I was a migrant child up until I was in tenth grade. For me going up north in the trucks with other families was exciting. We used to go up to Michigan for cherries and apples, and to Idaho for potatoes. Today I often tell people that I was very well traveled as a child. Now, as I'm invited to speak throughout the country, I end up going to the states where I was as a migrant child.

I don't think I was aware as a child of the poverty. Migrant children attend maybe four months of school a year as we move around with the crops. I didn't want to go to school up north. Because we were migrant, we didn't have the conveniences and the clothing that other kids had, and they looked down on us. That was very difficult for me as I was growing up. When we'd get back to the valley, we would go to migrant school from 7:30 in the morning to 5:30, and they would try to give us everything we had missed.

I met the Sisters when my father died. My mother was completely broken because my father was the one who used to take care of everything, pay bills, buy the groceries, make decisions. My mother never worked. She was 46 when my father died, and she just completely despaired. There were nine children. My oldest brother was 21, and I was the youngest. The Sisters used to come and visit, to console my mom. In retrospect, I can understand what was happening with her, but I was very appreciative that the Sisters would come around because we felt so lost. And I think at that time I probably subconsciously said to myself, I will want to do that for someone somehow.

Myself, my sister next to me, and my mom stopped migrating when I was in the ninth grade. That's also when we moved out of the labor camp into a house that we bought. My brothers and my other sisters continued migrating. They said that I ought to stay and finish high school. I am the only graduate from high school from my family.

When I was going to graduate, I had a scholarship for Mexico City for Spanish because I had wanted to learn languages. But when I decided to come to the convent, I had to forfeit. And that was a difficult choice, because for my family it was like this is the honor we never would have expected. My family loved the nuns, but when I entered, it was a letdown for the family. One of my brothers wanted me to be a cheerleader; the other one, a secretary, or a teacher, a nurse. Everyone had pooled so that I could finish, and so everybody felt they had an investment in me, and they had say-so in what was going to be my future. My choice to be a religious was in nobody's mind. But I finished high school in May, and I entered in August. That was in '66. They took my mom to California and then started migrating again. So I didn't see anyone for a year and a half, and my family was very, very, very difficult that first year.

I was really attracted to religious life. I wanted to be holy, and I wanted so badly to do everything right through those first formation years. The community was Mexican-American, so there wasn't any big change in terms of culture. But the food was different, because I had not been used to big breakfasts with oatmeal and melted butter on top. You see, when the community was begun in '46 there were only five members, so it was directed by the Sisters of Divine Providence, who were European. So the foods were their foods. But then after a few years the meals changed to more what we were used to. Eventually it became us. I go home to my family now and eat the same thing I eat at the convent.

I came at a time when it required that I be flexible and that I be open to the ambiguity, because nothing was settled. The habits were going out as I was coming in. I came in following Sisters whom I admired deeply and whom I loved dearly, and they all left. It was like: What am I doing here? But those moments passed.

My leadership probably began in 1972, when I was 23 and I was elected as secretary to the superior. I didn't know how to type. They said, "Well, you can learn." I sat among the leaders of the group and listened to how the decisions were made. I became familiar with the compassion and the sensitivity with which they dealt with the other Sisters. The opportunity to come into leadership at such a young age maybe softened the edges of judgment. You know [how young people] sit and say, "Who are *they*? Look at the decisions *they* are making." All of a sudden I was hearing the privileged information that led to a decision.

We were the first elected group. We were trying to learn how to be leaders and at the same time trying to address the issues. There was a lot of questioning. A lot of crisis. Those who had gone through Vatican II were beginning to feel the consequences of that in the early 1970s. So they were needing definite direction. The questionings that were going on throughout the country were happening in our small community as well.

There were other issues, too, for us. In '67 the superior general of the Sisters of Divine Providence had said to us: I think you may be ready to move [to being] completely on your own. We had been financially independent. We had had our own house. We were established with our own constitution. We had our own people in formation. But we had this canonical connection that said their superior general was our superior general. And so one of their Sisters would live with us in our convent. It was essentially psychological, like leaving a mother. Because practically speaking, we were doing everything by ourselves.

Nothing was going to change, but all of a sudden those decisions would be ours. So we had to face ourselves and [say to one another]: "Are you going to leave or are you going to stay? Because if you're not going to stay and we're going to disperse eventually, then it's not worth going through all of this." So we recommitted and renewed our own desire to be with one another. We felt strongly that if we wanted to model for our Mexican-American people, then we needed to take on leadership and say, "We're on our own in this congregation. You can do it, too. You can be your own person."

I was elected superior in 1984. It was in that term, from '84 to '88, that we submitted our request [for independence] to Rome. You know, we are Sisters of Providence, and I have lots of providence stories. The process was very complicated, and I knew nobody in Rome. So how in the world am I going to get these connections going? So the superior general of the Sisters of Divine Providence says, "Get in touch with Sister Mary Linscott, because she's the connection between Rome and the United States. She's going to be in Cincinnati [this summer]." This is the summer I am in San Francisco trying to finish my degree. So in this house where I'm living, this elderly Sister, Thaddea Kelly, keeps coming to me and telling me, "Honey, don't worry. If I can help you, I will help you." I think this elderly Sister wants to pray for me, and I keep telling her, "Sister, I really appreciate that. You pray with me."

Then I get in touch with Sister Mary Linscott, and she says, "Okay, Sister. Bring your documents with you." And I figure, "Documents? I'll give her the constitutions and whatever. Right? I mean, I don't know." So my assistant and I fly to Cincinnati. [Sister Mary Linscott is] very tall, very somber-looking, and she comes from Rome, and she's got all this authority. So I come with a little recorder, saying I want to record everything so I can bring it back and not miss anything. She sees us, and she says, "Now who are you? You're not on my list from Rome. When did you hear from Rome?" I say, "I haven't even written to Rome." She says, "Then you're not supposed to be here." She looks at this recorder and says, "You cannot tape this." I say, "All right, I won't tape it. But can you speak to me?" I think she felt very badly for us, so she ended up speaking to us.

She tells us, "You need to work with a consultant." [One of the two consultants she names] is a Sister Thaddea Kelly. Well, I know a Thaddea Kelly, but it can't be her. So I say, "Where from?" And she says, "San Francisco." So I go back and find Thaddea, and I say, "Why didn't you ever tell me who you were?" She says, "Honey, you never asked me." I say, "I worry all this year, and all you tell me is 'Let me help you, Honey.' Why don't you tell me who you are?"

Anyhow, Thaddea Kelly became the piece that connected us with Rome. Then Monsignor Galante was appointed undersecretary for the Congregation of Institutes for Consecrated Life. And Monsignor Galante—he's now Bishop Galante here in Beaumont—was the chancellor in Brownsville when we were there, and he knew us well. So these two people, Monsignor Galante and Thaddea Kelly, became extraordinary figures in the process—right at the moment we needed them.

During that same term as superior, in 1987, I was serving on the Planning Committee for the General Assembly of LCWR [Leadership Conference of Women Religious], and the theme for that assembly was enculturation. They asked me if I would write a song. I said okay, but I had never written a song. I write poetry and I play guitar, so I put the two together and wrote the song, "Holy Is the People." They had asked me to write the song, so that a black choir and a mariachi choir could both sing it. The great Thea Bowman—you know, the black Sister who was a tremendous, tremendous figure in the Church?—she performed the song, and the mariachi came in and did their piece in Spanish. It was wonderful to hear 900 people singing this song that was the very first song I had ever written.

That threw me into visibility at the national level. And so in '91 I was one of the nominees for president of LCWR. My mom and I had remained very close. At the time I told her, "Mother, what do you think? Do you think I should accept this nomination?" She knew what LCWR was, and she knew what kind of work I was doing. She said, "Do you know why they are asking you to take it?" And I said, "Probably because there's a new consciousness, and because I am there, and because I can make a contribution that is going to be different than what has been." So she said, "Well, if you can help them, do it." So when I gave my speech for the nomination, I shared this with the group. My mother became almost a hero for them.

We had the voting on one day, and the next day they were to announce. I didn't think that I was ever going to become president. But I had been grateful for the moment to stand before the conference, and I had done it with a lot of pride. So when they told me, "You are elected," I couldn't even move. All I kept thinking was, "This is a predominantly white organization. I cannot be a voice for them."

It had been an overwhelming vote. It usually goes three or four ballots. This was a one-ballot election. So it was announced. The translator broke down and couldn't translate, so the [Hispanic Sisters] who had earphones didn't know what was going on. They're looking around; everybody is clapping; and I stand, and then they realize that I probably had been elected. So they start crying. At that moment I realized, "This is not for me. This is for them." Four Sisters from my own congregation were there; but I couldn't find them, because people started coming from all over. I kept thinking, "Where are they? Where are they?" Almost at the end of the line, they're all standing there with big tears coming down from their eyes. I looked at them, and I said, "How come you didn't come over?" And they said, "Well, we were waiting because we figured you had now become the Conference's and you were no longer ours." I said, "How dare you think that!" [And then I said,] "You were as paralyzed as I was. You couldn't move."

I called my mother, and I said, "Mother, you're going to have to be on your knees for the next three years." She started crying, and then she said, "Well, I expected that you would be elected." My mother had tremendous, tremendous confidence in me. When I was elected superior to the congregation, I called her and she said, "I knew it. I think you could be elected pope one year." She felt I could do anything and everything. She was a very, very big influence in my life.

There were moments that were difficult through the next three years. The women [in LCWR] were really, really wonderful. But then you get down to the practical stuff. I don't have a Ph.D., and all these women sitting around this table have Ph.D.'s from notable universities. My process of working and thinking through things is different. It's a struggle for me to have to do everything in English for a month at a time, not to go into Spanish for a few days. I think the queen of languages within my heart is Spanish, but no one understands Spanish. My prayer is usually in Spanish, and that prayer had to be in English. The music that I'm used to, that inspires me, is not written by Jesuits. But that's the music we use, because that is what is predominant. So you have to develop this extra sense, jump into this other person while you're there, and you become that person for that moment. So at the end of the meetings, I would be very tired.

My dealings with Rome were far easier than I had anticipated, because Spanish is the language for dealing with everything within the Congregation of Religious in Rome. Now the Church in the United States is a different story. I do not know for sure whether I was totally accepted or whether I wasn't. And I don't know whether I will ever know. The issue that came up during those three years was the approval of the new council, the Council of Major Superiors of Women Religious, in April of '92. It was a parallel conference established and approved by Rome. So, to represent women religious, the United States now has two organizations, which are divided by a school of thought. The Council of Major Superiors—well, they are more conservative. You have to be in the habit in order to be part of them. You have to live in a convent with other religious. There's a variety of criteria they have. I was with them for several meetings as they became approved, and we got together for some social time with them as well. They are definitely of the school of thought that they are there to serve the bishop and the priests. It is a different sense from what we [in LCWR] are used to, which is [that] we're here for the people.

It was a very difficult time. I would have to say, though, that being president of LCWR was a positive experience. I think it's also a very rare experience. It'll probably be another generation before another minority person gets up there into leadership at that level. In order to get into those positions, you need to be visible, and we don't have enough trained Hispanic or black women in congregations. And then I think there has to be another graced moment for a conference to look at someone and to single them out and say, "We're giving you this opportunity. We're ready for you."

That was one of the things that I said in the evaluation at the end of my term—that I truly hoped that if they ever invited another person of color, they would be ready for them. I said, "You really lucked out, because I'm mild and I'm willing to bend every which way." I was willing to adjust to the way the conference does things, and I was not there to push my agenda. That is not to be taken for granted with anyone else. In the process I got a little hurt here and there, but overall it was positive. I think that my experiences in my life have been such that I at this point am not an angry and resentful person. But that is not going to be true for many others.

It's probably very significant, and very, very important that when my mother died, she chose—and I say she chose because I really think she did—she chose to die in February of '92, when the LCWR was having a national executive board meeting here in San Antonio. My mother knew everything about LCWR. She kept telling me, "This is the time when you're supposed to be in your meeting. Why don't you leave?" She was in intensive care—she was only there three days; she died very quickly—and I'd tell her, "That's okay. Someone's taking care of things."

So the president, the executive director, and the vice president of LCWR were able to go to the funeral. Three very white, very tall women from out east. I wanted badly for them to meet my mom. They had heard so much about my mother through me, but when they finally made it, of course she was already gone. And she looked beautiful. She loved jewelry, so she wore all her jewelry, and she wore a beautiful dress. She had always said that she had not had enough time with my father, but when she died and they reunited, she was going to dance because they loved to dance. So we got her a real pretty dress that she could dance in. Within my culture, death is like a transition of life. It's part of who we are, and we move with it. And so my little nephews and nieces were going up to the coffin to kiss my mom. The day that we buried her, she had been in the coffin already at the funeral home for a day and a half, so her hair was all messed up because everybody had kissed her and touched her. It's what they always do. But this is not part of what these women do. So then I tell them, "Come meet my mom." They joined us at the celebration, and they joined us at the funeral, and afterward I thought it was probably traumatic for them to be among all these black-haired people. My family has continued to be very poor— my extended family also. But it was very, very beautiful; and that probably was the most transformative moment of my work with LCWR: to have the leadership experience who I am at home, and who we are as people. I think my mother probably said, "If I'm going to go, I'm going to go in style. I'm going to have these national figures to my funeral." (November 1994)

Sister Anita died of cancer in 2006 at the age of 59. She was teaching at Our Lady of the Lake University in San Antonio until a month before her death. In 2003, she published her first book, which grew out of her experience as a Texan of Mexican descent. She had plans for many more books.

14

THE DECISION
TO LEAVE

THERESA PADOVANO

Theresa Padovano has traveled a long road, from Missouri to Kansas to Oklahoma to Montana to Texas to New Jersey. She has also taken another journey—from community life in a large convent in Leavenworth, Kansas, to family life in the hilly suburbs of northern New Jersey.

Mrs. Padovano, 50, is a full-time mother of four (not including a Latvian exchange student who, at the time of the interview, was staying with the family for eight months). Her husband, Anthony, a professor at Ramapo College and an adjunct professor at Fordham University, has written more than 20 books and was the first president of CORPUS, an organization of 10,000 members that advocates reforms within the Roman Catholic Church, including full ministry for married priests and the ordination of women.

The Padovano home has over the years been a gathering place for men and women who serve the Church in a variety of ministries—some traditional, some far from the mainstream. Mrs. Padovano described her husband as a bridge-builder—"he tries to keep people together"—and she herself has made an effort to connect the two parts of her life. She keeps in touch with several women who were friends in the community and has taken her entire family to visit her former motherhouse in Leavenworth. "They couldn't have been more wonderful," she said. "All the doors were open."

You have to understand, my background is from a very pious German, middle-western family, a large family of seven—six brothers and myself. And I guess my parents out of sheer need turned to God frequently. We were daily Mass and communion people. Rosary every night. It was a very religious kind of upbringing. I really felt called by God, and I wrestled with it in high school. I clearly remember sitting up in bed one night, and saying "Yes!" And that was it. There was never a question in my mind after that. I was about a junior in high school at that point, dating and so on.

I became a Sister of Charity of Leavenworth, Kansas. It was a very young, vibrant community, as I knew it in my elementary and high school years: a top-notch group of ladies. They were very much alive and dedicated—happy and joyful and involved with helping the kids. They loved what they were doing. How could you not be attracted to them? I entered in 1958. I was 16.

I look back on my mistress of novices and [my mistress of] postulants and say, "Oh my God, how did they take it?" But they kept us so busy all the time. It was a very rigid schedule of rising early and prayer and manual labor and study. There was a group of about 80 of us. Can you imagine 80 teenagers together? We had a ball!

What I remember was the opportunity for meditation and study and prayer and getting to know a lot of wonderful people. That's what I got from it. I was very happy for the opportunity. I would do it all over again.

We were close to being college graduates by the time we got out. But at that point, when I left the juniorate, I was still 19. I went out into the classroom in Oklahoma City, teaching second and third grade, all these little people. I loved it, but I don't know what they learned.

The following year I went to St. Patrick's in Oklahoma City, which was a very vibrant parish. There was a pastor there, a very charismatic fellow, and he was in the midst of having the people build the church there. I mean, these people were cutting down trees and making pews, laying flagstone and doing the whole thing themselves. I don't know if you've ever been to Oklahoma. It was still missionary territory at that time. So the people there were not people of long-standing tradition. They were new Catholics, and they were, most of them, from Baptist backgrounds, very much involved in scripture. Wonderful people! The theological mentality was similar to the geographic territory, which was open, flat—you could see forever.

[The pastor] had his church built with the altar facing the people before the [Second Vatican] Council was over. He used to meet with the Sisters regularly, every week. And he would discuss the liturgy, the scripture readings for that Sunday, and talk about what they were going to do with the homily. So we were very involved in the total ministry of the parish. I was really spoiled.

When the community decided that it was time for me to move to [a diocese in the northern Rockies], it was quite an adjustment. Because, again, the mentality was very much like the geography. There were tall mountains and valleys, and [some of the people] couldn't see beyond their valley. If it hadn't been done before, they couldn't think of doing it.

I was in East Helena; I taught seventh and eighth grade there. Then that school closed, and I went to the diocesan office. At that point the bishop was Bishop [Raymond] Hunthausen, who was wonderful to work with. Just a beautiful guy. I was in the religious education office, and we traveled the whole western third of the state of Montana. We were on the road a lot, working with priests and their people. I met a lot of wonderful priests—some of whom had serious problems with alcohol, loneliness. Some were eccentric, having been left out in the boonies all alone too long.

Then, let me see, I was working there in the diocese a couple of years and I decided it was time I ought to finish up my college education. So I applied for a leave of absence from the diocese to go back and finish, so that I could start a master's program in religious education. That summer I started a master's program down in St. Mary's Seminary in Houston, Texas. And that is where I met my husband. He was a priest, teaching on the staff there.

And it was like being knocked off a horse. Like Paul. It was a very difficult, very scary time in my life. Because here I was, this good kid who'd been good since she was this high and had everyone's approval. As a matter of fact, when I was getting ready to enter this master's program, there was a faculty advisor who was supposed to go through the process with you. She wanted me to go to Loyola. And I said, "No, I don't want to go there. I've heard too much about the priests and the nuns dating [there]." So I went to Texas to avoid all that, and guess what happened? I got knocked off my horse.

I met him at the airport. Another group of people were going to pick him up at the airport. And—I can't remember—he was coming from another summer assignment, and there was a work stoppage, and the plane was delayed, so they called and said, "We're starving. Can somebody else come out and wait for this guy?" So myself and another member of my community jumped in the car and went down to pick up this new professor. And I've been running to the airport ever since.

So then he taught me Christology. And we started talking and walking, and the relationship blossomed. This was a difficult, very difficult decision. Because I loved my community; I loved the work I was doing. He loved the work he was doing. It took years to decide that this was what we had to do. But I felt that this was a call from God just as much as my vocation to religious life [had been].

We were both committed to what we were doing, enjoying what we were doing. But, you know, it's a very complex thing. I saw what was happening to the Church, I saw what was happening in the ministry, and I saw that it wasn't good. And I felt nudged by the Spirit to maybe help to bring about this change in ministry in the Church in some small way: to help people see that ministry and marriage can function together, and that they're not mutually exclusive involvements. Loving a person doesn't keep us from loving God and loving the Church.

When I was ready to leave the community, the mother general asked me to go and see somebody [for spiritual guidance]. And I went to see him, and he didn't make sense to me. His idea was: This is God dangling a carrot in front of you to test you. But that's not my kind of God. He doesn't do things like that. I'd never said no to love before, so I thought that this was the right thing for me to do. And I didn't leave with any kind of a sense of bitterness or anger or anything like that. It was the next step for me on my journey.

I think there was confusion on the part of some of the older Sisters. They didn't understand, because I left and I didn't tell them that I was getting married right then and there. I took a leave of absence for a year. Those who were closest to me were wonderful. They didn't care what the situation was. They accepted me; they loved me; they sent me off with fond farewells and moral support. The mother general at that time looked at it as God using the community to prepare these women to go out into society, to do something for the world. So she was beautiful about it. I think that was a big help to me and to a lot of the other gals that left at that point.

These were people that I loved and trusted, and it was a real leap of faith [to leave]. What was I going to do with this guy, if perchance somehow in the Church they would not accept his ministry? I really felt deep in my heart that he had such a charism that the Church wasn't going to turn its back on him at that point. He was so well-known through his writings and lecturing that I felt the Church didn't care whether a minister was married or not. What they wanted was ministry from him and his gifts. And I was right. They never did isolate him or turn their back on him. They continued to call on him, more than we would like at times. He's done more lecturing and writing since he's been married than before.

He told them, "The reason I'm leaving [the priesthood] is that I want to marry and I want to continue to serve the Church, and I'm going through this process out of respect for the Church and its procedures," and he got his papers. Then we got married right here in this house. My brother came from Kansas City. He said, "What can they do? Throw me in jail?" I have two brothers who were priests. One of them is married now and has three adopted children, and the other is still pastor at St. Patrick's in Kansas City.

I think for me it was that leap of faith, trusting that this was okay with God. I'd had all kinds of support and approval as a youngster and a young religious. There were no social supports for what we were doing. That was the difficult part of it. Some people didn't see it in the same vein that we saw it. They just saw two people who left, who broke commitments. They thought it was involved in sex or something.

My family was incredible. My parents said they didn't care what we did as long as we didn't lose the faith. That was all they were interested in. Now, these are not people with theological backgrounds; these are just people of faith. They would have been disappointed if we'd walked away from the Church. We assured them that that was not the case, and they were very accepting.

Some people did not have that support. They came from parents whose identity was tied up with their being a priest or a nun, and God help you if you left. It was like a comedown or a loss of status for them. Some people were very hard on their sons and daughters.

And I must say we've never met with a lot of nasty reaction. From the time we went to a parish, people knew of our background. And they were wonderful, accepting. I used to be a cantor in the church. People would say, "How did you learn to sing like that?" I would say, "Chant class in the novitiate many years ago. Gregorian chant." So they knew my background, and Tony would give a background for the readings, and they'd know that wasn't an ordinary layman up there. People for the most part were accepting of us. They didn't care whether we were married or not.

Spiritually, I think there is a carryover [between being in the convent and being married]. Living in community is a difficult task, and living in a family is a difficult task. At least in the community you had a group of people who had one vision and purpose, and that's a beautiful thing. In a family you sometimes feel a little isolated, especially if your husband is gone and you're one against this thriving group of kiddos.

Mark Anthony is 16 now, Andrew is 15, Paul is 12, and then this month Rosemarie is 10. And we have a guest from Latvia, a 16-year-old—a very quiet but very impish young man. They're good kids for the most part. The summers, most of the time, Tony is away because he has a chance to do his own theological work at different universities all over the United States. But most of the winter he's home, except for an occasional trip for a few days.

I'm a full-time mother. I think being a mother is a pretty important vocation. I'm not the kind who thinks you can have it all. I think we're limited human beings, and we have to make some choices. And I feel that giving them some time is important when they're young. There'll be another time for me to do other things when they're out of the house.

They all go to the public schools. We did that purposely. We felt like they shouldn't be subjected to the prejudices or biases of the priests and Sisters in the parish. We thought we'd like them to have an opportunity to be themselves at school, without any baggage with them. They know our backgrounds. We told them when they were little. This doesn't make any sense [to them]. "Why can't daddy celebrate in the big church?" They don't understand that at all—why being married to their mother makes it impossible for him to be a minister in the Church.

That's the way it was in the early Church. The priests were married. You look at scripture, and Jesus went to heal Peter's mother-in-law. In the early Church they were married for the most part. It's something that could change. It's not a doctrine of the Church. It's a disciplinary law that could change, like not eating meat on Friday. It could be that simple.

[Being in the convent] was a wonderful opportunity to grow as a person and as an individual. I think a lot of girls go right out of high school into whatever and [then into] marriage and really don't have too much of a sense of themselves. You can live without a man. That's not a big problem. A lot of women don't think they can. [You need to] have a sense of your own worth and talents and your own weakness. So you don't go into marriage and think [that] if it's not fun, it's all his problem. You pick up experience dealing with people that's very valuable. I used to say that the miracle of religious life is not poverty, chastity, and obedience, but living with a whole bunch of other women and not killing each other. I've never regretted that time. I'd do it again.

The transition was difficult, but I think it's been worthwhile. I still see our calling as something that has to do with the renewal of the Church. What we've tried to do is be a concrete witness to the fact that ministry and marriage are not incompatible, that we can be productive members of the Church and give to the world without being celibates. (January 1992)

This interview took place at the same kitchen table where we had talked 18 years ago. The Padovano home is still as hospitable, but quieter. Their children are grown and living around the world, in Shanghai, California, Tennessee, and New York. Theresa says, "They are all so different. It's just been phenomenal to watch them develop." She and Anthony have two grandchildren.

Voice of the Faithful [VOTF] has been my main occupation in the last seven years. Until that time I was involved in a local parish. I did some education; I did some liturgical ministries like cantor and lector. When Voice of the Faithful started [in 2002], I tried to introduce it there, but the pastor was not too charmed with the idea. He didn't want to hold the bishops accountable for what was going on. That was the end of my parish involvement. [Laughs.] I just felt uncomfortable there.

[Some of us here in New Jersey] heard about what was going on in Boston and we went up there for a VOTF conference. We just felt like it was time for us to do something on the local level. As a mother, all these stories the survivors [of clergy sexual abuse] tell, they really tug at your heart. These children were terribly abused, and no one believed them. They were punished. "Don't you ever say anything like that about Father So-and-So. He would never do anything like that." I wanted to help educate. The laity needed to hear that this form of almost idolatry of the priesthood had to end. When it started impinging on the way children were being abused, I just couldn't [not act].

My community was an offshoot of the Nazareth Sisters of Charity, from Nazareth, Kentucky. They decided they wanted to respond to the needs of the pioneers who had moved further north. I think that urge to forge forward and address the evolving needs of the church is deep in my psyche. These Sisters, who grounded me from the time I was 16 until I was 28 or so, were people who were always looking toward the future and looking at needs that were not being addressed and trying to respond to them. I see that as the connecting link [between my years in the convent] and my work now in this reform movement.

If we look back at the Church's history before the Roman Empire, it was a very egalitarian, very open society. Open to women and men. If it has been done once before, then it can be done again. I am very hopeful because I see the people in the Church have grown in their understanding of this possibility and the need for it. I think the problem is we look too much at the institution. That's discouraging. If we look at the people church, we see wonderful things going on. People are proclaiming their own liberty and developing their own communities of faith. It has been my contention that the bishops are way behind, that in fact they have excommunicated themselves from the people of God. But some day we will welcome them back. They are still held hostage to this system, just as we have been. I would love to see them flourish in their spiritual life and in their life as leaders of the church.

The Gospels feed my hope. If you don't have that, you certainly lose confidence that anything good can happen in this church. But this, too, will pass. This group of so-called leaders will pass. And I will pass. The Spirit is in charge. (November 2009)

THE REVEREND JANE FLAHERTY

Jane Flaherty followed an improbable path—one that took her out of the Midwest, where she was raised; out of religious life; and ultimately out of the Roman Catholic Church. On the wall of her office in the stone parish house where the interview took place hung a plaque: "Be it known to all the faithful throughout the world that on the 15th of February, 1992, in Trinity Church, Moorestown, New Jersey, Jane Frances Flaherty was consecrated to the sacred order of Priests in the One, Holy, Catholic, and Apostolic Church and in accordance with the Constitution and Canons of the Episcopal Church."

The Reverend Jane Flaherty, at 54, is tall, strikingly attractive, with short gray-black hair and large blue eyes. As a priest in the Episcopal Church, she can perform the full range of pastoral and sacramental activities, including presiding at liturgies.

In September 1995, Jane Flaherty became rector at St. Christopher's Episcopal Church in Portsmouth, Virginia.

I grew up in a very devout Roman Catholic family. My father studied for the priesthood but left before he was ordained. My mother died when I was six, of cancer. My father really fell apart after that, and eventually moved away and left me with an aunt. He was found dead of a heart attack [when I was in sixth grade]. I think all of that has a lot to do with who I was and who I am. I've had a very healthy view of death, and I think at a young age I began to identify very much with Jesus suffering on the cross and wanting to give my life to God and to other people. I couldn't have said that at that time, but I think that was a lot of the motivation for going into the convent. Most people who have those kinds of experiences tend to resist getting close to people, because they've been hurt. I felt if I got close to somebody again, then I might lose them again. And so a celibate life didn't seem difficult to me.

[In 1955,] after my sophomore year, I went into the convent. I was 16. I think the real reason I became a School Sister of Notre Dame was [that] they had an aspiranture which accepted high school students. That was more similar to a boarding school than it was to a convent, except that we were separate from the other day students who were not intending to be nuns. So there was an element

The Reverend Jane Flaherty is hugged by two young admirers after presiding at a Palm Sunday Procession and Eucharist at St. Christopher's Episcopal Church in Portsmouth, Virginia. Rev. Flaherty served nine years as Rector at St. Christopher's, nine years during which she highly valued her role as celebrant at Holy Eucharist.

of being with the religious community, but we also went home for the summer and for Christmas and Easter.

I can't really ever remember being unhappy there. I think as I got older, I began to find obedience a lot harder. Sometimes you were told to do rather stupid things. And there wasn't that encouraging people to think for themselves and make decisions on their own. This was pre–Vatican II, and in some ways you were kept as a child. The superior was your mother and made all your decisions for you. Once I got out and started teaching and became an adult in a lot of other ways, it began to annoy me a lot more.

I was more prepared to teach high school than elementary school, but I went out to elementary school because they needed an organist. I was at St. Aloysius in St. Louis for almost two years. In March the mother superior called and said, "We want you to leave there and fill in for someone else." I had to go and teach math and biology in a high school. That was difficult—to have to leave relationships and everything and go live somewhere else in the middle of the year. The superior at that place where I got sent really rubbed me the wrong way, and I was glad I was only there a couple of months. The kids [I had taught] had taken the Iowa Test of Basic Skills right before I left, and I was eager to find out how they did. She forbade me to even ask. I thought that was unnecessarily harsh.

This was the early 1960s, when a lot of things were happening. It was really a time of tremendous change, both in the Church and in society, when people were being encouraged to think for themselves. I can remember the civil rights movement of this period, during which whites went in to help the blacks, and then, as time went on, blacks became empowered to help themselves. And I think a similar thing [happened] to nuns.

Well, it was exciting. I loved [the 1960s]. Probably too much. That was me. I like to make decisions for myself and be responsible for myself. And so I think it naturally led me to feeling that I wanted to leave. It was also partly because I wanted to continue to work in the inner city. [I had been helping out on weekends, visiting in the Pruitt-Igoe Housing Projects], and the nun I was substituting for got well again, and I couldn't do it anymore.

To leave the order was a rather tortured decision because, as I said, I really wasn't unhappy. There were annoyances, but there are no matter what you do in life. I just wasn't sure I wanted to make a life commitment. It didn't have to do with wanting to be married. I was pressed because final vows were coming up. Either I stayed in and made a life commitment or I left. There was no in-between in those days. Actually, I had fulfilled the three-year commitment at that point, and I was free to go.

I prayed about it for about a year. There weren't too many people I could trust, who I could really talk with about it. I do remember a number of months ahead of time I went in to see the mother superior and told her. She was trying to discourage me from leaving, and the reason she gave was, "Well, you're taken care of here. You're never going to go hungry. You'll always have a roof over your head." And I still remember [her] saying, "But, Sister, what if you marry a drunk?" I thought it was so naive. I had always admired her before that, because she was a very spiritual person.

[After I left, I moved into one of the] residences for single women around St. Louis University. You had a room and a common bathroom and they served two meals a day at a very reasonable price. So I had a place to live and I had a [teaching] job. Then a priest—his parish was in the inner city in North St. Louis—came to the residence trying to find out if anyone living there would do some work in his parish. I said, "Oh great." So I helped him set up an adult education program on Sunday afternoons. During the next few years, those projects became funded through the federal government, and I was offered the job as coordinator of that center. So I left teaching and I helped out with a number of other things in the parish while I was there.

Actually, I fell in love with the priest. He was in an order, and he went back to New York. We talked about marriage, and I guess part of my leaving the

Catholic Church was that after Vatican II it was such a disappointment that they didn't move ahead on allowing priests to be married. That dashed any kind of hopes [I had]. He had very mixed feelings. He was a good priest, and he was not going to leave his commitment. And so at a certain point it ended. I haven't thought about that in a long time.

I guess I had gradually been moving away from the Church. And then I moved east. When I got here, I all of a sudden realized I didn't have peer pressure or family pressure to stay connected with the Church. There was a church about a mile away from where I lived, and when I drove past to see what time the Masses were, there was no sign that said what time the Masses were, but there was an enormous sign that said, "Bingo, Tuesday nights, seven o'clock." And it totally turned me off. So I stopped going [to church]. I got involved with a group of people who would get together in homes to have Eucharist on Friday nights. I call it the underground church. That was a lot of fun. And then gradually different ones started moving away, and the group fell apart. So I think it was 13 years I didn't go to church at all.

During that time my career was taking off. I had left teaching and [had gotten] a state department job supervising an adult education program. So I was really into adult education. Then I went on and got my doctorate at Rutgers [University]. I bought a condominium. I was busy with my career and with my studies and my friends and my house and all of that.

Then—it must have been about 1980—my uncle died. Now, my aunt and uncle raised me after my father died. And I remember going back to the funeral. I remember kneeling in that church and thinking, "I don't want to die without this. This is part of my tradition, and it means a lot to me. I want a funeral like this one."

But every time I would go to a Catholic church, there would be something that would tick me off. I was also reading the *National Catholic Reporter*, and about that time there were a lot of stories about some of the problems that religious communities were having with the pope. Well, that just fed [my annoyance] all the more. I had a friend [who was Episcopalian], and she said, "Well, you know, if you ever want to go to church with me, say the word. But I won't pressure you about it." So Holy Week came. I went to church with her on Maundy Thursday, and it was so wonderful. I didn't know anything about the Episcopal Church. I didn't know the Episcopal Church was different from other Protestant churches. Protestant was Protestant. It wasn't Catholic, so it was bad. But what I found there was all the good stuff of the Catholic Church, without the legalism and guilt and rigid authority.

It reminded me of Holy Week at the motherhouse. We [used to do] everything properly, according to the reformed liturgy after Vatican II. And they were doing practically the same thing. So I went on Good Friday, and I went to the Easter Vigil, and I went on Easter Sunday, and I went every Sunday after that. Pretty soon I was going on weekdays.

Well, it's great to go to an Episcopal church, but becoming an Episcopalian is quite another question. I mean you're really brainwashed; it's amazing how brainwashed you are. I remember going once to visit this older nun who we had all really admired. She was a lovely person. At that time I was deciding to become an Episcopalian, and as she walked me to the car, she said, "Now, remember. You can come back anytime, and I don't mean just for a visit." So the next time I went, I had to break the news to her. [Another time] I actually took the prayer book and explained to her that, yes, there were seven sacraments, and we do believe that Christ is present in the Holy Eucharist. And I read through some of the services with her, and she seemed a little more accepting. But I know she prays for me every day—that I'll see the light.

[While I was thinking about becoming an Episcopalian] I was having a conversation with one of the priests associated with Princeton University. He had started out as Episcopalian, became a Catholic, and came back to the Episcopal Church. And out of the blue he said, "Have you ever thought about being ordained?" I didn't even answer him. I thought, "What a funny question." I haven't been to church in 13 years; I don't know if I want to become an Episcopalian; and he's asking if I want to be ordained. I really ignored it and only came back to that later, because I couldn't forget it. From that time on, I really couldn't *not* think about it. I went on and became an Episcopalian. I got very much into pastoral care, becoming more involved in people's lives and ministering to people. And, you know, the more I got involved in it, the more I wanted to do it. The problem was that the rector of that parish was against ordination of women. I eventually had to change parishes, because your parish has to sponsor you—your rector has to sponsor you—before you can even go into seminary. I was very deeply involved in that parish and had a lot of friends there. That was a very painful time.

I guess these things repeat themselves through your life. It was another loss, going all the way back to my parents' dying, or feeling I had to leave [the convent], or moving from St. Louis and leaving friends and family there. By the time I [had to leave the parish] I had enough knowledge of psychology and spiritual direction to be able to understand what was happening. These struggles repeat themselves through your life, and you reenact it and reenact it, learning to let go and learning to forgive. What I learned about forgiveness is, you don't forgive by willing it. It's a whole healing process, and it took me several years.

There are a lot of things I think I understand because of things I've been through—the deaths of my parents and the spiritual life I learned as a nun. An interesting thing happened to me just in the last year. On Good Friday I was asked to preach on one of the "seven last words" [of Jesus], and I got the words, "I thirst." This phrase from a Psalm kept coming back to me: "As the earth, parched, lifeless, and without water." You know—that we long for God "as the earth, parched, lifeless, and without water." I kept looking for those words, and I couldn't find them. I finally went to my breviary, which I still have, and [there were] the exact words. That was the translation in the breviary. All those years in the convent, I can't ever remember the Office meaning very much to me. The Mass meant a lot to me, but saying the Office didn't. And yet those words were still deep inside of me.

My life now is fully dedicated to God's work. I think that's why I went into the convent in the first place. This isn't just another line of work. [Being a priest] means bringing God to people and bringing people into the presence of God, whether that's in church, or in the suffering they're going through, or in the joys they're going through. [The first time I said Mass,] it felt like I was destined to do this. It's my whole life. A priest is not something I do. It's who I am. (October 1993)

Rev. Flaherty remained at St. Christopher's until 2004 when she retired to Alton, Illinois, to be nearer to her family and friends. She bought a small home and loves to garden. She is now 71.

As I prepared to retire from St. Christopher's, one of the parish leaders said that they were a divided parish when I came and that I brought them together. I don't know how I did that! I can't say that I did something special. But I believe that God used me as I was, as God uses all of us at times.

I knew when I made the decision to retire here that I would be going to a conservative Episcopal diocese, where women priests are not particularly welcome. Since retiring, I have had some, but not many, opportunities to celebrate the Holy Eucharist and preach in Episcopal parishes. I have led worship and preached in Protestant and ecumenical situations. I attend an Episcopal church here in Alton, where I participate in the life of the parish, and I have been asked to do some teaching. I rotate with a Lutheran pastor and Episcopal priest in teaching a weekly Bible study.

During the past year, I have been attending sessions at the School Sisters of Notre Dame motherhouse in St. Louis to consider becoming an Associate for Mission to the order. Years ago, I was one of the School Sisters of Notre Dame. But I am still one of them in spirit. My spiritual formation as a young nun imbued me with these views and ways of living, which I have carried with me through life. I feel that I have come full circle.

Part Two

FROM THE PRESENT INTO THE FUTURE

15

STAYING THE COURSE

SISTER FRANCES MAUREEN CARLIN

Sister Frances Maureen Carlin, 83, lives at the Dominican House of Retirement in Amityville, New York. She also works full time in the Heritage Center there; she has assembled a large collection of memorabilia from her order's past. Her own photograph hangs on one wall; she was superior general from 1967 to 1973. She is sprightly and cheerful and talkative. Although she does not wear a habit, she tries always to wear something white—as a sign that she is a Dominican. The day of the interview, it was a white skirt with a blue-and-white blouse and a navy jacket.

Personally, if you ask me about myself, I like every single thing that happened. I would never, never want to go back to the way it was before. I always end that statement by saying I didn't die from it. I got a very good education right up to the doctorate. I had wonderful experiences. I met lovely, wonderful women. I've been given opportunities in leadership that I might never have had in the world. But I would never want to go back to the way we lived. Why? Because there was something about it that didn't allow me to be who I am.

I'll tell you what I would like. Before I die, I would like to be an ordained deacon, because I think it would be a verification of all that I have done in the Church and for the Church. [It wouldn't be] a reward—I don't mean that—but an affirmation of my role. I think we women religious are doing everything that a deacon does and ever did. If you look, you can find out that there were women deacons in the time of Peter and Paul in the early Acts of the Apostles. Of course, now they skim it over fast, because they don't want to acknowledge that women deacons existed.

The head of our maintenance staff is an ordained deacon. I don't know what it means for him and his family. I don't know what restrictions there are. But being an ordained deacon wouldn't change my life. What I definitely don't like is that they do not allow women to preach. We have Sisters with master's degrees in theology. I have no objections to [the hierarchy] saying you could only preach if you have a course in scripture. I have no objection to that. But don't say just because I'm feminine I cannot give a homily. That's what makes me think the pope is really, therefore, a sexist.

So what's going to happen? In 1967 we were 1,600 Sisters, give or take. I remember the years [when I was prioress]—every other phone call was, "May I see you?" I knew what that meant. Now we're not even 800. Laypeople are doing what we do. They are in the schools. They are the principals. They are directors of religious education. They don't need us from that standpoint. So we have to ask ourselves: "Why am I a religious?" That's the first question. My second question would be: "Why am I a Dominican?" Those are the questions we have to ask ourselves now. And if we know the answers, I don't think there's anything to fear. (March 1991)

Sister Frances Maureen died on October 9, 1997.

SISTER MARY ELISE TOAL

Sister Mary Elise Toal was my second-grade teacher at a large Catholic grammar school in New York City. Then she was a merry young woman with bright blue eyes and a rosy complexion; she wore the white Dominican habit. Now she is 70. Her auburn hair is touched with gray, and her color is not good; she suffers from failing eyesight and heart problems. The motherhouse of her Dominican community is in Amityville, New York.

I did not want [to be called] Mary Elise. A novice mistress had given me Sister Mary, Bride of Jesus, and I thought it was beautiful. Bride of Jesus. My mother came to visit me on a Tuesday just to see me all alone. And I said, "Mom, guess what my name is going to be? Sister Mary, Bride of Jesus."

She said, "Oh, how horrible." I said, "Mom, it's from Brigid, your mother's name." You know, all excited. And my mother said to me, "Uh-uh, I don't like it at all."

So we met with Mother Adelaide, who was the novice mistress; and my mother said, "Please don't call her Mary Bride. They'll be calling her Biddie all her life."

So Mother [Adelaide] began with other names. "How about Sister Mary Elise?" And my mother said, "That's beautiful; I like that." So Mother Adelaide said, "That's what it will be—Sister Mary Elise."

Then we had to write about our names, why we were choosing that name or why we accepted that name, and I wrote a whole five pages. Of course, this was the way they kept us busy in the novitiate. And I wrote all about the Visitation, about Mary and Elizabeth, which I think is a magnificent combination. I brought it to Mother Adelaide and she said, "Oh, no, you're going to be Sister Mary Elise from Elizabeth of Hungary." So I spoke: "Mother, this is about the Visitation." She said, "That feast falls in July, and it's very inconvenient for the Sisters to have a feast day during July. Everybody celebrates during the year. So you take November 19th, Elizabeth of Hungary."

So I had to look up Elizabeth of Hungary and rewrite the whole thing.

Once we changed our names, people kept saying, "Go back to your old name." And I said, "No. I have a combination that I love. I have a combination that I've lived my whole life—the Annunciation and the Visitation, Mary and Elizabeth. I'm keeping my name. My feast day is the Visitation. And, furthermore, that was my first act of obedience!"

I celebrated my golden anniversary a year ago. It was a great, glorious day, and that was the whole theme of my Mass. The priest spoke beautifully on it. He ended by saying, "Mary Elise, you have had many Visitations." I said, "Gee, I wish I could have used that 50 years ago with Mother Adelaide."

I do feel that each day the Lord [asks] us to bring him to life, to give his life to others. I believe that each one of us is called to give birth to Jesus, as Mary was called at the Annunciation. The Visitation—these two ladies met. One was pregnant in her old age, probably in menopause, which was a disgrace at that time. The other, as much as we want to build up around Mary and how beautiful she was—she's the Mother of God—Joseph was going to divorce her. I'm sure Joseph the man didn't understand it. And Mary didn't understand it herself. Yet here were two women: one who's going to be the mother of the forerunner of Jesus, John the Baptist; and the other one, the mother of Jesus. They could meet, and regardless of age, they could talk, they could love, they could understand each other. And I think that's what we are called to do as religious. (December 1991)

Sister Mary Elise died on March 2, 1997.

SISTER JOSEPHITA LARREA

Cuban-born Sister Josephita Larrea has been an Oblate Sister of Providence for 63 years. At 91, she is determinedly independent. On the afternoon of the interview she was very tired, because she had had a series of medical tests in the morning. The conversation lasted less than 10 minutes, but in that time she conveyed alertness, charm, and humor. At the end, she gestured out the window to a picnic where the guests were all patients from the infirmary. It seemed a point of pride to her that because she was so healthy, she had not been invited.

I've *never* regretted—*never* regretted—having entered. Do you know, in life everybody has ups and downs? We're not always sailing in a smooth sea. But with God's grace—and really I have the support of my community at every moment—I feel I have been happy. There were times . . .; but then, as I said, I was happy. If I were to start a life again, I think I would do the same.

Sometimes you wonder [about the future]. Young people can work in the Church and do much of the work that the Sisters do and still have their own freedom. It seems like in the Church itself, if we read history, there were times when things were very dark, and then the light came.

I know that my days are not really long—90 years, 91. You don't expect to live much longer. But many things happen. [I went to] the dentist a few years ago, and I said it's not necessary to do so much [for me]. He was 38 years old, and he died, and I'm still here. So I don't know what the Lord will want. I hope and I pray that I will see my community flourish again. I trust that many will join us. I hope so. I hope so. If it is God's work, it will continue. (July 1992)

Sister Josephita died on January 15, 2000.

FIVE SCHOOL SISTERS OF ST. FRANCIS

When I arrived at Alverno College in Milwaukee for a series of interviews, I was told that five additional women, all School Sisters of St. Francis, would like to speak with me. The only time remaining was lunch; the only place was a crowded faculty dining room; the only possible format was more a roundtable discussion than intimate interviews. Nevertheless, the women spoke thoughtfully and personally, focusing most clearly on their sense of community.

SISTER CELESTINE SCHALL

My overall experience has been very positive in religious life. I just think about what I would have not become had I not been exposed to the many opportunities that religious life has given me. I joined the order to do something with my life, to make a difference in this world. That to me is the core of why I became a religious—I couldn't do something alone that I could do with a group.

SISTER GEORGINE LOACKER

I've been a religious Sister since 1942, and I can't think of a better way of life for me. Way back, my mother taught me that problems are not things to gripe about; they're things to be solved, and difficult situations are things to make something out of. I think she knew I was kind of a stubborn person and that I often would kick against the ordinary and want to do something different. In fact, when I wanted to go to the convent, she thought I just wanted to try something different, that it would just be a fling.

I went to a high school where causes were very, very important, and I loved them. There was a lot of inspiration in the high school I went to, both by the teachers I had—who were religious in our community—and by the excitement I got from helping the poor and seeing some effect of what I could accomplish. Part of seeing the effect of what I could accomplish came from the fact that I was part of something bigger than myself.

I think then of the things that happened in religious life. Every time I got an appointment, I didn't want to go. I didn't want to teach in the first school I was sent to. I didn't think I was ready. I didn't want to go teach in college when it was time, because I so loved teaching high school. In fact, I hid on the roof when

I knew the appointment was coming. When it was time to go to graduate school, I think I was more open to it; but I was always fighting against the initial stimulus. That turned around, because certainly God helped me, but also because way back my mother taught me what to do with things like that. As a result, my life has been very, very happy. I have difficulties that I'm trying to solve every day, but I like the challenge of trying to solve them.

[One of the challenges today is] seeing our numbers decrease and wondering what it is that we can do to let other people know how great this life is. Because we don't have some of the other responsibilities, we can join our talents together and accomplish something together. Exactly what that is to be in the future is not always clear to me, but the challenge of trying to work that out with others has been very satisfying.

SISTER JUDEEN SCHULTE

I entered the convent in 1966. I think part of the reason I entered was a translation of Kennedy's "Ask not what your country can do for you. Ask what you can do for your country." I think this idea is probably similar [for] many religious women.

I grew up in a strong Catholic tradition; and as the oldest of seven children, and the oldest of five girls, I knew that the world for women had its own perils in the 1960s. Occupations were either teaching or nursing. Most women were expected to marry. I wasn't drawn to marriage, and I *was* interested in working. So I translated Kennedy's command into "Think what God has done for you and give back." That was why I entered religious life. I stay—have stayed—through different times because I have a sense that the talents I bring are enhanced by collaboration with others, and they are best when shared.

I had been in the community for one year when all of us who were postulants and novices were called together by our generalate and told that we essentially had three choices to make. We could leave; we could leave with the option of coming back; or we could choose to stay. Our officers told us that they believed because the community was changing very drastically, staying held a number of potential perils. In the group I was with, more of us chose to stay than to leave; obviously, I was one of them. We spent a lot of time talking to other Sisters, people who had been in longer [than we had], and we would talk about why we came. We came because there was something bigger we could—and had to—do as a collective.

I find that by joining with others, we can make a very strong impact on society and make a very different world for the women of today than the one I experienced when I was a teenager.

SISTER MARLENE NEISES

I'm from a small farm in South Dakota, and the School Sisters taught at the grade school and the high school where I went to school. I had the feeling of responsibility from grade school on that as a Catholic, as a woman, I needed to seriously consider being a Sister. I entered after high school in 1965.

Those were challenging times—if you think, 1965 to 1970—to join. Joining wasn't hard. Those were challenging times for our order. For me personally there was never any question about staying; it was more questions from others. Given that time in history, that time in the Church, others [were] always asking, "Why are you staying? Why are you doing that?" Which maybe made my commitment stronger, because others kept asking.

When I chose to be a member of a religious community, part of that was to offer myself—the talent I had, the talents I didn't know I had—to others. More people working together to have something happen can accomplish something bigger than one person alone. That's important to me.

SISTER ELIZABETH ENGEL

I entered the community in 1923. And at that time, while we were in high school we were encouraged to devote our Sunday afternoons to helping the poor. It wasn't called the inner city at the time. We called it the "fourth ward" and the "sixth ward," and we went down Sunday afternoons. I got the idea that the best way to help the Church was through education. So I gave up some things I really liked to do, and I entered the community. I'm going to be 85, so I've been here a long time, and I'd do the same thing all over again.

This may seem odd, but personally I never felt challenged whether I was going to stay or not stay. But I had a very difficult time during the 1960s. It was the saddest time in my life. These Sisters all came in before they left to tell me what had happened—it was so difficult to understand. They weren't convinced they wanted to go home. That's what made it even more difficult. It was just sort of suggested because [nobody knew] what they were going to do: you know, where they could go, whether they could get a position. That was a very, very, very difficult, very difficult, time; and it lasted a number of years before it was settled. And these were such fine young people that I thought had a vocation. [Long pause.] But then these stalwarts [gestures toward Judeen and Marlene] stayed with us. [Laughter.] (November 1992)

> Sister Elizabeth died on August 28, 2001. The other four Sisters remain in ministry and connected to their communities—the School Sisters of St. Francis and Alverno College.

16

LIVING IN THE PRESENT

SISTER CATHERINE BERTRAND

Sister Catherine Bertrand is executive director of the National Religious Vocation Conference. Because it is her job to assist religious communities across the country with their vocation ministry—that is, recruitment of new members—she knows well their current struggles. She supervises a staff of six at the Conference's headquarters in a secured building on Chicago's South Side. The neighborhood is unsightly and unsafe.

At 42, Sister Catherine, a School Sister of Notre Dame, has a job that entails long periods of traveling and almost constant speaking engagements. Even on a Saturday morning in November, in a leisurely one-on-one conversation, her vitality was evident.

In 1969, when I entered, it was the time of the great exodus in so many communities. Sixteen of us entered when I did; and we often say now that as we were trying to get in, we almost got run over as some others were trying to get out. That was the tone of the time. I don't think my motives for entering a community were very good at all. If I were a vocation minister interviewing me, I probably would have said, "Wait about 20 years." Ultimately I made my decision based on a dare; a friend said, "I don't think you'll stay."

The one thing I was very sure of was that I wanted to do something with my life that would make a difference. And that, too, was very much the tone of the time. I had considered the Peace Corps. But I was in the community at least two years before I really began to think this could work, that I could do this. I was beginning to have a sense of belonging to something bigger than just me—to a group of women who could make a difference, not just because they were the individuals they were, but because of how we did it together. I had a sense of a great vitality, that this was a place where people had energy they wanted to spend well. For me [religious life] continued to make sense.

The flip side of coming to appreciate what it is to belong to something bigger than yourself was the realization that I'd have to give up some of what I would choose to do or how I would choose to do it. Attempting to transform

Sister Catherine Bertrand cleans up a neighborhood in New Orleans after Katrina, joining other School Sisters of Notre Dame from the Mankato [Minnesota] Province as well as their lay employees and spouses on a two-week service trip. "We literally went from house to house helping people, gutting houses, cleaning out storage areas, whatever needed doing on the block."

independence into interdependence was a struggle. And I began to get in touch with how costly the vowed life was going to be. I didn't see religious life as my only option. So to look at a lifetime of being celibate—I was aware very, very early on that there were going to be trade-offs. You can't have it all.

I think [the struggle] was resolved, at least in those first years, by realizing how energizing ministry can be. When you're in your twenties, it's part of the human growth cycle to give a great deal of energy to career development. And in some ways there's a parallel to that in religious life, where you begin to discover the excitement of ministry. I loved the places where I was and the people I worked with and the things I was involved in. So the celibacy question is not always on the front burner.

I've only come to realize this as I've looked back, but I have the sense in my life that everything has connected to something else, especially ministerially. What I experienced one place proved to be very helpful in the next. For example, I taught primarily in junior high and high school, and you learn skills there that you don't learn in any other way. The next assignment I had was to be in charge of resident students in our girls' boarding school. Many of them came from very, very difficult family situations, and it was a real eye-opener for me in terms of the horrendous possibilities of family life. That proved to be an incredible background for moving into vocation work.

When I got a phone call one day asking me to consider vocation ministry for the School Sisters of Notre Dame, that proved to be a more significant phone call than I ever imagined that it would. There's something very affirming about having someone say to you: We believe that you have the skills to do this work. I certainly took my time in looking at the pros and cons, but it seemed very right to go ahead. The difficult part, I think, is that you are constantly working with people who are discerning a response to religious life. In dealing with anyone else's issues, you cannot help but deal with your own. So day after day after day, you yourself are confronted with the very questions that you keep asking other people.

I would say the most positive thing about my position was working within my own community. I loved the time I spent visiting the Sisters. I would invite them to tell their vocation story and to talk about why they continued to choose this life. It was exciting for me, but also encouraging for them to hear each other. Sometimes we need to hear ourselves articulate: Why am I doing this with my life? Media coverage today is so negative about religious life, you begin to believe a lot of it yourself. So to keep looking at, "What was my original desire in coming?" and "Why do I continue to choose it?" generates new enthusiasm. I found our Sisters very responsive and very supportive of me in that work. And I found myself saying again and again and again and again that *we* are the best or the worst inviters. Do we make the lifestyle look like it's something that someone would want to be a part of?

The worst question you could ever ask any vocation director is "How many are coming?" And certainly I was asked that question. But I moved into the position believing that it's as much the responsibility of the community to invite people to enter as it is mine, perhaps even more so. I was the one designated to work with people once someone else had invited them. There were times when I felt the pressure [to produce new members], but not necessarily pressure that anyone else was putting on me. The problem came more from my own desire to have people join.

After five years of working with our own community, I was asked to consider a position as assistant vocation director in the archdiocese of St. Paul. It seemed like a perfect time for a change. I did enjoy vocation ministry, so to continue in it, but in a different facet of it—working with both men and women—seemed like a good way to go.

There were certainly differences, in terms of overall issues. Probably it was again a confirmation of what I think I knew in theory: How different religious life and diocesan priesthood are by their very nature. I can remember interviewing my first priesthood candidate, and [he said], "I want to minister in the area where I grew up. I want to be among the people I know." I was sitting there with my "religious life" ears on, thinking, "There's no spirit of adventure here." But in essence, that's exactly what you are looking for in the diocesan priesthood, that desire to minister within the group of people you've been called forth to serve. So [for me] it was understanding some very definite differences. It was also moving into that whole arena of diocesan Church, a different experience of the modern Church, and certainly more Church structure than I had experienced within my community. And my sense is that there are some very fine people—men and women, priests, religious, laity—who are very concerned about the issues within the Church today. And to start stereotyping all bishops, or all priests, or all men does an incredible disservice to them, as well as to women and to the Church at large. So for me what may have felt a bit more black-and-white before I was in that position became very gray. The lines are not so clearly drawn.

I will never, ever be one of those people who will say I never had a moment's doubt [about my vocation]. I have had to rechoose many, many times to continue the religious life. I had to give a talk at World Youth Day in Denver [in 1993], and I shared this with a group there. I have come to the conclusion that God's gift to me is uncertainty rather than certainty. Not the kind of uncertainty that every morning I wake up and say, "Am I going to get through another day?" Nothing like that. But it's the kind that keeps you on the edge, so that I have to keep rechoosing.

I think it's been better for me to approach it that way. Is this really what God would want of me? Is this how I can best use the gifts and talents I've been given? I have to continue to look at the fact that, no, I don't have my own family. I don't have my own home. As much as community has been very significant in my life, and I feel very connected with the people in my community, there still are times when I think what life might have been like had I chosen something else. I've never taken this lifestyle for granted. People sometimes ask, "If you had it to do over again, would you do it over again?" I don't know. It's a nonquestion in some ways, because there's a context within which you choose. That context would be different now. But do I regret it? Oh, heavens no. I don't regret it. And have I been happy? Yes. I talk with my married friends. They have similar questions. You know: What if I hadn't married So-and-So? Or what if I hadn't chosen a particular career? We're not in a society that helps us live with limits very well. Sometimes [when you're] with people who share very similar values, it does raise questions as to what might have been.

Has there been anybody in particular who caused you to wish you'd done something different?

Oh, sure. One of the challenges to us as religious is to keep looking at interrelationships. How do we do it with a sense of integrity and respect for our own choices, but also for the choices of another person? That's been one of the joys as well as one of the challenges of my life. I'm deeply grateful for the people I have loved and who love me, and I think I'm a better religious and a better minister as a result of that. Again, when I made the vow of celibacy, it was my understanding that it was a way to love, not a way not to love.

Sometimes when people talk about celibacy, they think of it as abstinence from or lack of or giving up of genital activity. It is all of that. And some days that might be exactly what it feels like. But it's so much more than that. On a better day, it is a vow to love in a less particular way instead of loving *a* single person.

I've come to learn over the years that you don't skip life's stages. I don't care if you entered religious life at 18 or 28 or 58. If you're attentive to your own person and to what is happening around you, you go through the stages of human growth, whether you're in the community or out of the community. The challenges will be there, but so will the joys. It's difficult sometimes, whether you're in marriage or in religious life, to sort out what has to do with lifestyle choices and what has to do with human growth issues. But you don't push the questions under the rug because you happen to be a religious.

What is it you do now?

I'm executive director of the National Religious Vocation Conference. And basically my work involves working with vocation ministers from religious communities throughout the United States. We do a lot of program development and training sessions so that vocation ministers are as well equipped as they can possibly be to do the work they are doing. Another big piece of my job description is serving as liaison for a number of organizations that [are also concerned with] vocation ministry. Like LCWR [Leadership Conference of Women Religious] and CMSWR [Council of Major Superiors of Women Religious] and CMSM [Conference of Major Superiors of Men]. I also work with NCDVD, which is the National Conference of Diocesan Vocation Directors. I'm in contact with the campus ministry groups and also with the Bishops' Committee on Vocations.

People love to hear signs of hope. And I'm able to share some of those. They also want to hear about the factors that prevent people from considering religious life today—and what are the steps we can take to help turn that around? My sense is that [people] are very concerned that religious life be focused, that there's a clarity in identity as well as purpose.

From what I hear from people who are looking at religious life, they want to be part of something that's bigger than themselves. But they also want to be a part of a group that does more than gather once in a while to see how everybody's doing. They want to join a lifestyle where people pray together. They want to be a part of something that is going to sustain them. So it is an incredible challenge to a religious community to look at what can sustain not only those of us that have been here a little while, but especially younger people coming in.

There are many ways that religious life is being lived, and I'm not saying one way is better than another. But it is becoming clear that there is a certain, for lack of a better word, *structure* that needs to be there if we're going to sustain the new members. And that's not [provided by] highly independent living. It might be okay for some people who have been in religious life a while and have the kind of foundation that will allow them to move out and live more independently, because they know who their connecting links are. But for new people coming, they need that foundation.

The lamps are not going out on religious life. I don't think I have blinders on. I've been in this work a long time, and I've seen some of the best and some of the worst. One of the signs of hope would certainly be that we have some choices to make. We're not just helpless people who don't have any options. Religious life as we've known it is not going to continue to exist. It isn't existing now.

Certainly, I look back, and the community I entered is not the community that exists now. The community that existed for those who entered 25 years before me is certainly, certainly, not what exists today. The next 10 years are going to be very critical years. [Religious life] will demand a great deal of creativity, and some real looking at what has been, in order to move into a future that will continue to be relevant within the Church today.

Other signs of hope are some of the people who are coming to religious life: tremendously talented people who are not losers, people who had many options and still see this as a valuable way to live life. Some are still in college; many have been out of college two, three years and have found that the corporate world wasn't all that it was cracked up to be. But there are older people, too, second- and third-career people looking at other options.

Religious life still looks very white. But the numbers of multicultural candidates are slowly increasing, particularly Hispanic and Asian candidates. It's much smaller with African-Americans, and very, very, very small with Native Americans. The effort to reach out to men and women of color is vastly different from what it was a few years ago. But we don't always know how to do it, because we don't always understand the cultures well enough. In our organization we have a Hispanic vocation minister and an Asian—a Vietnamese—vocation minister who chair standing committees that work specifically with these issues. They need to be the ones to tell us how we do this. But the effort is certainly there. My hope is that it's there because we realize the richness [women and men of color] bring to the whole picture, not because it's a last-ditch effort.

Basically, I'm a hopeful person, and I have found many reasons in life and in religious life to be hopeful. I hope the work that I'm doing will have some long-term effects on the caliber of ministry in the Church. I'm also a realist. And there are days when I certainly do wonder, "Does this have any impact on anything?" I try to live by what I've come to call the "Gamaliel principle." In scripture, Gamaliel says, "If this movement is of God, it will last, and we will find ourselves fighting against God if we try to destroy it. And if it's not, it will fade away. It will destroy itself" [Acts 5: 34–39]. When I confront some of the things going on in religious life or in the Church, I often think of that principle and say, "Some of this is way bigger than I am, and I don't need to get bent out of shape about it." It will stand the test of time, and what really is of God, I believe, will last. (November 1993)

Sister Catherine was for 10 years the executive director of the National Religious Vocation Conference. From 2003 until 2009 she served as provincial leader of the Mankato Province of the School Sisters of Notre Dame.

I am more convinced than ever in the value of vowed religious life. But the context in which this commitment is lived out is indeed difficult. Women religious are struggling to "stay at the table," tables which are often not of our own making. But this is the time for creating our own "tables." Yes, we are fewer in number, and we are aging. But we are here! I joined religious life because I believed that these were women who were changing the world. We have. We are. And we will continue to do so.

SISTER ANCILLA MALONEY

In 1993, at the time of the interview, Sister Ancilla Maloney—a Sister Servant of the Immaculate Heart of Mary (IHM) from Scranton, Pennsylvania—was teaching at Holy Cross High School in suburban Delran, New Jersey, and living with 12 other IHM Sisters in a large convent on the property.

At 55, Sister Ancilla (pronounced "An-SILL-a") is lively and energetic. She talks fast and walks fast—more than a match for her teenage students. She is one of several women who mentioned being moved by Mary Jo Leddy's book Reweaving Religious Life; *and at the end of our conversation she expressed her intention to change her own style of living religious life.*

A year later, she had started down that road. In September 1994, she moved to the Bronx in New York City, where she now lives in an intercommunity house with other women religious and teaches in an inner-city high school.

Mary Lou, we've known each other since we were 18 and freshmen in college together. Did you know then that you had a vocation?

Yes, I did. I only went to [the College of] New Rochelle because my parents had said that they did not want me to enter when I finished senior year in high school. They felt I hadn't lived life, and they wanted me to go to college. The thought started to go through my head in freshman year in high school. Then in the middle of sophomore year, Dad nearly died. He was sick for four months. It was part of the culture at that time that maybe 100, 150 kids would go to Mass in the morning before school, and so that was something I did. After communion I'd pray that if God would allow Dad to live, I would be open to the possibility of a vocation. I loved Latin. I had a picture with the words "Ecce Ancilla Domine" ["Behold the Handmaid of the Lord"] from the Angelus, and I prayed those words.

The other day I was teaching a morality class, and this one kid said to me, "I can't see how anybody could give her life to somebody you could never see, couldn't talk to, couldn't touch." So I talked about having spent time building a relationship with God. [I told them that in high school] we had the opportunity to go on weekend retreats, and I remember spending as much time as possible in the chapel when it was very quiet and dark—just the candles. Those moments gave God an opportunity to move in and build on a relationship that had already been established.

Remember when we went to Dartmouth [Winter Carnival] together? I was telling [the kids] about that. I remember getting out of bed and walking down to church that morning. No one, not a soul, was awake. It was snowing; it was beautiful. I remember walking through the snow, and the presence of God really caught me up. It was this wonderful winter weekend at Dartmouth, and I was having a wonderful time; and this whole other relationship, this whole other part of my life, was developing. [At the end of that year], the day of class elections, I was nominated [for class president]. I remember standing up and saying I would not be returning to New Rochelle. That was the moment I publicly said what I was going to do. I entered in the fall of 1958. [When it came time to select a name, I chose Ancilla—the Latin word for *handmaid*. It all goes back to those high school experiences.]

In the novitiate, I met Sister St. Mary, who was a great woman of God. I was very much struck by her contemplative spirit, her sense of the Lord. She'd talk about God's action in our lives, and sometimes I'd just about be able to understand. I used to visualize this as if I were hanging on to the wings of the plane and she'd be taking off, and I'd be hanging there just trying to grasp what she said. I would spend time praying over what she would say. It would draw me deeper into my own relationship with God in a way that made me hunger for more and more and more, and really commit myself to that relationship, so that my priority in life has been pursuing that relationship with God. Out of that has flowed the rest of my life.

During the summer of 1968—that wild Democratic convention in Chicago—I was in Altoona, Pennsylvania, teaching in a high school there. I lived with four Sisters who were deep into American politics. Two of them were liberal Democrats, and two of them were archconservatives, so this dialogue back and forth was fascinating. I had totally missed the Vietnam War and the commitment to civil rights. Up to that time I had thrown myself into learning how to do elementary school. I was into think-and-do books. Then I was into economics, world history, boys' health, religion, the whole high school scene. I had no time to even breathe, much less know what was going on in the world. That's the way it was. I was just keeping my head above water.

I lived [with those Sisters] one year, and then I went to St. Dominic's in Oyster Bay. When I got to St. Dominic's, a Sister there was 150 percent into the civil rights movement, into African-American culture, into protest against the Vietnam War; and she didn't drive. So I took her to antiwar protests and civil rights demonstrations. I had never really questioned the position of the government, but now I began to look at it. Plus the Church was opening up; this was '69, '70, '71, '72. The Vatican Council was taking root. So we were looking at commitment. We were looking at the integrity of our own vow of poverty, relative to the real poverty of the world. The call of the Church, the call of God's people, began to fit with looking at what was happening in terms of justice and civil rights.

I had a lot of growing to do, because basically I was a conservative. I took my direction from my parents. I would ask Dad, "What would you do?" and that's how I would vote. Well, I began to really look at my own positions and opinions and concerns. In 1970, I decided that part of my responsibility in teaching high school was to open the kids to poverty. You aren't going to change their attitudes if they don't have direct contact with the poor. I asked a priest who had been working with the Christian Appalachian Project to come and talk to the kids. I got permission to go to Kentucky [to work with the poor there] for two weeks in the summer of 1970, and I've been going back ever since. I've probably taken more than 300 kids from college and high school over all those years.

Tell me about your work as vocation director for the congregation.

I was responsible for working with young women who thought they might be interested in religious life. I would say that, and people would say, "Oh, that's recruitment." I never, never defined the job as recruitment. I don't like that word. Actually, it was recruitment, but I just don't like that word. I saw myself as walking with those who were searching to understand God's voice in their hearts. I remember after I first started work in September, I went to Pittsburgh to visit my brother and he said, "Well, what you do is, you try to sell something nobody wants." I'll never forget him saying that. [I remember] driving home all the way from Pittsburgh thinking about that. I had to push that out of my mind.

I can't separate talk about vocation work from where I was on my own journey. For most of my life, I had a sense of success, of accomplishment, of being able to master things, meet challenges, whatever. A lot of that came from my Dad [saying], "There's always more you can do." That's part of my driven-ness. I was involved in leadership in the congregation, the whole nine yards of that. Then four or five years prior to vocation work, I was living with someone who was very, very difficult to deal with. Some of that certainly was myself, which I was not aware of. I was not self-aware at that time. But in the course of dealing with that situation, I met failure, as far as I was concerned, because I wasn't able to handle the situation. For the first time in my life I came to grips with something I couldn't do, and just at that crucial midlife time.

The year after that living situation ended, and before I started vocation work, I made a retreat with Sister St. Mary, and she raised the whole issue of control. See, this all fits together. I had not been able to control that situation. I was just coming out of the tailspin of those years, and then I moved into vocation work, where you have no control over what happens. When you're in school, you have control over your classes. You have control over what you're teaching. You have control over your schedule. You move into vocation work, and there's no control.

My whole life was turned upside down. I'm a day person. I have a lot of energy in the morning, but after prayer and supper in the evening my energies are down. I was doing a lot of work, a lot of traveling, at night. Never mind that I was trying to do a ministry that was at best a no-control situation. You would plan anything—a weekend, a retreat—and you could never tell how many would come. So I found vocation ministry, especially in the beginning, very difficult. I remember in front of our motherhouse there were these big pillars, and I got out of the car to put something in the mail, and I was so uptight and so anxious that I didn't put the car in park, and it went right into one of the pillars. I got in the car and drove away. I mean, any other time I would have been beside myself! But I was in such upheaval because there were no boundaries in that kind of life. You had to create it from scratch. No structure, no structure whatsoever. So I would sit in the office and wonder, "What am I going to do today?"

But as it got going, there was a whole pool of young people who were involved in things I did. Like river retreats. I would get about five or six Sisters and usually about 15 or 20 girls from our college and other colleges, and we'd get on the river in twos and threes in canoes, then stop and have prayer and a picnic, and then get on the river again, and maybe finish with Mass and some more prayer. It put the young people in contact with a whole group of Sisters in a fun way. You had a retreat or a day of prayer for vocations—few would come. You do a river retreat, you do a hiking retreat, or you go for a week in Washington or a week in Kentucky or a week in Mississippi—you could always gather a group of our Sisters and a group of young people and see if the chemistry would click.

Over the course of my six years, about 25 came into the community. A lot of talented women. Some have stayed; some have left after profession. But they were long years. We had two, three, four [women entering] every year, and that was good. I felt okay about that. Psychologically, having no one come would be very difficult for the whole congregation. Sometimes one woman has come and has not stayed, but still someone comes.

During those years I was very much into the control issue, into the call to let go and let God be much more of a director. All this was going on at the same time as the experience of vocation ministry and was triggered by the crisis I had experienced. So it was a whole transition in my life, letting go of a lot of things that I thought were important. Like leadership. I was able to look at myself and say there are gifts and talents you have, and there are other gifts and talents you don't have.

When I finished vocation work, I wanted to teach in a high school in a poor area, but we only have a couple [of schools in those areas]. And then in the midst of deciding, Mary Persico, who is the principal here [at Holy Cross High School], called and said, "I'd like you to come and consider opening up a Peace and Justice Center."

The Peace and Justice Center is not supposed to be just for the kids. I don't have a club. The concept is that all of us are called to be committed to peace and justice as part of the Gospel. It's been the clear specific teaching of the Church since the early 1970s, and it comes out of Matthew's Gospel [Chapter 25], where

Jesus says, "When you fed the hungry, when you clothed the naked, when you gave drink to the thirsty, you did it to Me. Come, you blessed of my Father." We try to put the kids in touch with other cultures, [so they] see that the poor have faces and hopes and dreams and the same kinds of needs that they have and their brothers and sisters have. But the goal of the Peace and Justice Center is really to involve all the Holy Cross community, to raise the consciousness of the whole community. Over the course of the years I think there has been some faculty support. But for whatever reason, out of 90 faculty, there have not been a lot of people [committed]. The thought of peace and justice seems to be threatening. [Faculty members] don't see it as essential, or they see the Peace and Justice Center as radical, liberal, communist—all those terms. Rather, this is the teaching of Jesus. Never mind that it's the teaching of the Church; this is the Gospel message!

My dream is to start a high school for Hispanic teenagers or black teenagers, marginalized teenagers, where you have a whole faculty committed to justice. Personally I'm ready to live a life that's simpler and also to live in community with people who have a common commitment to justice, who have the same desires for community prayer and community presence and simple lifestyle that I do. These are wonderful people here, wonderful people, but we do have different ideas about things. And that's fine.

I've said this publicly at meetings [of our congregation]. We're good folks; we're good people. We have good schools. We minister well wherever we minister. There is an excellence, a spirit, a goodness in what we bring to the Church and society. But I think that in ways that have just crept up on us, we have bought into the American middle-class way of life. And not just my congregation—a lot of congregations. I don't pretend to have the answers straight from God, but I believe that religious life has value, that religious life is not going to die. What is at the root of our call is this relationship with God that I've spoken of before: this passion, if you will. I think that's present today. I think God is calling women today. Then why are they not drawn [to religious life]? I think they're not drawn because we aren't countercultural.

I don't have a particular call to priesthood, but it's something I think needs to be part of the Church, just from a justice perspective. I've worked with many wonderful priests who are committed to the Lord and to God's people and who are wonderful human beings. Then you have the power structure of the Church, the hierarchical structure. I think they've made a lot of mistakes. They're making mistakes now, mistakes in terms of being dogmatic when we're still searching for truth. It breaks my heart to learn of more and more people who are leaving the Church because they're not finding community, they're not finding compassion, they're not finding good strong leadership in the ways of the Gospel. I don't have all the answers. The issues are really complex, but sometimes, many times, I just ask the question, "What would Jesus do?"

There are a lot of good things [at Holy Cross]. I walk into this house after school, and it's a good place to be. I like the folks I live with, and I like the rhythm of the life. Nobody's life is perfect. A woman who moves into marriage has all sorts of dreams about what she'd like marriage to be, and she deals with all kinds of things that weren't in the dream. That's the way I've lived with the hopes and dreams. But I have a sense that I'm being called to live more radically, to live the dream in a sense, not just for myself, but for the congregation and religious life. I'm so committed over here [at the school], I'm so busy all the time, that the way to make that happen is not real clear. I know people have the same dream I do. I'm so far away from people that putting it together seems overwhelming. But I'm at a point where I think now is going to have to be the time. (October 1993)

> *Sister Ancilla brought her passion for peace and justice work with her to Aquinas High School in the Bronx. In 1999, U.S. News and World Report named Aquinas one of the outstanding high schools in the country. The article paid particular attention to the school's community service; many of the programs they cited were the ones Sister Ancilla initiated. We spoke at St. Ann's Convent on East 109th Street in Manhattan, where she lives with seven other women religious from two different communities. Her mother died in 2010 at the age of 100.*

When I got here, I recognized that we had Spanish-speaking kids and the migrant workers [I'd worked with in North Carolina] were Spanish speaking. So I decided that in the summers I would take some students to North Carolina to do a Bible school program for the migrant kids. We would go out into the migrant camps and spread out a blanket or a big sheet. That became the classroom. We did religious instruction and Bible study and we had arts and crafts. It was wonderful for our girls.

For two weeks we lived in a trailer—six girls and three Sisters. You should have seen it. The kids slept all over in sleeping bags in this little trailer. I can remember one night one of the Sisters had to get to the refrigerator, and there was a rocking chair upside down and all the kids' laundry was hanging on the rocking chair. It was wild. [Laughs.] We did that every summer. Then around 2000, I was tired. I was really tired. Two weeks with teenagers, it was really challenging. Sometimes it would be really hot, and they didn't want to work. Also about 2000, Mom needed me. So I went home to be with her in the summers and that activity stopped.

Teaching in an inner-city school with these girls who come from so many diverse backgrounds has been so rewarding. I don't have a peace and justice office the way we had in New Jersey. We just do stuff. I got our girls involved in the community, in the neighborhood, right near Aquinas. We did tutoring and childcare with families who [had been homeless and were getting their lives back together]. We did Valentine parties and Halloween parties and Easter egg hunts and then we did week-by-week tutoring for the kids. We're still doing that.

Life isn't perfect. Every day isn't perfect. Sometimes the kids don't take the opportunity of the excellent education they're given. But one of the exciting things is that almost every kid goes to college. Graduation night is an experience I've never had in any other place because the parents and friends are so excited. In most instances, the girls are the first ones in the family going on to college. (March 2010)

MARY JO LEDDY

Although Mary Jo Leddy is Canadian, her book, Reweaving Religious Life, *has had a very strong influence on many American nuns. After it was published, she traveled throughout the United States speaking to groups of nuns at seminars, workshops, and study days, sharing her thoughts on what is wrong with religious life today and what could be made right in a new model, whatever that might turn out to be.*

In 1994, after 30 years as a Sister of Sion and at the age of 48, she left religious life. She lives now with a group of refugees and other volunteers at Romero House in Toronto, where she has perhaps found for herself a new model of religious life.

When I was at that age when most people made decisions about their life after high school, I had this basic sense that I wanted to give my life to God. It was very simple. It wasn't complicated. And I remember going to see the provincial to ask to enter. She asked me why, and I said, "God is really important to me, and I think it's worth spending your life living as if that were so." I can't believe there's any better reason than I gave then. I feel exactly the same way now.

I entered in '63, and it was completely the old style. As far as I knew, nothing had ever changed. So it was strict. But for me it was just a wonderful experience. It was a two-year period in which your life was completely focused. I didn't like the housework, but [my formation] stands to me as kind of a paradigmatic experience of what it means to have every aspect of your life and every moment of the day ordered toward God. I remember when we received the habit, we had this talk from the novice mistress. [She said] we would be buried in [those clothes]. In one year we were out of the habit and everything had changed. So early on I had that double experience of an ordered culture of belief and then the fact that it could change. Early on we had to sift and sort what was essential and what wasn't.

I'm embarrassed to say that at first I was extremely leery of the [changes]. I had no experience upon which to say why we needed to change. I thought the way the Sisters dressed was fine. So when the changes first happened, I really didn't see why we needed it. But after I started going to university, I could see; and then by the time the changes had really happened, I had internalized why they were necessary.

When I came here to Toronto, we were at the beginnings of liberation theology and I was influenced by that. But in terms of really kicking into my own life, I think it was my dissertation [that mattered most]. I had heard of this Jewish thinker at the University of Toronto, who was just excellent, a man called Emil Fackenheim. So the first year I was here, I signed up for his philosophy of Judaism class. And very early on, he said something like: [How is it] possible to keep on doing philosophy in the same way after the Holocaust? And that to me was the most provocative question I heard. The man was struggling with ultimate questions. So I took all of his classes, and then I asked him to be my thesis director. I wandered around a long time before I finally landed on the philosophy of Hannah Arendt [as a topic for my dissertation]. After three years of reading her and writing about her, and having to interface that with Emil who didn't like her, and facing the Holocaust and what happens when people are silent about systems, I had a moral resolve that I would take responsibility for my life and the times that I lived in. I was profoundly changed in the course of doing that dissertation. For me the crisis of faith was more about humanity than about God. What I saw was that very good people can be involved in systems in which the net result is murder—that most of what happened was because good people did nothing. It wasn't because of the evil. It was because good people did nothing. So I felt that I had to write, I had to speak, I had to act—and that I would.

I was writing my thesis, coming to this conviction about my [own commitments,] when the official Catholic paper in the country, *The Catholic Register*, came out with editorials supporting apartheid. An acquaintance, a Jesuit priest, had been working with the Task Force on Corporate Responsibility, where they would go to bankers and raise questions about apartheid. One banker said [to him], "Look, the Church supports [apartheid]. You're not representing the Church." It was really shocking. I frankly didn't even read the official paper at that time. But three of us were having lunch in a cafeteria, and we said it was terrible that [these editorials] would be considered as the voice of the Church. [Then we started talking about founding an alternative Catholic newspaper.] We said, "Let's each of us get four people." The 12 of us talked about it and at some point crossed the Rubicon and decided that we would start *Catholic New Times*, and we did.

For the first issue [which came out in October 1976], we ran 500 copies and passed it out at meetings. We had one phone and a desk in somebody else's office. I'd worked on a high school newspaper, and I had said I would [serve as editor]. I thought it would take one day a week. It was crazy. I was the Newman chaplain on campus and supposedly working on my thesis, but I worked on the paper at least three days a week at nights.

The issue that galvanized us was apartheid, but it wasn't central in a sense. The issue that hit us right away was women's ordination. As a campus minister, I had been preaching. The priest I was working with was preaching at five Masses every Sunday, and it was too much. He said, "Well, could you do some?" And

I said yes. I found it quite exhausting. I overprepared. I was nervous. I was tired at the end of Sunday, and I wondered, "Why would anybody want to do this?" Anyway, I was doing it. And at that particular time, the pope issued a statement on women priests and the archbishop issued a statement saying women couldn't preach. The whole Newman community was in an uproar. They wanted me to continue, and I felt I should. For the first time I really felt in my bones discrimination. What I was being silenced for was something I absolutely couldn't change: being a woman. And it seemed so ridiculous to me; I mean, I wasn't saying Mass. But the bottom line was that if I had continued, this guy would have lost his [priestly] faculties. I was prepared to take a stand for myself and for the people, but I didn't want him to be the one to pay. And since at the same time we were starting the newspaper, it seemed easy to move over to that. And the fact is that the paper became a way of preaching.

At the paper we had to deal with every issue in the Church. I had to think through everything. Ultimately there was a profound sense of being committed to the Church and the tradition, to a sense of sacramentality, but also a deep sense of our own justice—our own justice and equality of relationship. Some of our positions actually surprised people on the left more than on the right. Because, for example, we were strongly pro-life. But it was consistent with an ethic of life. Our strongest position, I think—and I'd have to say it was largely influenced by my own position—was supporting the peace movement in the 1980s.

I also started a column in the *Toronto Star*. It's a funny thing. Most of what I've done I've backed into. It's not what I planned. One day a lady called me up and she said, "My name is Basya Hunter, and I must see you." She was a playwright here in town, had done a number of award-winning plays. She took me out for lunch, and she said, "I've read everything you've ever written, and you're a writer. And if you don't write, you'll never be yourself." It just took my breath away. And she then produced all my articles with her commentary. I really felt as if this old Jewish angel had come into my life. I filed it away, because "Write?" About what? But three books germinated—all at that time.

One of the things you've written is that somewhere, sometime, each one of us has a prophetic moment. Where would you put yours?

It's hard to evaluate your own life. I guess I think mostly what I have to contribute is that for whatever reason, I'm not afraid of the unknown. Anything that begins is, by definition, terrifically uncertain and fragile. And I think the saddest thing I have seen in religious communities—because I've seen a lot of them, especially after *Reweaving Religious Life: Beyond the Liberal Model* was published—is that so many religious who are really good people, and genuinely want a future for their community, will go anywhere and will do anything if they just know where they're going. And by definition you don't know. If it's genuinely something new, it's not that predictable or definable. And I found that the most painful thing in giving talks to religious was always at the end. [Somebody would say,] "Tell us what the future model should be." Like maybe I have the secret. And I always had to say, "I really don't know. You just have to try." But they always kept saying, "Don't you have a sense of—?" And I don't. I think you just have to try and see how it turns out. A lot of what I've done, like starting the newspaper, is going out into the unknown. I don't want to call it a virtue, because I don't feel that way. I think it's something temperamental. I'm more comfortable with unknowns.

I'm uncomfortable with the number of people who are saying *this* is the future model of religious life. And all they're talking about is an inverse image of the present. Because I think the truth is we really don't know. The basic desire of living one's life completely in terms of God, I think, will always be there and will always give rise to some form of religious life.

How did it happen that that was no longer the way for you?

I'm in a strange situation, and I haven't really articulated this publicly before. But there's a way in which I don't feel I've left religious life—I really don't. I've left a particular congregation, but I haven't left religious life.

It was the darkest five years of my life, coming to that decision. Because I had grown up in [the Sisters of Sion]. It was in that congregation that I learned religious life, that I deeply internalized it. But it just reached a point where I couldn't live what I had learned from that congregation, in that congregation. That was very painful. But I'm profoundly grateful to that particular group of people.

At one point I looked around at different groups. But it's not like a set of clothes you take off and put on. It was artificial. As I was asking those kinds of questions, by accident I ended up living with these refugees. And one day—it was last summer, actually—we were on a camp [vacation] with the children, and I woke up, and I said, "This is everything I ever wanted to do." And I think it was only when that happened that I could leave the congregation. Because I couldn't leave [until] I really had a sense of being called *to* something. And I don't even know what it is. I know it's here; I don't know what it is.

I'm living probably more poorly than I ever have. I live with people who've been dispossessed, radically dispossessed, and we live with fundamental insecurity. We all rely on the food bank at least once a month. I think in this context that celibacy makes more sense than it ever has. These people don't understand anything about religious congregations. From their perspective [religious life] is irrelevant. What they know is what you're living—with them. They know that some of us are there for all of them. A couple of the Ethiopian women kept saying, "You are our mother." I thought, "I must be maternalistic. This is dreadful. This is against everything that's politically correct." But what they explained to me is that a mother loves each child completely. And that's what they saw me doing, loving each of them completely with no discrimination. Now, I'm not sure that's true. But it was a summons to me to do that. Obedience I don't know about anymore. I think it makes a lot of sense in a time when a congregation has high intentionality, when there's a clear mission, a mission that is shared and that's demanding. But I don't see most congregations have that. So then I'm not sure what the obedience is, other than just going along with stuff. I think it's the vow that's most in trouble—not because of bad people or even because of structures, but because the intentionalities of communities are not clear and focused and can't be at this point.

So I see Romero House, this little community here, as allowing me to live religious life in a way that makes a lot of sense to me in a very real, daily way. At the heart of Romero House is that we—people like myself, volunteers—live with refugees. I'm on this floor; there's refugees up here; there's refugees down here and in the basement; and there are three houses like this. What we do is we live together as neighbors. And sometimes we're friends even. It's that simple. Being together is radically liberating for all of us. For the refugees, having people—Canadians—living with them, liking them, gives them the confidence to begin again and to bridge into the rest of the culture. And it's liberating for us. We learn a lot about everything that's important. Most of them arrive just with an overnight case. They're from all over the world, mostly from Africa at this point, Ethiopia, Eritrea, Somalia, Zaire, Rwanda, Burundi, Sri Lanka, Iran, some Russians. Kind of a mix. Usually people come in through the airport and are referred by somebody in immigration. Or, up from Buffalo. They arrive into the States, and then go to Buffalo and claim refugee status at the border. It usually takes six to eight months [for that process to be completed]. And during that time they stay with us.

How did you first get involved with Romero House?

I had just finished a term as provincial and was thinking about starting a center for action and contemplation. I was talking to people; and then a friend, Anne O'Brien, who had been living at the Christian Brother Refugee House, said, "Mary Jo, if you want to do a center, why don't you try doing it among the people? Not at some university, where they usually have these centers, but just with the people." As soon as she said that, I thought: That makes a lot of sense. So within 24 hours I'd moved over and was living with these refugees. And the minute I was there, I thought: I love this. This is just great. To make a very long story short, the Christian Brothers withdrew from that work with refugees. By that time a number of my friends had become involved in the project, so when the Christian Brothers closed down, we set up Romero House, which basically continued the same thing. It had a sense of rightness, of continuing the peace work I do, but dealing with real people who have suffered from war. These people were all fleeing from war.

It's heartbreaking at times. All I know is that I understand the Gospel in a way I just wouldn't otherwise. Some mornings at prayer when we read the Gospel, it just leaps off the page—when it says, "Come to me, you that are weary and burdened" and that's really how you feel. We have to make an act of faith in the power of love and the power of truth. Some of the suffering drives you to prayer, and some of it drives you to want to do something, and I do. I do a lot politically. But there are some things you can't do, and that's hard. It's really hard. My heart just gets broken by these people—and I mean that in the best sense. There's no question about my being here. And at the same time, there's so much suffering. What I'm struggling with is how to live with that and how to pray with it.

I don't think any of us have a handle on the future of religious life, or of the Church. I believe that we're at one of those in-between times in history. But I think we know when we meet like-hearted people—I don't say like-minded, because we all think differently. We know the people who are asking the questions and with what heart and what spirit. I think there's a shared sense of a number of women religious: that religious life is important; that it's valuable, that there is a future. *What* is not clear. And that what's going on now is in ruins, basically. It's a combined act of faith and yet an assessment that the present is just not working, [even though] there are many, many fine women in the congregations, and I'm quite convinced that almost everything really good in the Church has happened because of women religious.

We live the present. I don't think it's like you're waiting for something over the horizon. I really believe that every time, like now, is the best time to live the Gospel. We will become Christians by living this moment fully, as much as people in the past or in the future. So it's not as if, when I say this is an in-between time, I mean it's less of a time. I think it's a very important time, and I think to the extent that we can live this moment now in its fullness with all of its burden and its blessings, there will be something in the future. And we don't really know what that is. But for us now, this is what we're called to live. What's going on in religious life isn't just about this, that, or the other thing; it's a shaking of the foundations. It's that we've become so much part of the culture that we can't get out of it. And [the problems we face] reflect the extent to which we've internalized our culture.

As I reflect on my own life—or even just what we've talked about—most of what's happened has been a surprise to me. It's been by indirection—in very, very ordinary meetings or conversations. It has happened in the in-between. That is how grace has worked in my life. The only other thing I would say is that at the same time as the Jewish prophet-actress came to see me, I was making my 30-day retreat; and I met a wonderful Mercy Sister, Kieran Flynn, who really challenged me. She kept saying, "You're so bored spiritually. You've just got to go deeper." I was with her when she died. It was clear to me that she was unconscious and she was praying. But it wasn't just that she prayed; she had become a prayer. And it always stands for me as some kind of a summons—that your life becomes a prayer. She really helped me [toward] a radical sort of spiritual freedom. Oh, she had this wonderful Irish accent, and she would say, "Mary Jo, the only thing you should ever squander is money. If you run out of money, you can always rob a bank. But [don't squander] your life." And then she would say things like, "It's really only God, *only* God, that should [claim] your complete heart and soul. Not the Church, not religious life, not this project, not the newspaper." That's the freedom we all need. Women religious, too. They ought to have the freedom not to get hung up on this or that form of living, or on things in the Church, positively or negatively. Just keep living until you're gone; the rest will follow. (September 1994)

Mary Jo Leddy continues her connections—and her service—to the refugee community in Toronto, particularly to Romero House, which now consists of four houses for refugees plus a community center in the west end of the city. Since its founding in 1992, it has provided housing, settlement, and advocacy services to more than 4,500 individuals and families. Mary Jo is an adjunct professor at Regis College. In 2002, she published Radical Gratitude, *a meditation on appreciating life's fullness.*

SISTER PATRICIA MARKS

For Sister Patricia Marks—the full-time director of religious education in a suburban New Jersey parish—the journey from a very traditional Italian order, the Religious Teachers Filippini, to a less structured noncanonical community, Emmaus Disciples, has been arduous. But she told her story with an air of composure and a light touch that put the bad times in perspective.

In addition to her parish work, Sister Pat is a marriage and family therapist and a certified divorce mediator. She keeps up this level of activity despite recurrent bouts of ill health that force her to limit her schedule. When we met for the interview, she seemed older than her 52 years. She still suffers from the rheumatoid arthritis that was misdiagosed when she was a young woman.

I was born and raised in Trenton, New Jersey. My mother is from a very large Italian Catholic family, and my father was Episcopalian, British. That's a unique combination. My father died when I was about nine. And then when I was about 12, my mother remarried, another Anglo-Saxon Episcopalian. My mother owned a restaurant for 30 years.

I went to a public school while my father was alive. When I was in the sixth grade, my mother thought I was getting a bit wild, and in those days people said, "Oh, the Sisters are going to straighten you out." You know, they were like the Gestapo. So she said, "I'm going to put you in [Villa Victoria,] a private school all the way on the other side of town near the river." I figured, "Well, I'll go, because I have to but I will break every rule they have, and I'll get thrown out, and that'll be that."

But the Sister principal knew what I was doing. She called me to the office, and she said, "I know you're trying to get out of here. You could get 56 demerits, and I'm not going to throw you out. You might as well like it." Then I fell in love with the place. And so when I wanted to enter the convent in twelfth grade, and I told my mother, and she was weeping and gnashing her teeth, I said, "I didn't want to go there, remember?"

I didn't really shine as a student until probably senior year of high school. I was very athletic, very social. I credit my mother's restaurant with making me social. Our house was connected to the restaurant by a corridor, and my mother used to pull us out in the restaurant to meet all these people. And I would go reluctantly. I can remember her dragging me down the hall, saying, "You have to learn to get along with all kinds of people. You have to learn to converse with them."

Why did I enter religious life? I think a lot of it is time-conditioned. In 1959, when I graduated from high school, young women were more mature, but they had limited choices. There were 25 girls who graduated from high school with me, and I think all of them knew at 18 whether or not they were going to get married right away, go to college and then get married, or enter religious life. Three of us entered religious life. If you wanted to work in the Church, you became a Sister. There was no such thing as lay ministry. And the Sisters [I knew in school] were very good. I found out later that [the Religious Teachers Filippini] sent their best there, the most educated, the nicest. They were very gentle. All these tales you hear of people getting hit by nuns—I never had any of that. We didn't wear uniforms; nobody hit anybody; they didn't yell.

[When I entered], I bought the whole package. I accepted everything. I think of myself now; it's like another life. I know it isn't, but that was another Pat Marks. And yet there's a sense of continuity. It was very, very strict. Just to show you how innocent and ridiculous our life was: We couldn't do anything on New Year's Eve, so at midnight [all the novices] went in and flushed the toilets for five minutes.

Everything was circumscribed with a ritual or a procedure of some kind. Let me give you one instance. After our night prayers we used to have to line up and ask the superior, "Can I have my permissions?" One night I said, "What am I asking permission for? Every night we line up and we ask you." "Oh," she said, "your permission to change your clothes, brush your teeth, go to the bathroom, take your bath." I said, "You're kidding."

If anybody asked me to do it now, in 1994, I wouldn't even remotely entertain the possibility. But I was 18, and it was just the way things were. My interpretation of religious life was one we had been taught: Keep the rule, and the rule will keep you. You don't have to do anything extraordinary. You just have to do whatever the rule says. And that guarantees you'll be a good person and you'll be saved. But that started to crumble. Some scandalous things happened. I found out that [one of the professed nuns] and one of the novices were having a very, very intense sexual relationship. I was very, very naive. Everybody's telling me that this is going on. And I'm going, no, not a chance. Well, one time I actually witnessed it. Then they both left.

I was not well at the time. They thought I had rheumatic fever, so I had to stay in bed for 10 months. I began to see what I considered really dumb inconsistencies. I couldn't have a radio for six months while I was ill, and they didn't allow me to read for two months, so I had nothing to do. The doctor said I could only get up and go to the bathroom twice a day. So for the first time in my life I was surreptitious. I asked my friends to smuggle books in to me. I would keep them under the bed. It was either that or I was going to go nuts. So I read my head off, and that was my salvation. I had studied Italian, so I read the life of our foundress, St. Lucy Filippini, in Italian. She was not even a nun. They called her "maestra," which in Italian was "teacher." She owned property; wore regular clothes; was out preaching in the streets, teaching girls to read, which was a criminal offense in parts of Italy at the time. I began to look at her life and at what the Vatican Council was saying about [returning to the vision of your foundress], and, my goodness, we were nowhere close!

The Filippinis had always been considered progressive. But when the Council came, there was a real shift in attitude. I think it had a lot to do with the fact that the mother general at that time was very close to Pius XII. When John XXIII came along, she told us he was an ignorant peasant. With Pius XII she was in like Flynn. But with John XXIII she wasn't. So I think it was a combination of her disdain for him and the fact that he didn't give her any privileges—she lumped him and the Vatican Council together and stood fast [against any changes]. I don't know whether we started going backward or everybody else moved forward. But the progressiveness that was there was lost.

The treatment for rheumatic fever in those days was cortisone. So they pumped me full of cortisone, which distorted my face. I was normal weight, but I had to eat regular meals, so I gained 75 pounds. I was just lying in bed and taking prednisone, which gives you water retention. I became a diabetic. After 10 months of that treatment, my aunt said, "Take her to Philadelphia." I went to a rheumatologist, and he said I had a very rare form of rheumatoid arthritis. They never were quite sure. But anyway, I had to get back up and reenter the world.

When I was active again, I made contact with a priest who had worked with our community. He was distressed that the community was not really doing anything in terms of renewal, so he encouraged a group of us to put together an experiment in community life.

[The experiment] was not revolutionary at all. The ritual permissions [that I mentioned earlier] would be gone. There was to be an identifiable superior, but also discussion about decisions and shared authority. At the time we had an Italian manual of prayers, which the Filippinis translated into English. We wanted to choose our morning and evening prayers from the Psalms. That's how harmless our experiment was.

We put together a perfectly canonical document, and I presented it to the provincial here, and they sent it to the mother general in Rome, and the general sent back, "No, we're not going to do any of this, regardless of what the Church said." The provincial called me and said, "You can't do this." I began to say, "Why?" And she gave me a big lecture about I shouldn't say *why*.

The leadership worked for about six months on everyone [in our group] and really made life hard for them. So in the end it was just myself with the proposal. The provincial said to me, "Well, we can't have a proposal with just one person, right?" I said, "True." So she said, "Write to the Congregation for Religious and tell them you no longer want this." I said, "No, I'm not going to write that. I do want it. I will tell them you drummed everybody else out and you are forcing me to rescind the application." [She said,] "You can't say that!" I said, "That's the truth." So we went back and forth.

I was angry. I knew that I wasn't happy anymore. But I still didn't want to leave. And I remember the provincial saying, "I'm sure you want to leave." I said, "No, I don't." So she said, "I don't know where to put you. Why don't you go to Harlem? Nobody wants to go there." At the time the Filippinis had a school in East Harlem. I said, "Sure, I'll go." Oh, my God! I didn't know what I was in for.

That was when I decided you learn from whatever happens to you. I've met people along the way who have not had one-eighth of the advantages I've had and have done better. When I went to East Harlem, I spent six months looking at those apartment houses and saying, "Oh, my God! I'm not going to have any influence here." I almost had a nervous breakdown. And then finally a priest said to me, "Why don't you just relax? There are many beautiful people here." But I had this savior mentality. We were there to save the people. He said, "Learn from them." I began to look at those children and how they lived, and think: Would Pat Marks have done as well if I had grown up this way? It was a very humbling experience for me.

I went to a Jesuit psychiatrist for two years while I was working in East Harlem. If I hadn't gone for counseling, I probably would have been suicidal at that time. I was very angry. I was angry at my father [because I found out he had died so young because he was an alcoholic]. I was angry because of my illness and how the doctors treated me. I was angry at myself for being so passive. I should have just gotten up out of that bed and said, "I'm going to another doctor." I was angry at the community. Those were my last two years in the Filippinis. [The psychiatrist] said, "As a therapist I usually don't tell people [what to do]. But you are absolutely in the wrong place. I'm telling you right out. You do what you want, but you're stupid to stay two days longer."

In the mid-1970s, a group of 10 of us left [the Filippinis]. We were going to set up an American province, a separate branch of the order under the bishop; but you had to have a minimum of 25 people. After a year together, we were in canonical limbo. We still had our vows, but we weren't going to get 25 people. Meantime, a group of women had left the Sisters of Christian Charity and started a community called the Emmaus Community of Christian Hope. We talked with some of them for about a year, and then eight of us joined them. What happened was, we didn't have the benefit of the money that goes with being in a traditional community. Our vows were considered private, so we had to pay income tax, and we couldn't survive paying taxes. All of a sudden, here we were with no money. Another community of Sisters gave us eight turkeys the first summer we were on our own. We would not have had anything to eat if it wasn't for them. To this day I'm tired of turkey. All summer we had it.

Initially we were going to work for the Church and live in convents that had been emptied by other orders. It looked like a great opportunity [for the parishes in the diocese]. More Sisters to run the schools. But then a lot of the gals had other aspirations. One wanted to be a lawyer. Some people just wanted out of Church work. We found out that the convents only go with the schools. Once the gals started getting into nonschool work, and the numbers dwindled, the pastors were very reluctant to say, "I'll let 10 of you live in my convent even though only one of you is teaching in my school." Which makes sense. So the next stage was those who lived in the convent paid rent to the pastor. But then as more and more found other jobs and moved out into their own apartments, then for two or three people to live in a big convent, it didn't make sense for the parish.

You know the term *asceticism?* The asceticism of the modern age is meetings. We spent three years in meetings. And it was real penance. It was like Lent for the whole year. We were supposed to write constitutions and rules. Who are we? What are we going to do? What do we believe? We were very good at leaving what we knew, but we took a lot of baggage with us, and didn't realize until we got out there that we didn't know who we were or what we wanted to be. It's the difference between running away from something and running toward something. What we were running away from was much clearer to us than what we were moving toward. So it was a real agony to figure all that out. Did we really want to get back into the same system of religious life that we had seen be so destructive?

We were a group of 35 at one point, living in four different convents, still very centered in the Church. The bishop of the diocese used to come and be with us all the time. At that time our age spread was 22 to 68, a typical range of religious life. I do couples' therapy now, and a lot of times a woman goes from home to marriage and then gets disillusioned in the marriage and has an affair. And everything explodes. She's making up for lost time, that time between home and marriage when she didn't have a chance to grow. We were like that. We were like kids let out of a box.

It's interesting how, once the center doesn't hold, it just keeps moving. I was satisfied with being liberal and a feminist, but still pretty much within the Church. But what happened was [that] a huge segment of the group simply moved out of the Catholic Church, because they were so disillusioned with the male leadership. So you couldn't identify the Emmaus Community of Christian Hope as Catholic anymore. People weren't going to Mass. The Eucharist had been very central to our initial vision, but then [the group seemed] not identifiable at all with Mass or Eucharist or prayer. That was a little farther than some of us wanted to go. That's what I mean by "the center didn't hold."

I remember one time we were having a meeting, and there was no time left in the schedule on Saturday or Sunday to go to Mass. I asked the leader, and she said, "Well, we just don't think it's important." I said, "I hear you." I wasn't going to [challenge] those who wanted to move farther than I wanted to go.

There were four of us who were [in agreement], but we were not about to establish anything else at that point. This was in the 1980s, and the Emmaus Community had gotten involved with sponsoring Vietnamese boat people; and I took charge of that project. For about five years I was so busy taking care of a Vietnamese family that my status just remained the same.

At first there were four of us Sisters and a Vietnamese boy and his father living together. Then the father ran away, and I became Hung's foster parent. Eighteen months later his mother came to live with us. Then two of the Sisters had to move out of state, so it was just Sister Marie and I and the Vietnamese. We had to move, too. We found an old house that was a real fixer-upper for $68,000. I don't know how they gave us a mortgage. Marie and I have been alone together for the past seven years. Just the two of us and our two cats. I'm very happy with the quiet.

My assumption when we left the Filippinis was very arrogant—that they had to be the way I thought they had to be. Who says that they have to be that? If the people who are in community feel that they have a purpose, who am I to say that they don't? I don't regret the years in the Filippinis. If I had it to do over again? Yeah, I would make a lot of different choices. But nobody gets to do it over again. I spent a couple of years very depressed, and I've learned as a therapist that depression usually means you're looking back at what you've done and regretting it. You need to say, "Okay, what's done is done." You've got to look ahead and get on with your life. I'm very friendly now with the Filippinis. I go up to their motherhouse; they see me; they're very nice.

I think I stayed with the Emmaus Community as long as I could. I'm still friendly with them, too. It's interesting. I do a lot of the same things as they do. I'm very concerned about the same issues. I'm a feminist. But for them those issues are more central than they are for me. There's a whole underground Church that's always been there. There's something all around us called Women Church, where women meet, usually ecumenically, and have their own rituals, paralleling Eucharist and using inclusive language. There's a whole host of resigned priests out there who have small house churches. All of this goes on—like the planets on the outer rim of the solar system.

I found [Women-Church] very comfortable. But it wasn't the mainstream. I think it's good for the people who are in it. But I guess what I call real life or real people is much more varied. I think the parish is the perfect place to be. Not that every parish is; but you have every age range, you have people in all kinds of dilemmas there, all states of education. It's really like a microcosm of the world.

I'm very happy doing parish work. I'm the full-time director of religious education here. But in order to make it financially, I'm also a licensed marriage and family therapist. With the counseling, I work about 60 hours a week. I won't take any more than 10 hours a week of counseling, because I won't be of help to people. The church pays me about $25,000, and my counseling brings in another $15,000. In my practice there are people I see for nothing, because they're homeless or they're old. I always have a few clients who can pay the top fee, and it balances out, so I don't worry anymore. Luckily, Sister Marie's aunt died two years ago and left her some money, so we paid off the mortgage. It's a blessing.

I've had to put an awful lot of time and attention simply into surviving financially. But I don't want it to rule my life, because money can. It can rule your consciousness and your intentionality. The traditional religious life has focused on the vows of poverty, chastity, and obedience. But basically you have the freedom in a religious society to take any gospel counsel and try to live it out. [When I made private vows] I took a vow of simplicity of lifestyle, of sharing resources. And a vow of celibacy. And a third, of obedience to the Word, trying to live your life according to the inspiration of scripture and Jesus Christ.

There are incredible options available to people who want to have a committed lifestyle in the Church. The Church actually allows more freedom in choosing a committed lifestyle than people realize. [The hierarchy] doesn't encourage it. You have to knock on their door and say, "I know I'm allowed to do this." There are actually over 500 noncanonical groups all over the country. They call them different things: *intentional communities, covenant communities, religious societies.*

After Sister Marie and I left the Emmaus Community of Christian Hope, I talked to the bishop about trying to form another group. We wanted to tap into the same tradition—of the disciples on the road to Emmaus—but we couldn't keep the same name, so we decided on Emmaus Disciples. The group would be very flexible, an open-boundary community where people would come in and out as they needed for mutual support. But the purpose would be to be peacemakers, to be people who consciously and intentionally try to heal relationships. Six people have called to inquire, and right now we're just going to meet once a month for prayer. What the future holds, only God knows. We're just going to let it develop; I'm not even worried about it. (August 1994)

Sister Pat still struggles with health issues, but she maintains a small steady practice as a therapist. She has retired from parish work.

Externally, my life hasn't changed that much, but it's amazing how much has changed in the Church and in women's roles in the Church. Religious life, as we knew it, is slowly disappearing. I have mixed feelings. I believe there is a place for people who want to dedicate more of their life to ministry. But women are finding other ways to live out the Beatitudes. They can still do ministry in the church without being controlled by the church hierarchy as women religious have been. I can't change the big picture. That's not what God is asking of me. I deal with people individually.

SISTER VIRGINIA JOHNSON

Sister Virginia met me at the door of Visitation House, a large private home in the neighborhood adjoining what is now Marydell Faith and Life Center and was once Camp Marydell. Visitation House has served as home for Sister Virginia and several elderly Sisters in recent years; its large rooms and wide doorways have easily accommodated the necessary walkers and wheelchairs.

Still spry despite a recent auto accident and lingering mobility problems from her illness, Sister Virginia, now 75 "and a half," served me homemade soup and bagels for lunch and then offered a tour of Marydell, where she moved up and down the winding paths with ease, often leaving her cane behind. Her love for the grounds and her community's past was evident at every stop. The future, however, was also in sight.

My mother was not able to take care of me until I was eight, so I was with different people as a small child. All of my foster homes were in Bridgeport [Connecticut]. They were very good and I remember them well—the O'Neills, the Palmers, the Masons. I moved 13 times, but I stayed in the same school—St. Charles School with the Sisters of Mercy.

When I was eight, my mother and father and I lived together, and then two years later my mother and father divorced. When I was 10, my mother was working and she was a single parent. She needed to find a camp for me to go to in the summer time, so we found Marydell Camp right here in Nyack. I came to camp every summer until I was 17. I fell in love with the Sisters.

I entered the convent on September 20th, 1951, my mother's birthday. She wanted me to be a nurse, and I wanted to be a nurse nun, but mainly I wanted to be with the Sisters of Christian Doctrine. I fell in love with them because they were so kind and so friendly. I loved their prayer life. We used to go and sit by the chapel, which was down the hill from the camp, and listen to the chanting. I remember when I entered, I looked down at my black dress, and I said, "Gee, I'm really here. This is really me."

I don't think that we knew it was strict. That was the way it was. Silence was very important. No eating in between meals, which was kind of hard sometimes. We liked housecleaning on Saturdays because we could put milk and cookies out for a snack. We'd get up at 5:15 in the morning to the greeting, *Ecce ancilla Domini,* "Behold the handmaid of the Lord." We'd answer in Latin, *Fiat mihi secundum verbum tuum,* "Be it done unto me according to Thy word." Then we would go to chapel. We'd have meditation and morning office and Mass. And then we'd go for breakfast. Meals were in silence. Reading was done at dinner and supper. We all had *manuali* [housework] to do. It was a very rural life. The motherhouse was in Nyack right by the Hudson River. Marydell was a large property, which had a farm on it. The farm was across the street from the convent. We had a big apple orchard and we made lots of apple sauce. We had our own chickens, probably 80 chickens.

You had a very unusual experience, I think—entering a convent and meeting, really knowing, the founder of your community.

I think that as I got older, I appreciated it more because of course at that time it was just part of the deal. Mother was very interesting. Her name was Marion Frances Gurney and she graduated from Wellesley. Wellesley had a strong influence on her life. She had been an Episcopalian and she worked in an Episcopalian church for a long time. She eventually became a Catholic in 1889. She believed very strongly that with so many immigrants coming into the country, they [should feel] welcome in the Church, and so she began human services for them as well as a catechetical program. In order to have a good catechetical program, she had to have trained catechists so she began a normal school for teachers of religion.

She had no intentions of founding a religious community, [but she had] traveled around to different religious communities trying to get them to take over the catechetical work. [Those Sisters] couldn't go out at night. They were teaching in the schools and they weren't free to do this other work. So, finally, in 1908, Mother—her name became Mother Marianne of Jesus—told these women who had been teachers and were interested in continuing the work to come together in September. They made an agreement to live the life of poverty, chastity, and obedience, to share everything in common, and to stay together as long as the Church allowed. [It took a few years for the group to formalize] so our foundation day is June 29, 1910.

Mother was very spiritual, very, very spiritual. She was a good organist and a real liturgist. So we had wonderful training in liturgy. Once or twice a week we would have Latin class with Mother Marianne. I was very good in class because I went up to Juvenal [third year Latin] in high school. I couldn't speak it, but I could read without any problems. I remember one of the novices was having a terrible time. She was so frustrated she threw the Latin book across the floor. Mother sent for me and I had to teach Latin to the novices who had never had Latin before. It was a big honor.

Mother was not well in those last few years. She never ate with us in the refectory. I entered in 1951, and she died February of 1957. She was 89. She died quietly while we were saying the rosary. We were all in the room with her. [Cries.] Then one of the Sisters went over to chapel and chimed the bell 89 times. It was late at night, nine o'clock. Our novice mistress, Sister Ursula, succeeded her as Mother General. She was kind but she was straight—you knew what to expect. She taught us how to pray and she taught us the Rule. We had the Constitution of St. Ignatius of Loyola [who founded the Jesuits] with only the pronouns changed.

I went to Fordham University forever, for 13 years. Of course, we only went on Saturdays. It took a long time to get that first degree, my B.S. in education. [My first ministry] was once a week I taught eighth grade Confraternity of Christian

Doctrine in Pearl River [New York]. I also did census work in parishes almost every day. We'd go to the homes in the parish. I found a lot of people who wanted to become Catholics, a lot of people who wanted to be back in the Church, and a lot of people who didn't want to bother with it at all. They married out of the Church, and that was it. They were happy out of the Church. I visited the sick, the homebound, that kind of thing. It was great. I loved it.

Our ministry was religious education. We did not teach school. Nobody paid anybody for teaching religion. There was no money. So we begged for food. We used to go [to New York City] in the truck once a week. We would go to Horn and Hardart, which was wonderful because they had these big barrels of cookies. I used to love the cookie bins! Then we'd go to the vegetable district and we would get cases of kale and cases of beets. I remember one of my learning experiences as a young Sister was throwing out all the beet greens and Sister Loretta, who was the cook then, told me, "No, no, no, no. You cook those greens. You don't throw those greens away." And they were delicious. I love beet greens now. Kale, I hated.

We would go to the meat district in the city. You'd go in saying, "Do you have anything to spare today?" And then you'd say, "God bless you." Whether they gave to you or not, you said, "God bless you." Sometimes they gave nothing. Sometimes they'd give us all these animal kidneys, and sometimes they'd give us a whole chicken.

We'd go to the coffee district and we would get maybe one or two pounds of coffee beans. We'd bring them home and put them in a big bin. Every now and then, we'd bring all these beans to the city to beg them to roast the beans and grind them up for us. We had Heinz coffee because there were all kinds of beans. Who knew? I guess half of it was chicory. The worst part of that was we had a cook who made coffee Jell-o with the leftover coffee. That was the worst thing I ever ate in my life, and we had to eat whatever was served.

What was the experience like when you were begging for money?

I found that kind of hard, a little embarrassing sometimes. But people were very good to us. You'd get permission from whoever ran the company to beg. You'd sit with your box, and you'd say, "Thank you. God bless you. Thank you. God bless you." [We begged] at a box factory in Nyack and at the Ford place across the river. In Yonkers we began by going to the insurance offices. The people in the offices there were very friendly. They gave me my *liber usualis* when I made my final vows. That's the book for the Divine Office [which we prayed every day].

[One day a week] we would go to the five-and-ten. We'd get there about eleven o'clock, and we'd sit there until four o'clock or four-thirty. [Sighs.] That was a long sitting. I did all my Latin work, sitting at that five-and-ten. That's where I learned to eat fried-egg sandwiches. Sister Baptista and I used to go to this little restaurant. We could never eat between meals, but we could get lunch, and we used to get this little fried-egg sandwich every Friday. It was a wonderful break in the routine.

Begging was just part [of the life]. I didn't know it before I entered, and I guess I felt ashamed to tell people about it. The bishop stopped it in the sixties. The Sisters who taught in the schools were getting paid and so then we got stipends, too. But it was prorated. The stipend was set for teaching communities and our treasurer would have to prorate which part of the day we would get paid for teaching. That was embarrassing, too. Because religion is not something you should have to be paid for. Mother Marianne never would have gone along with that. No, you preach the Gospel freely.

How did you feel about the changes during the 1960s?

You know, I don't remember having feelings. I think my feelings were deadened for a while. I remember Mother said feelings didn't count. They do. I know they do. But I don't think we were allowed to have feelings too much. When Mother died everything was still the old way. The changes were very gradual. We were allowed to make home visits. Even overnight home visits. We were allowed eating out with people. We were allowed to have an amount of money for ourselves. We were allowed to go on vacation. We were in short skirts but with a veil. [When I entered] we had no choice in names. My name was Maria Alma of St. Gabriel and Mother Marianne gave it to me. Alma means, kind, sweet, amiable. But it was hard to say because of those two A's. My baptismal name was Virginia Catherine and on August 10th, 1966, I went back to Virginia. I like my name. My mother chose that one. One time—I remember this was on a visiting Sunday at Marydell in Nyack—I said to my mother, "Mom, when are you going to call me Sister Maria Alma?" She said, "I'm not. God gave you that name. I gave you Virginia." I said, "Oh." You didn't argue with my mother.

I went to Beaufort [South Carolina] in 1961 or 1962, and I was there until 1969. We did catechetical work in a lot of different parishes. We went to Parris Island and I was very friendly with the chaplain on Parris Island, Father John O'Connor. [He later became Cardinal O'Connor, the archbishop of New York]. He was a mentor for me. When he first came to New York, it was amazing. He said, "We've come a long way, haven't we, from Beaufort?"

It was interesting because I developed MS [multiple sclerosis] when I was in Beaufort. I didn't know what was the matter with me. No doctor could diagnose it. Father O'Connor had left Beaufort and gone up to Triangle, Virginia. I wanted to see him. So I took my first airplane ride up to Triangle, Virginia, and he was very kind to me. From there, Mother Ursula made me come up to the hospital in Nyack because she wanted to know what was the matter with me. That was when they diagnosed multiple sclerosis, but they didn't tell me. You weren't allowed to know. It was still the old school. The superior saw the doctor.

[They said] I had peripheral neuritis, whatever that was. So I went back to Beaufort. The symptoms were gone, the hot spots and all that, and I was okay for a while. And then I completely lost my vision in one eye. It was the summer of 1968. I went to school all the time in the summer, to Fordham [University], and I remember driving there, and I remember my eye wouldn't open. I went to a couple of ophthalmologists and I had no idea what they said, because they didn't tell me. So I went back south. I was sick, but not sick in bed.

Maybe 10 years later, I was back in Nyack. I said, "Something is the matter with me." I went to see the neurologist. That's when he told me I have MS. I said, "Oh." I didn't know what that meant. So I said, "Okay." What else could you say?

Then I lost my eyesight. My eyesight went completely. Boom. I couldn't see anything. Blind, blind, blind. And that was scary. My ophthalmologist put me in the hospital for a few days, and the police came and took my driver's license away. I guess it has to be reported when somebody becomes legally blind all of a sudden.

I gave up religious education and I gave up running the camp [Camp Marydell] which I had been doing. I couldn't see, I couldn't drive, I couldn't do anything. Well, I could pray. I joined a parish mission team, a group of priests, lay people and Sisters—6 of us at first, then 12, and then we grew to 20. We would go to a parish and give a mission for four days. We each gave testimony stories and prayed for the people. It was wonderful. I told them about the experience of losing my sight and getting MS. I told them that it was like opening so many presents because people were so good. I had been on the ambulance corps, but I had to give that up. The chaplain for the ambulance corps was a Methodist minister. His mother was blind, and he gave me her Braille watch.

I stayed on the mission team for five years and gradually, my eyesight came back. I went back into religious education and then I took a job doing social work, which I love. I was elected president [of our community] in 1994 and re-elected in 1998. The big thing that happened [during my first term] was a mandate to build a house for our Sisters for active ministry and also for those in retirement and health care. The decision was to build it on our own property. We were too spread out for a little community. Those first four years, a lot of the work was on that kind of stuff, getting a builder, getting the funding, selling two houses that we had. We also had a lot of aging and health issues. It was hard.

We're talking now in 2010, your 100th-year anniversary, and the future is troubling. What's the mood of the Sisters?

It's unclear. We looked into merging, but it's not going anywhere. We're too few. It's too late. It takes 10 years to go through that process. We have to say we didn't do it. I think that the realization is we don't belong with another community. We would not be ready to submit ourselves to being a part of someone else's community. We wouldn't have the same tradition.

We want to start a trust fund for the care of our aged and infirmed and disabled. Well, everybody in the community is aged. Our median age now is 79. We have one person who's 62, and she's the youngest. One Sister is 67. Everyone else is in her seventies or older. We're 24 now. Actually, when we look around, there are 16 of us who are pretty good. The rest are too frail, too sick. We have five people [who need] nursing care around the clock. Taking care of the Sisters. That's our first priority.

We don't want this property to turn into condominiums or housing or anything like that, so we're looking into covenanting [with another religious community] or [establishing] a land trust to keep it forever green. If there is any money left when we're finished taking care of the sick, we were thinking we'd like to fund a trust for ongoing religious education or social work.

Till my time ends, I hope to continue my life as a Sister of Christian Doctrine and to be of service to the Church in any way I can. We've gone through hard times before. We'll get through them again. No matter what, I have faith, a belief that the Lord is really with us. (January 2010)

17

ENVISIONING
THE FUTURE

SISTER CHRISTINE SCHENK

The interview took place at the offices of FutureChurch, which occupies a narrow storefront in Lakewood, Ohio. A large wooden table for folding and collating mailings dominates the front room; Sister Chris' small office is next; and in the back is the multipurpose meeting room/ kitchen/supply room where we spoke for more than three hours.

Two full-time and three part-time staff members run a national organization from these three rooms. Sister Chris, 63, has served as executive director of FutureChurch since the organization's early days. During our conversation she was by turns pensive, outraged, patient, impassioned—as befits a woman who has spent years of her life as both a nurse-midwife to poor women and a community activist.

I was the oldest of four daughters. My parents were of middle class, maybe even on the low end of middle class because we always had money issues. We lived in a very small town, Lima, Ohio. One reason I ended up being who I am is that my father was one of only two or three men from his whole regiment to come back from World War II. Dad always felt that the only reason he came home was because of my grandmother's prayers and his sisters' prayers. He was never someone who wore his religion on his sleeve, but I always knew he had a deep faith.

My mom was without a doubt the smartest girl in her high school class. I think she really wanted to go to college, but in those times women didn't go to college. There was a war on. She didn't learn to drive until she was 50 because my grandfather didn't believe women should drive. But I can still remember her walking with me and my two sisters to the library. And she had such a heart for the down-and-out. At one time a black family was going to move in next door. My dad was very worried. I can still remember her saying, "Paul Schenk, we've taught our daughters our whole lives that black people are just as good as we are, and we are not going to change that now."

My dad was an insurance salesman, and he built his territory three different times to be at a point where he could feel comfortable supporting his daughters.

And three different times [the company] cut his territory in half. The third time he started to organize a union. He had four children. Two of us were in college, one was in nursing school, and one in high school. We were very lucky and got scholarships, but what kind of courage did it take to do that? [It was 1968] and I had just graduated magna cum laude from Georgetown University. I thought I was pretty hot stuff, and he had to take out a loan to bring the family to graduation.

I had been attracted to the Medical Mission Sisters in high school. We went to the summer schools of Catholic Action and they had a booth there. I can remember the Sister-doctor thing was huge. I thought that would be so cool. I loved the missionary thing, too, the idea of going to some of the most marginalized groups. I didn't see myself being stuck inside a convent. I had already seen too much of the big, beautiful world and had experienced the freedom and liberty of that to want to think I was going to spend it all behind closed doors, even for God.

[Several years later] when I visited the Medical Mission Sisters, I found a group of very committed women, a supportive communal environment, and in my own growth and development as a human being, I really needed that in my life. I began an adventure in stretching myself that I never would have imagined. Growing up in Lima, Ohio, [I was comfortable] with my identity as an American citizen, my country right or wrong. But I was meeting women coming back from Bangladesh, from India, and talking about the effects of foreign policy. Suddenly I had a whole other standard to measure what kind of a country we were. I learned how to do social analysis, and I have taken that with me every place I have gone ever since.

I spent six years with the Medical Mission Sisters and I internalized the peace and justice stuff, the passion to be about God's good news among the most marginalized. Among the most marginalized were the Farm Workers' Union. It turns out I had a great love for the farm workers because there were many migrant workers who harvested tomatoes and other crops right around Lima. When I was in high school, we went over to teach the kids religion. What a laugh! They were the ones who taught us because we had never seen such poor living conditions. Well, anyway, the union needed a community organizer [in Philadelphia], and I needed a break from nursing, and I asked Medical Missions if I could work for them full time for room and board and $5 a week. Surprisingly, they let me do that.

That was probably 1973 to 1975. I lived in West Philadelphia with various farm worker families and also with an outstanding Sister of Loretto at the time, Ruth Shy, who was the director of the Philadelphia boycott and taught me everything I know about community organizing. What I learned is that you can create something out of nothing. One quick example. Cesar Chavez was coming to Philadelphia for a rally, and Ruth told me that I needed to organize an interfaith communion breakfast for 200 people within three weeks, and we had to get everything donated. I looked at her like she was crazy, but sure enough over the next three weeks we got the place donated, the food donated, [volunteers] to cook the food, and each religious denomination gave $300 or something. To this day it astonishes me.

People used to say to me, "Why are you doing this because it's probably not going to succeed?" But you see Cesar had another thought. He said, "Where are we going to go if we don't work to make it better?" I learned how to change things I didn't like. That was the best education anyone could have gotten in terms of practical strategies for systemic change.

[At the same time] I also had some very, very hard emotional struggles. [In] the Medical Mission Sisters what was hard for me was the way people would come in and out of your life. At that point I really needed some solid friendships. I loved the women in the community. But it wasn't working for me personally. Your happiness has to come from inside, not just because you're around a bunch of neat people, you know? I still think leaving was the hardest decision I ever made. But I knew the rightness of it because my insides really settled down, and I was not as depressed and agitated and upset.

I went back to Hyden in eastern Kentucky to teach in a program at the Frontier School of Midwifery. I knew people there. I lived in a trailer by the side of the mountain. You live and you work with all the same people. I really was not up for finding my way in a new city after leaving the Medical Mission Sisters. I was still in a pretty emotionally fragile state. I grieved like I couldn't believe for at least a year.

There was a man I did fall in love with. He had been in seminary for a while, and he finally told me—after about a year of my having great hopes—that he was gay. It took me three years to finally accept that [marriage] wasn't going to happen. But when I look back now, I don't regret the experience whatsoever. I never understood the struggles of gay people. I would never have understood without this friend.

[After I had moved back to Cleveland and was working as a midwife] I had gotten involved in the Community of St. Malachi, part of St. Malachi parish in a low-income area of the city. The far-sighted priest who started the community [and was pastor to both groups] said, "We can't just have great liturgy." He challenged the laity [to take the Gospel message further]. We declared sanctuary for refugees from Central America. I helped design and lead the [decision-making] process. I did all the good stuff that I had learned from the farm workers. Now, mind you, Cleveland is the home of Jean Donovan and Dorothy Kazel. [Two of the four American women who were murdered in El Salvador on December 2, 1980, by Salvadoran soldiers at the behest of their government.] So the city itself was very sensitive to everything that was going on in Central America. I had gone to Dorothy Kazel's funeral Mass and had been so inspired.

When you're discerning nonviolent resistance, you have to make sure that you're doing it from the right spirit. You have to be sure you've got all the facts. We met once a month. We would bring speakers in from the INS [Immigration and Naturalization Service] so everybody was clear on what the risks were. [We knew that] in most cases political refugees were being murdered as soon as they went back without even having their story investigated. At the end, the community voted in favor of declaring public sanctuary, and the parish voted not to declare public sanctuary. Our community eventually helped 21 refugees—men, women, and children—find safe haven in Canada.

[All during those years] I don't think I ever stopped thinking about religious life. But it wasn't until I finally let go of my hope for this love affair with my friend who was gay, that I was open to really looking at it with some seriousness again. I always knew that if I joined any group it would be the Sisters of St. Joseph in Cleveland.

I entered the Congregation in 1988 when I was 42 years old. I said to the woman interviewing me, "It's not like I start out looking for edgy things, but it just ends up there. I don't think this is likely to change, so if that's going to be an issue in the Congregation, we had better get that out on the table right now." She looked at me and started to laugh. And she said, "No, I think that would be fine." When I made my final vows on June 13, 1993, it was the happiest day of my life. I never expected to have so much certainty about it. I knew, I knew this was right.

[During the time] I was doing my novitiate with the Sisters of St. Joseph, I was asked by the Community of St. Malachi to co-chair a committee on Church reform. Another parish in Cleveland had passed a resolution in response to a decision from the U.S. bishops to substitute communion services for Sunday Mass in places that had no priests available. [The resolution] basically said that Eucharist is more central to Catholic identity than the marital state or gender of the priest. They called on the bishops to look at other options, rather than doing communion services. Now this was in 1990. Some 28 parishes supported the resolution. At St. Malachi's, we decided to call together leadership from progressive Catholic groups in the diocese to talk about what was needed and on October 14, 1990, 36 people from 16 parishes gathered at St. Malachi church hall. That was the beginning of the FutureChurch network.

Our first public event was our rubber chicken dinner with Richard McBrien, who was the chair of the theology department at Notre Dame at the time. We thought if we had 350 people that would be a very good outcome. Well, much to our amazement, 689 people came. We call it the miracle of the multiplication of the chicken. It wasn't only the numbers, it was who came. Pastors brought their entire parish councils. There were staff and teachers at the seminary. People who were employed in the Chancery. It was one of those times where you knew this wasn't just a good liberal Catholic idea. This is more strongly rooted.

We had our mission before that first event: recognizing Eucharist as the center of Catholic worship and calling for full participation of all Catholics in the life of the Church. We knew then that if we failed to do anything about the priest shortage, the Catholic life we loved was going to be severely impacted because there would be no priests. It's pretty much the same mission that we have today. What we saw then has happened.

Can you pick out some highlights of your work with FutureChurch?

Certainly I think the Mary of Magdala [initiative] is one of the highlights. Let me give you some background. The push back from the official Church about the non-ordination of women had really started, I think, in 1976, right around the time that [some] Episcopalian women were ordained *contra legem* [against the law] in Philadelphia. Oddly enough, I was there because I was working for the farm workers then and Ruth Shy said, "Come on, we've got to go to this." That same year the Pontifical Biblical Commission issued its report saying that scripture is basically silent on the issue of women's ordination. Then the U.S. bishops tried to write a pastoral on women. They had listening sessions with women all over the United States. In this very diocese we probably had at least 10 or 12 listening sessions with 20 to 50 women each. The first draft of the bishops' pastoral said we should discuss the ordination of women. By the time they got to the third draft, having sent it to Rome, not only was "we should discuss" not there anymore, but [the draft said] the bishops must teach that women cannot be ordained. A group of bishops decided they could not pass this draft even though a whole lot of church energy had gone into it for over 10 years. And it did not pass—by a significant majority.

Then, in 1994, the Vatican released the document, *Ordinatio Sacerdotalis*, which said that the Church's definitive teaching is that women cannot be ordained. It became clear that if we wanted FutureChurch to continue to be as parish-rooted as we had been, we were not going to be able to talk about women's ordination. The Vatican had just spoken from on high. So that led to our efforts on women in Church leadership. We put the issue of ordination over on the side.

We took the 15 recommendations from the Benchmark study from the Leadership Conference of Women Religious about things that could be done right now to advance women's roles. It was everything from educating about the inclusive practices of Jesus to advocating on behalf of lay ministers in the church. Eighty percent of all paid lay ministers in the United States are women. And they are very often the subject of significant unjust treatment.

There are two things related to women's roles. One is the theology of women's ordination, which is still obviously in great flux. The other one is the history of women, and we are focusing on the history. We've done pilgrimages to the catacombs of Priscilla and Domitilla in Rome where you can view the beautiful frescoes of women's leadership of the early Church. This is often the only way you are going to find out [about these women], because they're not there in the literary record. [The idea is] to help women and men begin to see that, yes, women were there with Jesus. It was a whole cohort of both women and men.

We are trying to raise awareness of the historical data about women leaders in the early Church, beginning with Mary of Magdala, who was not a prostitute. She was the first witness to the Resurrection and a very pre-eminent woman leader. Since we started Magdala celebrations on July 22, 1997, it has been an extraordinarily successful campaign. I think we had 23 celebrations the first year. The next year it went up to 153 and ever since then we've had between 250 and 400 celebrations a year all over the United States and internationally.

We love the Church, we respect the pope. We respect the teaching of the Church. But some of FutureChurch's harder times have come because we did not withdraw from our call for discussion of women's ordination. It's not the same as saying, "Go get ordained." It is saying that we need to continue to talk about this. The media doesn't do nuance, so anytime they described me or the organization, it was about women's ordination [even though] we spend less than 10 percent of our time on women's ordination.

Two other highlights. When [the Vatican] started the preliminary documents for the International Synod on the Eucharist in 2005, the priest shortage wasn't even named. With the help of FutureChurch supporters and Call to Action regional chapters around the country, we spearheaded a survey of 14,000 priests in 57 U.S. dioceses and found that 67 percent of respondents supported open- ing the discussion of mandatory celibacy. We also collected over 37,000 signa- tures and presented them to synod leaders. Probably even more important, what we learned at the Synod on the Eucharist helped us lay the groundwork for our remarkably successful advocacy at the 2008 Synod on the Word. They had had no women scholars whatsoever at the Synod on the Eucharist, even though that would have been one place a woman could have served as an expert. So we started two years ahead of the new Synod, asking them to appoint women biblical experts. We provided a list of women biblical scholars. [Ultimately, there were six women experts at the Synod on the Word and 19 women auditors.] We asked for greater attention to Jesus' and St. Paul's inclusive practice. We asked them to restore to the Lectionary the stories of women who had been diminished or deleted. Much to my great gratitude, [there was] conversation among the Synod bishops who had never known that women were actively deleted from the Lectionary. And much to people's surprise, a Synod proposition did ask for opening the study of the Lectionary in light of current historic circumstances. Now we're doing follow-up with that. This is big. It's progress.

If I named the things that were highlights, we should also talk about the painful things. Certainly, the clergy sex abuse was huge. And if I had to name one thing that is driving reform of the Church now, that's what it is.

Catholic people have to look and say, "Something's not working right." These bishops are no longer the same as God in our eyes. There are so many people who are sure we need to have a married priesthood because if parents had been involved, some of these decisions about whether or not priests [who were abusers] should return to ministry would have been made differently. There was nobody at the table who was an advocate for children.

That's one of the engines [driving reform]. The other one is the priest shortage and the mass of parish closings. That's more subtle, but in the end it's going to be more impactful. Bishops are having to close parishes—to great turmoil. The Camden diocese [in New Jersey] just announced that they were going to close half of their parishes. Here in Cleveland, Bishop John Lennon is closing 50 out of 230 parishes because of financial difficulties and the priest shortage. The process was started under our former bishop, Anthony Pilla, but no one—I can tell you no one—anticipated that it would end up with 50 parishes closing. People thought that they were getting together to cluster and share staff, and that we would find more creative ways of ministering. But no one thought we would be closing vital, solvent communities. All of those 50 parishes are in the urban regions of Cleveland, Akron, and Lorain. They are the poorest areas.

This for me is far more painful [than anything else that has happened.] When we started FutureChurch, we were trying to prevent this from happening. And we were not able to prevent it. You say, "Did I just give the last 10 years of my life for nothing?" That's how it felt. I don't believe that, but that's how it felt. I know these people and these parishes. I know the pastors. I know the vitality and vibrancy of the community life that has led so many of these parishes to be really a light to whole neighborhoods. I served low-income and poor women in Cleveland for 20 years as a nurse-midwife. I get the deal in these neighborhoods. Yet we see the diocese turning a deaf ear. What is Church about, anyway?

I love the Catholic Church. I am a product of the Catholic Church. I am who I am today because of priests and Sisters and lay people who guided me in my spiritual awakening, who accompany me now, and who are sticking with the Catholic Church to this day, rather than let it succumb to its worst elements. I really love the idea that we are traversing through history as a community. If I had to name one image, that's what I would name. With all that happened in the early Church and in the Middle Ages and in the Renaissance and the Enlightenment, there was sin and suffering and sorrow and grace and glory through it all. We are traversing through history as a community and I want to be part of that community.

[Sometimes I ask myself] "Wouldn't I be better working on behalf of the most marginalized, the homeless, people in Africa or Latin America?" I aspire to be about proclaiming God's just reign. If the Church is supposed to be the visible face of God on Earth, then how much more important is it that the Church itself be just?

What's the most important issue in the Church? Far and away the most important issue is our continuation of the sacramental community, which is being called into question by the priest shortage. It's not just in the United

States. It's all over the world. Organizations representing 18,000 Brazilian priests petitioned Rome two years ago for open discussion of optional celibacy.

There may be an even greater need in the Church than either a married priest-hood or women's ordination. We need structures that incorporate the decision-making voice of lay people.

We will not continue as an effective community into the twenty-first century if we don't figure out a better way. You've got, at least in the United States, a highly educated laity, a very spiritually evolved people. And you have a leadership that isn't leading. Look at who is graduating from Catholic universities. Highly skilled, gifted [young people] called by God. And we're not going to involve them in shaping the future? What happens? People drop away.

What keeps you grounded?

I have a lot of spiritual supports. The Sisters in Cleveland. The Community of St. Malachi. I see my spiritual director regularly. I meet with women for faith sharing. I have to say that my rootedness comes from my hometown of Lima, Ohio. My family and my friends from when I was growing up knew me before there ever was a FutureChurch. They've been a really important balance because this work can gobble you up.

What's FutureChurch going to be like without Chris Schenk? I'm not going to last forever. The board is working on a transition plan so that whenever it's time for me to go on to the next thing, we can do the transition appropriately. But I really can't imagine not staying involved in the work I am doing now. (December 2009)

SISTER JOAN CHITTISTER

At dinner in a restaurant in Erie, Pennsylvania, with me and two other Benedictine Sisters from her community, Sister Joan Chittister was the complete extrovert—articulate, dynamic, charming. The next morning, in her office, she was no less articulate, but more introspective, personal, vulnerable.

Sister Joan, 58, has been prioress of her Benedictine community, president of the Conference of American Benedictine prioresses, and president of the Leadership Conference of Women Religious. She has become, through her many books, articles, columns, and personal appearances, a very visible spokesperson for an inclusive, collegial model of the Church.

Since the interview, Sister Joan has written several more books. Of note are Beyond Beijing: The Next Step for Women, *her reflections on the Fourth UN Conference on Women held at Beijing in 1995; and* The Fire in These Ashes: A Spirituality of Contemporary Religious Life. *In early 1996, she began a one-year visiting fellowship at Cambridge University in England.*

Sister Joan Chittister engages her audience as she gives a keynote address in Melbourne, Australia, in December 2009. Expressing both her commitment to her faith and also to improving the role of women around the world, Sister Joan spoke of the role of faith communities at a summit to end global poverty, sponsored by the International Women's Development Agency. *Fiona Basile*

My family was ecumenical before it was a word, let alone a virtue. My mother married the boy next door, Dan Daugherty. They had been married three and a half years, with a baby almost three, and my father died. My mother was a 21-year-old widow. She remarried a couple of years later, a man by the name of Chittister. He was Presbyterian. It was a major factor, I think, for the simple reason that those things weren't done in those days.

So I grew up very clear about two separate realities and the boundaries between those two places. She was ardent Irish Catholic, and he was just as ardent Reformationist. Neither one of them, incidentally, practiced religion. That is why it worked. I was sent to the Catholic school, and I went to Mass every day. My mother went very seldom. As a youngster I questioned her about it, and her answer was, "My marriage is more important."

At any rate, I have no memory of any time in my life when I did not know I was going to enter [the convent]. And my only explanation is [that] when my father died, my mother's family was very opposed to her taking me to the funeral home. And my mother said, "What the hell is she supposed to think? That her father simply left her? Her father died, and she has to get used to it like the rest of us do. She's going to see him in that coffin." So she took me to the funeral home. I remember the funeral home very, very well. She had to hold me up. At the far end of the casket, there were two Sisters of Mercy who had come to visit, because both my mother and my father were educated by the Mercys. I asked, "What are those?" And my mother's answer was, "They are very special friends of God's. They'll stay here to meet the angels; and when the angels come, they'll say, 'This is Joan's daddy. He was a very good man, and you should take him straight to God.'" I remember thinking, "Oh, that would be a wonderful thing to do in life. To give little girls' daddies to God." And so after that I just followed nuns around wherever they were. If they were on that side of the street, I'd cross the street. That was all there was to it. I have no other recollection of the decision. Zero.

My mother was brilliant. And I do not use that word casually. I've only known brilliance two or three times in my life, and she was definitely it. There was great intelligence, but she was totally uneducated. She never finished school. Talk about the woman's question. Talk about a waste of intelligence, and perhaps of a life. Dear God! From the age of three on, I got my marching orders: "You study. You read. That's your only road." She was telling me, long before there was a feminist language for it, that a woman has to be able to take care of herself, that you never know what's going to happen. And, of course, it had happened to us.

I was raised to be very independent. The prioress of this house said that she would not take me, because I was an only child and that someday my mother would need me. My mother looked at her and said, "Well, Mother Sylvester, that's very kind of you. But it is not Joan's fault that she's an only child, and her life is not going to be destroyed by that. I will take care of myself, and Joan will take care of herself. She has made up her mind to do this. She will do it."

[I entered] when I was 16, in 1952. I have to tell you that I was attracted to this particular community because it was a high-energy, high-love group. The Sisters showed a lot of joy among themselves. But when I entered, I found a rigidity, almost a neurosis, because we had a novice mistress who I think was a highly committed, very prayerful, extremely rigid, totally compulsive, completely neurotic human being. And her rigidity was just absolutely overwhelming to me. The *real* irony of my life might be that I entered on September 8th, and on the Feast of Teresa of Avila, in October, I got polio. When I got polio, my life became a series of exceptions. Nobody liked it, least of all me. But those exceptions probably [kept me in the community].

I didn't walk for four years. I lost the right arm; it came back very quickly. I lost the lungs. I was in an iron lung for several months, I guess. I lost the left leg, and it was the hardest of all to bring back. I was in braces for several years. The subprioress of this community, who had been an RN before she entered— and this is the second time in my life when I encountered brilliance—took over my care. She used to exercise me every single night for an hour and a half. I was rolled into the exercise room during the "grand silence." You weren't supposed to talk, and we didn't, of course. But one night I had had it. I whispered, "Sister Theophane, the books in the novitiate are terrible! They should be burned! Every book there should be burned! They're awful!" She said to me, "I think they would be very much for your good." Well, two days went by; and one night when she took me off the exercise table, put me in a chair, and put the lap robe over me, she slipped a book under it. And then after that she gave me books regularly. She became my spiritual mentor, and I really needed it.

When your question is, "Were you the good nun?" the only possible answer is yes and no. I kind of did what I was kind of told. But I never did it with the kind of commitment that turned it into the real image of the nun. I did not understand why I was to walk with my hands under my scapular; it seemed silly to me. Therefore, I did and I didn't, you know. Everything was like that, I'm afraid.

When I set out to explain what happened, it was perfectly clear to me, as a slightly used history teacher, that up through the 1930s, the life of a woman in a convent and the life of a woman in a home were not all that different. The only differences were children. The good woman in the 1930s was not out on the street alone. A good woman did not have financial independence. A good woman was not autonomous. It was a very circumscribed life. Then the 1940s came and the war. The patriarchy needed a different kind of woman, so they created one. You had Rosie the Riveter and the WACS and the WAVES, who were all doing the boys' jobs. So they leave the home. They're out at night; they go to meetings; they're making money. Social institutions are created to sustain the women who are sustaining the male system. But in the 1940s the image of the 1930s was still the ideal. So when the boys come home, the woman is expected to relinquish this, because this really wasn't natural, normal, or nice for her; and so she goes back to what she was supposed to be. Except women never went back. They were put out, but they never went back. They always knew there was something else. The difference then between the laywoman and the woman religious is that the woman religious never gets a new social framework. So I maintain that up to the 1930s what [women religious] were doing was never questioned. In the 1940s it was still being internalized. When my crowd came in the 1950s, we didn't internalize. I wanted to be a Sister so badly that if that was the game you had to play, I'd play it. But I could never—nor did my group— internalize it. Then came the 1960s, and not only did they not idealize it or internalize it; they didn't accept it. They began to say, "Why do you do this? I can't live like this." So you have two parallel systems. The irony of it is that the high-level, educational professionalism was in the convents. The laywoman was getting the unprofessional salaried autonomy without anywhere near the professional preparation. In the 1960s, the young women see two things: religious professionalism and the female potential. They put the two of them together. But they come in [to the convents] and they find professionalism without potential. That's when the system begins to break down.

[The period of the 1960s] was wonderful and it was terrible. It started with hope and excitement and ended in a lot of bitterness and difficulty for a long time. There was deep resentment from people whose lives were being taken away from them, people who had internalized the system. Remember that you are dealing with people who were not professionally educated theologians. That's the Church's own fault. Let's put the blame where the blame lies. They never permitted a woman to get a degree in theology. We had psychologists, historians, sociologists, all prepared to examine their lives. But almost nobody was trained in theology. That really was the problem.

I think I should make it very clear up front that I did not lead the [renewal in our community]. I was very excited about it, and I wanted to be part of it. But I'm so rational—I don't do anything without a reason. When somebody like me would ask, "Why would you ever want to eliminate the habit?" the answer I got was, "Because." That's not an answer for me, to this day. At least I have learned I have to get my answers for myself. But at that time it was very difficult. I was very young, and I was the cautious introvert in the community. I was not prepared to move until I had better answers, and those answers for me had to be both historical and theological.

In the middle of this, I was dumped—and I mean dumped, I'm choosing my words with great care—into Penn State. I was sent to get a doctorate I didn't want in communication theory, with an emphasis on organizational and social psychology. I cried all the way on the bus—sobbed—because I didn't want to leave my high school teaching position.

I had come out of Notre Dame with a master's degree in communication arts. I went to Penn State and learned the theory I needed to know of personal development, institutional development, and social change. And sitting in this public classroom, I began to understand my own life. What I could not hear in my own community, I was now being taught, three credits at a time, at the local state university. I was being taught the whole notion of organizational deterioration and organizational renewal and revitalization. I was finding out what was happening both structurally and personally to religious life.

Then I came back to Erie. And I'm sure that the people who had seen me as at least a burden, if not an obstacle, [to renewal] were more shocked than anybody else. Because I went from person to person and said, "I want you to know that I have come to the point where I understand, and I must [go along with the changes]." I was very understanding and very sympathetic toward people who could not justify change in their lives. It is also true, however, I was very naive. I genuinely thought that once people saw the reasons, change would come immediately. Which is my problem with the Church right now about women. It's so clear to me. If we know, then of course we must [change].

Can you pick up the thread of your feminism?

My mother's a very strong influence on my life, as you can tell. My mother's also an Alzheimer's patient, and for all practical purposes I lost my mother 21 years ago. We just simply haven't had the opportunity for a funeral. That's very hard. We went through all the stages, slowly, painfully—paranoia, outbursts, withdrawal, you name it. So she and I never had the chance to talk about these things in any kind of academic terms. But she taught me plenty. The feminist literature has taught me nothing that I didn't know at the age of three. Nothing. Zero. That woman laid it out to me. What she didn't have—because of her lack of education—was a historical filter through which to feed this rational child. But I came across a book—a tiny book, about 75 pages—by a Sister Albertus Magnus McGrath, a Dominican from Rosary Hill College. I'm not sure of the title anymore, [something like] *Women in the Catholic Church: Women in a Man's Church.* It's out of print, so far as I know. I started reading that book one night—I can even tell you the year; it would have been 1973—and I read the entire book that night. The priest headmaster of the school [where I was teaching] is the third time in my life I encountered brilliance. This man was very much a father figure to me. I went to school at 7:15 the next morning to be there when he came in. I was sitting in a chair—full habit. He came in, and I said to him, "Father, I have something I want you to read." He said, "Oh, that's terrific. Did you bring it?" I handed him this little book, and he looked at it. He said, "'Women in the Church?' I'm not going to read something like that. That has nothing to do with me!" My life changed at that moment. Do you know what happened to me? What I wanted was the corrective on that history, and what I got was confirmation of that history in two sentences. He threw the book down. I remember the hurt; it was not anger.

But then after that [other things happened]. He instituted a demerit system. Teachers were supposed to fill in a slip for kids who were chewing gum or talking in the hall, and so many demerits resulted in a detention or something. He reviewed the demerit slips of only the Sister teachers, because "You know how women are. They're very emotional." I taught a senior economics class, and I had quite a reputation. I never raised my voice, but they had passed the word around: "You don't cross her." One of my favorite tricks was the old nun trick. I went to the door of the room, and I watched my watch. When they figured out I was there and everything was in order, I figured out when the bell had rung and when order should have started. I went to the board and wrote, "Seven minutes wasted times five: 35 minutes of detention tonight." So I had done this, assigned these kids 35 minutes detention. And a kid came back to me two hours later and said, "Father says we don't have to stay. We'll miss our bus." Seniors! I said, "My heart bleeds. You be in that room." [He said,] "No. Father said we don't have to stay." I packed up all my books and I walked into his office. I said, "I have been told by one of the students that you have excused them from detention. Now I presume that is incorrect, but I need to check it." He said, "Ah, yes, Sister, they can come tomorrow night. It's the same." I said, "No, it's not the same. But you are absolutely right, Father; they can come tomorrow night. However, if they come tomorrow night, you own the class. You own all of my classes, as a matter of fact." We had detention. The world didn't end. I wasn't fired, and the relationship was not destroyed. But I was radicalized. I began to see clericalism, and I began to see patriarchy. I began to see history.

The question of the role of women, the nature of women, is emerging all over this globe. It is not true that feminism is a fad of a few white Western women. This is a global issue. It is *the* radical human issue, because if you accept the notion that God built inequality into the human race, that God made some humans more human than other humans, and they're in charge, and we know who they are, then you have set up domination. Then a theology of domination becomes the fundament of your whole institution and your life. And it's wrong.

The question of domination and control at the price of literally millions of lives has somehow or another embedded itself in my soul. Those two issues—justice in the Church and justice in society—I just seem to be stuck on them. I can't seem to put them down. And as long as this community has a corporate commitment to these issues, I don't even have a right to put them down.

The concept of corporate commitment began in '78. The day I was elected prioress, I went to a microphone and said, "Sister Mary Margaret [the former prioress] enabled us all to grow up. It's time for us to ask what we grew up for. I will be pursuing that question."

And I began to teach them social psychology. The function of a group is to enable us to do together what we cannot possibly do alone. I created in my mind the concept of the corporate commitment, and then I set out to have the community answer the question: What public issue should the Benedictine Sisters of Erie be concerned about as a result of their charism? It was not for me to answer. I had raised the question. We came up with categories like peace, homelessness, hunger; and then we voted. After the vote I announced, "The Benedictine Sisters of Erie, Pennsylvania, have adopted a corporate commitment to nuclear disarmament."

We met at the end of the first year and reviewed what had happened. There was an awful lot of pain; [the community] took a lot of battering. Families, priests, institutions! They took kids out of our schools. The mail, day after day after day, said: "You people are crazy. I don't want my family to have anything to do with a bunch of radicals." Some Sisters were taking such an assault from their families; I felt so sorry for them. One night I sat in that office, out there alone in the dark—and I'm not given to stuff like this—and said to myself, "Joan, you must resign. You had no right to do this to this community. They were a nice, normal crowd before you started something like this. They have to have a chance to start over, and you must resign." I wrote a letter of resignation, but the people around me pointed out that this was the community's decision and if I resigned, it would certainly deepen the turmoil.

My favorite phrase is, "You just put one foot in front of the other." You just keep going. We held each other up. We had only ourselves. Now if you ask [people in Erie], "Have you ever heard of the Benedictines?" at least half of them will say, "Yes." And if you say, "What do they do?" they will tell you it has something to do with peace and the poor. They know. They know. We don't work *for* people anymore. We work with them. You know? Everybody learning as we go. Twenty-five years ago, you and I would never have had this conversation.

This community, at the present time, looks extremely healthy. And I believe, as the Chinese say, that if they stay on the road they're on, they shall surely get where they are going. The vocations have been steady and regular. The absolute salt of the earth is walking in off the street, saying, "I want to be one of you." I think it says something about the clarity of definition of the community. That's absolutely essential. A person has to have a reason to lay down her life, and it's got to be more than a clean well-lighted place. People don't do those things. So the community is defined; it is authentic; it is vibrant; it is spiritual. And it seems to have a very healthy future.

Religious life in general will definitely last. There's no way to nuance that. Why? How can I be so darned sure, when everybody tells you everything's dying? Because there has been celibate communal life in every major culture that we know of since the beginning of time. There is a spiritual dimension to life that will be the conscious pursuit, the single-minded pursuit, of some people. It has changed forms multiple times. It is changing form again. A lot of what you see now will go to the dust.

My own feeling is that a third of the religious communities in the United States are already dead. It's just a matter of a dignified burial, and any good actuarial student could tell them just how long it will be. They haven't had anybody come or stay for years and years. They're living their dignified lives, and they're doing a fine job, but at some turning point they did not change. That's all I know. The task is also finished. The task of the labor force in the Roman Catholic Church is, for all practical purposes, over because institutions no longer function the way the institutions once did. One-third of the communities in the United States, I believe, have rounded the corner. They can make it, probably will make it, and are leading the pack running. Another third of the communities still think they have the time to make up their minds. I don't. I think it's time to stand and be counted.

I say in an NCR [*National Catholic Reporter*] article in February [1994] that there was a time when all individuals were invisible and communities were the social reality. Now individuals are carrying their communities in too many places, and the community itself is totally invisible. We know this person and this person and this person, but we do not know these communities anymore. Until the communities take hold of their own personalities and presence, we do not have a right to the vocations in the Church. And I don't know that individuals will stay long in groups where you don't have the energy of the group carrying them. What you've got is coexistence without a common soul, a common mind, a common direction, a common energy. You've lost the fuel, and you've lost the motor. The thing's not running.

I don't believe that religious life exists for its own sake. I don't believe you can witness to the Gospel without living the Gospel. And when I say "living the

Gospel" I don't mean everybody has to be in a street demonstrating. There are styles and moments and ways. But I do believe that witness is of the essence. If the unacceptable question is to come from anywhere, it should come from the religious community. If all those years of prayer and service and immersion in the scriptures are to mean anything, then the Jesus who raised questions to the Pharisees must not die in religious life. It is a question of naming the questions. That is the function of religious life.

I refuse to be silent about the questions, because if we are silent now about the questions, it will take another 50 years simply to legitimate questions again, let alone answers. I'm not sure we have 50 years. I really mean that. I am experiencing the hemorrhage of the Church. My problem now is that my own studies have dragged me ahead of even some of the questions. So that now I look as if I'm somewhere beyond, outside, unconnected. It's absolutely false. I don't know what the public image of me is, and I do not care. But anybody who believes that what they're looking at is a high-level leaper doesn't know me at all.

My agnostic advisor in graduate school was a second father figure to me, 25 years my senior. I was one of his most favorite students, and he wasn't shy about telling people that. Just before I left campus with my shiny little doctorate in my hands, he said, "I'm going to tell you what your talent is, and you mark it down. Don't you ever forget it. Your gift is to see what's in front of you and say what you're seeing. Some people can see it, but can't say it. Some people who say things can't see at all. Your talent is to see what's in front of you and say what you're seeing." To this day, when I write an article, my mantra is, "See what's in front of you, and say what you see—no matter what it costs you."

There's something out there in front of me that hasn't dimmed, that I keep moving toward, that I know is possible, that I know is powerful, that I know is absolutely necessary. I will go to my grave, wherever my grave is, and I will still be working toward that vision and maintaining those questions at any cost. That I know. (September 1994)

Sister Joan still maintains a rigorous schedule as an international speaker. She is the author of 42 books, writes a column for the National Catholic Reporter, *and serves on numerous commissions embracing the causes of global peace and women's rights. We spoke in Huntington, New York, just after she had delivered the morning address at the 2009 national Voice of the Faithful Conference. In our interview, Sister Joan, now 74, displayed the same energy, wit, compassion, and ability to articulate what she sees, as she had in delivering her keynote.*

Erie has just been named the poorest city in the state of Pennsylvania, and I live in the poorest neighborhood in Erie. That's where I belong. It's terribly important to me to be there. I do not get a chance to interact with those people moving past the window in our little priory, or organize them, or even become one of them like so many holy people have been able to do. But my heart comes from there.

My breath and soul come from Benedictine spirituality. This is a tradition in which one young man in the sixth century saw the system and didn't attempt to reform Rome. He simply called people around him to live differently. He allowed no slavery where he was. He demanded the sharing of goods where he was. He immersed these small communities in the word of God so that they'd have a different view of the world. That notion of sacred reading, *lectio divina*, turns the whole world into the sacramental for me.

The glory of God at work in all the people gathered in one place is overwhelming to me. If you really want to know what worship sounds like, go to a huge interfaith meeting where all of these voices and all of these languages and all of these dances and all of this incense are praising God together. You don't lose an ounce of your own faith. You know that God has come to you in your tradition and your culture in one voice and is operating in another tradition and culture in another voice. What is perfectly clear is that God is working in those cultures, and I must learn from the way God works there. I get to see my own life and tradition with a crystalline insight that is so sharp around the edges that it's frightening. Now, do we believe the same things doctrinally or metaphorically or scripturally? No, we don't, but are we all on this single path together going through these same exercises in the discovery? Yes, we are. I want to be there as a presence of God in Christ. I am not afraid that any place I've gone or anything I've done has been less than that.

There is no separation for me between my so-called religious life and my secular political life. There is none. If it is true that there is a separation, that somehow or other this use of the words "contemplative" and "cloister" as synonyms is correct, then Jesus, who walked from Galilee to Jerusalem raising the dead, teaching women, empowering the lame, curing the lepers, was not a contemplative. But nobody can convince me of that. What is a contemplative? A contemplative is someone who sees the world as God sees the world. It is not dressing up for Halloween and hiding in a hole some place.

I can tell you that when I was in a medieval dress doing everything by the book, I could feel the separation. People were polite, people were even compliant. Their children were obedient. But now I feel so much real love. I've come to understand what real respect is all about, and it's not about the things that we used to think it was. I am not sure that in my lifetime there's ever been more respect and more love for women religious. [In Erie] the Sisters are deeply loved. All sorts of people pour into our chapel every Sunday for Mass. We have almost 200 oblates in a community of 110 [nuns], do you know? I mean, don't tell me that people aren't interested in monasteries and convents.

[Women religious] have often been in trouble with the Church because they are always going somewhere else. They're always out on those streets looking for the new poor, the new abandoned, the new outcast. It seems to me if we are going to be authentic, we're always going to be ahead of the system. Women religious know their history. They know that they are in a long line of troublemakers. [In the 1960s and 1970s] while we were being scolded for coming out of uniform and leaving the schools, we were the people opening the peace and justice centers and the halfway houses for women and the soup kitchens and the retreat centers and the spirituality programs. The apostolic nuns have been suppressed over and over and over again in Church history. But this time you're trying to suppress the most educated, independent, self-confident, purposeful group of women in the Church.

The big question right now is will these "investigations" or "assessments" or "inquisitions," whatever your euphemism is, have a positive or a negative effect? I pray it will be positive, that somebody would finally say, "These are our beloved daughters in whom we are well pleased." If that doesn't happen, you will see the organized seeding of new kinds of religious life that will be outside the control of and the identification with Rome. I'm not saying that it will be in huge numbers at first. But the seeds are already there. In almost every parish there are small faith-sharing groups within the system that are functioning outside the system.

Women religious will bring their traditions and spiritualities from this older model into mixed groups of lay and religious. As a Church we're so used to these categories that we can't even imagine that those barriers can come down and merge. And yet the dynamism is in the merging. I'm seeing more of a symphony.

You said back in your 1994 interview, "I am experiencing the hemorrhaging of the Church." Did you have any idea then what the next 10 or 15 years would bring?

I knew exactly what was happening. I used to say to bishops in that period, "The Joan Chittisters of the world are not your problem. Keep your eye on the women in first grade right now, because by the time they're 21, the Church will be the last bastion of sexism in their lives. And their major spiritual questions are going to be, 'Why?' and 'Why would I go there?'" And it is happening. It is happening everywhere.

We're at this wonderful new dawn of Christianity that is beyond a narcissistic concentration on the system. And [the Church] has a real chance to be a Christian presence in the world. It's a real moment of opportunity. My sense of tragedy lies in the fact that we may delay it for one moment. I'm not saying that a very powerful patriarchy cannot stamp this out, like stamping out the sparks after a marshmallow roast. You can stamp them out there in the fire pit, but they are going to fly someplace else. These are questions all over this globe. There's a very strong women's movement in Saudi Arabia. There's a very strong women's movement in the Philippines. There's a very strong women's movement in Russia.

The saddest thing for me [these past 15 years] is the heartrending awareness of the position of women as lesser animals on the globe. I really can't get beyond that. The female human being as a class in every single society has been a beast of burden and a bearer of the sins of the world with no opportunity to shape the world for the children she bears. I call that the sin of every male organization and religion on earth. They have denied the world half of the resources of the world. As a result, they've seen with one eye and heard with one ear and stood on one leg and decided with one-half of the human mind, and it shows.

You are well-known for your wonderful deep laugh. What makes you laugh now?

Oh, my gosh, almost anything. I collect jokes. I tell stories. I listen for them. They help me see the silly irony of the human condition. And I get to another appreciation of life through animals. I really love animals. I just bought a baby parrot we named Bennie. She's the perfect pet for this time of life. She doesn't have to be walked.

Have we captured some of things that are on your mind?

Absolutely. Immersion in the scriptures, the value of religious life, the end of patriarchy, Church renewal, the development of women everywhere, finding life beyond the human—and, yeah, a stubborn insistence on finding humor in everything. [Laughs.] (October 2009)

Epilogue: Where They Are Now

Anyone who seriously searches for the pulse of the American Roman Catholic Church must look beyond the statements of bishops, the controversies over dogma or discipline, and the number of bodies in the pews of parish churches. The American Catholic Church is not simply what the hierarchy says it is, or what the media say it is, or what radical spokespersons on the right or the left say it is. Contemporary Catholicism is complex, multifaceted, and rich in diversity.

The same must be said about the lives of today's women religious. As these oral histories demonstrate, nuns defy stereotypes. Readers can compare the cloistered life of Sister Florence Vales with the ministry of activist Sister Anne Montgomery; the Mexican-American heritage of Sister Anita deLuna with the African-American legacy of Sister Mary Alice Chineworth; the different paths Sister Margherita Marchione and Sister Patricia Marks, both members of the same community, followed.

When the Sisters from LCWR first suggested to the Smithsonian Institution an exhibit focusing on the contributions nuns had made to American history since the first women religious arrived in 1727, they were greeted with amazement. Is there really a story there? The Sisters overcame benign ignorance and immense financial hurdles to present the story they knew was indeed there; and the exhibit, "Women and Spirit: Catholic Sisters in America," began touring museums around the country in 2009. The exhibit must fill a huge vacuum; few Americans are aware of the varied roles nuns have played in the country's past three centuries. Where their contributions have been recognized, it has primarily been for teaching generations of Catholic school children or serving as nurses and administrators in Catholic hospitals. But nuns who left the classroom brought a Catholic presence to places, issues, and events where it had not been. Those contributions to our shared past must also be preserved, and oral history offers one still-available avenue where we can hear, in the women's own voices, what happened.

These oral histories, selected from 96 interviews, represent only a sampling of the diverse stories that deserve to be told. In the interlude between the years when the original interviews were conducted and this second edition, we have learned much more about how our memories work, what we repress, what we retain, and what we choose to share. These years have also produced many historical accounts of the events the women religious describe, both in the Catholic Church and in the country. Updating the interviews offered me an opportunity to re-evaluate the original conversations. Perhaps because the oral histories were collected as the women were already growing older and speaking with some perspective; perhaps because honesty was so much a part of their lives and many of them viewed the interview as just one more tool of self-evaluation; or perhaps simply because they were indeed where they said they were, the facts of the narratives, without any notable exceptions, still hold up.

TWO PERSPECTIVES

If we use a wide-angle lens, what emerges from the histories are insights into the character of the American Catholic Church and perspectives on many of the changes that have occurred in American society during the last 50 years. If we then focus on the personal dimension of these histories, we can observe the texture of lives lived in the midst of uncommon change.

As these histories recount, the relationship between nuns and their Church during the decades since the Second Vatican Council has often been uncomfortable. During the early 1960s Vatican II mandated dramatic change for the entire Catholic Church. But the Church measures its existence in centuries; human beings measure theirs in decades. Thus, change that comes too quickly for the institution can seem painfully slow for the individual. The tension between the two exacts its toll. In the original interviews and in the second edition updates, my questions about the Church were met with ambivalence, anger, sadness, puzzlement, wariness, and pain.

As the decades have gone by, the backlash against the Vatican II *aggiornamento* has become more entrenched. Two divergent paths have led from the Council documents. The hierarchy, during the papacies of both John Paul II and Benedict XVI, has chosen to emphasize doctrinal correctness and continuity with centuries-old pre-Council values, bringing back earlier liturgies and pieties and shutting down any discussion of change in the celibate male priesthood. To those Catholics who believe that Vatican II called the Church to respond to "the signs of the times," such a return to the past is not what the spirit of the Council intended. Women religious in the United States, most of whom responded with their own renewal in the 1960s, have found themselves once again on the front lines as the struggle between the differing interpretations of Vatican II has intensified. Many women religious, trained now in theology and Church history, understand the two Vatican investigations into their lives, which were begun in 2009, as expressions of this wider tension.

What *is* the relationship between these nuns and their Church? Have they changed its character? Or have they themselves changed so much that they have moved beyond its boundaries? Is the Catholic Church so sexist, so mired in patriarchy, that no change is possible? These are significant questions—the kinds of questions the nuns themselves continue to ask.

In having to defend their way of life for the last 40 years, women religious have come face to face with the choices they've made and the theology on which they made those decisions. Sister Sandra Schneiders traces the roots of their lives to Jesus and his followers. "Anyone examining the life of ministerial women religious in the United States today should have no difficulty recognizing their choice of and commitment to the pattern of life to which Jesus called his original band of itinerant disciples."

In these oral histories, we hear that the women believe they remain faithful to the Gospel and to the Church where their roots go deep. One woman said, "The Catholic Church is my Church, and I love it. Who ever said everything we love has to be perfect?" But many of them spoke of their commitment to the "Gospel message" or to the "people of God," thus distancing themselves from hierarchical structures. Some also believe that asking tough questions is the critical role they must play now within the Catholic Church. Sister Joan Chittister put it succinctly: "If the unacceptable question is to come from any-where, it should come from the religious community. . . . That is the function of religious life."

The roles women religious have played in American society have often flowed from their roles within the Catholic Church. Some of them were able to do the work they did because they were supported by a Catholic social service agency, such as Catholic Charities. Others received financial backing from their religious communities, which may, in turn, have been supported by Catholic institutions and Catholic laypeople. But history now shows that their work and their influence reached far beyond the confines of Catholicism. During the 1960s, '70s, '80s, and '90s, nuns marched in civil rights demonstrations; protested the war in Vietnam; served time in jail for civil disobedience; worked with addicts, prostitutes, AIDS patients, and the homeless; and spoke out against anti-Semitism, sexism, and the Gulf War. Their presence, in smaller numbers, has continued into the twenty-first century. As the oral histories show, women religious were *there*. They may not have been the first or the most important or the only ones there, but their stories ring true. Their accounts contain little hubris.

Sister Rose Thering, for example, spent close to 40 years trying to improve Jewish-Christian relations; her oral history offers a fascinating perspective on an international struggle, complementing both news accounts and historical analyses. Other women dedicated their efforts to national issues—such as civil rights, health care, and immigration law—where systemic change is critical; the histories of nuns like Dr. Marilyn Aiello, Sister Mary Heinen, and Sister Fran Tobin can still contribute to our public discussion of those topics.

The updated oral histories add more evidence that women religious continue to speak their conscience and respond to contemporary issues. Sister Rosemarie Milazzo and Sister Anne Montgomery have both served as members of Christian

Peacemaker Teams in war-torn countries like Congo and Iraq. Sister Anne has also continued her active presence at demonstrations for nuclear disarmament and justice for prisoners at the Guantanamo Naval Base.

American Catholic nuns have demonstrated a remarkable ability to move gracefully through life's stages. Women religious in good health do not retire at 65 or 70 or even 75. They may leave one job, especially if their employer has a mandatory retirement policy, but they find another. If they need new credentials, they go back to school; if they have to relocate, they do. Sister Marie Lee was in her mid-sixties when she started Project Regina to teach Hmong refugee women to sew. Sister Carita Pendergast was 87 when she published her first book. It would seem that, having confronted significant changes in their earlier lives, they developed a resilience that serves them well in old age.

That observation, drawn from the original narratives, is reinforced by the updates. Sister Mary Rose McGeady retired as President of Covenant House because of ill health; she moved back to her community's motherhouse where she could receive the care she needed. Then, in her late 70s, she helped five Lutheran women open a shelter for homeless women with children.

Nuns have matured in other ways, too. These oral histories demonstrate that since the 1960s women religious have achieved a keener sense of themselves, deepened their spirituality, and nurtured warm personal relationships.

In most of the interviews, I was impressed with the women's willingness to tackle sensitive personal subjects, such as depression and cancer. A few of them thanked me for offering them an opportunity to reflect anew on their lives; they called it a "gift." Nuns were taught that they had to give up their individuality when they entered the convent; they have reclaimed it, and they seem to treasure it and nurture it in themselves and in each other.

The women were happy to be asked about their spiritual lives, to let me know that they had left behind rote prayer and found comfort and inspiration in scripture. In many different ways, using eloquent metaphors and simple clichés, telling stories where they could, they talked about finding God in their daily lives. Sister Noreen Ellison's description of her encounter at a gas station in rural Texas is a notable example.

Even as they face disapproval from the hierarchy and disappointment from some Catholic laity who wish they were still staffing parish schools, the Sisters spoke to me of hope, which they said was firmly rooted in their adherence to the Gospel.

The most painful topic, the one around which we danced most often in the original narratives, was women's liturgies. As one woman told me when she declined to talk about her experiences, "It's the last taboo." Other women did speak about the subject, but I sensed a high level of discomfort and found no consensus. The topic is clearly connected to women's ordination, an ongoing divisive issue in the Catholic Church.

In one of the two new oral histories, Sister Christine Schenk provides the factual background that explains the difficulties of discussing this topic in public. Women's ordination is, in fact, one of the three doctrinal issues for which the Vatican began its investigation of LCWR. The centrality of the subject, which affects all Catholics, not just women religious, suggests that the tension surrounding it will not abate. And nuns will remain on the firing line.

Another controversial issue in the Church in recent decades has centered on the issue of sexual abuse of minors. The numbers of clergy credibly accused of abuse and the numbers of bishops accused of covering up the evidence have horrified not only Catholics but people around the world. Women religious have spoken out in favor of the victims, served on newly mandated diocesan oversight panels and become active members of Voice of the Faithful, an organization formed in 2002 in response to the stories of victims first in Boston and then worldwide. A few communities of women religious in the United States have also had to deal with abusers in their midst. The numbers of women abusers, Theresa Padovano told me, "are smaller, much smaller. But their communities don't want to deal with it either. The financial repercussions to their work, the bad publicity—it's a human thing to want to protect what you've built. But, as with the bishops, you can't choose the institution over people."

On personal relationships, two areas are worth noting. Many of the women spoke of rebuilding ties to their families; of interrupting ministries and going home, sometimes for a year or longer, to care for elderly parents. The women also spoke of their love for one another. Sister Gloria Perez put it well: "I love my community deeply. They are definitely my family. They're the women that I will live and die with. . . . I find God very much in my Sisters." The significance of these two developments becomes apparent if we recall that when most of these women entered the convent, they never expected to go home again, and they were forbidden to demonstrate affection for one another.

I often saw this affection when I visited motherhouses and observed the tender way the younger Sisters treated the elderly among them. In the updating interviews, several of the narrators, no longer young themselves, spoke of the joy they felt when they visited their Sisters in nursing homes or infirmaries.

WHAT THE FUTURE HOLDS

The women in this collection, reflecting current demographics, are almost all in their 70s, 80s, and 90s. They left behind the holy separate space they entered as young women, also leaving behind their status as "beloved daughters of the Church," their illusions of security and guaranteed respect. Most of them have no regrets. As Sister Kathy Quigley said, "I think women religious in the Church are at our finest moment in history. I have no regrets about our lifestyle because we have matured spiritually, we have matured emotionally, and we've matured ministerially."

But the long-term future character of religious life is unclear. Sister Annmarie Sanders has a vested interest in that long-term future; at 50, she is one of the new generation of leaders of women religious—old enough to have some perspective on the past, young enough to understand the needs of her peers and those who might consider entering religious life today or in the years to come. She was too young to be included in this oral history collection. But when I spoke with her in early 2010 in her offices at LCWR in Silver Spring, Maryland, where she works as director of communications, she provided a necessary perspective.

She readily confessed to being envious of the lives of women religious who had come before her, who lived during eras when they had a vast pool of gifts to draw upon and resources to go meet any need. But, she says, "It can't be what it was. How can we build on that legacy and take it into the future?" There is no clear roadmap—and so few women to make the necessary decisions. She has sensed a hunger among younger people for prayer and community, not just joining together for ministry. "People want to come together to be more attentive to God's work in our lives and in each other."

Sister Annmarie believes that the future will require women religious to answer the question: "What is the unique perspective we can bring to our global world as women grounded in our faith, as women steeped in the Gospel, choosing a communitarian way of life?" It is important, she adds, for women religious to be articulate about what they have intentionally chosen. They will need to be educated to defend the life they are leading, but also to be able to respond to all the new questions facing society. "The world is moving forward. Do we want to be on the sidelines? Or be relevant in finding answers to all the new moral and ethical questions?"

What we hear in the oral histories—and what I also heard from Sister Annmarie—are four general areas that the women think have been essential to their expression of religious life and will remain essential, in some form, in the future.

Whatever their ministries have been or will become, the women cherish the contemplative dimension of their lives. Sister Janet Ruffing and Sister Joan Chittister were articulate on that subject. And the narrators clearly believe in community, in what they can do together. The communitarian bonds might be envisioned in different ways, but, as Sister Annmarie put it, "The important thing is being part of something bigger than ourselves." There is a three-century history of what American women religious can accomplish when they work together.

A third non-negotiable for all the narrators is a commitment to the underserved. Although the focus has changed many times and will change again as the world's needs change, that commitment will always be at the heart of religious life. Ministry, however, is also the dimension most at risk these days as so many communities struggle with overwhelming financial burdens and others merge or die out.

The fourth essential, the women said, is grounding in the Gospel. But, a few women added, they must also be open to participating in the global community, to learning from other traditions. As their numbers in the United States grow smaller, many congregations, like the Sisters of Mercy and the School Sisters of Notre Dame, have come to cherish their international Sisters and draw on their insights. In another sign of global solidarity, which has been enabled by the technology now available to all, Sisters around the world and across congregational lines are gathering together to share their stories, support each other, and search for new ways to minister together.

Some of these questions about the future of religious life are chiefly of concern to the nuns themselves. Others, I think, have broader relevance. If we accept what the oral histories show—that nuns have become an integral part of American society, even though they may criticize it and struggle against its excesses—then the loss of dedicated lives affects us all. What would it mean for the Catholic Church—and American society—if nuns were no longer around? Would it matter?

The oral histories also make clear that nuns are more than what they do. Sister Janet Ruffing said, "Religious life is supposed to be an icon—a window onto the sacred." Can we live without icons?

These oral histories contain richly textured lives from which we can extract more than a few history lessons—and perhaps also courage and hope. Nuns may have left behind their chalk and erasers, but they are still teaching.

Appendix A: Narrators

Sister Bonaventure Burke; interviewed June, 1991
Sister Gloria Perez; May, 1991
Sister Marlene Brownett; March, 1992
Sister Rosemary Rader; June, 1994
Sister Margherita Marchione; February, 1991
Sister Carita Pendergast; March, 1991
Sister Rosemarie Milazzo; August, 1992 and January, 2010
Sister Noreen Ellison; June, 1991
Sister Mary Heinen; October, 1992
Sister Marilyn Aiello; November, 1994
Sister Judy Ward; May, 1994
Sister Marie Lee; October, 1992
Sister Fran Tobin; March, 1994
Sister Jeanne Cashman; November, 1992
Sister Peg Hynes; October, 1993
Sister Mary Rose McGeady; September, 1992
Sister Marie Gilligan and Sister Kathy Quigley; November, 1994
Sister Irene Garvey; March, 1991
Sister Janet Ruffing; November, 1993
Sister Annette Covatta; September, 1992
Sister Vilma Seelaus; January, 1995
Sister Margaret Traxler; November, 1993
Sister Jeannine Gramick; December, 1992 and February, 2010
Sister Anne Montgomery; May, 1994 and December, 2009
Sister Rose Thering; February, 1992
Sister Florence Vales; December, 1991
Sister Irene Mahoney; July, 1991
Sister Helen David Brancato; December, 1993
Sister Mary Alice Chineworth; July, 1992
Sister Gwynette Proctor; February, 1995
Sister Germaine Fritz; May, 1992
Sister Kathleen McNany; December, 1992
Sister Theresa Kane; August, 1994

Sister Anita deLuna; November, 1994
Theresa Padovano; January, 1992 and November, 2009
Rev. Jane Flaherty; October, 1993
Sister Frances Maureen Carlin; March, 1991
Sister Mary Elise Toal; December, 1991
Sister Josephita Larrea; July, 1992
Sister Celestine Schall; November, 1992
Sister Georgine Loacker; November, 1992
Sister Judeen Schulte; November, 1992
Sister Marlene Neises; November, 1992
Sister Elizabeth Engel; November, 1992
Sister Catherine Bertrand: November, 1993
Sister Ancilla Maloney; October, 1993 and March, 2010
Mary Jo Leddy; September, 1994
Sister Patricia Marks; August, 1994
Sister Virginia Johnson; January, 2010
Sister Christine Schenk; December, 2009
Sister Joan Chittister; September, 1994 and October, 2009

Appendix B: Religious Communities

NOTE: The 96 women interviewed for this research project are (or were) members of the following religious communities. Listed first is the official title of the group, according to the *Official Catholic Directory*, 1995 edition. If there are other names by which the group is commonly known, those follow. The initials that are given below and that women religious use after their names do not necessarily correspond to the English words; they may be based on an original Italian or French name or on an alternative usage. (For example: O.P. stands for Order of Preachers, another title used for Dominican Sisters and priests; and the initials used by the Religious Teachers Filippini—M.P.F.—come from the Italian, *Maestre pie Filippini*.) Asterisks indicate communities represented by women in the text.

  Adorers of the Blood of Christ (A.S.C.); Precious Blood Sisters and Adorers of
      the Precious Blood
*Benedictine Sisters of Baltimore, Maryland (O.S.B.)
*Benedictine Sisters of Elizabeth, New Jersey (O.S.B.)
*Benedictine Sisters of Erie, Pennsylvania (O.S.B.)
*Benedictine Sisters, St. Paul, Minnesota (O.S.B.)
  Carmelite Nuns of the Ancient Observance; Hermits of Carmel (H.O.Carm)
*Discalced Carmelite Nuns (O.C.D.)
*Sisters of Charity of Cincinnati, Ohio (S.C.)
*Sisters of Charity of Leavenworth, Kansas (S.C.L.)
*Sisters of Charity of Saint Elizabeth of Convent Station, New Jersey (S.C.)
  Sisters of Christian Charity (S.C.C.)
*Daughters of Charity of St. Vincent de Paul (D.C.)
  Daughters of Mary Help of Christians (F.M.A.); Salesian Sisters of St. John Bosco
*Dominican Sisters, Amityville, New York (O.P.)
*Dominican Sisters, Sinsinawa, Wisconsin (O.P.)
*Dominican Sisters, Racine, Wisconsin (O.P.)
  Dominican Sisters, Adrian, Michigan (O.P.)
*Emmaus Disciples (noncanonical)

Franciscan Handmaids of the Most Pure Heart of Mary (F.H.M.)

Sisters of St. Francis of the Holy Cross (O.S.F.)

Sisters of St. Francis of Assisi (O.S.F.)

*School Sisters of St. Francis (O.S.F.)

Grey Nuns of the Sacred Heart (G.N.S.H.)

Community of Holy Spirit (C.H.S.)

*Sisters of the Holy Names of Jesus and Mary (S.N.J.M.)

Sisters, Servants of the Immaculate Heart of Mary, Monroe, Michigan (I.H.M.)

*Sisters, Servants of the Immaculate Heart of Mary, Scranton, Pennsylvania (I.H.M.)

*Sisters, Servants of the Immaculate Heart of Mary, Immaculata, Pennsylvania (I.H.M.)

Congregation of the Sisters of Charity of the Incarnate Word (C.C.V.I.)

*Sisters of Loretto (S.L.)

*Maryknoll Sisters of St. Dominic (M.M.)

*Medical Mission Sisters (M.M.S.)

Medical Missionaries of Mary (M.M.M.)

*Sisters of Mercy of the Americas (R.S.M.)

*Missionary Catechists of Divine Providence (M.C.D.P.)

*Congregation of Notre Dame de Sion (N.D.S.); Sisters of Sion

*School Sisters of Notre Dame (S.S.N.D.)

*Sisters of Notre Dame deNamur (S.N.D.deN.; also S.N.D.)

*Sisters of Our Lady of Christian Doctrine (R.C.D.)

*Oblate Sisters of Providence (O.S.P.)

Religious of the Passion of Jesus Christ (C.P.); contemplative Passionist nuns

*Sisters of the Presentation of the Blessed Virgin Mary (P.B.V.M.)

*Religious Teachers Filippini (M.P.F.)

Religious of the Sacred Heart of Mary (R.S.H.M.)

*Order of Saint Clare (O.S.C.); cloistered Poor Clares

Sisters of St. John the Baptist (C.S.J.B.)

*Congregation of the Sisters of St.Joseph (C.S.J.)

*Sisters of St. Joseph of Carondelet (C.S.J.)

*Sisters of St. Joseph of Chestnut Hill (S.S.J.)

*Society of the Holy Child Jesus (S.H.C.J.)

*Society of the Sacred Heart (R.S.C.J.); Religious of the Sacred Heart

*Ursuline Nuns. Roman Union (O.S.U.)

Visitation Nuns (V.H.M.)

Glossary

abbess. Superior of a monastic community of nuns. Elected by members of her community, an abbess has general authority but no sacramental jurisdiction.

abbey. In most essentials, an abbey is the same as a monastery. *See* monastery.

altar. Central table in a church building. Eucharist is celebrated at the altar. *See* Eucharist; Mass.

apostolic communities. Also called ministerial communities. Those engaged in ministries that answer a need in society. Prior to the 1960s apostolic communities for women commonly interpreted their mission as education or health care.

apostolic visitation. An examination, initiated by the Vatican and carried out by its delegated representatives, into a troublesome situation or into the lives of a particular group of Catholics, e.g. American nuns. Visitators report back to the Vatican on their findings, which may or may not be made public.

associates. Members of the laity, women or men, married or single, who join with a religious community to share in their mission and prayer life. They do not take vows or vote in congregational matters. For the Benedictines, called oblates.

bishop. Most frequently, the pastoral leader of a diocese. Only ordained priests can be consecrated bishops.

canon law. Body of laws that govern the Church. Revised most recently in 1983.

canonical status. Recognition that a religious community has official standing in the Roman Catholic Church. *See* noncanonical.

Carmel. Mount Carmel is a mountain ridge in Israel long regarded as a holy place. The Carmelite order, a hermit way of life that emphasizes solitude supported by community, began there in the thirteenth century. By extension, the term *Carmel* also means a Carmelite monastery.

celibacy. Unmarried state required of Roman Catholic priests and women and men who are members of vowed religious communities; also, abstention from sexual intercourse. The term *celibate* refers to one who practices celibacy.

chapter. Assembly of delegated members of a religious community for elections and decisions on other governance issues.

charism. Gifts or graces given by God to individuals or groups like religious communities, which are to be shared with the world.

chastity. One of the three vows taken by most women religious. For religious, it is sometimes called *consecrated chastity*, reflecting a belief that all Christians are called to be chaste, whatever their chosen state of life. *See* vow.

Church. At first, the Church was the young, dynamic Christian community of the New Testament. Later, as it spread, the emphasis on governing structures and jurisdiction increased, creating an institutional Church and a hierarchy. In the twentieth century, particularly after Vatican II, there has been a new focus on envisioning the Church as the "people of God," a servant community.

clergy. Men ordained to holy orders. There are three levels: deacons, priests, and bishops.

cloister. An enclosure. Areas of a convent or monastery reserved exclusively for members of the religious community.

community. Colloquially, and in the context of this book, a generic term used to describe members of a religious group or the group itself. Living "in community" no longer necessarily means living in the same geographic place but does imply other commitments to the group. Official distinctions designate the kind of vows, charter, and governance a particular community might have and whether it is technically a congregation or an order. *See* congregations; orders.

congregation. All religious communities begun since 1752 are officially designated congregations (as opposed to orders, such as the Carmelites and the Ursulines, which were chartered before that date).

contemplative life. In the strict sense, a life dedicated to work and prayer in a cloistered community. Since Vatican II, the term has been explored in a broader context; many women religious who are not cloistered nuns feel that they too are called to be contemplative women.

convent. Officially, a residence for women religious. The term has most frequently been used to describe the rather large buildings where Sisters who taught in parish schools lived. Nowadays two or three nuns living together might call their inner-city walkup apartment a convent.

deacon. A *transitional* deacon is a man on his way to priesthood; a *permanent* deacon is a layman who is considered a cleric but who will remain a deacon for life. Permanent deacons may be married.

deaconess. Woman in the early Church who was appointed and charged with performing certain ministries. An example frequently mentioned is Phoebe (Romans 16:1). The role of women deacons, which centered on liturgical ministry to women and children, flourished in the early Church; the Council of Chalcedon, in the year 451, speaks of their ordination. In western Christianity their role ceased to exist around the sixth century.

desert experience. The desert not only is a physical reality but also carries symbolic meaning. In spiritual imagery, the desert is the place where solitude and community confront each other, where the human and the divine meet.

diocese. Geographic Catholic community under the pastoral care of a bishop.

encyclical. Formal pastoral letter written by a pope and usually addressed to members of the Roman Catholic Church. (Pope John XXIII addressed encyclicals to all persons of goodwill.)

Eucharist. From Greek for *thanksgiving.* Sacramental celebration of the death and resurrection of Christ. Often referred to as the Mass. *See* Mass.

formation. Program each religious community designs to train its prospective members. *See* novice.

Gospel, Gospels. Accounts of Jesus's life and ministry produced by the evangelists Matthew, Mark, Luke, and John and included in the New Testament.

habit. Distinctive clothing worn by religious communities.

hermit. One who lives a life of prayer in solitude.

hierarchy. In general usage, the term refers to those in positions of authority in the institutional Church—bishops, cardinals, and the pope.

homily. Part of the liturgy. Formerly called a *sermon.*

inclusive language. Use of words and phrases that designate all members of a group. This is a controversial issue in churches today, because English-language liturgical and biblical texts use androcentric terms—for example, *man* for *human being.*

juniorate. Place where *junior* Sisters—those no longer postulants or novices; that is, those who had made first vows—lived while they continued their education. The need for such places disappeared in the 1960s, when the number of young women entering religious life was no longer large.

liturgy. Public and official prayers and rites of the Church. Colloquially, the term is often used to refer to the Mass. *See* Mass.

magisterium. Teaching authority of the Roman Catholic Church; also, the hierarchy holding this office.

Mass. Traditional term for celebration of the Eucharist.

meditation. Mental, as distinguished from vocal, prayer. It implies both silence and listening and is meant to bring one into closer union with God.

ministry. The public service rendered by members of a religious community.

monastery. The place where certain orders of nuns—such as the Benedictines, the Poor Clares, and the Carmelites—live. A monastery may have autonomous rule, under an abbess or prioress; its members usually remain permanently attached to it.

monastic. Spirituality and way of life followed by members of monastic communities. One of the basic tenets is a daily balance of prayer and work.

monsignor. Honorary title given to a priest in recognition of services rendered to the Church.

mother superior, mother general. Titles given in some religious orders to the woman in charge. Today, many communities prefer to use the title *president.* Others have a collegial style of management, with no designated superior.

motherhouse. This may be the place where the religious community originated. It also means the community's headquarters or base of operations—where the mother general or president lives, where the novitiate is, and where chapter meetings are held. Increasingly, it is the site of infirmaries and residences for elderly Sisters.

noncanonical. Term for religious communities that are not officially chartered by the Church. Many noncanonical religious communities, however, have the approval of their local bishop, and members take private vows before him.

novice. Woman preparing to profess vows in a religious community. Canon law requires that every novice must have at least one full year of *canonical novitiate,* during which the candidate studies scripture, theology, and the history of the religious group she is joining.

novitiate. Place where or period of time (usually two years) during which a novice is trained.

nun. In the strict sense, a nun is a member of a contemplative religious order who meets certain other obligations. In general usage, and throughout this book, *nun, Sister,* and the more recent term *woman religious* are used interchangeably.

obedience. One of the three traditional vows taken by women in canonical religious communities. Its meaning now varies widely from one community to another, as is evident in the oral histories. *See* vow.

orders. Religious communities of women founded before 1752, often in connection with orders of men. The Dominicans, Benedictines, Franciscans, and Carmelites are orders of both men and women.

parish. Geographic division of a diocese.

pastor. Person responsible for the pastoral care of a parish.

Paul. St. Paul. As Saul of Tarsus, he persecuted Christians until he was mysteriously blinded and knocked off his horse on the road to Damascus (Acts 9: 3–18). Accepting his experience as a revelation from God, he then became a great Christian missionary. A reference to "being knocked off one's horse" has thus come to mean a conversion experience, an encounter with God.

postulant. Candidate for membership in a religious community. A woman was a postulant before she received the habit of the community and became a novice.

poverty. One of the three vows traditionally taken by women religious. Property is owned by the community, not the individual. *See* vow.

priest. Ordained minister in the Catholic Church.

prioress. Woman in charge of a priory. *See* abbess; monastery.

priory. Kind of monastery where orders of religious women live.

profession. Pronouncement of vows. Usually a formal ceremony which members of the religious community, family, and friends attend.

provincial. Woman in charge of a region or geographic division of a community. An elected office. Nowadays, depending on the size of a community, provincial teams help govern a province.

rectory. House where a pastor and priests in the parish live.

religious life. Life in a vowed religious community.

retreat. Withdrawal from everyday life for a time of prayer. A spiritual experience which can be undertaken by an individual or a group.

sacristy. Room, adjoining the sanctuary, where ministers assemble for liturgies and where altar linens, vestments, and eucharistic vessels are stored.

sanctuary. Area of a church immediately surrounding the altar.

Second Vatican Council, Vatican II. Convened in 1962 by Pope John XXIII to open the Church to the modern world, Vatican II was an ecumenical council, an assembly of official representatives from the worldwide Roman Catholic Church. John XXIII also invited observers and auditors; Protestants, Jews, and Catholic laymen and laywomen—including some nuns—were among the groups permitted to view the sessions, though not to participate.

Sister. Specifically, a woman who is a member of a religious congregation, not a cloistered order. However, the term is used interchangeably with *nun* and *woman religious.*

spiritual direction. Process of trying to understand one's relationship with God, with the help of a trained director.

spirituality. Lived expression of one's ultimate beliefs.

Vatican II. *See* Second Vatican Council.

vocation. From Latin *vocare, to call.* Inclination toward a particular way of life, which Christians see as a call from God. Since Vatican II, no one vocation, specifically to religious life as opposed to married or single life, is seen as superior to any other.

vows. Most generally, solemn promises made to God. More specifically, public promises made by members of religious communities. These are most frequently the vows of poverty, chastity, and obedience. Some communities take additional vows.

woman religious. Member of a religious community. Used as an alternative—and often preferred—term for *nun* or *Sister.*

women's liturgies. Religious rituals for, by, and with women. The most controversial are those that parallel eucharistic celebrations, making use of bread and wine, with a woman serving as celebrant. Other noneucharistic liturgies celebrate special seasons or events in a woman's life, or the life of a group. Women's liturgies may take place within the context of a religious community, but they are just as likely to be ecumenical, multicultural gatherings where nuns are simply women among women.

For further information, consult *The HarperCollins Encyclopedia of Catholicism,* Richard P. McBrien, ed. (New York: HarperCollins, 1995).

Selected Bibliography

Abbott, Walter M., ed. *The Documents of Vatican II*. New York: Herder and Herder, 1966.

Beane, Marjorie Noterman. *From Framework to Freedom: A History of the Sister Formation Conference*. Lanham, MD: University Press of America, 1993.

Brennan, Margaret R. *What Was There For Me Once: A Memoir*. Toronto, CA: Novalis, 2009.

Chittister, Joan, et al. *Climb Along the Cutting Edge: An Analysis of Change in Religious Life*. New York: Paulist Press, 1977.

Chittister, Joan. *The Fire in These Ashes: A Spirituality of Contemporary Religious Life*. New York: Sheed and Ward, 1995.

Chittister, Joan. *The Way We Were: A Story of Conversion and Renewal*. Maryknoll, NY: Orbis Books, 2006.

Davis, Cyprian. *The History of Black Catholics in the United States*. New York: Crossroad, 1990.

Dolan, Jay P. *In Search of an American Catholicism: A History of Religion and Culture in Tension*. New York: Oxford University Press, 2002.

Fiorenza, Elisabeth Schussler. *In Memory of Her*. New York: Crossroad, 1983.

Fisher, James T. *Communion of Immigrants: A History of Catholics in America*. New York: Oxford University Press, 2008.

Gluck, Sherna B. *Rosie the Riveter Revisited: Women, the War, and Social Change*. Boston: Twayne, 1987.

In Good Conscience. Barbara Rick, dir., prod. Out of the Blue Films, Inc., 2004.

Johnson, Elizabeth A. *She Who Is*. New York: Crossroad, 1993.

Leddy, Mary Jo. *Reweaving Religious Life: Beyond the Liberal Model*. Mystic, CT: Twenty-Third Publications, 1990.

Mahoney, Irene. *Encounters: A Book of Memories*. Bloomington, IN: Author House, 2010.

Mahoney, Irene, ed. *A Company of Women: Journeys through the Feminine Experience of Faith*. Liguori, MO: Triumph Books, 1996.

McGrath, Albertus Magnus. *Women and the Church*. Garden City, NY: Image, 1976. (Originally published as *What a Modern Catholic Believes about Women*. Chicago: Thomas More, 1972.)

McNamara, Jo Ann Kay. *Sisters in Arms: Catholic Nuns through Two Millennia*. Cambridge, MA: Harvard University Press, 1996.

Neal, Marie Augusta. *From Nuns to Sisters*. Mystic, CT: Twenty-Third Publications, 1990.

Neal, Marie Augusta. *Catholic Sisters in Transition: From the 1960s to the 1980s*. Wilmington, DE: Michael Glazier, 1984.

Nygren, David J., and Miriam D. Ukeritis. *The Future of Religious Orders in the United States*. Westport, CT: Praeger, 1993.

Philbert, Paul J., ed. *Living in the Meantime: Concerning the Transformation of Religious Life*. New York: Paulist Press, 1994.

Quinonez, Lora Ann, and Mary Daniel Turner. *The Transformation of American Catholic Sisters*. Philadelphia: Temple University Press, 1992.

Rogers, Carole Garibaldi. "Overlooked Narrators: What Women Religious Can Contribute to Feminist Oral History," *Frontiers: A Journal of Women's Studies*, Volume 19, (3, 1998): 157–70.

Ruffing, Janet. *Uncovering Stories of Faith*. New York: Paulist Press, 1989.

Schneiders, Sandra M. *Finding the Treasure: Locating Catholic Religious Life in a New Ecclesial and Cultural Context. Religious Life in a New Millennium*, Volume One. Mahwah, NJ: Paulist Press, 2000.

Schneiders, Sandra M. *Selling All: Commitment, Consecrated Celibacy, and Community in Catholic Religious Life. Religious Life in a New Millennium*, Volume Two. Mahwah, NJ: Paulist Press, 2001.

Schneiders, Sandra M. "The Past and Future of Ministerial Religious Life," *National Catholic Reporter*, October 2, 2009.

Sister Rose's Passion. Oren Jacoby, filmmaker. Storyville Films, 2004.

Sisters of Selma: Bearing Witness for Change. Jayasri Hart, dir, prod. PBS Home Video, 2007.

Suenens, Cardinal Leon Joseph. *The Nun in the Modern World*. Westminster, MD: Newman, 1963.

Ware, Ann Patrick, ed. *Midwives of the Future: American Sisters Tell Their Story*. Kansas City, MO: Leaven, 1985.

Weaver, Mary Jo. *New Catholic Women: A Contemporary Challenge to Traditional Religious Authority*. San Francisco: Harper and Row, 1985.

Wittberg, Patricia. *The Rise and Fall of Catholic Religious Orders: A Social Movement Perspective*. Albany: State University of New York Press, 1994.

Index

THE OXFORD ORAL HISTORY SERIES

J. TODD MOYE (University of North Texas), KATHRYN NASSTROM (University of San Francisco), and ROBERT PERKS (The British Library Sound Archive), *Series Editors*
DONALD A. RITCHIE, *Senior Advisor*

Doing Oral History, Second Edition *Donald A. Ritchie*

Approaching an Auschwitz Survivor: Holocaust Testimony and Its Transformations *Edited by Jürgen Matthäus*

A Guide to Oral History and the Law *John A. Neuenschwander*

Singing Out: An Oral History of America's Folk Music Revivals *David K. Dunaway and Molly Beer*

Freedom Flyers: The Tuskegee Airmen of World War II *J. Todd Moye*

Launching the War on Poverty: An Oral History, Second Edition *Michael L. Gillette*

The Firm: The Inside Story of the Stasi *Gary Bruce*

The Wonder of Their Voices: The 1946 Holocaust Interviews of David Boder *Alan Rosen*

They Say in Harlan County: An Oral History *Alessandro Portelli*

The Oxford Handbook of Oral History *Edited by Donald A. Ritchie*

Habits of Change: An Oral History of American Nuns *Carole Garibaldi Rogers*